SNAKES, DRUGS
AND
ROCK 'N' ROLL

Advance Praise for the Book

'Rom Whitaker is one of India's greatest conservationists, and this beautifully written book is the story of how he developed his passion for nature, especially of the reptilian variety. At a time of mounting alarm over the state of the environment, in India and globally, Whitaker's enchanting memoir shows us that we can live in greater harmony with forests and animals—we can love our planet rather than destroy it.'

—Akash Kapur

'I grew up in Avadi, a suburb of Chennai, from 1966 to 1983. Every year the school trip included a visit to the Snake Park, followed by a stopover at the Crocodile Bank. I don't know what my classmates thought of these places, as they were more keen on getting to the beach, but for me this was the highlight of the trip. Especially if there was a venom extraction on that day. I knew of Romulus Whitaker, and if there had been a poster of his available, he would have joined the Eagles, ABBA and Karen Carpenter on my wardrobe door. Romulus Whitaker's memoir of his boyhood and early adulthood spent in India and America tracing his fascination for snakes (and reptiles) turning into a calling is extraordinary. Vivid with detail and replete with experiences that range from fishing to cleaning decks, from acid trips to snake bites and the celebration of wilderness, this is not just any memoir. It's a bloody good read and unputdownable!'

—Anita Nair

'People who still don't believe that truth is wilder than fiction should read Rom Whitaker's jaw-dropping memoir. As someone who grew up catching snakes in the Everglades, I look at someone like Rom as kids of my generation looked at Mickey Mantle or Willie Mays. That he is now dedicated to saving king cobras—the most feared reptile on the planet—is a fitting coda to his astounding story.'

—Carl Hiaasen

'Without doubt, over the past half a century, Rom Whitaker has been one of India's most passionate and dedicated naturalists. His has also been an unconventional and colourful life in two countries and cultures, full of fascinating encounters and hair-raising adventures. All this makes his memoir both exceptional and thrilling.'

—Jairam Ramesh

'Romulus Whitaker: the name rolls off the tongue, part sage, part adventurer. The man who bears it has carved a place for himself among the world's great naturalists and herpetologists. There is a touch of the Crocodile Hunter mixed with encyclopaedic knowledge akin to that of east Africa's legendary snakeman "Iodine" C.J.P. Ionides. Whitaker's story, co-authored with his talented wife Janaki Lenin, is an enthralling account of a life well lived that would be hard to match today. For many, a virtual world of tablets and Facebook has become the new reality, one disconnected from the wonders of nature. Caution has replaced the quest for adventure. Many youngsters rarely leave their bedrooms, let alone venture into the unknown in search of themselves. Whitaker found his true calling in nature's endless creativity. After reading this book, so will you.'

—Jonathan and Angela Scott

'Rom Whitaker's professional work as the "Snakeman of India" has been truly legendary. What is so special about Rom is his deep passion and extraordinary skill as a naturalist. He mastered these in the first twenty-five years of his remarkable life, which are covered in this volume. This set the stage for his career in India, during which Rom inspired—and launched—many of India's acclaimed herpetologists. Going beyond that, this book is also a riveting social narrative, richly embellished with Rom's colourful adventures (and misadventures) all along the way.'

—K. Ullas Karanth

'I replaced my usual books with *Snakes, Drugs and Rock 'n' Roll* as my mandatory bedtime read. With rather unfortunate effects, I must hasten to add—for, instead of putting me to sleep, the narrative was so engrossing that it kept me up until the late hours. I do not know if I'm blinkered by the fact that, being a naturalist since my boyhood, I could relate so much to many of Rom's early exploits, but, boy, what a life he's had! An absolute roller-coaster ride of a book that is sure to leave the reader thirsting for more!'

—Manoj V. Nair

'A fascinating and important glimpse into the wonder years and the making of one of India's conservation pioneers, *Snakes, Drugs and Rock 'n' Roll* is a wonderful and original achievement of writing. It teems with stories and glitters with images of Bombay and Kodai, and learnings from his mentor in Florida. The narrative form and Rom's voice are a splendid fusion of accumulated wisdom, wistful nostalgia and intimate prose. Reading Romulus Whitaker's brilliant memoir, I encountered a Rom I had never met.'

—Pranay Lal

'A hell of a ride with an adrenaline junkie ... An honest read that captures Whitaker's extraordinary, diverse and dramatic life experiences—from his wild youth of huntin', fishin' and lovin' to becoming India's best-known herpetologist, or simply "India's Snakeman".'

—Prerna Singh Bindra

'Growing up watching Rom in wildlife documentaries, I had always wondered what the story behind this peculiar gentleman dressed in funky printed shirts, permanently armed either with a snake stick or a snake, would be like. If you, too, have wondered how a trigger-happy boy from New York could go on to become a Padma Shri-winning herpetologist in India, *Snakes, Drugs and Rock 'n' Roll* is just the book for you. And if you've met Rom, the book will feel like an extension of a fireside conversation he may have had with you, his natural flair for storytelling making this autobiography a "breezy" ride!'

—Rohan Chakravarty

'Rom Whitaker is a legend in India and, indeed, around the world. His founding of the Madras Snake Park in 1969, and his leadership role in crocodilian and snake conservation set standards for the global conservation community, as did his groundbreaking research on king cobras. His evolution from a hunter to one of the most significant conservation figures worldwide makes for a compelling story and is a must-read for anyone in our field. I had the privilege of visiting Rom in India more than forty years ago, and he stimulated my interest in crocodilians, which continues to the present day, and we have remained close friends ever since.'

—Russell A. Mittermeier

'To read *Snakes, Drugs and Rock 'n' Roll* is to encounter an antic life, filled with adventure. The saga of how Romulus Whitaker became an institution in Indian natural history is a lesson in the virtues of a curious mind and a warm heart. A fizzing, entertaining and vastly rewarding read!'

—Samanth Subramanian

'This unapologetic chronicle of the formative years of India's "snake missionary" reveals a young life lived to its fullest. This "breezy", evocative memoir reads like a novel, where characters, places and adventures come alive in one's mind's eye with ease and ingenuity. Protected by the "God of Idiots", Rom's adventures lead him to recognize his inability to reform to a life of an "automaton", and to fulfil his true calling and embrace the great open wilds. So much of Rom's story resonates with me, not the least his claim that he "was more an Indian at heart than a Whitey". I can't wait to read the second volume of Rom's memoir, where "the twenty-four-year-old hippy with no education" returns to Bombay to face the daunting reality that awaits him with promises of even greater adventures!'

—Sanjna Kapoor

'Though Rom Whitaker is barely twenty-four when the first volume of his memoir ends, he has already packed in more experiences than most people will in a lifetime. Rich in adventure and travel, filled with hardy exploits that take every chance to turn foolhardy, and driven by an infectious love for life and the living, this is an extraordinary account of an extraordinary life.'

—Srinath Perur

'Snakeman and naturalist who refuses to conform to the mainstream notion of conservation. This memoir is a must-read, as it is about the passion it takes to make nature work for people and livelihoods. Rom Whitaker may not have had a grand plan for what he did. But we know that his life's work in practice has shaped the very idea of coexistence and the solutions we desperately need to live lightly on Earth with nature.'

—Sunita Narain

'An irreverent, candid page-turner! Rom Whitaker upends the sombre hunter-turned-conservationist trope with a memoir brimming with animals, adventure, humour and self-reflection. This is one wild trip.'

—Zeenat Aman

SNAKES, DRUGS

AND

ROCK 'N' ROLL

Romulus Whitaker

with Janaki Lenin

HarperCollins *Publishers* India

First published in India by HarperCollins *Publishers* 2024
4th Floor, Tower A, Building No. 10, DLF Cyber City,
DLF Phase II, Gurugram, Haryana – 122002
www.harpercollins.co.in

2 4 6 8 10 9 7 5 3 1

P-ISBN: 978-93-5699-712-7
E-ISBN: 978-93-5699-711-0

Typeset in 11.5/15 Bembo Std at
Manipal Technologies Limited, Manipal

Printed and bound at
Replika Press Pvt. Ltd.

To

Doris Norden, Gail Wynne, Nina Menon and
Neel Chattopadhyaya

CONTENTS

Introduction   xiii

SECTION 1: GROWING UP

1. The Big Move   3

2. A New Life   23

3. Lovedale   29

4. Freedom   37

5. Kodaikanal   47

6. The Middling Years   53

7. The Year of Fishing   61

8. The Year of Stuffing Birds   77

9. The Year of Vices   95

10. Tryst with Explosives   111

11. The Final Year   125

12. Mysore   133

13. Gumtapuram   148

SECTION 2: FINDING MY FEET

14. Arrival in America   167

15. Cut Adrift   182

16. Odd Jobs   197

17. Seasick Seaman   209

18. Seasoned Seaman   223

19. Miami Serpentarium   233

20. Snakeman   254

21. Drafted   272

22. A Colour-Blind Lab Tech   289

23. Snakes, Drugs and Rock 'n' Roll   308

24. War Duty in Japan   322

25. Commercial Snake Hunter   332

26. Homeward Bound   345

    Epilogue   358

    Acknowledgements   359

    Bibliography   362

    Index   363

INTRODUCTION

FOR YEARS I'VE RECOUNTED parts of my story for willing listeners. Often, these sessions would end with a request to write a book. At the best of times, writing is a daunting task. It becomes even more so when I have to remember events from my life on the page without pruning the unsavoury bits.

As long as I can remember, snakes have been the focus of my fascination and love. I was so lucky to grow up in the northern New York countryside, where harmless snakes were common. The wilds of the Kodaikanal hills in south India, nurtured that love to an obsession during my schoolboy years.

Many conservation pioneers started their careers as ardent hunters, a phenomenon captured in the 1978 book *The Penitent Butchers*[1] by Richard Fitter and Sir Peter Scott. Fitter was then secretary of Fauna & Flora International (FFI), the world's oldest conservation organization. It was started in 1903 by 'an assorted collection of big game hunters who realized they were running out of things to shoot and despite their self-interest, kick-started international wildlife conservation'.[2] This isn't an anomaly. The world over, conservation has its roots in hunting.

1 Richard Fitter and Sir Peter Scott, *The Penitent Butchers: 75 Years of Wildlife Conservation* (Cambridge, UK: Fauna Preservation Society, 1978).
2 'Raiders of the Lost Archive: Episode One' by Tim Knight, https://www.fauna-flora.org/news/raiders-lost-archive-episode-one/

I'm perhaps the last of the dying generation of converts. As a high school student, I killed and skinned birds for a museum collection, which put me on the fringes of scientific research. For a year after I graduated, what people call a 'gap year' these days, I shot spotted deer and blackbuck to eat, stalked a marauding leopard and guarded crops from elephants. In Wyoming, I spent more time hunting and fishing than getting a college education.

When I drifted to Florida it was still a wild place, where I learnt about snakes from the best. Commercial snake hunters like me took thousands of snakes out of the Everglades and adjacent farmlands. The pet trade had begun, and the gigantic surge that would threaten snakes like the eastern indigo was a few years away. As I honed my skills, Carl Kauffeld, whose book *Snakes and Snake Hunting*[3] served as a guide, lamented revealing the locations of snakes, as even then hunters were devastating their populations. Snake numbers had a chance of rebounding as long as the habitat was intact. But that was not to be.

The development boom started soon after I left the States in the late 1960s. In Florida, real estate developers tore up large swathes of wilderness to build condos for retirees flocking to the Sunshine State from the north. The state also drained the Everglades to reclaim land. All these activities were far worse for the reptiles. Conservation laws in later decades protected wildlife and their lands, but not before snakes had suffered a serious decline.

You may wonder how a boy who grew up loving snakes could exploit them. It's for that reason this is not a memoir, but an autobiography. If I were to cleave to the single track of how I am viewed—a reptile conservationist, educator and researcher—a lot of back story would be missing. In an autobiography, authors are caught between extolling their virtues and achievements, and camouflaging their raging egos. It would be dishonest to chronicle the awards and applause, and airbrush my bloodthirsty past off the record. The simple thing to do would be to leave out these inconvenient parts as they are not acceptable activities for a conservationist today. That way I'd escape

---

3 Carl Kauffeld, *Snakes and Snake Hunting* (New York, US: Hanover House, 1957).

the criticism that's sure to come. By revealing my bloody hands and early love of destruction, whether it be of animal life or explosives, you, the reader, can see the real me with all the warts. I make no apologies, since I don't view myself as a conservationist—that's a label others have bestowed upon me. I've always done what I loved, whether fishing, hunting, catching snakes or championing the cause of habitat protection and protecting snakes.

This was who I was, and still am to a large extent—contradictions, complexities and all.

SECTION 1

GROWING UP

1

THE BIG MOVE

Dreamtime at Age Eight

INDIA WAS IN MY blood long before I was born. Aunt Elly, Ma's eldest sister, married H.H. Abdul Razzack in the 1920s. I don't know the story of how the paths of an artist of Swedish descent and an Indian engineer crossed in the States. Their East Village digs attracted visitors from the Indian subcontinent. When Rama, who would later become my stepfather, landed in New York City, on his way to the Massachusetts Institute of Technology, which was also Razzack's alma mater, it was inevitable that he would knock on the door of 248 West 11th Street, Greenwich Village. In the course of Rama's frequent visits, he and Ma fell in love.

Before that, Ma married Dad, not once but twice. They, Romulus Earl Whitaker Jr and Doris Norden, met as students at the Columbia University School of the Arts, New York City, in 1932. Their relationship was tumultuous, and they divorced the first time soon after Ma gave birth to Gail, my elder sister. But they had second thoughts and got hitched again, resulting in my existence.

In May 1943, I was born at Kew Gardens General Hospital in Queens and christened Romulus Earl Whitaker III after my father, whom everyone called Earl. Ma called me Breezy since Romulus seemed too pompous for a little brat. I was one of a foursome—

my sister Gail, an Irish setter Tempest and the cat Zephyr, all named for the wind. Don't ask me why Ma did that.

That year, Dad, a down-home North Carolina boy, enlisted in the army, and we moved to live with Ma's family in Wollaston, on the outskirts of Boston. After basic training in Camp Croft, South Carolina, he trained to be a paratrooper, and his unit was dispatched to Europe. He broke his back during a jump and was discharged. When the Nazis shot and killed one of his buddies while he was floating down to earth over Belgium in the Battle of the Bulge, he felt ashamed and guilty. Had the army not relieved him, Dad was sure he would have also suffered a similar fate. But he had conflicted feelings. In a letter to Ma, he wrote, 'Better him than me.'

After Dad's discharge, Ma, Gail and I moved to live with him at Sea Cliff on Long Island. He worked in his father's store, Whitaker and Higgins, on Bleecker Street in Manhattan's East Village, supplying bandages and pharmaceuticals to the US Army. Marrying a second time had been a mistake.

Ma didn't proclaim to be a left-leaning liberal, but Dad subscribed to right-wing ideology. He had been a member of the pro-Nazi German American Bund before the war broke out. I didn't ask him about it for fear of jeopardizing our tenuous relationship. Besides these political differences and failings, Ma's strong will was too much for my father. Despite the closed door and Gail's hands covering my ears, I heard loud voices, followed by long silences and then aching absences. He was an alcoholic and beat Ma, while Gail and I cowered in our room. That did their marriage in, and they separated in 1945, when I was two and Gail was six.

We moved back into Ma's family home in Wollaston, where the Nordens wrapped Gail and me within their fold.

My grandfather, Samuel Norden, 'Pappa' to the family, arrived as a merchant marine in the States from Sweden in 1889. Augusta Ericsson, 'Mumma', had been a passenger on the same ship on her way to join her uncle, Captain John Ericsson, the inventor who built the ironclad battleship the USS *Monitor* for the Union Army. But he died before the ship docked in the States. Mumma and Pappa got married in Atlantic City, New Jersey, and moved to Wollaston, where he got a job as a longshoreman. My grandparents spoke English with an accent, Mumma's thicker and harder to understand than Pappa's. Of their seven children, Elly was the oldest and Ma was the youngest.

The two-storey wooden house must have been crowded. Besides Mumma and Pappa, Ma's sister, Aunt Edna, and her husband, Dick Babson, also lived there. Their daughter, Joanie, was a few months younger than me. Family lore says I swatted a wasp before it stung her and stopped her falling out of an upstairs window by holding on to her. As a toddler, I spent hours in the backyard with Pappa, watching the wars between black and red ants with a magnifying glass. My main memory of this house was the aroma of bread, which Mumma baked every day.

Dad largely disappeared from my life after the separation. I remember he took Gail and me to a rodeo at Madison Square Garden, where we sat in the front row. All of a sudden, Lone Ranger and Tonto in costume rode towards us. Having watched their adventures on Mumma's round-screen television, I was excited to see them in real life. To my astonishment, Tonto greeted Dad, 'Hey Earl! Howya doing?' *How on earth does Dad know Tonto!* Dad introduced us.

'Pleased to meet you, Gail and Breezy,' Tonto said as his enormous hand swallowed mine,

I gaped speechless. I looked at Dad with awe for the rest of the outing. Later on, I learnt he was a member of a dude ranch where he had met the actor Jay Silverheels who played Tonto in the television series. Another exciting trip was fishing for bluefish in Long Island Sound. But the other specifics of those memories are as lost as any real feelings of love.

A few months later, Ma rented a country home in central New Jersey near a village called Three Bridges. I'm not sure why we made the move. Perhaps she felt cramped in Wollaston, or she didn't want to burden her parents. I loved wandering in the fields, watching butterflies and birds while Ma read a book. I was too young to have more than a few fleeting memories of this period and place.

There was that time when Tempest bounded up to Ma, who was returning with her arms full of groceries. He stepped on his glass food bowl, which flipped over and shattered, and a flying shard sliced open a vein on her foot. Blood splattered everywhere. While she phoned a neighbour for help, Gail pressed a cloth over the cut. Even as a little kid, I was struck by how gutsy Mummy was in raising two children on her own in the country.

Did we live on alimony and child-care payments from Dad? How did we get around when we didn't have a car and Ma didn't know to drive? I don't have answers. She had a few close friends who visited from New York. Otherwise, the three of us had only each other for company.

Within a few months, we moved again, this time over 320 kilometres to northern New York state, near the Vermont border. Aunt Elly and Uncle Razzack had bought a twenty-two-room mansion, built in 1813, surrounded by forty acres of land nestled among endless forests in the tiny village of Hoosick. The house had a pillared porch, a carriage house, servants' quarters and an enormous barn. After Elly and Razzack bought it, the locals changed its name from the Big House to the Ambassador's Residence.

H.H. Abdul Razzack wasn't an ambassador, although he had the demeanour of one. The soft-spoken man with an authoritative and reassuring baritone voice came from Hyderabad, south India. During the Second World War, he was the principal planning engineer for the Board of Economic Warfare in Washington. Later, he became the chief technical and industrial adviser to the governments of the high-profile and wealthy Nizam of Hyderabad in India and the King of Jordan. The family joked the Nizam paid Razzack's consultancy fees by the minute.

Elly and Razzack, along with friends from the city, and the Babsons, visited Hoosick on weekends and for a few weeks in summer, but otherwise, the idyllic place was ours, where we lived for the next three years. By then, the Babsons had an addition, Joanie's brother Johnny.

Gail, Joanie, Johnny and I spent hours in the attic despite the stench of bat guano, rummaging through boxes stashed there for over a century. We pulled out framed pictures of strangers, ancient coins, antique candlesticks and a damaged spinning wheel, catching glimpses of an earlier era. Like putting together a jigsaw puzzle, we glued together broken Blue Willow china plates that depicted the love story of a Chinese girl of royal birth and a Japanese commoner. We even found a handful of pointed bullets and pretended to shoot by throwing them at each other.

The vast barn became a supersize playhouse, where we kids climbed the ladder to the loft and, yelling the paratrooper's 'Geronimo!', swung on a thick rope to land on the soft, earthy-smelling piles of hay that the previous owners had left behind. Mummy warned a thousand times, 'Watch out for pitchforks.'

We imagined trolls and other fantastical beasts from fairy tales lurking in the dark, dank cellar. When Mummy told us an escape tunnel had been dug during the Revolutionary War, we descended the wooden steps as a group, finding security in numbers, to look for it. We knocked on walls, hoping to hear the hollow sound of a hidden hole. Any little noise sent us screaming and stumbling upstairs. Needless to say, we never found that underground shaft, then or later, when we outgrew our fears. Mummy probably made up that story, one of the many that kept us occupied and out of trouble as children.

One early morning, I lay awake in bed thinking what we could do that day. No one else was up and the house was silent. A strange noise from outside disturbed my thoughts. It seemed to be coming from under the carriage house. I hurriedly threw on shorts and a sweatshirt, pulled on my sneakers and tiptoed downstairs. As soon as I opened the kitchen door, the cold winter breeze froze my nose and cheeks. I followed the animal's tracks on the fresh snow leading to the carriage house, where they disappeared inside a narrow gap under the step. I grabbed a rake that was leaning against the wall of the carriage house and poked the handle inside. It touched something soft, and before I could think of what it could be, a loud screech scared the pants off me. I had no time to step back as the vilest-smelling liquid caught me full in the face. I knew what it was right away. A skunk. I jumped back and ran to the kitchen door. Mummy was putting on the kettle when I thrust my head through the door.

'My god, what is that stink?' she demanded.

Without waiting for a reply, because she knew that smell could have come from only one creature, she marched me to the bathroom. No matter how much I scrubbed myself with soap, that stench lingered on me for a few days. Lesson learnt—I never molested skunks again.

When the Babsons left, Gail resumed drawing, and I spent my days outdoors in a perpetual wonderland. I stuck my hands into tree holes, watched butterflies and beetles, and suffered itchy rashes from poison ivy. Bees stung and ants dug their sharp jaws into me. A spider I had caught with a tea strainer bit the tip of my forefinger, teaching me a lesson for nudging it. Down in the stream leading to the Little Hoosac River, I turned over rocks to find crayfish, grabbed slippery frogs and squeezed toads to hear their peculiar 'let me go' calls.

It wasn't only the tiny creatures that interested me. Woodchucks dug holes and chased each other around the yard. 'How much wood would a woodchuck chuck if a woodchuck could chuck wood,' I chanted under my breath while watching their antics.

Deer often grazed at the forest's edge, which made me imagine beasts like lions and tigers lurking in the dark wilderness. Mummy told me of an encounter with a mountain lion while camping with a friend in the Catskill Mountains, which she scared away by shooting a shotgun in the air.

Mummy started me fishing when I was about four years old. She rigged a long straight stick with a length of string and a bent pin. I collected worms by turning over rocks in the yard and kept them in a jelly jar half full of soil. As I headed for the stream, she warned me against touching the electric cattle fence that blocked the shortcut. I chucked the rod over and gingerly crawled through the strands of wire. After making it unscathed to the other side, I was overcome with curiosity and touched one of the electrified wires, which gave me a jolt. Shaken but none the worse for wear, I continued across the railroad tracks.

The tips of a willow tree dipped into the water and thorny blackberry bushes bordered one of many pools in the stream. I had seen yellow perch and sunfish in that particular pond on previous trips. Settling on an overhanging log, I tried to get a worm on to the pin. Not an easy task, since the sharp point had no barb like a fish hook to hold the slimy, squiggling creature in place. I dropped the bait into the water and waited.

Dragonflies touched and rippled the water, their transparent wings glistening in the sun. Above me, two blue jays on a birch tree cackled at each other. A hawk circled high in the sky. The sunny warmth felt good. *Would Mummy have baked blueberry pie for dinner?*

A sharp tug startled me. With a swirl, a fish almost took the stick out of my hand. I hauled with all my strength and flipped a struggling yellow perch on to the grassy bank next to the log. Before it could wriggle back into the stream, I dove on it, and the spines on its dorsal fin pierced my hands. Wiping the drops of blood on my shorts and ignoring the pain, I carried the fish home.

I burst into the carriage house, which Mummy had turned into her workshop, dangling my catch in front of me, excited and proud.

'That fishing rod worked?' Mummy asked in surprise.

'Can we eat it?'

'It's too small and there are lots of tiny bones.'

Before I felt a twinge of disappointment, she suggested, 'Why don't I make a soup with it for Winken and Blinken [the cats]?'

I agreed.

Hooking that fish set me on a lifelong obsession, which included catching barramundi in New Guinea, mahseer in the Himalayas, largemouth bass in the Everglades and channel catfish in the Mississippi River, to name a few.

Another day, on my way to the stream, I ran into a group of fellow four-year-olds from the village. I joined their game of hide-and-seek among the rows of corn while chomping on the milky kernels of the ripening ears. If we heard the distant thunder of an approaching train on the way to the pool to fish, we waited for it and waved furiously. No one even noticed us, let alone wave in return. We all dreamt of riding in one, better still, riding in the engine with the train driver. My friends had small fishing rods, which were much better than my home-made one.

One let me borrow a hook, which made fishing easier. I coaxed Mummy into buying me a proper fishing rod. This was when a decisive incident set me on my course as a snake missionary.

We rolled over rocks to find earthworms, what my buddies called 'angleworms', for fish bait. One flipped a flat rock and yelled, 'SNAKE!' We crowded around, and they pounded it to death with stones, screaming, 'Kill it, it's poisonous!' I didn't stop them, nor did I join in. Not having seen one before, I was fascinated but afraid. After the boys stepped back, I squatted near the battered creature and examined it. I carried it home on the end of a stick against their advice.

Mummy and Gail were in the kitchen when I walked in.

'The poor thing!' Gail exclaimed.

'It's a harmless garter snake, Breezy,' Mummy said. 'It wouldn't have hurt you.'

'I didn't kill it, Mummy. The other kids did.'

'Promise me you won't kill a snake,' she said.

I readily did. Perhaps this was when I became fixated on the reptiles and vowed to be their champion.

After that episode, I took to turning over every stone—not for earthworms but for snakes. When I found one, I took it home alive in the jelly jar.

'It's a milksnake,' Mummy said.

She took a photograph of a four-year-old me holding it, recording the event for posterity. As cold spring merged into warm summer, I caught gorgeously patterned milksnakes that the village kids called checkered adders, tiny delicate ring-necked snakes, Dekay's snakes, sleek and fast ribbon snakes, and garter snakes. I tried different handling techniques, eventually learning to move one hand over the other as the snake slithered. The excited ones shat and musked on my hands, and each species had a distinctive odour. For instance, garter snakes stank worse than skunks, but milksnakes weren't so bad. I also got bitten a lot, making the local boys react, 'You're gonna die. You're a goner. Just wait and see! A checkered adder bite'll kill you in an hour.'

Mummy bought *Snakes of the World* by Raymond L. Ditmars, who later became one of my heroes. Of course, I couldn't read it by myself.

She read aloud the chapter titled 'The New World Harmless Snakes' several times. Before long, I had memorized their names and every detail about these creatures' habits and temperaments.

Mummy helped me convert an old aquarium into a terrarium in which to keep snakes as pets. To feed them, I caught grasshoppers and small frogs in the fields. She let slip many decades later how distressed she had been to hear the frogs squeaking pitifully. But she said nothing then, not even when I carried snakes in my pockets. Elly got a fright when she drove to the local post office and reached into the glove compartment to get her purse. I had been playing with a garter snake in her Buick and forgot that I had left it there. Mummy must have given me a talking-to, a memory that escapes me now.

Another time, I found a shed snakeskin under a rock. Back at home, I examined it with my plastic magnifying glass. The skin was inside out.

'Mummy, snakes shed their skins the way we take our socks off,' I announced my discovery.

The eye of the snake was covered by a single rounded lens of skin. Everything about them was so wonderfully different. I made out faint long lines down the back. A garter snake.

I found other sheds, but many were difficult to identify. It would be a long time before I learnt about counting scales to figure out the species of snake.

Years later, I asked Ma if my interest in snakes had worried her. Any other mother would have been quick to shout 'Leave them alone!' to discourage such a dangerous passion.

'I wasn't surprised or worried at the time,' she replied. 'Violet [Ma's sister] had also been crazy about snakes. When she was young, she used to carry them in her pocket.'

As her parents had encouraged Violet, Ma reinforced my curiosity. Everyone expected I'd outgrow snakes. As a teenager, I became enamoured of motorbikes, but my interest in snakes didn't wane. Ma confessed she had her moments of doubt.

'How could I as a mother have allowed him to do all this!' she confided to a friend.

'How could you have done anything else?' he had asked in reply.

That to her mind settled it. She couldn't have prevented me from pursuing snakes.

In summer, my friends and I skinny-dipped at a swimming hole in another part of the stream. We balanced on an overhanging branch and jumped off like monkeys and doggy-paddled ashore. Sometimes, a huge snapping turtle lay basking on a half-submerged log or stuck its head out of the water to take a breath.

'That big old turtle's gonna bite your pecker off,' said my buddies every time we saw it.

While wandering alone, I found a six-inch snapper crawling along the shallows of the stream. Instead of shoving a finger in front of its face, I poked it with a twig. The head shot out and snapped it in two, startling me. *If this little cooter could do that, imagine what that big old turtle could do?* Thereafter, I wore my undies while diving, and nothing the other boys said could make me take them off.

What did Ma do while I was running off into the fields and to the stream? She worked on wood in the carriage-house workshop. At other times, she was bent over her sewing machine, or she and Gail were baking something delicious. I was so engrossed in my world that I don't know what she did.

In the evenings, the three of us listened to radio programmes, or Mummy put a fast-spinning 78 rpm vinyl record on a Victrola with a wind-up crank on the side. Since the appliance was temperamental, she didn't want me to touch it. I sat back as the music filled the room, such as Paul Robeson's bass voice singing *Ol' Man River* and *Old Black Joe*. Mummy also played Nat King Cole, and she often hummed his *Nature Boy* as she worked.

There was a boy, a very strange enchanted boy,
They say he wandered very far, very far over land and sea.

Once a month, Gail, Mummy and I caught the Greyhound bus into New York City to stay for a few days with Elly and Razzack in their four-storey Greenwich Village brick house. Elly, a tall, lovely woman with classical Swedish features, was a successful commercial artist.

She worked in her first-floor studio with her horn-rims perched high on her aquiline nose. On a table beside her easel lay a row of trendy shoes. They were singles, never a pair. She specialized in sketching them for ads in fashion magazines.

A natural-born hostess, Elly entertained a lot. If I asked her what was for dinner, she often replied in Swedish, 'köttbullar', with a giggle. I didn't know what was funny about 'small balls' then. When the smell of a baking cake drifted up, I still had time to pound down three flights of carpeted stairs to lick the mixing bowl. Since the kitchen was set below street level, I could see people's legs as they walked past the window. As an adult, I was reminded of the calls of ragmen and newspaper boys of those late-1940s' New York streets on hearing Robbie Robertson sing *Rags and Bones*.

Comin' up the lane callin'
Workin' while the rain's fallin'
Ragman, your song of the street
Keeps haunting my memory.

Mummy, Gail and I often visited the American Museum of Natural History, my favourite place in New York. The dinosaur skeletons captured my imagination on every visit, and I never tired of staring slack-jawed at their immensity. When asked what I was going to be when I grew up, I replied, 'bone-digger-upper'. I lived out those prophetic words as a palaeontologist's assistant for a few months more than a decade later in Wyoming. After a picnic lunch at Central Park, Mummy and Gail read books or sketched while I stalked through the bushes, surrounded by imaginary slavering dinosaurs. My weird brain morphed tadpoles in the pond into baby crocodiles.

This was my world when handsome and jovial Rama arrived with presents and fun. Elly and Razzack sponsored him at MIT and invited him to stay with them during his vacations. It would be years before I could wrap my tongue around his unpronounceable Bengali surname, Chattopadhyaya. He threw me up in the air, to my hysterical delight, and made me laugh with his nonsensical word games.

'Big Bug Breezy, with the boy, boy,' he called.

The wispy tendrils of hair curling out of his large ears fascinated Gail and me. We loved him, and he doted on us. He became the father I never had.

Although I enjoyed visiting my aunt and uncle in the city, my heart was in Hoosick. *Why can't we stay in the country, where there are so many snakes and fish to be caught?* Mummy seemed happy and excited when Rama was around, and he was around a whole lot. His entry into my life would change the course of my destiny forever.

Before long, Rama's parents came to visit 248, but they didn't arrive at the same time because they were divorced. Rama's mother, Kamaladevi, was a freedom fighter, feminist, actor, writer and colleague of Jawaharlal Nehru and Mahatma Gandhi. She had just settled hundreds of thousands of refugees fleeing Pakistan in the township of Faridabad, near Delhi. I didn't know all that then. She didn't seem like anyone else I had met so far in my young life. Since Rama wore suits like other men, I hadn't considered his Indianness. But his mother dressed in gorgeous saris, colourful glass bangles tinkled on her arms and a large red dot decorated her forehead. Her English had an accent, although I had no trouble understanding her.

Harindranath, a poet, actor, politician and comedian, had enormous ears, an impish laugh and a trove of songs. Kamaladevi and Harindranath were gentle people, and I took to them both, at that age oblivious to their greatness.

In May 1948, Granddaddy Harin wrote a poem for Gail and my birthdays, which are four days apart:

Two children on their natal day awaken
To find that they are a year older than
They were a year ago …
To them I send my greetings glad and warm,
The poet-father of a grown-up man,
Ramu—who says Breezy and Gail have taken
His heart by storm:
Now, tell me, Gail and Breezy, is that so?

Yes! Warmest greetings from my poet's pen
To Gail who has this day completed nine
Which means, next year, this day, she will be ten,
So, once again this rhyming pen of mine
Will have to write at least another line
Of equally warm greeting ...
Now, little girl! Though time be ever fleeting
May everyone around you say: 'To Gail
Life always seems a rainbowed fairy tale
Since she has got the knack of lending wings
To the most foolish, ordinary things.'
And now, we come to Breezy-Boy, alive
And kicking at the tender age of five.
A favourite pastime with him, I declare,
Is 'Come on, Ramu, "trow" me in the air!'
A charming lad who, under a magic wand,
Became a blue-eyed angel-boy—and blonde!
His one desire of all his keen desires
Is just to meddle with electric wires
(Which often gives the home a shock or two
Far greater than electric wires do!)
But he himself needs none, the little scamp,
Since he himself is an electric lamp
Self-kindled with a joy that never tires
Without the help of long electric wires!
God bless you both, my loves! God bless you both
And bless your education and—your growth!

Ma may have rued giving *Boy's Book of Snakes* by Percy Morris as my Christmas present because I became an obnoxious five-year-old know-it-all, holding forth to adults about the wonders of snakes. And, of course, in my day and night dreams, I faced hooded cobras, black mambas and enormous pythons.

Soon after New Year, my days of running footloose ended. Mummy enrolled me in kindergarten at St. Luke's School in Greenwich Village.

Surrounded by brick buildings, the school's tiny open area had lots of trees but hardly any space for kids to run around and play. I missed Hoosick's expansive fields and clear streams. We made occasional weekend visits when I fished and caught critters, but there was never enough time to do everything. Months flew by and I moved to first grade.

Mummy and Dad divorced again. For some reason, she had to travel all the way down to Arkansas to finalize it. She brought back a Cherokee Indian turtle shell rattle, which I treasured for many years. By then, Rama had graduated from MIT. In the summer of 1949, Mummy and Rama married. The quiet event didn't register in my mind since Rama was around so much, but I remember digging into apple pie topped with vanilla ice cream at the dinner party. Mummy became Doris Norden Chattopadhyaya, but the closest she came to pronouncing her new Bengali surname was 'Chattopajya'.

Though Dad and I exchanged Christmas and birthday cards, he also remarried and had a baby daughter, and seemed far away in every sense. He sent a ten-dollar cheque every year without fail, which Mummy cashed for me to spend on toys, comics and other treats.

Rama dreamt of setting up a motion-picture colour-processing lab in India, a vanguard move for what was to become Bollywood, the foremost producer of feature films in the world. To learn the fine points of the business and technology, he got a job at Technicolor in Hollywood. In mid-1950, our family of four sped along Route 66 in a brand-new two-door maroon Ford sedan headed for Burbank, north of Los Angeles, California.

At 80 kmph, Rama covered 500 or 650 kilometres each day. The 4,500-kilometre trip would have taken at least a week. Either we were nice kids, or Ma and Rama were patient parents and made up lots of games to keep us occupied. Rama entertained us by mimicking his father, making fun of radio programmes or inventing silly word games. 'Wata wata wistakata wata wata way,' the first sentence of a long rhyme is the only one that sticks in my mind.

For much of the way, I curled up by the back window of the car, watching the scenery zip by. The dark forests of the east captivated me, but I was bored by the monotony of the vast cornfields of the Midwest. We stretched our legs in scenic spots and stopped for hamburgers. Signboards offered some amusement, especially the Burma-Shave ad boards. These ads sped past with one line per board spaced a hundred metres apart.

DROVE TOO LONG
DRIVER SNOOZING
WHAT HAPPENED NEXT
IS NOT AMUSING
Burma-Shave

DON'T STICK YOUR ELBOW
OUT SO FAR
IT MAY GO HOME
IN ANOTHER CAR
Burma-Shave

NO LADY LIKES
TO DANCE OR DINE
ACCOMPANIED BY
A PORCUPINE
Burma-Shave

The boards zipped by too fast, but Gail read them aloud as much for my benefit as for her own pleasure. As we drove through the deserts of New Mexico and Arizona, I recalled the Roy Rogers, Lone Ranger and Cisco Kid westerns on television at Wollaston. Rama gave in when I wanted to spend a night at a motel shaped like an Indian teepee. As exciting as the move across the country was, I'd miss Hoosick.

We lived in Burbank for almost a year. Gail and I were enrolled in Bret Harte Elementary School, where I was in second grade. Unlike St. Luke's, this school had a wide, open playground, where we played marbles, softball and kickball. But I missed fishing, catching critters, and cousins Joanie and Johnny.

Burbank was hot, arid and barren. I moved rocks from the roadside into our yard as shelters for creepy crawlies. I turned these stones over again and again as I had done at Hoosick, but except for a few crickets, nothing ever came to live under them. The lizards basking on rocks were skittish and too fast to catch. But snakes were not far from my mind. For a writing assignment, I wrote, 'The garter snake is non-poisenous. You can pick them up, if you handle them with care.'

I fell in love with cacti, and Mummy, who was pregnant, encouraged this newfound interest by buying tiny pots of the desert plants. Mummy's friend said a rock with a white ring around it would bring me good luck. Hours of scouring sidewalks and empty lots didn't yield one, but I learnt to appreciate the colours and patterns of rocks, which I called 'minerals', and built a sizeable collection.

In March 1951, my sister Christine was born. With blonde fuzz, dimples and blue eyes, she took after Mummy's side of the family. Everyone fell in love with this adorable doll-like angel.

For my eighth birthday, my father sent the usual ten-dollar cheque and a diary with the inscription, 'Happy Birthday! Here is a diary for you. When you write in it, think of me and write to me once in a while. Daddy.' I still have the diary, but it doesn't have a pen scratch on its blank pages, not even to mark my birthday. I treasured it enough to keep it, but the lack of entries illustrates my troubled relationship with him.

When Christine was nine months old, we drove back to New York, where Rama and Mummy began preparations for the big move to India. I left my cacti collection behind at Burbank, but stuffed all my minerals into my trunk.

Since we were leaving for the other side of the world, we celebrated Christmas early. Rama's mother Kamaladevi joined us for the festive occasion. My heart skipped a beat when I found a big box with my name on it underneath the decorated tree. An electric train set, complete with bridges and a miniature station, was the most spectacular present of my life, thanks to Rama. Kamaladevi gave me a cowboy outfit with a hat, boots and a toy six-gun. Mummy's gift to me was another book, *The Dinosaur Book: The Ruling Reptiles and Their Relatives* by Edwin Colbert.

While the adults talked about the events and politics in India, I became a cowboy railway engineer orchestrating catastrophic collisions.

I exclaimed, 'Holy cow!' at a particularly noisy crash.

'When you are in India, Breezy,' said Razzack with a big grin, 'you cannot say "holy cow" because they really are holy.'

The others laughed, but I was confused. *How could a cow be holy? Or is Uncle Razzack pulling my leg?*

After Rama left for India to prepare for our arrival, Razzack organized a film screening for family and friends. *The River* by Jean Renoir was about an English family in Bengal. In a subplot, Bogey, the seven-year-old blond kid, plays a snake charmer's flute, which attracts a cobra. It bites him and he dies. The movie made my family concerned about our move to India. Everyone had the same thought—would this snake-smitten eight-year-old survive in the Land of Snakes? By a strange coincidence, Richard Foster, the cameraman with whom I partnered in 1992 to make *Rat Wars*, my first film for National Geographic Television, had starred in *The River* as Bogey.

Mummy eyed my minerals and suggested I take only a few small ones. While she had to pack everything we needed for our new life, I agonized over which stones to choose. After several rounds of elimination, I got the collection down to ten. I left the electric train behind as well, since Mummy said it wouldn't work in India, where 220 volts was the norm.

On 15 December 1951, my sisters, Mummy and I boarded the liner SS *Independence*. The choppy Atlantic Ocean made me queasy. I couldn't understand why the taste of bile in my throat wouldn't go away.

'How many days does it take to reach India?' I whined.

In my misery, I didn't see Mummy was in worse shape and had to care for Christine at the same time. Gail, however, didn't suffer at all. On the second or third day, my symptoms passed. I explored the vast ship, which felt like a desolate city. Most of the passengers remained out of sight, seasick in their luxurious cabins like Mummy, for much of the trip. In the hallways, I befriended other kids who were also at a loose end.

In the playroom, we played card games and swapped comic books. When we couldn't sit still any more, we sang songs as we loitered around the ship. I tried to impress them by pretending to be a seasoned traveller and polyglot, singing familiar tunes such as *Mocking Bird Hill* and *On Top of Old Smokey* with gibberish lyrics. If they thought I was a fake, they didn't call my bluff. When we grew hungry, we wandered into the cavernous dining hall. For two or three days, we were the only ones there. I don't remember if the adults ate in their cabins, came to the dining hall later or had no appetite at all. We kids chased each other through the hallways, with the uniformed stewards tut-tutting, 'Be careful, children. Don't run.'

I had plenty of time on my own. Stir-crazy, I wandered the long corridors, swaying like a drunk as the ship rolled. I stood on the open upper deck, holding the railing and watching the endless, restless ocean for a few freezing moments before racing below, where it was warm. I may have daydreamt of catching many snakes once we arrived in India but had no premonition of becoming a merchant seaman working on rust-bucket cargo ships crossing that same sea fifteen years later.

Gibraltar was the highlight of the voyage. When the liner anchored, small boats selling scarves, bracelets and other knick-knacks pulled up alongside. Heaving lines flew from the dinghies, which the crew knotted to the railings. Adult passengers I had not seen since we embarked in New York appeared. With shouts and gestures, they leaned over the railing and bargained over their purchases. Trinkets and greenbacks went up and down in tiny bags tied to ropes. I bought a white soapstone turtle for a dollar, and seventy years later, that figurine sits on the sideboard at home. It seemed as if the ship had stopped for the express purpose of buying souvenirs.

When the shopping frenzy abated, we headed into the Mediterranean. Its deep blue waters sparkling in the sun were a startling contrast to the Atlantic's dirty-grey choppy waves. Rocking gently like a cradle, the ship rode the big swells. The Mediterranean was a welcome change. Passengers stayed out on the deck as the cold gave way to warmth.

A few dolphins followed the vessel, while some raced ahead at the bow. We children ran from one end of the ocean liner to the other to watch them. When a half-grown dolphin broke the surface, we squealed, 'There's a baby!' Soon, the pod vanished, leaving us gazing at the empty sea.

When the *Independence* docked in Naples, we were relieved to stand on land once more, none more so than Mummy, who hadn't enjoyed the rolling ship at all. After waving goodbye to our new friends, we boarded a train for Rome, where we stayed a day or two, taking in the sights. At the Vatican, we visited St. Peter's Basilica.

'Do you think the pope's nose is around that corner?' asked our irreverent mother. 'Go and see if you can find it.'

I knew pope's nose was a chicken's ass but didn't know the Pope was a person. Wandering all over the immense building, I peered into every crevice for a poultry body part. Gail didn't believe Mummy, but went along with the joke.

'Aww, Mummy,' I said finally in exasperation. 'There's no pope's nose.'

We boarded our first aeroplane, a twin-engine Air India DC-3, for the next leg of our trip. I was excited to be travelling in this sleek and magical machine. The roaring plane climbed high over the Rome airport, and I pressed my nose to the porthole, watching people, parked aircraft and buildings become smaller and smaller. We made one stop at Dhahran, Saudi Arabia, before touching down many hours later at Juhu in Bombay.

As soon as we stepped out of the plane, the blast of heat felt like opening an oven door. The scent of flowers, spices, wood-fire smoke and other mysterious smells assailed us. By the time we walked to the metal-roofed Quonset hut that served as the arrival hall, my hair stuck to my scalp and sweat trickled down my back, an unfamiliar experience. Customs officials couldn't make head or tail of the American household items in our trunks. Mummy lied with a straight face, claiming the liquid in the baby bottles was Christine's medicated formula. If an officer had taken a good sniff of that stuff, he'd have keeled over. The bottles contained a precious fifth of Johnnie Walker Black Label Scotch whisky,

Rama's favourite, and pure gold in India in those Prohibition days. Eventually, after what seemed hours, customs and immigration waved us through.

I was delighted to see Rama waiting at the exit.

'Big Bug Breezy, with the boy, boy!' he said hugging me. 'You've become such a big girl, Gail,' he commented to her delight.

He lifted Christine from Mummy's tired arms and baby-talked as she gurgled in response. While he organized the loading of our trunks into a taxi, we piled into the familiar flashy Ford, which had been shipped over from New York. I sat in front while the ladies took the rear seat. I was startled to hear Rama talk in what sounded like gibberish. I had been pretending to speak a foreign language on the ship, but he could actually communicate in one. It was so alien to my ears, I couldn't make sense of what he was saying.

When Rama started the car, I was ready to relax—we had finally arrived. We were exhausted from ten days of travelling. Little did I realize this was the beginning of the real journey.

2

A NEW LIFE

Life's a Beach

RAMA DROVE THE MAROON left-hand-drive Ford through Bombay's Santa Cruz airport exit gate and merged with the manic traffic on the main road. I felt like I'd landed on another planet.

I gaped at the chaos. Lots of people everywhere. Kids walked, raced and played without adult supervision. Red rusty, dented double-decker buses spewed thick black exhaust and listed dangerously to one side. Cows ambled across the thoroughfare, with traffic swerving around them, while a few others stood on the sidewalks, using their tongues to peel garish posters off the walls. Oblivious to the humans and vehicles, they chewed as thoroughly as they would in the peace of a meadow. Razzack had been right—cows must be holy, since everyone dodged and made space for them. But nobody shooed away the half-asleep donkeys huddled in groups. Nor did anyone care about goats mingling with pedestrians. *Are they holy too?* Cars honked non-stop and narrowly missed crashing into jaywalkers. Someone was sure to get killed, and I didn't want to miss it. My new home and country were far more exciting than anything I had experienced in the States in my eight-year existence. I was deaf to the conversation between Rama, Mummy and Gail, with all my senses focused on what was happening outside the window.

Rama parked at Hotel Miramar, right on the coast in Colaba at the southern tip of Bombay. Until our house was ready, we were to stay here. It was a hotel only in name. It didn't have a front desk and was really a block of furnished apartments.

I wrote to my cousins back in Wollaston. 'It doesn't seem very different here, except that the people wear different clothes and sleep out on the streets at night, and even on the city streets cows and goats just walk along. I haven't seen any snakes yet, but before we go to school Rama is going to have a snake charmer come here and show us his snakes.'

Why did I write 'It doesn't seem very different here' when almost nothing seemed familiar? Was I reassuring my cousins or myself? I couldn't help gawking at everything. Even the birds behaved differently. Crows cawed aggressively from the window sills, and if no one paid attention, they boldly flew in and stole from the dining table. Outdoors, black kites nicked food from my hands.

Those first days were a whirlwind, as Rama drove us around, introducing us to the city. We visited the marine aquarium, where I gaped at stingrays, octopuses and small sharks; a fair, where we rode the merry-go-round and the Ferris wheel; and the film laboratory, which was still under construction.

One day, we were getting ready to go out, when two teenage boys armed with air rifles knocked on our front door and asked if they could shoot pigeons from our balcony. Before I could throw the door wide open and ask them in, Mummy crossly told them to leave. Those rifles stayed in my mind with the persistence of an itch. I tried to talk Mummy into buying one for me. When she wouldn't commit, I badgered Rama, even though there was little chance of succeeding.

I resigned myself to tamer pastimes. Low tide left pools on the rocky sea edge. I slipped as soon as I set foot on the mossy rocks and scraped my knee. Lesson learnt, I began to tread carefully. Strange marine creatures were trapped in the pools—everything from sea anemones to colourful fish. The many hours of being in the tropical sun broiled me. Over the following days, my skin peeled off in patches, making me feel like a snake. Mummy's warnings about spending too much time in the sun didn't prepare me for the novel experience of getting sunburnt.

After an afternoon of exploring the tidal pools, I ran into the two pigeon-hunting boys at the entrance of the hotel and introduced myself. For some reason, they called me 'Burger' even after I corrected them. They let me handle their air rifle, and for a moment I imagined stalking tigers through the forest with a high-calibre rifle. The other residents in the building considered pigeons pests and let them shoot the birds, which the guys took home for the pot.

Rama organized a second Christmas celebration, which doubled as a welcoming party. After dark, the apartment filled with a bewildering crowd of uncles, aunts and cousins. Although I missed the warmth and affection of the Swedish family back home, I had gained a whole new one here in India. They spoke Konkani with each other, but switched to English with us. My eyes popped on seeing a long gift-wrapped parcel with my name on it. A BB gun! It wasn't an air rifle, but I was delirious with joy. Another present was a box of fireworks. I couldn't wait to set them off. After a sumptuous dinner, Rama pulled out a tabla and, sitting cross-legged on the floor, drummed with elan as he sang. The rhythm and the lightning movement of his fingers hypnotized me. Rama seemed like another person among his relatives than when he was with us.

A few evenings later, we drove to Ruia Park at Juhu Beach to check on the progress of the house renovation. I waited impatiently for darkness to fall when Rama would help me set off the fireworks on the beach. The sparkling display made Christine laugh, and her eyes glitter.

We missed our Indian grandparents Kamaladevi, whom everyone called 'Amma' here, and Granddaddy Harindranath. Since arriving in India, we hadn't seen them. Kamaladevi was based in Delhi, but Granddaddy lived nearby with Sitamma, who had reared Rama when he was a child. Granddaddy had stood for elections the previous year and won a seat to India's first Lok Sabha, the lower house of the Parliament, as an independent candidate representing Vijayawada of the then Madras State. So he was often away in Delhi too. Sitamma, however, more than made up for their absence.

On Sundays, Rama drove us to Matunga, a locality in Bombay, to his cousin Tara Aunty's house, where we sampled hot Indian gravies, rich sweets and fried savouries. Our many questions, 'What's this?', 'What's that?', amused the relatives. I became firm friends with Tara Aunty's sons Naren and Sunder. No one from Granddaddy's side of the family lived in Bombay, and I didn't get to know any of them.

Two weeks later, we moved into what was to be our home for the next few years—a three-bedroom, Western-style bungalow, surrounded by rows of banana and coconut trees. I had my own room, with ample space for my minerals and books. The beautiful sandy beach was empty except for fishermen. This northern enclave was not yet part of Bombay, now a 20-million-strong megapolis known as Mumbai. Most of our neighbours were white expatriates from England, the States and Australia, employed by General Electric, Burmah Shell and Caltex.

Since my parents were away during the day, they hired Kumar to manage the household, answer the door, cook and make sure we kids didn't get into trouble. The young, unmarried Malayali man lived in the servants' quarters behind the house and spoke English. A Tamil governess, or ayah, looked after Christine. In later years, Ma told me she had to instruct the lady that smearing opium paste on the nipple of the bottle was not the way to get the baby to sleep. I had thought this was a myth, but apparently, the practice was common then.

The din of cawing crows and crowing roosters roused us from bed every morning. After a breakfast of toast and eggs or a bowl of cornflakes, Rama and Mummy left for the city. I watched the fishermen on the beach hauling in their nets, while Gail didn't lack for subjects to draw.

In the afternoons, I shot my BB gun at an empty can. Pretending to be one of the heroes in the westerns on television back in Wollaston, I stalked crows as if they were the bad guys. But the smart birds never let me get close enough.

Kumar made sandwiches for lunch and Western cuisine such as meat and potatoes, casseroles and baked macaroni and cheese for dinner. Food was the one familiar thing in our changed lives.

I was mucking around in the backyard one afternoon when a big snake slithered out from behind some planks leaning against the garage. *Is it a cobra?* It had a thin neck but didn't have a hood marking. *Is it a rat snake?* But it had already zipped away.

'*Samp, samp* [Snake, snake]!' I excitedly called to the neighbour's gardener, the only human in sight.

By then, I had learnt the most important Hindi words from Rama.

'*Kahan* [Where]?' asked the neighbour's gardener.

'*Udhar* [There],' I said, stretching my arms out. 'This big.'

'*Shayad dhaman tha* [It was probably a rat snake].'

The incident with the snake surprised Mummy, who had assumed there would be none in a bustling city. Downtown Bombay may have been busy, but Juhu was a laid-back residential suburb. She was more concerned about our safety from another animal, warning Gail and me to be careful of the skinny, sometimes sore-covered, mongrels wandering on the beach. Despite our best efforts to stay away from them, a mutt we named Jellybean attached himself to us and became a fixture at home.

Amma visited Bombay, staying with friends in the city so she could attend meetings. She dropped in, bringing gifts from her travels around the country. I faced a problem: How to address her? For some reason, perhaps at her bidding, Kamaladevi never became 'Grandma'. *Should I call her Amma, like everyone else?* I nicknamed her Amma Doodles, a frivolous name for a stern lady to whom everyone was obsequious. But when she heard my name for her, she giggled. And the name stuck.

I overheard the adults talking about Granddaddy's notoriety and acerbic wit in Parliament. He made fun of the ministers, not even sparing Prime Minister Jawaharlal Nehru. I had only vaguely been aware of his involvement in the Indian political and cultural scene. Decades later, in 2009, reading Sadanand Menon's piece in *Business Standard*, I learnt more about him:

Harindranath or 'Baba' as some of us knew him passed away in 1990, unsung and unacknowledged for all the services rendered to a series of cultural/political causes. He had been among the founding fathers of both Progressive Writer's Association and Indian People's Theatre Association. … in the 1942 Quit India Movement … it was Baba's songs (like *Shuru hua hai jung hamaara, shuru hua hai jung / Yudh karenge shuddh marenge nar-naari ek sangh*) [Our fight for justice at last has begun, has truly begun / A battle that will claim martyrs, both men and women as one] that were on the lips of the hundreds of thousands who marched down the streets.[1]

Granddaddy visited occasionally, and Sitamma played a big part in our lives, sometimes living with us when Granddaddy was in Delhi attending Parliament. Not only did she make the best sweets, but she had everything under control around the house. She didn't speak much English and I didn't speak much Hindi yet, so we communicated in gestures.

Meanwhile, Rama was busy every day at his motion picture processing lab in Parel, making preparations to move it to a huge, brand-new building designed by Mummy, on Dr Annie Besant Road, where it still stands. It was called Ramnord Research Laboratories, a meld of their names—Rama, with Mummy's maiden name Norden.

This dream world ended soon. Gail and I were to go to Lawrence School, in Lovedale, a hill station 7,000 feet up, 900 kilometres away, in south India. A family friend had recommended it as one of the best schools in the country. What followed was the worst time of my life.

---

1 Sadanand Menon, 'Re-Visiting the IPTA years', *Business Standard*, First published on 17 April 2009, https://www.business-standard.com/article/opinion/sadanand-menon-re-visiting-the-ipta-years-109041700102_1.html

3

LOVEDALE

Military School from Hell

I N FEBRUARY 1952, A little more than a month after we landed in
India, the five of us arrived at Victoria Terminus. The station was a
chaos of passengers rushing about and uniformed railway staff pushing
trolleys loaded high with boxes. As soon as the driver parked, porters
hemmed us in.

'Sahib, sahib,' they pestered in chorus.

'Carry all luggage, ten rupees,' offered one.

'Nine rupees,' said another.

Rama bargained in Hindi with the head porter. Two men piled our
suitcases and bedrolls on a cart and led the way with surprising speed
through the crowds to the platform. Linking our hands so we wouldn't
be separated, we hurried behind them. There was no time to gape at
anything as we dodged people sleeping on the floor, squatting in groups,
and rushing in every direction carrying boxes, trunks and bags.

We shoved our suitcases under the seats on the train and threw our
bedrolls on the upper berths. As an eight-year-old, I was enamoured
of trains and was excited to finally travel in one, especially on the two-
night ride to Madras, watching villages, farmlands and forests whizz
by. We carried plenty of snacks and, when the train stopped for a few
minutes at any of the big stations, we bought lukewarm soda pop from

vendors calling out 'Cooldrink, cooldrink, cooldrink' as they rolled their carts along the platform, running a metal bottle opener across the glass bottles. *Tring, tring, tring.*

In Madras, we boarded another train for Mettupalayam, at the foot of the Nilgiri Hills, where we caught a mountain locomotive that chugged up scenic hillsides to Lovedale. It was so slow that a few passengers ran alongside and hopped aboard again. The cool air, almost like Hoosick, had the pervasive minty scent of eucalyptus.

The housemaster ushered us into Kailas House, the dorm for fourth and fifth graders. We followed him down the long room lined with two rows of barracks-style beds until he stopped at the bed that was to be mine. A wooden trunk at the foot of it would hold my things. There were no desks or chairs, and any reading or writing would be done in the study hall. Gail would live in another dorm, called Girls' House. Mummy promised Gail and me that Rama, Christine and she would rent a cottage near the school soon and live there for a while. And they left. I had never been on my own before and I didn't know what to expect. That was for the best.

Except a few British kids, most pupils were Indians. Gail and I were the only Americans. We may all have spoken English, but the cultural differences extended beyond our accents.

Lawrence School started as an orphanage for the children of British soldiers and clerks. For almost a century until then, it had been a military school. Only three years earlier, it had turned civilian—not enough time to shake off its old ethos of heavy-handed discipline, which included caning. Despite his cordiality in our parents' presence, the housemaster receded to being a distant figure of authority. The prefect, an older student who was in direct charge of all the kids in the dorm, was his henchman.

The daily routine was regimented. At 6 a.m., a senior student played the bugle: *Charlie, Charlie, get out of bed, Charlie, Charlie, stand on your head.* We shot out of bed and got dressed, pulling on green shirts, which was the colour of our dorm, brown shorts and canvas shoes. Without a moment to lose, we assembled in the playground for PT, or physical training. We did callisthenics for half an hour, followed by chota—

bun and tea. This was odd, since at home Mummy said I was too young to have tea or coffee.

Often, the stale bun had weevils. As a new kid, I didn't want to attract attention by complaining. The others chomped into theirs, neither noticing nor being bothered. When I pointed out the bugs to another kid, he shrugged. Too hungry to throw it away, I swallowed it and took a gulp of the sweet, thin tea to lubricate its passage down.

Then we returned to the dorm to make our beds and straighten our lockers. The bedspread had to be stretched taut as if it had been ironed. I ran around my bed, pulling and tucking in every corner, but couldn't get rid of the wrinkles. On my first day, the prefect took one look at my bed and thrashed my bare calves with a switch.

'No snakes in the bed,' he shouted, making the creases seem cute.

The others snickered and looked away. Red welts bulged where the thin cane had made contact with my skin. More than the physical hurt, the humiliation of being beaten in public stung.

'Pull it tight,' he ordered.

I did as told, with tears pricking my eyes. If I was a wimp, it was because no one had raised their hand against me until then. This was only the first of several beatings to come. But I'll admit there's nothing like the fear of being whipped to make one learn quickly.

We plastered our hair with Brylcreem and changed into our day uniform of khaki shirts, shorts, woollen jackets and dark brown ties. I was befuddled by the tie and somehow knotted it right by mimicking the others. Then began the laborious process of putting on footwear—over the woollen socks, we wore hose tops, which looked like tight leg warmers, up to our knees, and folded the edge over. Then we put on our ankle-high, spit-polished black boots with steel horseshoe soles that made a military-like 'clamp, clamp' as we walked. Next, we wound puttees, a strip of khaki cloth about three inches wide and two to three feet long, from the top of our boots to the folded edge of the hose top. The tapered end of the puttee tucked into a fold. We had better be done with this elaborate preparation by the time the bugle call announced breakfast. If my puttee didn't meet the prefect's standards, or if I took longer than the others, the switch came out. A few lashings later, I mastered the style and speed.

We couldn't saunter into the dining hall. That was for normal people. Since we were being schooled to become automatons, we lined up according to our houses outside the hall and marched in. We couldn't sit anywhere we liked either. We each had our spots allocated at the table. All that drama for a pitiful breakfast of semolina porridge. With the mandatory worms. Twice a week, we got a treat—a boiled egg and toast. Eggs were special, and the others bartered with each other: 'I'll trade marbles for your egg [pronounced "yegg"].' Forget marbles, I was prepared to kill for another egg.

As if this regimentation wasn't unbelievable enough, there was more to come. We were all by default in the NCC, the National Cadet Corps. An older student taught a group of younger students to march and hold a rifle with military precision. Of course, we didn't have real firearms but wooden replicas. He occasionally disappeared, and upon his return would adjust the position of our heads up and down with a hand that stank of shit. I grew to hate these drill sessions and, by extension, the school itself. I had nightmares of marching cadence with the instructor barking 'Left right, left right, left right', and woke up in a sweat when I missed a step, fell out of line or turned right instead of left.

Much later, I understood this was the way of the military. They instilled discipline from the beginning, so there would be no nonsense. You don't say 'no', nor do you question. You do as you are told. In wartime, if you didn't obey the sergeant, you might get killed. But I was an eight-year-old gringo kid, unaccustomed to such a rigid regimen.

With our minds numbed from this stomping back and forth, we lined up and marched to our classrooms. I had missed third grade and was in the fourth 'class', as they called it in this school. Each desk came equipped with an inkwell and a dip pen. Dropping the pen and bending the nib annoyed the teacher, another terrifying human. Despite missing a year of school, I didn't do badly in academics, nor did I excel.

We marched into the dining hall for lunch and dinner of traditional spicy south Indian meals of rice, sambhar and some vegetables. In the month I had been in India, I wasn't yet used to chillies, which were chopped fine or ground into a paste and mixed with everything at the table. The only thing that didn't set my mouth on fire was the dhal. The frugality of my diet left me hungry all day.

In the evenings, we raced to the playground for sports. At first, the teacher made me try horse riding. He put me on a horse and whacked its rump, setting the beast off at a trot. I sat, terrified, bouncing up and down and holding on to the reins and saddle for dear life as my bones rattled. To give him credit, he might have tried to teach me to ride, which was lost on me. He probably recognized after the second or the third attempt that I wasn't right for the cavalry. Before I quit horse riding for good, an exciting incident took place.

Carpenters had erected a huge, flimsy castle out of canvas and plywood for a theatrical play at a sports field next to the forest. Along a bridle path, which skirted around this structure, a horse threw off a student and bolted on hearing or smelling something near the spot. Soon everyone chattered with excitement about a leopard holed up in the castle. Some boys boasted of seeing the animal; a few claimed it had charged at them. They might have been making up stories, but the school didn't want to take any chances. The principal announced we were to walk in groups. Horse riding was suspended until further notice, much to my relief. Hunters arrived to shoot the leopard, which they did.

We marched in order to see the big, scary animal stretched out on the grass. The boys ahead of me in the line pulled a whisker out as a souvenir. When it was my turn, I ran my hand along its bristly body, ears, teeth and claws. The beautiful leopard seemed huge, and I wished it were alive. It reminded me of a realistically mounted one at the Natural History Museum in New York a lifetime ago. I had only a minute or two, and then it was time to move on.

After the short-lived lesson in horse riding, the sports master made me try boxing. The end of that ordeal came when I slugged my opponent in the nose, causing a distressing amount of blood to stream down his chin and on to his white T-shirt. I had overstepped the bounds of behaving like a sportsman. In my defence, he had hit me first, and it had hurt.

Between evening activities, kids played with spinning tops, but I didn't have one. I tried to use a carrot, which didn't work at all. If someone shared their top with me, I forgot about my troubles and enjoyed myself. That didn't happen often enough. I'd have to save my allowance to buy a top for myself.

Our weekly allowance of one rupee and eight annas came in Chinese coins. We weren't allowed to have Indian currency, and the prefect confiscated any he found on us. We exchanged the coins at the tuck shop for candies called goose eggs, bull's eyes and Extra Strong peppermints. I craved this sweet stuff and couldn't get enough of it.

For a week, I resisted these sweets, the one joy in my life, to buy two tops. We wound a length of string around the grooves at the narrow end of the top, and on the count of three threw it down with force to set it spinning within a circle. The one that spun the longest was the winner. But if any didn't spin or wandered out of the circle, we placed it within and the other kids let loose their tops on it until it was pockmarked. This action was called 'goonch', to make holes. We were such savages that instead of making a goonch or two, we tried to cleave the top in two.

We also played marbles, or, as we called it, mibbles or mibbs. I ditched the American style of shooting, by placing the marble on the curved forefinger and using the thumb to flick it at another one. The Indian way was more dynamic. You drew the mibble back on your middle finger and let it fly. The force of this catapult action could even shatter other mibbles. We had names for each one, depending on their appearance. The glass ones were called aggies or shinies, and the steel ball bearings peeries or steelies.

For a change, we attempted to play cricket. Since we didn't have a kit, and sticks and planks didn't cut it, we gave up and stuck to tops and mibbs. I didn't take part in any other sport because, as I sadly wrote to Johnny, 'I am slow in running, and in jumping I will fall.'

Besides games, there was nothing to look forward to. We did homework in the evening in the study hall before going to bed. No music, radio or television. And no reading storybooks in bed. In every aspect, life at the school was far from enriching, with its many rules and punishments.

We were unleashed on weekends. Of course, we did homework and wrote letters to our families, which had to follow a format: 'Dear mother and father, how are you and all at home? I am fine. I like my school very much. Everything's lots of fun here.' I'm not sure if I complained to Mummy, or if the school censored my letters. Her cheerful letters about Christine, Jellybean and other news from Bombay—with no further mention of coming to live in Lovedale—made me even more dejected.

Although jungles covered the neighbouring slopes, no one went hiking. So my introduction to the wilds had to wait. The devout Christian kids attended church on Sunday, but I played marbles and tops in the playground with the other boys. Despite these games, I didn't form any close bonds with my playmates. I was despondent from the awful food and severe discipline, which perhaps came in the way of making friends.

The final straw came during a cross-country run. After running a long way, I shuffled on exhausted feet down the home stretch. A boy lay on the ground as if he were sleeping. Thinking he was taking time out, I nudged him with my foot to make him get up before he got into trouble. But he had passed out. I called the nearest adult for help.

Later, another student told a teacher that I had kicked this boy when he was down. Summoned to the headmaster's office, I went with trembling knees, knowing nothing good was in store. Without asking for an explanation, Mr K.I. Thomas told me to hold out my hands and caned my palms. I fought the urge to curl my fingers. In my fury and bitterness at being punished for something I didn't do, I blinked to keep the tears back and swallowed the sobs. He didn't stop with one, two or even three raps. My refusal to cry seemed to make him more furious. My palms burnt with pain and then became numb. The only sounds in the room were the whine of the cane through the air, punctuated by a dull slap as it met my hand. When he had finished, beads of sweat dotted his forehead and he dismissed me from his office.

The other boys stopped whatever they were doing and watched me head back to the dorm. Although no one said anything, I felt I had risen in their estimation. But that did nothing to quell my humiliation, pain and unhappiness. I had enough of the school and wanted to get out.

By evening, my sore hands were swollen so thick that I couldn't close them. I marched with the others into the dining hall for dinner, but barely ate anything. I didn't have an appetite. That night in the dark, I finally allowed the tears to flow.

When Gail and I met after lunch the next day, I showed her my hands. She was horrified. A few days ago, her classmate had been caned on her palms on the stage in front of all the students for using another student's toothpaste without permission. Gail had objected to the extreme punishment for such a little mistake and complained to her housemother. So when I was caned, she was livid and called Mummy from the school phone and reported the incident. I continued with the motions of what was expected of me, but I was depressed.

I cheered up on hearing Granddaddy Harin was to be a guest at the school. In preparation for the event, we learnt a song written by Rabindranath Tagore, *Kharabayu boy bege charidik chai meghe*. Although I don't know its meaning, I can still sing the whole song with enough gusto to rival any Bengali.

The big day arrived, and the entire school applauded as Granddaddy took the stage. I felt comforted seeing his familiar face. The ultimate showman, he had everyone enthralled with his poems and jokes. After the show, I met him backstage and he asked me about the caning. By then my hands had almost healed, but my emotional hurt was still raw and came pouring out in a torrent. He was appalled and angry that I was being beaten. Since Granddaddy had already planned to visit Lovedale at the time of Gail's call, Mummy had urged him to bring me home to Bombay. Gail stayed on until the end of the school year.

Decades later, Thomas became the principal of Sishya, a posh school in Madras, and I was tempted to give him a shock, or a sock. The rumour was the sadistic prefect had been committed to an insane asylum. Although I can't vouch for its veracity, I took some satisfaction in it.

Despite the misery of those months, Lawrence School prepared me for my stint in the US Army fifteen years later and planted the seed of aversion to uniforms, military discipline and organized violence.

4

FREEDOM

Back to the Beach

BACK IN BOMBAY, I lost no time in shaking off the misery of Lawrence as a bad dream and dove headlong into a carefree existence on Juhu Beach and the wonderful sea. Every morning I drank a glass of fresh, creamy buffalo milk, scarfed a scrambled-eggs-and-toast breakfast and raced barefoot on the sand to watch the loincloth-clad fishermen.

A man stood on the shore with one end of the net's thick, braided coconut-fibre rope wrapped around his waist like a belt, while other men in a rough-hewn plank boat rowed out into the sea, laying the heavy shore seine in a huge semicircle, about 300 feet across. Lead weights at the bottom and balsa floats on top turned the net into an invisible underwater curtain. When the boat returned to shore, the men jumped out with the other end of the rope. Chanting in unison, two dozen men dragged the net ashore. The bunt, a conical bag of fine mesh at the back, trapped the fish. The men threw pufferfish, jellyfish and sea snakes on the sand, where they would die. So I flicked them into the water with a stick. Sometimes Christine and her nanny joined me. My sister was delighted when I showed her how the puffers inflated themselves when you pressed their tails. The jellyfish were goners by this time. The fishwives opened them and took the small fish they found inside. Divvying up the catch, the ladies loaded their baskets and made for the city's markets.

After watching the men for a day, I offered to help haul the net ashore. The amused fishermen made space for me in a line of heaving, sweaty bodies, even though I didn't have enough strength to make much difference. In return for my assistance, the men paid me with a mackerel or a handful of sardines. At home, Kumar fried the fish for me, since there was too little to go around.

Sometimes, two guys with a smaller net stood behind the main shore seine, catching anything that jumped over or escaped under the net. These fish were fair game, and it was a case of catchers, keepers. On many days, nobody trapped the escapees. It seemed like a fun thing to do, so I nagged Rama until he bought me a twenty-foot net. I recruited Atul, a fisher kid, to help me stretch it between two bamboo poles behind the seine. After sharing the catch with him, I took the rest home, often adequate for a meal for the entire family.

One day, Atul and I hit the jackpot, netting several mackerel that had leapt over the big net. A fishwife stomped over, screaming in Marathi and grabbed them from my net. I couldn't understand why she was upset. The watching men said nothing while Atul shifted from one leg to the other. She took what was ours and stacked them in her basket. I didn't know the language to argue. In anger, I flipped her basket, scattered the fish and strode away without a backward glance. She screeched until I was out of earshot, but she never messed with me again.

Most of the morning was gone by the time the catch was unloaded and the fishwives set off. I hung out with Atul and the other kids, bobbing in the waves and body surfing until my eyes stung from the salt, while their fathers repaired their gear. The water was clean, with none of the plastic garbage and tar you see nowadays. I learnt to swim in the shallows, which extended half a kilometre from shore. My skin turned dark brown and my hair bleached white from the hours spent in the sun. I picked up a smattering of Marathi and Hindi words while trying to converse with my friends.

On weekends, Mr Crombie, an American neighbour and a corporate honcho at Standard Oil, joined me in the sea. One Sunday morning, we were bobbing in the water when he called me in a strangled voice. He had a hard time keeping his head above the surface.

'Breezy,' he sputtered, 'I have a cramp in my leg.'

Slipping my arms under his armpits, I dragged him ashore and laid him on the sand. His leg was bent at a strange angle and he grimaced in pain. I rubbed the tense muscles until he felt able enough to hobble home by leaning on my shoulder. After that incident, I got to know Mr Crombie and his wife well.

Time passed slowly in the afternoons, with no neighbourhood games or sports, and I invented new pastimes. Sometimes, I fired the BB gun at a target in the garden, or let loose arrows fabricated with sticks. When that got boring, I spiced up the game by adding a sharpened nail to the dull end of the darts and shot at a garden lizard. I didn't expect to hit it and felt sick as it writhed and died at my feet. I was too ashamed to tell anyone what I had done.

To make amends, I learnt to catch these hefty foot-long reptiles, with flamboyant spikes on their backs, without harming them. If they were basking on coconut palms, I estimated how high they were by counting the number of rings on the trunk from the bottom. Then I snuck behind the tree and whipped my hand around to grab them before they scuttled away. The spines hurt my hands, and I got bitten a lot. After inspecting their rough scales, sharp claws and stiff tails, I let them go.

Borrowing an idea from the two boys who hunted pigeons, I hired out my services as a self-styled 'pest' controller to the neighbourhood. Here, residents didn't object to pigeons but to sparrows, which roosted inside houses in the gaps between the rafters and corrugated asbestos roofs and rained shit on the furniture below. Any neighbour irritated by the unhygienic conditions just had to call me. It sounded easy.

My first client was Mrs Crombie. I climbed a stepladder after dark and grabbed a bird while the others twittered and flew off into the dark. Now that I had a sparrow in my hand, I wasn't sure what to do next. *Should I release it outside? But it might fly back into the house. How do I kill it?*

'What shall I do now?' I asked Mrs Crombie.

'Let me show you,' she replied, holding out her hand for the bird.

She wrung its neck with practised ease and handed the limp body to me. It was as simple as that.

In those days, chicken wasn't available in supermarkets. People bought them live and killed the birds in their backyards. At home, Kumar did the deed. Twisting the neck of a sparrow wasn't a big deal.

I charged four annas per sparrow and eight for rats, which I caught using traps. In the currency of those days, four pice made an anna, and sixteen annas made a rupee. Mrs Crombie was my best client. Mummy likely ignored my part-time job, but it's also possible I pleaded with Mrs Crombie not to tell my mother, even though they were good friends. Besides paying me for catching birds, she fed me brownies and cookies. No surprise, I was at her home often. Perhaps she indulged me since she didn't have kids.

Although Rama had promised to ask a snake charmer to come around, he was far too busy. I finally met two charmers at a neighbourhood birthday party. They looked like princes out of a children's story, with glittering turbans and vests, and their dark, kohl-rimmed eyes flashed when they exaggerated their expressions. I sat impatiently through their performance of sleight-of-hand tricks, waiting to see what was in the round, closed bamboo baskets. Their mongoose, tied to a table leg with a length of string, was also restless. When one charmer opened a container, an excited murmur buzzed through the crowded lawn. He prodded a scrawny cobra to spread its hood while he played his 'been', a weird double-toned musical instrument made from a gourd. To my astonishment, the snake swayed to the music. They were deaf, since they had no ears. But here was one, responding to sound. *Could it hear some notes?* This performance mystified me until I realized the snake was not responding to the tune but to the movement of the charmers' 'been'.

At the end of that session, the two men cleared the space to stage a fight between the mongoose and the cobra. An argument arose among the kids—which one would win. To our disappointment, the grown-ups, perhaps worried it might turn gory, told the charmers to stop and pressed some money into their hands. The snake went back into its basket and the men began packing up. By then the other kids' attention had drifted to games, and I chatted with the two men.

The older, one-eyed and talkative Asmeth spoke more English than I knew Hindi. He narrated fantastic stories of snakes taking revenge and cobras with jewels in their heads. The one about the blunt-tailed red sand boa was the best. He claimed the snake had a head at each end, and it travelled six months in one direction and six in the other. This tale is so popular that years later, when I began giving talks about snakes, people still believed it to be true.

'If the snake has a head at both ends, how does it shit?' I would ask.

But that's getting ahead of the story. As a nine-year-old who had to learn a great deal about snakes, I was taken in by some of these myths. On returning home, I referred to Ditmars's book to separate the bullshit from the facts. Although the charmer was full of imaginative stories, he was the first person with whom I could converse about snakes.

Asmeth opened another basket to reveal a beautiful trinket snake. I took in its velvety yellow-brown head, pretty black stripes running down its eyes, and the startling black and white bands along its body. He took a coin and scraped the teeth off before I could stop him.

'It's not poisonous,' I protested.

'If it bites, you'll bleed,' he said in his defence.

Despite my sadness, I was touched when he gifted it to me. I kept the trinket snake, my first Indian snake pet, for two or three days and let it go in a vacant lot nearby. Before leaving, Asmeth told me where to find him—at Gandhi statue near Juhu Airport.

'Everyone there knows me,' he said. 'Just ask for Sapera Asmeth.'

A week later, Rama's driver took me to see Asmeth and his snakes. I picked up a non-venomous checkered keelback water snake from his basket without realizing what a biter it was. It latched on to my thumb, and blood dripped. Asmeth pried it off my hand and got bitten too. I suspected he did that on purpose to make me feel better. Whenever I got a chance, I met Asmeth to chat about snakes and play with the ones he had.

Mrs Crombie called me one afternoon about a snake crawling in her backyard. Her housekeeper pointed out the rat snake lying still under a plant. It was nearly as long as I was tall.

'I need something to put it in, Mrs Crombie,' I said.

She had a bright idea and directed her housekeeper, 'Bring a pillowcase.'

Little did she know that this was the start of a history of ruining Mummy's pillowcases. I leapt on the snake, grabbed it by the neck and wrangled it into the cloth bag. Mrs Crombie and her household staff, who stood at a distance, applauded, which boosted my ego. I took it home to show Mummy, who urged me to let it go. Word spread that I caught snakes besides sparrows and rats, and people called me to remove them from their homes and gardens. As a young punk new to the country, I was a snake rescuer lucky not to run into any venomous snakes.

When the monsoon began, I was stuck in the house for most of the day, rereading my books and magazines. There was no television in India yet. I grew nostalgic for Hoosick as boredom set in. That had been paradise—an easygoing family, cool weather and lots of creatures. We had made snowmen in winter, and popped popcorn and toasted marshmallows in the living-room fireplace. I missed my grandparents, Mumma and Pappa, and the Babsons at Wollaston, and Elly and Razzack in New York. With little to do, I was happy to be dropped at Tara Aunty's apartment for the weekends, where Sunder, Naren and I flew kites from their roof when the rain stopped. It wasn't a benign game of sailing these paper contraptions in the sky as we did in the States. We used a special string called cutting manja, since it was coated with ground glass. If I let it slip through my fingers, it cut them with the ease of a scalpel. Slicing another kite string took artistry, giving the manja a jerk at the right time without severing my digits. The aim of the sport was to be the last kite flying.

Only when darkness fell and we couldn't see the kites any more did we go inside the house, hungry and tired. After the enforced diet of hot Indian food at Lovedale, I relished the delicious Saraswat cooking at Matunga. When I complained about the hot chillies, Tara Aunty replied, 'Just pick them out before you put food into your mouth.'

Easier said than done. I carefully set aside green beans thinking they were chillies and bit into a fiery piece of 'tomato' or 'eggplant'. Aunty couldn't understand how I could be so blind. The problem was colour-blindness, but no one knew of my affliction then.

Another pastime was listening to Sitamma narrate rambling tales from the Ramayana. The smattering of Hindi I had acquired was adequate to draw me into the mythical world of Rama, the hero after whom my stepfather was named, Sita, after whom she herself was named, and Lakshman. Decades later, Granddaddy had a son he named Lakshman.

After Christine began babbling, one day she declared while pointing a finger at herself, 'Name name Nina, name name Nina.' No one knows where she had heard the name, and henceforth, she became Nina. Around this time, she demanded a pair of fluffy chicks, which were on sale on the roadside, and named them Cocky and Frisky with the same conviction that she had renamed herself. The chicks joined Jellybean in the garden. Mummy was pregnant with brother Neel during this time. While she rested, I spent the rainy afternoons playing with Nina and the chickens.

Twice a week, I rode into Worli with Rama to spend the day at Ramnord, watching my friends, the visual and audio special effects guys, at work. Or I hung out with the editors, who let me splice pieces of film together. Little did I know that I'd someday be splicing my own motion picture. I hopped on the back of the lab's Triumph motorbike, accompanying driver Ramdas as he delivered reels of 35-mm film to the old Parel lab, where some work continued to take place. If Nina came along, both of us sat in the sidecar. At the lab, I pushed her in film carts down the long, tiled hallways between the processing, editing and special effects rooms, where the acrid smell of chemicals and celluloid film hung heavy.

If a movie was showing in the lab's preview theatre, I hunkered in a plush seat and sipped a soda while being transported into some crazy melodrama. At the end of the last reel, when the lights came on, it was strange to see actors such as Nimmi, Vyjayanthimala and Raj Kapoor in real life as they rose from their front-row seats and walked down the aisle, looking so different from their screen roles. I knew them as my parents' friends from the occasional dinner party, and they stopped to chat. But their stardom was lost on me, and I never thought to ask for an autograph.

'Breezy!' Mummy called one afternoon while I was reading in my room.

'Yes, Miss,' I blurted out with military briskness, as I would have at Lawrence School, instead of a relaxed 'Yes, Mummy', and went to the kitchen.

Mummy looked stricken, her flour-covered hands motionless on the dough she had been kneading.

'We should never have sent you to that school,' she said. After a moment, she asked, 'Would you go with me to a premiere this evening? Rama can't come.'

People jammed the road leading to the cinema for a glimpse of the movie stars. Although two men in safari suits accompanied Mummy and me through the back entrance, we didn't escape the jostling and she clenched my hand so we didn't lose each other. The waiting fans enquired of our escorts if the stars Nimmi and Dilip Kumar had already arrived. Inside the theatre, I sank into the allocated seat with relief. Sitting beside me was Nimmi, who chatted as if we were at Ramnord, while I sat tongue-tied, seeing her as a demigoddess for the first time. That was the moment I realized how popular movie stars were in India. I didn't like the scrambling and shoving at the premiere and refused to go to another one, happy to be wrapped up in my own world.

Later that year, a curly-haired, freckled and gap-toothed American kid returned home from boarding school for winter vacation. Craig's family lived in what was called a 'shack', a posh house with a palm-leaf roof, on Silver Beach, about a half-hour's walk from ours, in the vicinity of the houses of actors Raj Kapoor and Dev Anand. I forget how Craig and I met. Perhaps our mothers, who knew each other, introduced us. We became inseparable, wandering barefoot to the beach to help the fishermen haul their nets, swim in the sea, catch fish and goof around all day long.

North of Juhu, not even a half-kilometre's walk from home, was a brook that residents now call Irla Nullah. To us, this was 'The Creek', a great place to dive from the sandbanks into deep water. Schools of small fish flitted along the edge, but my net was too short to catch them. Back at the house, I found a roll of one-foot-wide mosquito netting, left over from making window screens, which was perfect for what we had in mind. We mimicked the fishermen with their seine nets—Craig stood on the shore holding one end, while I walked into the water without spooking the fish. Then we herded them ashore by dragging the screen. We didn't eat these tiddlers, so we gave them to the fisher kids who watched our strange antics.

One boy was clearly impressed with the screen and wanted it. In return, he offered me his throw net. It was not an ordinary one that I could buy from a shop. His father must have spent many days making it. I couldn't believe my stroke of luck and was delighted with the exchange.

Craig and I returned to my house and sat down for lunch when there was a knock on the door. It was the boy who had given me the net, his face wet with tears and snot, accompanied by his father. The man demanded the throw net back, which I reluctantly returned, and he handed me the roll of mosquito screen.

Another area we frequented was a desolate place we called 'six-inchie territory', after a grove of acacia trees with two- to three-inch-long thorns, which we pretended were longer. We carried slingshots or catties, short for catapults, hoping to shoot birds. Neither of us was skilled, so we rarely hit anything. We soon found out why it was eerily empty.

One evening, we arrived to strange sounds and smoke filling the air. We hid behind some bushes and crept closer to see what was going on. A group of people were gathered around a burning pyre; a priest chanted while some men consoled others who were crying. It was a cremation ground. The smell of charring flesh, like barbecue, wafted towards us as we watched, spellbound. When the flames died, a man fished the skull out and broke it with a staff. Craig and I nearly jumped at the sight and sound. We couldn't tear our eyes away from the scene. Eventually, we slipped away before anyone spotted us. That was the first dead body and cremation we had seen. Spooked, we didn't go back for a few days.

We returned home with thorns in the soles of our feet. Mummy worked on my foot with a needle and tweezers. When I winced, she demanded, 'Why don't you wear shoes, Breezy?' Since we spent a lot of time on the beach, footwear wasn't practical.

With Craig's help, I added one more job to my resume—filling potholes. The municipality would dig trenches across roads to lay a water pipe or an electric line and then haphazardly refill them. At first, cars bumped over the uneven surface, but the rains eroded the soft earth, leaving craters. Craig's little brother had a small red wagon, which we used to haul stones and dirt to fix the approach road to Ruia Park. We then went door to door, asking to be paid for our unsolicited labour. When we collected enough coins to make two rupees each, we spent it on ice-cream floats, dunking the ice cream into the soda. Within a few days, the potholes needed repair again. We had hit upon a source of easy money.

In the meantime, Rama and Mummy were enquiring about schools. Craig told me about his school in Kodaikanal, which sounded a lot better than Lawrence. Mummy promised to speak to his mom.

A few days later, Mummy spoke on the phone to the school's representative and enquired about the 'snake situation'.

'It's too cold up here,' he replied with a laugh. 'Snakes don't like it.'

Relieved that her son would be safe, she planned for Gail and me to study at Highclerc School, started by American Protestant missionaries in 1901. I traded military training for a good Christian upbringing. But if that's what the missionary teachers thought, they couldn't have been more wrong.

5

KODAIKANAL

Missionaries and Misfits

MUMMY, NOW HEAVILY PREGNANT, didn't want to travel, and was relieved when Craig's parents offered to take Gail and me to Kodaikanal, 'Kodai' for short. Soon after New Year 1953, we caught the train to Madras from Victoria Terminus, and two nights later, boarded the *Pandian Express* at the Madras Egmore station. Early the next morning, we arrived at the Kodai Road station, at the bottom of the Palani Hills, where porters took our luggage to the nearby bus stand. There was no mountain locomotive like the one that chugged up the Nilgiris. The bus crew tied our bags on to the roof rack, and Craig's father guided us to seats in the front. The rear rows were the worst, he said, since they bounced hard over potholes and the puke of passengers sitting ahead came flying through the open windows. I sat at a window seat in case I felt sick.

The bus zigzagged up the switchbacking ghat road. The initial few sharp turns made me queasy, and several fellow travellers hung their heads out and threw up. After the first few mishaps, I averted my face to avoid getting splattered.

The stop at Oothu, halfway up the ghat, was a welcome relief from the swaying and bouncing.

'Blums, blums,' called the hawkers with baskets of plums.

Though the fruits were tempting, my tummy didn't feel good. Vendors balancing trays of neatly arranged newspaper packets stuffed with peanuts shouted 'Penus, penus', much to Craig's and my merriment, while embarrassed missionary ladies looked away. As the bus climbed, the heat of the plains gave way to the cool of the hills.

We arrived in Kodai at last and got off the bus when it stopped at the Highclerc School gate. Craig's folks retired to the Carlton Hotel next door, where they stayed until they left for Bombay. Craig and I shouldered our bags, and I followed him to Kennedy Hall, the dorm for grade-schoolers, where we would share a room furnished with bunk beds with two other boys. Not only was I to join fifth grade more than halfway into the academic year, but I was almost a year younger than my classmates.

Most students were American WASPs (White Anglo-Saxon Protestants), with two or three Indians and Southeast Asians. There wasn't even one African or African-American kid.

For the first few days, when the gong of the first bell reverberated across the campus at 7 a.m., I woke up thinking I was in authoritarian Lawrence and a feeling of dread came over me. When the realization I was in Kodai cut its way through my sleepy mind, relief made me relax. I didn't have to agonize over wearing the right uniform, hose tops and puttees. No one would cane me if my bed wasn't made to military perfection or if my shoes weren't polished to a mirror-like sheen. In fact, tennis shoes didn't need buffing at all. I could be normal, wearing comfortable jeans and T-shirts. Only on Sundays did I have to wear a wretched suit, choke myself with a tie and lace up well-polished leather shoes. Since this was a once-a-week requirement, I didn't grudge it much.

We sat anywhere in the dining hall and with whomever we pleased. Three times a week, we had hot semolina or oatmeal porridge without a garnish of weevils. On other days, the kitchen staff served toast and eggs, pancakes or good old south Indian dosais and idlis that I had grown to love at Matunga. The sambhar was mild, to appeal to our delicate Western palates. Compared to Lawrence, the fare at the Highclerc dining room seemed heavenly. Everything about the school, an outpost of the States in south India, was much more relaxed. I counted my blessings—the absence of prefects, callisthenics and mind-deadening marching. Every day at mealtimes I met Gail, who lived in Boyer, the dorm for grade-school girls. If I didn't have anything to say, I waved to her across the room.

At 9 a.m., we trooped into our classrooms, which faced the Quadrangle, or the Quad for short. This was where the all-important bell hung. What was it about ringing it that we hero-worshipped the bell ringer? I don't know. I wasn't the only boy who dreamt of becoming one someday.

My class of sixteen kids had American textbooks handed down from previous years for every subject. There was nothing about India at all, which would only come later in high school. Since I had missed most of fifth grade, I had a lot of catching up to do, especially in math.

Our classteacher caught me passing a note to Craig and sent both of us out of the classroom. We stood in the Quad, feeling ashamed as our classmates smirked. After they forgot about us, we snuck away into the boys' bathroom. Wetting wads of toilet paper, we threw them as hard as we could at the ceiling, so they stuck. At break time, when students swarmed into the toilets, the now-dry clots of paper rained on them. In Lawrence, they would have turned the school upside down to find and punish the pranksters. But here no one made a big fuss, nor did anyone discover the culprits. This caper was mild compared to what was to come.

After a long day of academics, the 4 o'clock bell announced an hour of sports. We changed into shorts and sneakers in our dorms, ran down the slope to the main road and crossed to the grassy sports field called Benderloch, Bendy for short.

The wizened old Halva Man, whose real name I never found out, sold sweet halva and peanut brittle by the roadside. Our stomachs were empty, and after the hours of tough lessons, a sugar rush was welcome. Since we didn't have cash on us, the vendor had a little book in which he noted down the amounts owed, which we paid at the end of the month. He made a killing off us.

After indulging our craving for sweets, we played kickball and baseball, and for the first time I enjoyed team sports. Sweaty and dirty, we returned to our dorm around 5 p.m. Batches of naked boys stood under the long line of showers. Not only was I embarrassed to strip in front of the others, but their vulgar talk mortified me. I had never heard anyone speak like that before.

'You call that a dick?'

'He's a needle-dick bug-fucker.'

It took me a few weeks to get used to this ritual and join the banter.

In the evenings, I was either in the Social Room, listening to Mrs Chell, our housemother, read aloud from books such as *My Friend Flicka* and *Thunderhead*, or stayed in our room and read books borrowed from the Reading Room. *Tarzan of the Apes* and Zane Grey's *Fighting Caravans* were favourites. Our reading staple was comics, which we traded with each other. The day a parcel of comics arrived from Bombay felt like Christmas.

When there were no more comics left to read, we walked ten minutes to a pokey scrap paper shop at the top of the bazaar. The owner always wore an oversized overcoat that made him look like a tramp, and the other kids called him 'Walawala Big Chief' behind his back. The origin of the name was already lost by the time I joined the school. His name was probably a tongue twister, like Muthuramalingam, which the students couldn't pronounce. He had an enormous collection of comics set aside from the stacks of cardboard and old newspapers. We traded two of our comic books for one of his. Occasionally, he had magazines such as *Boys' Life* and *Field & Stream,* which we coveted.

I made good friends, learnt dirty words, and homesickness was a thing of the past. In March 1953, Mummy wrote to say our brother Neelakantan, Neel for short, had been born. Gail and I would have to wait until May vacation to see him.

Although I liked Highclerc, there was one miserable aspect to it. It was a school for children of American missionaries and therefore steeped in religion. We said grace at every meal and attended daily Religious Education classes and prayer sessions at the chapel. Most of my fellow students had a Christian upbringing and accepted this as part of normal life. But for the few 'non-mish' kids like me, this atmosphere was stifling.

When my classteacher enquired about my denomination, I didn't know what she meant. After much head-scratching, I remembered overhearing Mummy say she was Unitarian and believed in a divine being but not in any Holy Ghosts or Sons of God. Saying I was Unitarian didn't go down well. The teacher's look of horror said it all. To any further questions about my religion, I shrugged.

Throughout Friday, my friends and I plotted how to make the most of Sundays, when precious hours were wasted in interminable morning and evening church services. We took to wearing jeans under our formal clothes, so we didn't lose a moment whipping off our suits. Picking up our tops, marbles or Dinky Toys, we raced to spend the rest of the day competing with one another.

My new friends played by staid, polite American rules, and I introduced them to the more exciting Indian style of playing. I taught them skills such as goonching and 'short sparks', spinning the top through the air and unleashing it to land on our palms. We went a step further, replacing the blunt nails on the tops with a screw filed to a sharp point. We had to be careful performing short sparks with such lethal tops, or we'd get a goonch in our palms. Every top became pocked with holes, and some cracked open under furious assault.

The school year ended, and Craig's parents came to fetch the three of us. I looked forward to the vacation in Bombay and meeting Neel, but I had also grown fond of Kodai. It would become my home for the next seven years, and only three of us from that cohort of fifth-graders would stay all the way through to graduation.

* * *

In Bombay, Gail and I met our little brother, Neel. For two-year-old Nina, he was the perfect doll. She gave him his bottle, patted his back to make him burp and sang lullabies in gibberish. Rama worked twelve-hour days and was hardly at home. I didn't know it then, but he had convinced the Maharaja of Baroda to invest in Ramnord, setting in motion a chain of events in which he'd lose the lab in later years. On my regular visits to the lab, I had fun watching the special effects technicians work on movies such as *Alif Laila,* which was inspired by *The Arabian Nights,* with Nimmi starring as the genie.

The film-processing operations had moved entirely to the new lab on Dr Annie Besant Road in Worli. Mummy started a factory to manufacture wooden toys at the old Parel lab and hired a carpenter named Mukund. But her main interest was photography. With her big-format Linhof still camera, she took photographs of some choice pieces from Amma's spectacular collection of indigenous Indian art. She had converted a bathroom into a darkroom, where I watched with amazement as images appeared when she dipped the white photo paper into the developer. She tried to sell the beautiful prints she made with the enlarger shipped from Hoosick. Although Mummy had great ideas, she had little business sense, even with Amma helping to market her products. Amma had by then become the chairperson of the newly created All India Handicrafts Board.

Craig and I spent the vacation at our old jobs of road repair and pest control to make some extra cash for Cokes and ice cream. On weekends, I visited cousins Naren and Sundar to fly kites and trade comics. Soon after I turned ten, it was time to return to school.

6

THE MIDDLING YEARS

Coming of Age

I HAD SKIPPED THIRD GRADE, quit Lawrence before completing the fourth, and attended only the fag end of the fifth, but the school let me move to sixth grade along with my friends.

In June 1953, Gail and I made our way back to Kodai with Craig and his parents, a routine we would follow until the end of eighth grade, when his family left India. I knew the drill of changing trains and boarding the bus, since I was a seasoned traveller by then.

The hill station bustled with missionaries escaping the heat of the plains, where most of them worked. Among them were parents of several classmates, and on weekends, they invited me to their homes, where I stuffed myself with home-baked cakes, cookies, and pies. When the visitors disappeared, I had to resort to powdered milk to indulge my sweet tooth. I kneaded it with water to make plum-sized laddoos or ate the powder by the spoonful.

I struggled to cope with lessons despite the best efforts of my teachers. Maybe the sporadic schooling of the previous years left me with poor foundations. But that was only an excuse, since I was indifferent to academics, doing only reasonably well in English, general science and art. I was physically present at my seat by the window, but my mind wandered to the trees and hills. Craig, however, was a good student, and I copied from his notebook at every opportunity.

A gang of high school boys from Boys' Block bullied us. If any of us had been sassy with them during the day, they showed up at our dorm in the middle of the night and marched us to the bathroom for a cold shower. Or they pushed our heads down the toilet and flushed. Fed up of being treated like shit, we decided to fight back. After classes, these big guys descended a flight of narrow stairs next to Kennedy Hall to reach Bendy. This is where we set up an ambush. We stuffed bags with the bell-shaped hard nuts of the eucalyptus trees and lay in wait above the stairs. When they reached the bottom of the stairs, we pummelled them with a barrage of nuts. But it was a losing battle. They overpowered and marched us to the toilets to flush our heads. This didn't stop us from trying again and again, until we eventually graduated to Boys' Block ourselves. Kennedy Hall became a girls' dorm then.

I looked forward to playing marbles, tops or kickball in the evenings and stayed clear of the boring track and field events. When Field Day approached, other students trained with feverish enthusiasm for months, leaping, sprinting and heaving. Participation, however, was mandatory. I opted for baseball throw as it was the least competitive. Although it didn't require any skill, I practised until I was blue in the face to build my strength. On the momentous day, I was proud to get a third-place yellow ribbon, but there were only five contestants in my age group.

Every Saturday was Social Evening. I expected movie nights to be fun, but I was often wrong. Religious films such as *The Robe* made me fidget until the ordeal was over. Hilarious movies such as Bob Hope's *The Paleface* or exciting ones such as *The Greatest Show on Earth* and *Ivanhoe* were an occasional treat. Another option for Saturday evenings was the ridiculous square dance. I grudgingly mastered do-si-do, allemande and promenade, but it bored the daylights out of me.

Roller skating, however, looked far more enjoyable, until I tried it for the first time and fell. It wasn't as easy as my friends made it appear. They had learnt to skate while I had been busy killing sparrows and filling ditches during vacation. Even Craig could skate. If I was to have as much fun as they, I had to learn but in private, away from my snickering buddies. I snuck into the gym, which was also the theatre, roller rink and auditorium, clamped Craig's skates on to my shoes and tightened them with a skate key. After bruising my knees and falling on my ass plenty of times, it was exhilarating to glide. I picked the best pair of skates at Field House from the ones discarded by students who had left. It would have to do until Mummy flew to the States and bought me a set, along with the fish hooks, candy and 45 rpm records on my wish list. Now, on Social Evenings, I careened with my friends around the shiny wooden floor of the gymnasium to the strains of *How Much Is That Doggie in the Window, Don't Let the Stars Get in Your Eyes*, and *Eh, Cumpari*.

Some senior boys fabricated a crude but ingenious go-cart by screwing bent-out-of-shape roller skates to a wooden frame. It looked like the rickety carts that lepers with bandaged hands and feet pulled along the streets of Madurai. But in this bobsled-on-wheels, the rider shoved his feet into two 'stirrups' hanging from it and held on to the 'reins', ropes nailed to the swivelling steering board. The footholds padded with old shoe soles acted as brakes when pressed down to the ground with the heels. Some crazy kids shot down steep roads such as Observatory Hill on this primitive contraption, which resembled something out of *Mad Max*. When it was my turn, I struggled to control the rickety cart flying downhill. I jammed on the brakes, smelling burning rubber before it slowed enough to pull over to the side of the road. My heart pounded with the adrenaline rush. The other guys taunted me, 'Chicken, chicken', but I didn't care. At least I was a live chicken.

Our favourite mischief took place in the dorm bathroom, a long, open room with eight to ten showers along one side of the wall. We blocked the drains with towels and flooded the floor by turning on the showers. Sliding naked across this puddle was a riot until the sudden arrival of the women janitors. We screamed hysterically as we rushed around to hide our bare bodies. They didn't tell our housemother what we were doing. Sometimes our screams were loud enough to draw her attention, and we suffered 'detention', grounded in the dorm on weekends with no playtime.

Every month, the class hiked all day to one of the many places that would later become popular tourist destinations, such as Pillar Rocks, Pambar Shola and Silver Cascade. Not a bird or animal stirred in the vast, boring plantations of eucalyptus, wattle and Spanish pine, fast-growing foreign trees planted by the forest department. Beyond lay the small magical pockets of native hill forests called sholas, dense growths of stunted trees between extensive stretches of grassland. I lagged way behind everyone else, as these were my first visits to a tropical jungle and everything was new and utterly fascinating. As in Hoosick a few years ago, I turned over rocks, peered into holes and watched for any moving thing—maybe a shieldtail snake, a giant pill millipede we called rollie poochis, an orb spider in its huge golden web or any other creepy-crawly.

The chaperone, either a teacher or a high school senior, berated me with 'Catch up, Breezy!', 'C'mon, slowpoke!' They probably cursed me for slowing them down, but I didn't care. Somehow these little creatures were lost on the other kids, and even the adults marched as fast as possible to the destination. I had no interest in racing from A to B, which was apparently what these treks were about. Every hike was rated with points, and everyone vied to tote up 100 points, or something inane like that, by hurrying through one of the lushest hill ranges in the world to earn a precious 'Thar pin', inappropriately named after a desert in north-western India. In later years, I successfully argued for the spelling to be corrected to 'Tahr', after the endemic mountain goat that inhabits these hills. I wished we could go on these outings more often, but I was in the minority. Most students snivelled at scrambling down steep slopes and being stung by nettles. I couldn't wander in these forests on my own to find snakes until I was older.

I coasted through the sixth and seventh grades, even though I did poorly in academics. I didn't share the other kids' enthusiasm for sports and developed a reputation for being a social oddball.

In seventh grade, I had a pet for a while. I had bought two mouse traps at the bazaar, or the Budge as we called it, and set them every night. A small mouse that got trapped lived in a cardboard box, and I called it Spark Plug. Craig gave me some cheese to feed it so I could handle it without getting bitten. I didn't keep it for long and released it.

* * *

My family had moved to a ground-floor apartment in The Cliff on Pochkhanwala Road, Worli, since the long commute to the Ramnord lab every day had been too tiresome for Rama. The relocation from Juhu Beach to the middle of the metropolis disappointed me. I could no longer benefit from Mrs Crombie's baking efforts, nor comb the beach with Craig. I couldn't haul nets with the fishermen or body-surf in the sea. Nor was there anywhere to roam around in the cramped city. The only salvation was the Worli Sea Face, a road meandering along the rocky coast, a ten-minute walk away.

In a repetition of my escapades outside Hotel Miramar in Colaba, I sliced my bare feet walking over the barnacle-encrusted rocks at low tide to peer into pools with a range of marine critters, from rock crabs to anemones. In one of them, a large, brightly coloured moray eel opened and closed its jaws to force water through its gills. *How to catch it?*

I smashed a hermit crab against a rock and dropped a piece, which the eel snatched. Next, I fashioned a simple noose with a fishing line and lowered it into the pool, but the alert moray quickly withdrew out of sight. I shattered the shell of another poor crab and tied it to a piece of light fishing line. Holding the noose in front of the eel's hiding place with my left hand, I dropped the bait with my right. I stood still, watching it sink. The moray emerged from a crack in the rock and stretched straight through the noose to reach the crab. I jerked the noose tight around its neck, but the struggling eel's tail had a firm hold inside its hidey-hole. The nylon line was taut enough to break, but I kept up the pressure until the moray gave in. I dragged it flopping and wriggling on to the rocks, and avoiding its snapping jaws, wrestled the slippery body into the fish bag tucked into the waistband of my shorts. Only then did I feel saddened by what I had done. It was so snake-like. Since it was injured by the hook, it wasn't fit enough to be released. I took it home to eat.

Everyone baulked at the idea, and Mummy tried to talk me out of it.

'Who will clean it?' she asked.

'If you clean it, I'll fry it,' said Padma, the cook, to me.

He, perhaps, assumed I'd give up.

In the backyard garden, I saved the head and cleaned the rest of the slimy eel, as I had seen fishwives do. True to his word, Padma fried it, and everyone, with some misgivings, ate a bite of greasy but good meat.

I boiled the head until the flesh fell off, but so did the tissue that held the fragile bones together. I laid these pieces of skull on a newspaper to dry in the sun and then stuck them together with rubber cement. The teeth were impressive, especially the two enlarged, rear-curving ones in the centre of the roof of the mouth. A bite would have been painful. I loved the meditative nature of assembling the delicate skull, and over the following years, pieced together skulls of road-killed snakes.

Back in the tidal pools, I deployed the same technique to entice spiny lobsters whose feelers stuck out from crevices. No matter how devious my methods, they evaded me. But I didn't spend all my time catching creatures. The other marine life exposed when the tide receded also enthralled me, such as a stranded octopus making its graceful way along the bottom of a pool before disappearing under a rock.

Amma visited Bombay to attend official events. By then, Prime Minister Jawaharlal Nehru had offered her several prestigious posts—ambassador to various countries and even vice president of India.[1] She turned him down, saying her work in handicraft and handloom was more important. She won the Padma Bhushan, India's second-highest civilian award, in 1955, when I was in the seventh grade.

Despite the august company she kept, Amma offered us stale snacks and mouldy nuts from her handbag, a compulsive habit acquired during India's fight for independence, when she had been imprisoned. The lack of food in prison had traumatized her, and she hoarded snacks wherever she went, whether to official banquets or fancy hotel dinners. We knew to accept and set them aside without offending her. But she often put Mummy on the spot when she emptied these nibbles into a bowl and offered them to guests. Mummy discreetly removed the container before anyone could eat from it.

---

1 Sakuntala Narasimhan, *Kamaladevi Chattopadhyay: The Romantic Rebel* (New Delhi, India: Sterling Publishers Pvt. Ltd, 1999).

Based on her work in designing Ramnord, Mummy got commissions from big corporate offices to do interior decorating. She was away during the day, and I ran footloose and fancy-free.

I shot sparrows with my piddly BB gun in the adjoining compound, a vast open place with abandoned construction workers' quarters. One day Mummy came out of the back door into the garden just as I winged a sparrow. I picked up the squawking bird and wrung its neck without realizing she was behind me. She stomped over, grabbed the gun from my hands and slammed it against the dhobi stone. The stock broke on impact. I had never seen her so furious and probably promised never to do that again. The lesson, of course, was to kill surreptitiously.

I taped together the gun's stock, but it was useless. For a time, I shot stones with the catty in my urban hunting ground next door, using trees, tin cans or old bottles as targets. My accuracy improved, but I was bored.

Salim, the son of a fisherman, was my age and a regular at the rocks, where he pried limpets and mussels with a chisel-like tool. When I mentioned the lack of fishing spots, he led me to a deep pool where I could use a line and hook. He liked the new Mustad hooks Mummy had bought in the States, so I gave him a few. I pulled mostly striped piggies while he hunted nearby. Fishing became a morning routine. When I struck the first catfish, his warning shout startled me.

'*Hato* [Move]!' Salim yelled. '*Kanta hai* [It has thorns].'

He demonstrated how to grip the fish and remove the hook without getting stabbed by the pectoral and dorsal spines. Despite this lesson, I got spiked by another catfish. Boy! Did it hurt!

Besides Salim, my other friends were the sons of drivers and house servants working in the apartments. The park, now called Lion Garden on the other side of The Cliff, afforded plenty of space to play marbles and tops. When we grew tired of these pastimes, we took to competitive kite-flying. The park was wide open then, with no big trees to snag the kite or the string. We cheered when decapitated kites floated off. Gangs of street kids dodged traffic and climbed trees or electric poles to be the first to get them. I didn't find out what they did with them. Although I had a stash of half a dozen kites at a time, I lost them all within days. Either my string got cut by someone else or the flimsy paper of the kite ripped. I may have been among the first to fashion a durable kite out of a plastic bag, a rare object in those days, stretching the material across the thin broomstick-and-bamboo frame of a store-bought kite. The trick to not losing kites was to duck my strings out of the way of another or be the first to yank when our twines crossed. My new friends helped improve my Hindi too.

Every vacation followed the same pattern—mucking about in the tidal pools of the Worli Sea Face with Salim, hanging out with my kite-flying friends at the apartment, and visiting Naren and Sunder at Matunga. At the Ramnord lab, I observed my special effects friends superimpose puffy clouds on drab scenery, where the hero burst forth into a love song and chased a girl around a tree. When Bombelli's opened its ice cream parlour next door, I had another good reason to visit the lab. For a youngster with a sweet tooth, it was heaven.

Gail, Nina and I became members of the Breach Candy swimming pool, the first one of my life. Until then, I had swum only in the sea at Juhu Beach and in jungle pools at Kodai. We visited it almost every day. By the end of the summer, I became comfortable in deep water and especially loved holding my breath and swimming underwater, at first alarming the lifeguard, who thought I was drowning. After an afternoon of splashing, we spent our five rupees on a snack.

Life grew exciting when I returned to Kodai for the eighth grade.

7

THE YEAR OF FISHING

Studies Be Damned

I WOULD HAVE PASSED THE eighth grade in my normal semi-comatose state had it not been for the English teacher who encouraged me to read classic American novels. I read by flashlight late into the night, after 'lights out', with the covers pulled over my head. Writers such as John Steinbeck and William Faulkner sucked me into their sagas, but Ernest Hemingway was my hero. The fisherman in *The Old Man and the Sea* and the hunter-narrator of *Green Hills of Africa* inspired me. Clipping the author's photograph from a magazine, I pinned it to my dorm-room wall. I loved writing reports of my favourite books. For the less exciting ones, such as *Silas Marner* and *A Tale of Two Cities* ('Sale of Two Titties', we called it), the school library offered a shortcut. The *Classic Comics* edition gave the visual summary of the story without me having to read the whole boring book. The term paper, however, required several weeks of serious research. When I turned it in, the teacher commented, 'How predictable you are, Breezy.' The title was 'Hunting for Tyrannosaurus Rex'.

For the assignment, I flagrantly copied from the book Mom had given me as a Christmas present four years earlier, *The Dinosaur Book,* with some paraphrasing to make it sound like my own writing. I wrote about the adventures of palaeontologists in their pursuit of fossils.

61

My enthusiasm for the subject got me an A+, pencilled in red on the front page, the highest grade I ever earned.

Math deficiency syndrome, with the additional torture of geometry and algebra, continued to plague me. A classmate took pity and offered to tutor me after school. For a month, each evening we sat together in a study room while she tried to din the basics into my thick skull. But the pressure of her leg against mine was too distracting. Sadly, she gave up on me as a lost cause.

If academics was boring, religion was mind-deadening. The two-hour Sunday services were jam-packed with students from all the Christian mission schools in Kodai. I fidgeted at the very back, bored and impatient. During one service, I noticed lice crawling through the hair of a boy sitting in front of me. I held the programme card against his head and three parasites crawled aboard. I spent the rest of the service watching them scurry around looking for a scalp.

Besides the weekly torture by boredom, we had daily Religious Education classes and the mandatory chapel attendance. Although the handsome brothers Dave and John Paul (JP) were my classmates from the beginning, our restlessness helped us bond. They were crazy about sports and among the first boys in my class to reach puberty. Both had dark hair, were the same height and muscular. Befriending these popular guys changed my self-image. I may have been a maverick, but hobnobbing with them made me part of the 'in' crowd.

Bolstered by each other, the brothers and I gave the RE teacher a rough time. When he declared, 'The Bible never contradicts itself,' we spent hours after school flipping through the pages for discrepancies. We flummoxed him the next day in class with our findings. For all my troubles at learning the Bible, even if only to nitpick, I received an anonymous note in my mailbox, 'You are in danger of hellfire!' That was like adding jet fuel to my irreverence.

I substituted the hymns with sarcastic words. For example, 'While shepherds watched their flocks by night' became 'While shepherds washed their socks at night'; and 'What a friend we have in Jesus, all our sins and griefs to bear' transformed into a sarcastic 'What a friend we have in Jesus, Christ Almighty, what a pal'. Despite our best efforts to contain our laughter by holding our noses closed with our fingers, others sitting nearby shot us dirty looks.

I perfected the art of speaking like Donald Duck, specializing in the Lord's Prayer and bringing this talent to church, singing:

We three kings of Orient are
Smoking on a rubber cigar
It was loaded and exploded
And now we don't know where we are
O Star of wonder, Star of light
Star of Holy dynamite.

As soon as the service ended, Dave and JP went to Bendy to play whatever sport was in season and Craig practised playing his trumpet with the band. Once, Dave and JP invited me to go for a bicycle outing on a Sunday, but I couldn't ride one. It was time to learn. From Shadrach's bike rental stand outside the school gates, I rented a cycle by the hour and pushed it to Lake Road, which was devoid of traffic in those days. Learning to ride a cycle was like learning to skate, a lot of falling and picking myself up. Soon, I was riding at full speed along the two-kilometre road, and ventured down the steep and bumpy Consumption Ghat, mimicking the brothers, and barely escaped breaking my neck.

One day, I banked sharply at the ferry landing when a boy ran in front of me. I braked hard, but we collided. 'Sorrryyy, thambi [little brother]!' I yelled, even as I flew into him. We picked ourselves up, shaken but not injured, and the poor kid magnanimously shrugged it off. I paid extra to cover the bike's bent fender. The accident taught me a lesson that saved my life in later years when I caught the motorcycle bug.

While my friends were otherwise occupied on Sundays, I hiked to forests such as Bear and Bombay Sholas, revelling in being in the jungle on my own without having to hear the yapping of other kids and the chaperone prodding me along. I searched for snakes, discovered birds' nests and observed lizards sunning themselves on branches. Under a log,

I scooped up my first snake of the hills, and it twisted and writhed in my hand, revealing the bright yellow squiggly markings on its underside. At first I couldn't tell the shield-tailed snake's blunt tail from the head or what it ate. At least part of the mystery was solved when I came upon one swallowing an earthworm.

Besides beautiful delicate green vine snakes in the grasslands, other species were scarce in the highlands. The weather was too cold for them, as the school representative had told Mom a few years ago. Absorbed by the sights, sounds and smells of the forest, I had to tear myself away to be back in time for dinner. I couldn't wait to get into high school to go on overnight camping trips.

On one memorable class trek, we found my first venomous snake, a bright green pit viper lying on the road with its head squashed. I was about to open its mouth to see the fangs.

'Don't touch it, Breezy,' the chaperone said. 'It may be dead, but it still has poison.'

I dragged myself away from it and trailed behind the group. Within a few metres was a live one coiled on a branch next to a small stream. Its triangular head made it obvious that this was not a harmless vine snake, but a venomous pit viper. The teacher leading the group was too far ahead to stop me from examining it. But I was nervous. *What if it bites me?* I admired its beautiful green colour and the large overlapping scales on its head and left it alone. I would learn much later that it was the large-scaled green pit viper.

On our way back, the pit viper was still there, immobile in the same place. I pointed it out to the others, but they had a hard time seeing it. Its green colour and sinuous body blended with the mossy tree limb. My friends took a while to see vine snakes too. Years of squinting into bushes had trained my eyes to spot them. Later, I read colour-blind people were better at recognizing shapes, since they had learnt not to depend on colour. Maybe there was something to that.

My Hindi was useless in Kodai as the local people spoke another language, Tamil. Shadrach, the cycle rental man, knew some English, and with his help and hand gestures, I learnt one Tamil phrase at a time.

When he heard of my interest in fishing, he invited me to fish with him and his friend, Velu, at the Kodai Lake ten minutes away.

I had brought hooks from Bombay and put together the rest of my fishing rig by buying a long bamboo pole, stripped peacock feathers for floats, and lead weights from my newfound friends. Their choice of bait to catch carp was vadai. Most south Indians know it as a spicy doughnut-shaped snack. But this vadai, an inch-thick, fried dense pancake of lentil and peanut flour mixed with spices, was specially made for fishing bait as it stayed on the hook when tiddlers nibbled. Shadrach swore the smell of the masala enticed the fish.

Without a reel, casting the bait took some manoeuvring. I laid the eight-foot rod on the ground and stretched the full length of the line across the road after making sure no car was in sight. Back at the 'handle' end of the pole, I whipped the filament over my head. The bait arched and splashed about twenty feet away from the bank. I aimed for clear water, avoiding the stands of lily pads, but still lost many a hook when the line became tangled.

Resting the rod on a forked support stick, as a bite could take half an hour or more, I baited a smaller pole with a tiny ball of sticky peanut flour paste to pull out tiddlers. The fishermen caught them as a fallback option for dinner, in case big fish were elusive. Since my meals at the dining hall were assured, I didn't need an alternative. But catching these tiddlers like the older fishermen made me feel as proficient as they were. At the end of each fishing session, Shadrach or Velu took them home.

One Sunday, I sat on the lakeshore, staring at the quivering peacock-feather float. I imagined the little ones nibbling at the bait and attracting the big fellows. A hefty fish surfaced and gulped a swimming insect. *That would be a good size to catch. What kind are the big ones? Could they be bottom feeders? In that case, I would be better off without the float. Is the vadai any good?* My thoughts came roaring to the present when the peacock feather bounced twice and dunked forcefully under. Something huge had grabbed the bait. I raised the long pole and struck. It didn't give. *Had I hooked a log?* Then, with a swirl of water, a large fish surfaced and shook its head, trying to dislodge the hook. Shadrach and Velu, who were smoking beedis and minding their floats, leaned forward to watch. As it tore back and forth, I struggled to keep the line from getting tangled in the lilies. The fish had a lot of fight left and wasn't coming ashore soon. I grew worried. It might snap the filament or the rod.

Shadrach had once described landing a big carp, and I followed his example. I tossed the bamboo pole into the water and ran to the Kodai Boat Club, which was about five minutes away. A boatman I knew lounged in his skiff, which I requested him for. In my hurry and breathlessness, my words were jumbled. But he understood and helped me untie it. I grabbed the oars and rowed furiously, following Shadrach's and Velu's excited gesticulations towards the western side of the lake, where the rod bobbed like a giant fishing float. When I got closer, a large tired mirror carp rose to the surface, mouth gaping from the effort. I picked up the pole and pulled the line until the fish came alongside. I wasn't afraid to slide my thumb and two fingers into the gills, since carp are toothless, and haul the three-kilogram fish into the boat. It was the biggest one I had ever caught. I stared at its huge, glossy golden scales, my heart pounding with excitement and exertion. Then a strange sadness enveloped me. I grieved killing the fish that had been going about its life underwater. *But how can I give up the thrill of the hunt?*

The guys on the bank laughed and clapped as I rowed back, exhausted. The boatman pumped my hand. 'Very good, very good.' After promising to pay later, I trudged down the road, elated by the fishermen's enthusiasm about the big carp. *What am I to do with the fish now?* Since I had no way of cooking my catch at the dorm, I gave it to Shadrach, a gift for teaching me how to fish that lake. I felt a kinship with these men that I didn't share with any of my classmates.

After that rite of passage, I fancied myself a great fisherman and lived a dual life—one in school, doing the 'done thing' with Dave, JP and my other buddies, and another on my own. Encouraged by the experience of landing the carp, I frequented the lake during the week at the end of the school day. Fishing was so much fun that I was surprised none of the other kids were into it.

I pinned an ad on the school noticeboard, asking interested people to place orders for fish I'd deliver fresh over the weekend. To my disappointment, I didn't get many, but my entrepreneurship impressed a visiting parent, who told Mom about it.

After one Sunday service, I got a four-anna ferry ride to the other side of the lake and walked to the far end to a spot called 'Laughing Waters', where my cronies were already settled. While enquiring whether the fish were biting, I let the bamboo pole slide to the ground and hooked my thumb. On hearing my cry, Shadrach came over to have a look.

'I get it out,' he said.

'If you pull it out, the barb will rip my thumb open,' I protested.

'I take out hooks many times.'

He asked another fisher to watch his rod while he rummaged through his bag. *Would it be better to go to the Dishpan instead of letting Shadrach mess with my hand?* But he knew more about removing hooks than anyone at school. Before I could decide, he returned with a quarter bottle of rum and a pair of needle-nose pliers. Scenes from movies flashed through my mind, of tough men chugging down a quart of whisky before someone dug into their chest with a knife and extracted bullets. I had no time to be disappointed.

Shadrach dribbled the alcohol on my thumb, which burnt as if on fire and made me squirm. I obeyed when he told me to look away, but I couldn't help glancing out of the corner of my eye. He gripped the hook with the pliers. *Would he rip it out?* He pushed it through my flesh. I sucked in my breath and gritted my teeth. When the barb came into view, he cut it off with the pliers and slid the hook backwards out of my thumb. The relief was instant. Shadrach sloshed more rum on the bleeding holes, sending a fresh wave of piercing pain.

'You give me a quarter [bottle of rum] next time,' he said with a grin and handed me a crumpled handkerchief, which he insisted was clean.

He took a hearty swig from the bottle and went back to minding his rod.

I wrapped the hanky around my hand and returned to school. Miss Annie Putz, the kindly Austrian nurse at the Dishpan, as everyone called the dispensary, gave me a tetanus shot and bandaged my thumb. By now I had lost at least two hours. I picked up another hook from the dorm, swearing never to make the stupid mistake of snagging myself again.

On the way to the ferry, I picked up a discarded wine cork outside the ritzy Carlton Hotel and jammed the sharp end of the hook into it to prevent any further accidents. Later, I gave Shadrach three rupees from my allowance to replace the quarter bottle of rum.

On the banks of that lake I learnt there were other ways of fishing than the conventional line-and-hook method. One morning, the Maharaja's Boat House, opposite the Boat Club, presented a strange sight. A string stretched across the entire width of a finger of the lake, tied to tree branches on both banks, from which a sizeable chunk of vadai hung on the water surface. A man in a safari suit reclined on a cane chair, cradling a shotgun and staring at the bait. *What on earth is he doing?* Then he raised the gun and shot at the water. When the splash settled, a fish floated dead. A young man, standing behind him, stripped to his loincloth, swam out to retrieve a large mirror carp. I hadn't seen anyone shoot fish before. I went up to the well-dressed man and introduced myself. He was the Nadudorai, meaning 'middle chief' in Tamil, but his formal name was Maharajkumar Radhakrishna Thondaiman of the Pudukkottai royal family. They owned Tredis, a vast property nearby, where they spent the summer months.

I asked Nadudorai about his unorthodox fishing style. Since a rifle bullet would ricochet off the water surface, he used a ball cartridge in a 12-gauge shotgun as it could penetrate the water and kill the fish. Although shooting fish was fascinating, I preferred the traditional hook and line. I hadn't yet heard of spearguns.

On my way to the lake one evening after school, I overheard a skinny, dark-haired German classmate, Christian, speaking Tamil with a local shopkeeper. Most of the other white kids at school didn't speak the language. We became friends, and I learnt German and Tamil swear words from him. Unlike the rest of us, he wasn't a boarder but lived with his family in the German Settlement. Having a day scholar for a buddy offered many advantages. On weekends, I hiked for half an hour to his house to gorge on the home-baked goodies his mother offered.

Apple strudel was a treat after a week of school food. When we entered high school, I could stay overnight with Chris.

Hunger often drove me to accompany Chris, Craig, Dave and JP to the Budge. Our first stop was a Brahmin hotel for hot dosais, vadais and coffee. Then, in search of entertainment, we walked into V.T. Pillai's general merchandise store, where the owner, Pillai, claimed he could get anything we needed. Smart alecs that we were, we ordered black-and-white striped paint and a left-handed screwdriver, which he swore would be delivered the following week. We checked later, only to be told it would take a few more days. Our order still awaits fulfilment.

The next stop was Mariappan's forge at the bottom of the Budge, where we watched the blacksmith heat metal rods on coal while his teenage son pumped the bellows. The distinctive smell of burning embers and molten iron filled the air. He pounded the white-hot metal into shape and plunged the sickle or tongs into water. With a loud hiss, steam shrouded everything. Hypnotized by the whole operation, we never tired of watching Mariappan at work.

At the nearby granite quarry, the blasters hand-bored three-foot-deep holes into the rock using a sharpened steel crowbar and a sledgehammer. Watching their work took me back to Hoosick, where I had listened to a song many times, Paul Robeson's *John Henry*, an African-American folk hero. As an employee of a railroad company in the late nineteenth century, he competed against a newly introduced steam-powered rock-drilling machine and won, but died from the effort. Each pit took these workers several hours, and the crater resounded with the clanging of steel pounding on steel. They worked like dogs, sweat pouring from their brows despite the cool weather. Then came the fun part. They filled the hollows with black blasting powder and left a length of the fuse dangling. The men showed us where we could watch the explosions without getting hit by flying or falling rocks. One guy lit a cigarette and trotted from fuse to fuse, lighting five or six at a time. The black tobacco brand Charminar was the best, he said later. The fuses sparkled and fizzled as they burnt, and he hurried back to where we sat huddled together, waiting with bated breath. Some exploded with a muffled underground boom that shook the ground, but the odd massive one sent huge rocks sailing through the air. The explosions thrilled us, and we returned often to the rock crater.

An old quarry behind the school gym was pocked with a few shallow cavities. I grabbed a hammer and chisel from the workshop and set to work, aping my dynamiting friends. I clobbered until my hands got blisters, but could do no more than scratch the granite. My respect for the quarry workers grew. If they had been the cool dudes for playing with explosives before, now they appeared superhuman for punching through the impenetrable rock by hand.

At this time, Tenzing Norgay and Edmund Hillary's feat of scaling Mount Everest captured our imagination. The five of us emulated the mountaineers on the steepest rocky slopes below Coaker's Walk. That none of us broke any bones and escaped with a few scrapes and scratches says more about our good luck than any skill.

Emboldened by our success, we made pitons out of some old railway spikes in the school carpentry shop and borrowed a length of rope from the tree cutters, who were trimming the gigantic eucalyptus trees. We tied the cord to a wattle tree growing on the edge of a twenty-foot cliff, and Craig rappelled down first. Then, heavy-set Dave took his turn. As he descended, the tree toppled and its roots ripped out, which sounded like the rope was shredding. We shouted, 'Watch out, Dave!', and he grabbed hold of an outcrop on the cliff face. He was too high from the ground to leap, nor could he climb. Three of us hauled on the cord and told Dave, 'Let go. We'll lower you down slowly.' He was heftier than we could handle, and his descent was too swift for his comfort. He yelled profanities at us, thinking we had deliberately let him fall with a thud. That was one of several times that the God of Idiots saved our skins.

One weekend, Dave, JP and I hiked to Kistnamma Naik Tope, which everyone called Tope, at the base of the hills. The fifteen-kilometre route followed the old Coolie Ghat, a rough zigzagging trail. Before the motorable road to Kodai was carved, White folk travelled up in litters, called doolies, borne by four men. The fat missionaries would need six men to hoist them, we joked as we headed downhill.

At a stream where we stopped for a break, a large black snake crawled along the opposite bank oblivious of us. I waded across the water without alerting it and grabbed the rat snake's tail as it tried to zip into a crevice. It resisted capture with all its strength, and I tugged hard, determined not to let it go. I didn't know this was the worst thing to do to a snake. When it finally relaxed and gave up the struggle, I shoved it into an empty pillowcase I carried with me and called out, 'non-poisonous', over my shoulder to the other two boys. After a picnic and a swim in the natural pool, we walked several kilometres to the main road and caught a bus back, having no energy to climb the 7,000 feet to Kodai.

When I opened the bag in the dorm, the snake lay dead. I was devastated. *What had caused its death?* There were no obvious injuries. I palpated the length of its body and came to a lump more than halfway down. It appeared to have suffered a broken back. This was a bitter lesson on the fragility of snakes. Never again would I pull a snake out of a burrow. This unfortunate creature became the first snakeskin I tacked out on a board to dry and hung on my dorm-room wall.

An outdoor life needed a Bowie knife. But Mom didn't travel between the continents as often as I would have liked. A tattered copy of the *Popular Mechanics* magazine gave detailed specifications for a twelve-inch knife modelled on the one used by Jim Bowie, the famous American frontiersman and defender of the Alamo. We watched blacksmith Mariappan forge it out of an old lorry leaf spring. Then I badgered the school carpenter to fabricate a handle out of a sambhar deer antler picked up on a hike. My friends each wanted a knife and kept Mariappan and the carpenter busy. The school cobbler made leather sheaths, complete with belt loops. Again, the God of Idiots looked over us when we goofed off on every forest trek with these knives we had honed to razor sharpness.

Not satisfied with a knife alone, I wanted a spear. An illustration from an old *National Geographic* magazine of a Masai warrior served as a model. My lust for weapons may have surprised Mariappan, but he didn't comment. 'Five rupees,' he said. The spear became popular too.

The weekend after the Masai spears were ready, we nimrods trekked to Bear Shola stream and cut long wattle staffs as shafts with our Bowie knives. We jumped from rock to rock, imagining we were hunters stalking large game in the savannahs of Africa. In reality, there was nothing except wild pig we could have gone after. Then I slipped on a rock face, and the sharp point of the spear pierced the base of my thumb. Embarrassed and bleeding, I wrapped my dirty handkerchief around my hand and told the rest I was heading to Dishpan.

'Douse it with peroxide,' suggested Dave, while the others snickered.

'No, no,' countered JP. 'Iodine burns better. That's what you need for a nasty cut.'

They burst into howls of laughter.

If Miss Putz at Dishpan was concerned about my many cuts, she didn't say anything more than 'You again, Breezy?' Gail and I met often, but she never heard of half of the mischief that I got up to. This time, however, I couldn't hide my bandaged hand from her.

'What happened to you?' she asked.

'A wild boar attacked my friends when we were on a hike,' I replied.

She shook her head and laughed, not believing a word of it.

Eighth-grade kids joined the high school students in formal social events. I gathered the guts to ask a ninth-grader, the tall and athletic Sylvia, to hold hands with me while we skated around the gym to the latest pop songs such as Bill Haley's *Rock around the Clock* and *Ballad of Davy Crockett* by Fess Parker. Later in the evening, I walked her to her dorm. For the awkward and socially inept boy I was, this was a major milestone.

For the much anticipated Junior High School Dance, I wore a colourful printed shirt that had been a gift from Mom, chino slacks, a pair of striped socks and polished black loafers, looking more presentable than I had in months. Sylvia looked gorgeous in a full skirt, and when she twirled during the dance, her many petticoats swished around. Slow songs gave boys the chance to hold their girls close, a new and exciting adventure. New at dancing, I stepped on Sylvia's toes a lot and was grateful she didn't complain.

The next morning, after Sunday church service, we held hands as we walked around Coaker's Walk, a scenic lane overlooking the plains. That was the limit of the romance. Except for these few dates, we never went steady, although we remained pals over the next few years.

Predictably, with so many extracurricular activities, my academic performance suffered. I wrote to Mom, 'You won't be pleased with my report card, but Miss Unruh said not to get discouraged.' That didn't mollify Mom. She reminded me that I would be entering high school soon and that I needed to get better grades. I made up my mind to try harder, not for the first time, even if the effort killed me.

When vacation rolled by, Craig's parents didn't come to take us back to Bombay. Instead, we were to travel in groups without an adult chaperone. Our parents sent first-class train tickets that my friends and I traded in for third-class ones. With the difference in fares, we had plenty of money to spend on sodas and mutton biryani on the trip home. Gail would travel with her group of girlfriends in the first-class coach.

When the locomotive pulled into the Kodai Road station, the noise and power of the steam engine awed Dave, JP, Craig and me. We stashed our bags in the compartment and sought the locomotive engineer at the tea shop while the engine filled up with coal and water.

'Could we ride in the engine, sir?' I asked.

We expected he would say it was against the rules.

'Sure, but only until Trichy,' he answered.

We couldn't believe our luck. Our first time travelling alone and we had struck the jackpot. We swung on to the engine behind the engineer and had the time of our lives, shovelling coal into the furnace and pulling the cord that blew the shrill steam whistle. I had dreamt of this as a kid in Hoosick.

At Trichy station, true to our word, we disembarked. We crowded around a vendor's cart that sold samosas and biscuits, when a faint 'meow, meow' came from under the cart. It was a tiny kitten that looked like it hadn't eaten since it was born. I fed it a biscuit. Mom, who liked cats, didn't have one, and it would make a delightful gift. *How am I to carry it back?* I bought an empty basket from a hawker selling oranges and lined it with newspaper. The container had sacking material stitched to the rim, which acted as a lid, so there was no danger of the kitten escaping. It travelled in that basket to Madras and then on to Bombay. It puked and shat in there, and I changed the paper lining.

If Mom was taken aback when she set eyes on her bedraggled gift, which looked more like a rat than a feline, she didn't show it. But the gesture touched her, and she named the kitten Trichy. No one would know then that that scrawny thing would transform into a gorgeous tortoiseshell Persian cat. Throughout its long life, Mom would proudly tell everyone who commented on the beautiful pet the story of her son picking it up from a train station.

Craig and his family returned to the States that summer, and I lost touch with him for the next few decades. We were old fogies when we caught up with each other in Australia in 2014, but we didn't have much time to swap stories. A year later, he died.

The first thing I did in Bombay was buy a German Diana air rifle. Despite the expenses on snacks, firecrackers, kites and sundry other things, I had saved enough money from my allowance and trading in my first-class ticket. M. Saleh, the friendly arms dealer on Abdul Rehman Street opposite Crawford Market, recommended the 35M model.

'It is accurate even from a hundred metres,' he said.

That sold it. On the way home, I couldn't stop running my hands over the flashy carved wooden stock.

Mom wore a worried expression, but said nothing when I proudly showed her the rifle. Perhaps she thought I'd remember my promise of not killing birds. I stashed it in my cupboard, where it stayed until my return to Kodai. The itch to try it out was strong, but I didn't want to run the risk of upsetting Mom.

Rama bought four-year-old Nina a small bicycle with training wheels. I took her to the park and supervised her as she learnt to ride. When she seemed to have mastered it, I removed the training wheels and steadied her as she pedalled. Then I let go without telling her.

'Are you still holding me?' she asked after she had cycled several metres.

Not hearing a reply, she looked back, lost her balance and fell over. Luckily, she didn't hurt herself. After she recovered from the surprise of riding by herself, she rode with confidence. Two-year-old Neel ran around the house. If Mom hadn't made a wooden gate, he would have tumbled down the steps to the garden below. Rama teased him with spoonerisms.

'A temple in the sea,' Neel said, pointing to the offshore Haji Ali Dargah as we drove along the coastal road.

'No, that's a semple in the tea, baba,' Rama replied.

'That's right,' I joined in. 'Semple in the tea.'

Eventually, Neel realized we were teasing him. Perhaps out of frustration or revenge, he invented a secret language he called 'Madiga', and entertained everyone by narrating entire stories in gibberish that he refused to translate. He was the centre of attention, with all the girls and ladies eager to pinch his cheeks and ply him with sweets. No wonder he was getting chubby.

Sometimes Nina, Neel and I visited the lab with Rama. The kids loved watching the processing machines, eating ice cream at Bombelli's and being pushed on the film carts down those long, smooth hallways. Gail had her own interests and friends. My sisters and I frequented the swimming pool two or three times a week. Neel wanted to go too, but Mom said he was too young.

By then, the driver had wrecked the old Ford, and Rama had bought a Fiat car, which became cramped with all of us on board. The new driver, Abdullah Jan, a self-possessed Pathan from near the Khyber Pass, taught me bad words in what I assumed to be Pashto, including '*shekal da ruksha*' and '*chupsha deri kabbari makawan*'. I suspect they were gobbledegook to entertain me, but I mimicked the guttural sounds with panache.

Then Rama got a brand-new '56 Plymouth, a flashy car with flamboyant fins on the back, luxurious seats, air-conditioning and plenty of space. I'm not sure if he bought it or if it was a gift from Abdulla Bassam, one of Amma's wealthy admirers. Abdullah Jan was more excited by the car than we were. He polished it every spare moment he got and posed beside it as proud as a boy with a new toy, much to the envy of the drivers in the parking lot of the apartment block.

For my twelfth birthday, Amma's present was a beautiful pelt of a snow leopard that Sheikh Abdullah, her colleague in the pre-Independence Indian National Congress, had gifted her a few years earlier. It was an accepted form of honouring a guest in those days. As the Prime Minister of Free Jammu and Kashmir, he vehemently protested India's annexation of his state and was imprisoned in 1953. I ran my hands through the luxuriant fur, scarcely believing my good fortune in receiving this extravagant gift.

Life in Bombay was fun, but I looked forward to returning to Kodai at the end of the vacation in June 1956. I was to enter high school, old enough to go camping in the hills by myself. And I had a brand-new airgun.

8

THE YEAR OF STUFFING BIRDS

The Field Naturalist Awakens

AS A HIGH SCHOOL freshman, I moved from Kennedy Hall to Boys' Block, the dorm perched on a steep slope overlooking Kodai Lake. I was now in the big boys' club and assumed the superior attitude of my peers towards grade-schoolers. We didn't bully them the way we had been in previous years, but we felt grown up and disdainful of associating with mere kids. With the move to high school came more freedom, which I grasped immediately, and probably more responsibilities, which were best ignored.

There were no rules against keeping an airgun in the dorm. Neither did anyone in Block bat an eyelid at the snow leopard pelt draped over my bed. Animal furs were common. Banday Brothers, a Kashmiri artefact shop across the road from the school's entrance, had silver fox and snow leopard skins on display.

Had Craig been there, I'd have roomed with him. My new roommate was the sophomore Chuck, a short, non-athletic comedian. The first thing we did was plaster our walls with pictures of motorbikes and fast cars. With the snake skins hanging on the wall, my dorm room was like a taxidermy museum. JP and Dave, whose voices had transitioned to a masculine gruff, hung banners of football and baseball teams. Classmate Phil didn't want such tame decor. Instead, he wanted street signs, which he had seen in a Pat Boone movie.

After 'lights out', we snuck out of the dorm with a screwdriver and a pair of pliers from the carpentry shop, and avoided the watchman by ducking behind trees until we slipped past the school gate. The plan was to unscrew an eight-sided STOP sign from near the lake road and escape before anyone caught us in the act. But the rusty screws seemed to have fused with the metal board. We took turns pitting our strength against the rust until a screw came loose. By the time we removed the others, we had bent the screwdriver out of shape.

Not content with one road sign, Phil coveted the bright red Communist Party of India (CPI) flag with the hammer and sickle. The party had been banned in Kerala a few years earlier, but it was active in Tamil Nadu.[1] We idolized the revolutionary heroes of the Cuban revolution, in particular Fidel Castro and Che Guevara.

A few days later, after everyone had gone to sleep, we again crept out of the dorm. At the junction of Seven Roads, a CPI flag fluttered alongside other party flags. We worked fast to cut the rope with a Bowie knife before a sleepless soul caught us red-handed. The weight of the cord brought the cloth down. We jammed it into a knapsack and slunk back into our rooms with no one any the wiser. The mere act of stealing it made us feel as subversive as our guerrilla idols.

Mrs Gibbs, our strict, matronly English housemother, was oblivious to much of what took place under her watch. We didn't dare get up to any tricks with her, but her Alexandrine parakeet was fair game. Every time I passed by its cage on the front porch of her house next door, I made sure its owner wasn't around before trying to teach it to talk. 'Eat shit ... Eat shit,' I said over and over again. But it was a wasted effort as the bird only knew how to whistle and shriek. Only the other boys in the dorm were entertained by my juvenile behaviour.

My admiration for anti-establishment figures and sentiments extended to the literary world as well. I became especially enamoured of

---

1 Parliamentary Debates (Part II—Proceedings Other than Questions and Answers), Official Report, Volume 1, 1952, p. 1552: 'Shri R. Velayudhan [representing (Travancore, Cochin)]: What happened in my State? The Communist party is banned. Not only is the Communist party, but 42 other political organisations are banned.'

Bertrand Russell, whose pronouncements on religion counterbalanced the school's religiosity. For instance, 'So far as I can remember, there is not one word in the Gospels in praise of intelligence …'[2] If I was in danger of hellfire back in eighth grade, I was irredeemable now.

After settling into the dorm, I lost no time in trying out my new air rifle. I crawled on my belly after spotted doves on the open land near Laughing Waters, no doubt fancying myself Jim Corbett stalking a man-eating tiger. On hikes down to the Tope, I shot a coppersmith, a white-breasted kingfisher (now called white-throated kingfisher) and even a gorgeous chalky male paradise flycatcher with long tail plumes, becoming Enemy No. 1 to the bird community. I slipped a fallen green pigeon into my jacket pocket. A few minutes later, something wriggled inside, and before I could thrust my hand in, the bird burst out and flew off, giving me a fright. I hung colourful feathers of the coppersmith from our dorm windows, stuck blue kingfisher wings in my hat and ate the breasts of doves. I was as avid about killing birds as a dedicated twitcher checking species off his life list.

* * *

I learnt much more from the older students in Block than I did in class. A senior brought several issues of the *Mad* magazine from the States, and its subversive humour and parody of pop culture captivated me. The *Mad* aphorism 'What, me worry?' became our cynical response to getting nabbed for doing anything stupid.

A sophomore returned from vacation with a 33 rpm vinyl record, and I listened to the satirical lyrics of a song called *The Old Dope Peddler* with rising disbelief.

> *He gives the kids free samples*
> *Because he knows full well*
> *That today's young, innocent faces*
> *Will be tomorrow's clientele.*

---

2 Bertrand Russell, *Education and the Social Order* (London, UK: George Allen and Unwin Ltd., 1932), p. 115.

The verses of 'Lobachevsky' and 'The Irish Ballad' blew my thirteen-year-old mind. *Who is this guy Tom Lehrer?* The record cover said he was 'a bon vivant, man about town, idol of three continents and Madagascar, where half a million gibbering natives think I am God'. Until Frank Zappa's psychedelic *Freak Out!* album released a decade later, I remained enraptured by Lehrer.

Sophomore Merrick, an electronics genius, made pillow speakers from empty tins of Kiwi shoe polish. We helped him string wires from his room to ours. He played DJ, stacking a dozen 45 rpm records that played in sequence on a turntable or tuning a shortwave radio to Voice of America or Radio Ceylon. It was a luxury to lie on our beds, listening to the latest hits after 'lights out'.

Another dorm mate, Mike, a slight boy with jet-black hair, had a remarkable talent for mimicking French and German accents, which had us in splits. One of the few non-mish kids like me, he was obsessed with airplanes, reading about them or drawing them. The clock in his room hung upside down.

'That's an easy way to tell Greenwich Mean Time,' he explained.

Apparently all pilots followed that time zone. Fifteen years later, he flew hundreds of fighter-plane sorties during the Vietnam War. To my delight, Mike was an excellent mimic of bird calls as well. He crowed like a jungle fowl, standing outside Block at the top of the hill. When we spotted a crested serpent eagle gliding overhead, he imitated its high-pitched cries. Although his calls were realistic enough to fool me, none of the birds responded, much to his frustration.

One night we were watching the moon rise over the lake when a jackal started howling. A different one answered from elsewhere in the valley. The sound was so clear it sounded as if they were calling from nearby. Mike joined their chorus. On another evening, he howled first and jackals responded from all around. I practised for hours, but my howls were nowhere near as good as his.

***

We had long admired JP's talent for farting on command. One of his capers was to place a vase against his ass, let loose and then light a match to see if it ignited. As I was walking by his room one day, I heard a loud 'Prrrrrrp', and he came charging out, shouting, 'It burns, it burns!' Flames shot from the jar. He laughed himself silly on seeing my incredulous face and confessed to lighting toilet paper inside the vase. *How could I better his prank?* This would require some thought and planning.

We were in the Budge most evenings, eating at restaurants or tormenting Pillai with some idiotic request or the other. One evening, Chris and I passed a small crowd of people being entertained by a magician. He took a surreptitious sip from a bottle of some clear fluid while his partner kept the crowd's attention. The magician lit a long match with a flourish, held it in front of his face, pursed his lips and sprayed the liquid. An enormous ball of flame erupted, and the audience gasped. That looked like a cinch to pull off.

I bought half a Coke bottle of kerosene for a rupee. Back at Block, a few guys, including JP, were sitting on the wall outside my room.

'You think your fart really burns, huh?' I said to JP. 'Watch this.'

Slipping into my room, I took a sip of kerosene, not big enough to puff out my cheeks and give the game away. I stood at a distance from the others, lit a match, held it about six inches from my mouth and blew out a spray. The burst of yellow flame was pretty dramatic.

'Howdja do that?' asked an impressed JP. 'Was that gasoline you spit out?'

'Magician's secret,' I replied with a smirk.

Even he agreed this trick was better than his fart in a vase. But I had to live with the consequences of that prank. The kerosene taste wouldn't go away easily, no matter how much I rinsed my mouth. An Extra Strong mint finally overpowered that sick flavour.

The trick gave me an idea for another one. We drew kerosene into a 10 cc syringe borrowed from the biology lab. I struck a match in front of the needle while Chris steadily pressed the plunger. The result wasn't nearly as dramatic as atomizing the fuel with my mouth. We tried the same gimmick with petrol. The dramatic stream of fire shot as far as ten feet, our first flame-thrower. It's a wonder we didn't set each other ablaze. This marked the beginning of our experiments with fire and explosives.

* * *

I shot a gorgeous barbet-sized woodpecker but didn't recognize its yellow crest. The biology teacher hadn't a clue either. He suggested the best people to ask would be at the natural history museum at the Sacred Heart College, Shembaganur, a few kilometres down the ghat. Luckily, it was a Friday. On Saturday morning, I went down to meet the kind and patient museum curator, the Jesuit monk Brother Daniel, who identified the bird as a small yellow-naped woodpecker. He led the way to his specimen preparation room and pulled out drawers to reveal rows of stuffed birds, while mothballs rolled around like marbles. Picking up a stuffed yellow-naped, he showed me how it differed from the other woodpeckers of the Palanis. He skinned the woodpecker I had brought and rubbed it with a pink paste, which he said was arsenic soap. He opened a cupboard meant for drying skins, and an acrid odour suffused the room. The woodpecker skin joined the others.

'Do you want to learn to preserve birds?' he asked, turning to me.

I nodded.

The next weekend, I shot a laughing thrush on the steep path called Priest's Walk to Shembaganur and took it to Brother Daniel for my first lesson in skinning. It was easy enough to remove the meat and peel back the skin on the legs. He showed me how to drape the neck skin over the bird's head, slice the skull open and scoop out the brain. Thereafter, I spent several weekends with him, learning the intricacies of stuffing birds.

The ones with thin necks and large heads, such as the flameback woodpeckers, required care and patience.

'Go easy now,' Brother Daniel directed as I peeled the skin over the neck. 'Pull gently, or you'll rip it.'

Brother Daniel, whom I nicknamed Father Tanner, introduced me to Salim Ali's *The Book of Indian Birds*.[3] Decades later, when I met the famous 'Birdman of India', his stories of making curries from a vast variety of birds, including some rare ones he shot for the immense collection at the Bombay Natural History Society, amused me. I felt kinship with this great man, and years later married his niece, Zahida.

Doves and pigeons were worse than woodpeckers, since their skins tore easily. I saved the succulent breast meat to cook with chilli powder, garlic and salt on the Primus kerosene stove at the dorm, making as good a delicacy as any served at a fine-dining restaurant. Healthy school food left me famished. These tiny bird breasts didn't fill my bottomless stomach, but they were an unbeatable snack.

Aside from getting occasional care packages of sweets, biscuits and powdered milk from home, I ran up a tab at the local Hamidia general store, buying chocolate, condensed milk, and, when they had it, tins of Kraft cheese. Banday Brothers added a dhaba, where I gorged on twelve-egg omelettes. On the rare occasions they got a consignment of Coca-Cola, I swigged a bottle with my feast. I frequented the Spencer's store on allowance day for special treats such as chunks of dark cooking chocolate and sliced ham. Although I had started the school year with clothes one size too big, wearing them with pant cuffs and sleeves unfashionably rolled up, I outgrew them fast.

A wheeler-dealer at the Budge sold a three-kilogram tin of cheese for twenty-one rupees. It was a lot of money, but it became affordable when several boys chipped in. The box was embossed with the American flag and the words 'Gift from the people of America—not to be sold or exchanged'. None of the local residents knew what cheese was or what to do with it. As long as the black market lasted, we had a ready source of processed cheddar.

After stuffing myself at the dhaba one evening, I bought a rose-ringed parakeet chick from a roadside vendor without realizing the chicks had been taken from their nests to be sold as pets. The young bird was easy

---

3 Salim Ali, *The Book of Indian Birds* (Bombay, India: The Bombay Natural History Society, 1941).

to tame, comical and smart, and it ate everything I did, even bits of ham and chocolate. Perched on my shoulder, it went everywhere within the school—except to class—resulting in a lot of shit-stained shirts. Its high-pitched screeches made my ears ring. Just as I had endeavoured to teach Mrs Gibbs's parakeet to talk, friends tried to train my pet to swear with similar results. But Mike persisted when the others gave up. He sat nose to nose with the bird and repeated the words 'Shit, shit, shit, fuck, fuck, fuck'. When he was unsuccessful, he changed tactic and gurgled, cheeped and whistled at it. The chick's pupils dilated and constricted, and its shrieks blasted his eardrums.

I hadn't clipped the bird's wings, so eventually it started flying clumsily around the dorm room. A few months later, someone left a window open, and it was gone. I hoped it survived. This was the first of many parakeet chicks I reared over the following years, and they all flew away on reaching adulthood.

I was between parakeets when JP and Dave suggested an epic bicycle ride down the ghat to the plains. Early on a nippy Saturday morning, we sped downhill on the fifty-kilometre windy road. There was no time to savour the passing scenery. We had to concentrate on the sharp corners and squeeze the brakes. At Oothu, we tucked into a welcome dosai and a cup of strong, sweet filter coffee. Perhaps energized by our repast, JP led the way. Dave and I struggled to keep up, but he was gone. We coasted around a bend and came upon JP lying sprawled on top of a thick lantana bush. He looked dazed as we helped to disentangle him.

'I took the corner too fast,' he said, more embarrassed than hurt. 'I didn't want to fall on the road and get scraped.'

So he had wisely gone right over the edge and landed on the bushes. After straightening the handlebars, we set off at a more reasonable pace. An hour later, when we reached the plains, we hitched a ride on a lorry back up the ghat to school. Although the trip had been exhilarating and we resolved to do it more often, I didn't do it again. I was busy with hunting and learning to stuff birds on weekends, and, unlikely as it may seem, I had also taken up a new, more literary vocation.

I expanded my reading from novels to poems, and I memorized verses that moved me, from Henry Wadsworth Longfellow's

Paul Revere's Ride to Alfred Lord Tennyson's *The Charge of the Light Brigade* and Percy Bysshe Shelley's *Ozymandias*. This ability to recite from memory earned me roles in plays. I discovered a flair for showmanship and revelled in acting. Until graduation, I was in a play every year. As a junior, I played the joker Launcelot Gobbo in Shakespeare's *The Merchant of Venice*, and as a senior, I was King Pausanius, who executed the impious, rabble-rousing philosopher Socrates in *Barefoot in Athens*. For the final staging of the latter play, I wore a kingly costume resembling a mini skirt.

I gave the Saturday night formal dance a miss. Sylvia was going steady with another guy, and the dance was no fun without a steady girlfriend. I didn't possess the gift of the gab, nor was I into sports. My fishing and hunting exploits didn't appeal to girls. Dave and JP bragged about making out in the dark, which sounded exciting, but the girl thing would have to wait.

Every weekend I looked forward to the company of Father Tanner. Arsenic soap, to cure the skins, wasn't available in any shop. He whittled a bar of soft soap, preferring Lifebuoy to any other brand, to a pile of shavings with a knife. Then he mashed it with a pestle and mortar until it became a thick paste. He may have heated it over a stove, a detail that escapes me now. After ladling in two tablespoons of white arsenic powder, he stirred until they blended together. Although it is a deadly poison, he handled the stuff with neither gloves nor mask.

Father Tanner mounted most of his birds as reference specimens for study by serious ornithologists, and these were stored in large wooden drawers. But the special ones, such as an adult white male paradise flycatcher, he installed in a lifelike pose on a small branch set on a pedestal for display at the museum.

When he heard of my interest in snakes, he led me to another room with several floor-to-ceiling shelves containing rows of jars with creatures pickled in formalin. He took one down, in which the massive head of a king cobra floated. It had been killed at the Tope a few years earlier. These huge serpents lived in my backyard! Ditmars hadn't mentioned south India as being king cobra country. Henceforth, the thought of one was never far from my mind on my treks.

On occasions when Chris and Chuck went with me, we hiked to the Tope. Instead of following the switchbacking path, we cut straight down the hill, making it in less than half the time. Our legs were wobbly and knees reduced to jelly. We stripped to splash in the refreshing water and terrorized the colonies of rock crickets, which we nicknamed 'crotch crickets'. Grabbing our groins in mock fear and yelling, we zipped past them bare-assed on a rock slide in the middle of the stream. Then it was time for a picnic. If we still had a tin of peaches or pears from the care package sent from home, we put it into the cool stream before digging in. Chuck came up with one of his innumerable ditties:

Yum, yum, piggy's bum,
Chew it up like chewing gum.

If we had no tins left, we ate fresh fruit bought on the way. After our exuberant play, we stretched out, exhausted, on flat rocks. On one trip, a butterfly swooped down from a tree without flapping its wings. It landed on another tree trunk and scurried up. *A lizard that could fly?* I hadn't known such a creature existed. Later, Father Tanner confirmed it was a flying lizard called Draco, meaning dragon. A living pterodactyl in miniature. I took a close look at a preserved specimen in the museum.

Many more rat snakes and cobras lay squashed on the road down on the plains than in the neighbourhood of Kodai, which made me think these large snakes liked the warm lower altitudes. I took the roadkills back to the dorm for skinning. Stretching the hides on a board with dozens of little nails, I rubbed salt into them. Later, when they were dry, they decorated my wall. A dead Russell's viper was too far gone to save anything but the fangs. But of king cobras there was no sign. In fact, I have never heard of another in that area since. That unlucky snake at the Shembaganur museum remains an enigma.

Tredis, the overgrown grounds of the Pudukkottai royal mansion, was the closest patch of jungle to the school and a perfect spot for shooting small birds. I took to trespassing until Nadudorai caught me one Saturday afternoon.

'I'm learning to do taxidermy at Shembaganur,' I replied shamefacedly. 'I need specimens, so I was shooting birds here.'

'Don't sneak in here like a thief, Breezy,' he said. 'Come hunting with me tomorrow.'

When the church service was over, I raced over to Tredis with my air rifle. We drove in Nadudorai's old 4WD Jeep to the Ten Mile Round to hunt imperial pigeons. They were out of my rifle's range, and he shot a brace of six fat birds with his Savage .22 rifle with a six-shot magazine. The .22 was quieter than a shotgun, and he was an excellent marksman. He handed me his rifle, but my aim wasn't nearly as good as his.

Back at Tredis, while lunch was being prepared, I wandered through the house, fascinated by the trophies, including a full tiger skin, a huge gaur's head and skins of all kinds of creatures. In the garden, Nadudorai showed me what a crack shot he was with the .22. He jammed an ace of spades card into the cleft of a stick. I expected him to shoot it through the middle, but he turned it edgewise and poised himself about twenty paces away. Without bracing the rifle, he took aim and shot. The card fluttered and fell in two pieces. The bullet had scored through it.

'Whew!' I exclaimed. 'That's some shooting.'

Later, I set up paper targets at Bear Shola and practised, following Nadudorai's instructions on how to breathe while squeezing the trigger. But I never reached his level of expertise.

Decades later, his son, Vijaykumar Thondaman, said Nadudorai learnt his shooting skills from Gunboat Jack, an African-American boxer who lived in Bangalore for many years and was famous for his flamboyant style.

As my obsession with hunting grew, going after little birds with the Diana didn't satisfy me. I wanted a shotgun to hunt bigger game. Discreet enquiries at the Budge led me to a clerk at the Kodai Missionary Union, a fine old fellow named Robert Kasi, who had a vintage double-barrel 12-gauge shotgun, given to him by a retired missionary who went back to the States. We had a delicate conversation, since he knew I couldn't have owned a gun licence, but we arrived at an agreement. In exchange for the firearm, I would share the kill. He also showed me how it could be conveniently taken apart. If that wasn't encouragement, what was?

Early Saturday morning, I shoved the stock and forearm piece in my knapsack and the barrel in my pant leg, so I couldn't bend my knee. I limped through the back gate of the school without anyone catching me. On reaching the forest, I assembled the shotgun and was ready for action. Imperial pigeons and grey junglefowl were now accessible game; I took them to Shembaganur for skinning and later shared the meat with Robert. I killed a beautiful giant squirrel and instantly regretted it. Besides, its meat was as tough as leather. At the Ten Mile Round, I was on the lookout for barking deer, which the locals called 'kaattu aadu' and the English-speaking hunters literally translated as 'jungle sheep'. Though I heard their distinctive loud bark-like calls many times and caught glimpses of them, I never got close enough to shoot.

Father Tanner quizzed me when he saw the squirrel pelt I had salted and brought for tanning, and I confessed to borrowing a shotgun.

'Where do you get the cartridges?' he asked.

'I use the old ones that Robert has,' I replied. 'Often they are duds.'

'I can teach you how to reload cartridges,' said the kind monk. 'We have a machine and birdshot. All you need to do is buy some black powder from the quarry fellows. And if possible, bring some old used shotgun shells. The plastic Remington ones from the States are the best; the Eley Kynoches come apart eventually.'

On the following weekend, I arrived at the museum with a bag of black powder and learnt how to reload cartridges, making number 6s and 8s with small birdshot, SGs with nine big pellets and LGs with six large lead slugs. The SG and LG were the preferred loads for game such as deer.

One thing in short supply was the primer, a cylindrical metal cap inserted into the bottom of the shell casing. When the gun's firing pin strikes it, it bursts, igniting the black powder in the cartridge. No shop sold these in Kodai, so it would have to wait until I went home to Bombay on vacation.

One day, as a group of us relaxed after the long walk to Berijam Lake, a fat, colourful snake swam past near the shore. I jumped up and grabbed a net from Bill, a sophomore who was crazy about butterflies, and scooped up the creature, noting its large, triangular-shaped head and the distinctive chain of oval circles along its back.

'What is it?' asked Bill.

'Russell's viper,' I squeaked, my throat constricting from nervousness.

I twisted the butterfly net closed and emptied the contents of my lunch box. Holding the net in one hand, I somehow manoeuvred the cold, sluggish two-foot snake into the container and shut it without getting bitten. I pretended to be a pro, hiding my excitement at catching my first venomous snake. I hadn't known this species lived so high up in the hills, and much later I would learn that it kills more people than any other snake in the world.

Back in the biology lab, the teacher let me use a large empty aquarium to keep the viper for a few days. *What possessed him to allow this?* A regular stream of students came to see it, and I gave my spiel about how it was dangerous but wouldn't bite unless it was frightened or hurt. Later, I released it on the Ten Mile Round.

With a growing reputation as the 'snake boy', I fielded questions from other kids.

'What's the long black snake that moves fast? Saw it on my way to the Tope.'

'That's a rat snake, not venomous and yes, very fast,' I'd wisely reply. 'Maybe the fastest snake in India.'

'We found a little snake under a rock … Looks like a big earthworm but with a colourful belly. What is it? Is it poisonous?'

'Those are shield-tail snakes. They eat earthworms and they are all harmless.'

Some sophomores searched the jungles around Rat Tail Falls (also called Thalaiyar Falls) for orchids to make into corsages to present to their dates for the annual prom. Bill, who had helped me with the Russell's viper, saw a green snake and caught it for me. His capture technique was clumsy: He grabbed its tail with one hand and caught its neck with the other. But the snake was faster, biting the tip of his right forefinger. Although in an account he wrote for the fiftieth reunion of his class he said he let it go after being bitten, I have a distinct memory he somehow coaxed it into his US Army canteen. Following the American Boy Scout first aid protocol for snakebite, the school chaperone made two neat crosscuts over the puncture wounds with the knife they were using to cut flowers, and sucked the blood. This was dangerous to do, since we now know some viper venoms mess with the clotting factor in the blood. Depending on the species, it can either cause blood to ooze freely from any wound or coagulate it so it hardly flows. Another problem is venom causes necrosis, dry gangrene, which destroys tissue. Cutting could aggravate these symptoms. Besides, using an unsterilized knife to slice the finger could lead to sepsis. The group reached the road and flagged down a lorry to drop them at Kodai.

Later, we dumped the snake out of the canteen. It was a large-scaled green pit viper, a species I had seen before. Bill was in tremendous pain and his hand had swollen up. Eventually, he lost the tip of that finger, but whether that was caused by the venom or the cutting is debatable. I kept the viper in the biology lab, straightening a wire coat hanger to use as a snake hook. As with the Russell's viper, I let this one go in a nearby forest after a few days.

Although high school gave us more freedom than in lower grades, my friends and I continued to chafe at the restrictions. Perhaps influenced by Castro and Che, some students took their discontent to an extreme. They hung an effigy of the principal from the flagpole one early morning. The tension in the school was palpable. Social evenings and movies stood cancelled, and everyone had to stay in their dorms. I couldn't sneak into the forest until they found the culprits. Those kids were sent to detention, meaning extra hours of study hall. At least they didn't get caned. I still shuddered at the memory of the punishment in Lovedale four years ago.

In science class one day, the teacher said, 'Turn to page 42 and read the word aloud.'

'Onion,' called each student.

Is this some sort of trick? Why do I alone see something different? I strained to make out 'onion' among the coloured dots, but no matter how much I squinted, the only word in my book was 'color'.

I hesitantly said, 'Colour.'

The teacher explained what colour blindness was, and I finally understood the years of confusion.

Where others saw red rhododendron flowers, in my vision the blossoms merged with the green foliage. Or the many times I had hurt myself and had thought little of it until I returned home, and everyone exclaimed about the bleeding. *What blood?* I had looked down at the brown spots of dirt. Those strange incidents made sense now—I was colour-blind. Strangely, if someone points to a flower and says it's red, I can see the colour. Whether it is a question of vision or recognition I cannot say.

I was always one of the slowest pupils in the class. At the end of the year, Chris's grades were so low the school wouldn't promote him to the next grade with the rest of us. He had to repeat the ninth.

When Mom came for Gail's graduation, she was astonished by how tall I had grown and was embarrassed by my ill-fitting clothes. My pant cuffs rode above my ankles and my shirt sleeves hung below my elbows. I wet my small shoes and then shoehorned my big feet into them. All of us boys learnt these tricks to last through the school year. Before we left for Bombay, I begged Mom for money. My meagre allowance wouldn't cover the enormous tab at Hamidia. She couldn't believe I had eaten so much and came to the store to see for herself and settle my bills.

I packed the stuffed birds, about fifty species, in a box cushioned with cotton for the trip to Bombay. The collection was too large to keep hidden from Mom. She might have been disappointed I hadn't honoured my word. Or she might have recognized their scientific value and excused me. She kept her thoughts to herself, and I took it as a licence to continue. Eventually, the specimens went with me to the States, and I donated them to a museum in Seattle.

The evening before we were to leave, Mrs Gibbs made cookies and juice for all the boys at the dorm. She would lay out this treat before every vacation throughout my time at Block. Despite her strict rules, she was a kindly soul.

***

After Gail's graduation ceremony, we returned home together—I on vacation and Gail to go on to the States to study art at Syracuse University. This was no surprise as she was always drawing and painting. Since both Dad and Mom were artists, it must be something in the genes that I missed out on.

Meanwhile, the family had moved to Cumballa Hill, a ritzy part of Bombay. Our apartment building, Shangri-La, sat on the edge of a forested hill overlooking the vast spread of the Mahindra factory. Peacocks called in the early mornings and rat snakes occasionally showed themselves. Leaning over the balcony wall of the second-floor flat, I shot hefty bandicoot rats with the airgun. Although this wilderness was within sight, I still missed the open spaces of Juhu.

Padma and Mom struggled to feed my gargantuan appetite. They made a roast chicken for me and another for the rest of the family. I demolished mine with no difficulty and had space for more. I cadged second helpings of anything going, even coaxing Nina to give up her dessert. At the end of the meal, there were no leftovers. Mom joked I must have worms. I was taller than everyone in the family and was well on my way to reaching my eventual six-foot height.

I couldn't buy shotgun shells without having a gun licence, but Saleh sold me the primers sorely needed for reloading the 12-gauge shotgun shells.

Perhaps to distract me from my obsession with hunting, Mom gave me her German-made Robot, a 35 mm still camera. It exposed half-frame pictures, so a roll of thirty-six frames would give seventy-two photographs. She taught me the basics of composition, preparing solutions for developing and fixing in her dark room, and printing and enlarging the photographs.

Halfway through the vacation, Rama, Mom, my sisters, my brother and I travelled with Amma to Kashmir. We went by train from Bombay to Amritsar, and then drove in two cars over a trashed road. We drove up the ghat road through Banihal Pass and had almost reached Srinagar when the police stopped our vehicles. Although Amma and Rama tried talking them into revealing what it was about, the uniformed men were tight-lipped. They seemed to be waiting for higher officials to arrive, so there was little to do but wait. A white Ambassador car with a red flashing light on its roof arrived. The policemen saluted and opened its door. A man alighted and rushed over to greet Amma. He was Bakshi Ghulam Mohammed, the prime minister of Jammu and Kashmir, who had heard of Amma's visit.

We followed his car through town, past souvenir and carpet shops with signs such as 'Savanna the Worst' and 'Suffering Moses', which were stuffed with all sorts of animal furs. Dal Lake was an enormous expanse of greenish water, with patches of lilies. We loaded our suitcases on several shikaras, as the gondolas are termed, and the boatman poled past houseboats with their names painted in large colourful letters. One called itself *Do It Again* and touted its speciality 'full spring beds'. Later, I heard these amusing names were the mischief of British soldiers sojourning in the pleasant climes of Kashmir after the rigours of the Second World War. The prime minister insisted we stay in a fancy houseboat moored in Dal Lake, which had the same name as our apartment building, 'Shangri-La'.

Shangri-La, with its three bedrooms, stately stuffed chairs and sumptuous Kashmiri wool carpets, was fit for a maharaja. A bowl of red apples took pride of place on the dining table, where the hamal (waiter) in a white uniform served meals.

While the others were busy settling in, I stood on the prow, watching carp rise to the surface. Mogla, the son of the boat keeper who was about my age, showed me how he caught fish. He threw a hook baited with peanut-flour dough over the side and swished a big stick back and forth through the water, chanting, '*Aow maachh, aow.*' When I taught him the English translation, he chanted, 'Comeon, feesh, comeon.' This disturbance unusually attracted the fish.

Catching carp was fine, but I had my heart set on trout fishing. Some streams in the upper reaches of Kodai also had trout, but I hadn't tried angling for those yet. At school, a teacher had described how eggs of rainbow and brown trout were brought in ice-chilled tubs to India from Scotland aboard sailing ships in the late nineteenth century. From the seaports, they travelled by train to the foothills, and then donkeys hauled them into the high hills, where the water was cold enough for fingerlings to hatch and grow. The effort to pull this feat off seems fantastic to this day. The colonial Brits also stocked trout in the higher reaches of Kashmir.

For my fourteenth birthday, Rama arranged for a guide, fishing gear and a car to take me to Pahalgam. While the rest of the family enjoyed a leisurely stay on the houseboat, I gazed at the fantastic vistas of snow-capped mountains and pine forests zipping by. The waters of the Jhelum River glittered in the sunlight, and I hoped the fish would bite. When we came to a stop next to a small bridge across what looked like a perfect trout stream, the Lidder River, a tall, skinny Kashmiri approached and introduced himself in broken English, 'I am Ali, trout fishing guide.' He handed me a spinning rod and reel, battered but functional. When I asked about spinners, he had other ideas. '*Mandooks*,' he replied as he opened a milk powder tin to reveal a dozen small frogs inside.

By the lovely stream, Ali pointed to the boulders where the rushing water created riffles, the ideal spot where fish might wait for a meal. My first cast didn't get any bites. On the second, I hooked a fish, which tore some of the line off the reel and dove deep into the middle of the pool. I played it for a few minutes. Since we didn't have a landing net, I flipped it on the bank, where it lay writhing.

'Not big,' Ali said with a smile. 'Next one, maybe.'

After unhooking it, I let it go and cast again at the bottom of a rock slide, where the water foamed white. This time I knew I had hooked a big fish when it stripped line from the reel. When I finally hauled it up on the bank, where it lay thumping, excitement and triumph washed through me. Ali said it was big enough to keep. I could do this all day every day for the rest of my life. For the next few hours, we skipped from rock to shore to rock along the stream, reeling in fish. We kept the big ones and released the tiddlers. I returned to the houseboat at dusk, elated with my legal limit of half a dozen fat trout for dinner. It had been so much fun that trout fishing in Kodai was next on my plans.

9

THE YEAR OF VICES

Smoking Beedis

ITRAVELLED WITH A GANG of other students from Victoria Terminus
to Kodai with a suitcase stuffed with primers, camera and a new
wardrobe of clothes. A few packets of dry yeast to make pear wine,
an underground high school tradition, found space in a corner.

We were re-rigging our room-entertainment system, running wires
from Merrick's to ours, when an excited Chris arrived at the dorm.

'Come home with me,' he said. 'I have something to show you.'

Leaving the others to complete the wiring, I clapped my arm on
Chris's shoulder as we walked to his house, wondering what was in
store. He was tight-lipped and wouldn't tell me more. *Did he get a
companion for Moosa, his pet toddy cat? Or maybe he's got a shotgun.*

In the front yard, Raju, the mechanic from the Budge, sat on his
haunches assembling an assortment of mechanical parts. It was a moped,
but in reality a bicycle with a tiny engine. The missionary colleagues of
Chris's parents had brought it piece by piece from Germany to India
to save on import duty. We waited with rising excitement as the two-
wheeler took shape. Then we zipped around the lake that evening,
overtaking pedestrians and delighting in the wind whipping our hair.
We imagined we were riding a motorcycle instead of this humble
motorized bike.

Chris and I took to spending time in Raju's mechanic shop, where
we ogled his collection of old cars and bikes. From hand-me-down
magazines, I recognized the various makes, the American clunkers such

as Harley-Davidson and Indian, and the trim British motorcycles with evocative names such as Triumph Tiger 100, BSA Golden Flash, Norton Manx and Vincent Black Shadow.

Raju rarely combed his long wisps of hair, which you'd think could get caught in machinery. The fifty-year-old wore thick glasses tied around his head with what looked like a bra strap. He wasn't voluble, but answered our many questions. His career had begun as a 'cleaner', or the driver's assistant, on an ancient truck that delivered supplies to ration shops in the hills and took produce from the hill plantations to the plains. He graduated to become a driver, and when his eyes dimmed, he started the garage.

While helping him change clutch plates on the local church pastor's old English Ford or dismantle an antique Jeep that a planter had brought in for a total overhaul, I dreamt of owning a motorbike like the ones rusting in his workshop. I wanted one so badly I could taste it. These flights of fantasy kept what was a futile dream alive.

Girls were the subject of interest at the dorm. Some boys had steady girlfriends, and I wished to join their ranks too. To get anywhere with girls meant keeping up with pop trends. As kids growing up in American culture but far away from that country, we yearned for the latest fashion in clothes, games, music and comics. Mish kids visited the States on furlough every two years and returned with whatever was the rage. I sent detailed instructions to Mom, who was going to the States with Gail, to buy shirts with button-down collars, black jeans and chinos with a buckle on the back.

If the cracks of our asses weren't on display, the jeans weren't slung low enough. Cleats on our shoes clicked as we walked, and at night sparks flew from the friction. We gave Muthu, the barber, elaborate instructions to copy our favourite movie star's hairstyle. Far from being overwhelmed, he had already become skilled from hairdressing previous generations of Highclerc kids. I had Elvis Presley's flat top without fenders, one lock falling forward on my forehead and a duck's ass in the back.

The next stop was Raja, the jeweller, who made silver ID bracelets. I asked him to embellish the nameplate with small black onyx stones in which Russell's viper fangs were embedded. Despite the lengths we went to keep up with the latest US teen fashions, we always lagged.

Decked out in my new clothes, fancy hairstyle and silver bracelet, I set out to conquer girls' hearts. To my utter disappointment, most didn't give me a second glance. Actually, I wasn't sure if they even gave me a first glance. Since sporty types like Dave and JP had no trouble dating girls, I blamed my lack of interest in sports for my failure. When a girl returned my smile, I missed no opportunity in asking her to the movies or skating at the gym. I probably frightened her off with my overeagerness. Some classmates were already shaving. Maybe my dismal fate was down to my smooth chin, indicating I was still a kid. I took to scraping it with a razor, hoping to encourage hair growth, but it didn't sprout a whisker. The truth was I didn't spend enough time pursuing girls to be successful.

Mike, the bird mimic, who had the same luck with the opposite sex, and I conspired to play stupid pranks. Late one evening after dinner, we crept out of Block and, avoiding the lighted hallways, made our way to Lower Boyer, the high school girls' dorm. Mike did his best rendition of a jackal, with high-pitched yips and a long-drawn-out yowl. I howled along. Gratified by the terrified screams, we chuckled all the way back to Block. The next morning at breakfast, the girls narrated how a nasty beast had shrieked outside their windows the previous night, and their lives had been in danger. Mike and I looked away to avoid bursting into laughter. Despite the prank's success, we didn't torment the girls any further.

We had other targets, however. Couples necked against the retaining wall of the Flag Green, the wide open entrance to the school. Mike stood facing the wall, and, crossing his arms across his chest all the way to the back, he pretended to be smooching a girl. Twenty feet away, I did the same ruse. When a teacher on night duty came along, the couples fled while Mike and I continued making loud kissing noises. Of course we got 'caught', but the laugh was on the teacher since we had no girl.

* * *

I photographed my friends, Field Day events and picturesque scenes around Kodai. Mr Doveton, who owned Doveton's Photo Studio in the Budge, let me help in the darkroom, developing and printing the photographs.

I took the Robot camera on a four-day annual class trip to Mandapam on the east coast. The eighteen students and accompanying teachers rented an old beach bungalow belonging to a corporate house. This was the first time we saw our girl classmates in bathing suits, and tried hard not to stare.

A teacher taught us to snorkel after we found a stash of masks, fins and snorkels in a corner cupboard. The tidal pools in Worli had been a small portal to the marine riches. But this, my first view of underwater life in their coral reef element, mesmerized me. Schools of colourful fish darted about while large groupers eyeballed us before disappearing with a swoosh of their tails.

We found two spear guns with which we supplied fresh fish to the kitchen. I blew the last film roll taking photographs of my classmates on the beach. Film rolls were too expensive for photography to become a serious hobby, so I put away the camera for the rest of the year.

One perk of tenth grade was being allowed to go on unsupervised weekend outings. It was mandatory for three boys to travel together. Although the school didn't give an explanation for this rule, I assume their thinking went like this: Should anything happen to one, the second guy could stay with him while the third could seek help. These journeys had an additional advantage—since we were away, we couldn't attend church services.

Chris, Chuck and I applied for permission to visit Periyar Wildlife Sanctuary in Kerala. The other reason for visiting the state was alcohol. Tamil Nadu was dry, and we knew several teachers disappeared to Kerala or Pondicherry (now Puducherry) for the weekends. A quarter bottle of cheap Old Monk rum mixed with Coke could get the three of us pretty woozy. Chris and Chuck, however, had other plans. At Theni, they insisted on going to Munnar. The girls working in the fields and tea estates didn't wear blouses. Our fevered sexual appetites got a thrill from seeing their breasts silhouetted through the thin fabric of their saris. Although the pleasures of ogling women and drinking were heady, we visited Munnar only thrice and Periyar not even once.

The need to get away into the wilds after a week of classes was strong. But I wanted to go alone, which was against the school's rules. I cajoled Chris and Chuck to sign up for a camp and stay out of sight until Sunday evening.

On that first solo trip, I went trout fishing. A teacher had told me Gundar stream, where we had swum on class hikes, was a good spot. I don't know when he fished, since I didn't run into anyone on my weekly treks. Perhaps he was guessing. In my knapsack were a loaf of bread from Jacob's Bakery in the Budge, two boiled eggs, a roll of hand line and some hooks. Carrying a long pole through the forest would have been an obstacle course. I climbed three kilometres up the steep Observatory Hill and stepped on to an animal trail leading off the Ten Mile Round.

That dirt track to Gundar Valley led me to another world. I spooked a sounder of wild pigs rooting around in a small patch of shola forest, sending them snorting and snuffling as they ran. From Neptune's Pool, I followed the stream's course downhill. At a promising spot, I stomped on the grass to disturb grasshoppers, grabbed one and flung it into the stream. A trout snatched it. It was just the place.

A long, deep drink of the cool, clear water that would become polluted in later years was refreshing after the hike. After hanging the knapsack on a tree branch, out of reach of hungry animals, I tied a hook to the line, crimped a piece of lead and skewered another grasshopper through the thorax. I flipped the insect into the stream and watched the current carry it. It had hardly gone a few feet when the flash of a fish broke the surface and the nylon filament tightened around my fist. The frantic trout fought and tugged. A rod would have made it so much easier. A wave of satisfaction washed over me as I yanked the ten-inch catch flip-flopping on to the grassy bank.

I tied a piece of canvas between trees to form a shelter and roasted the fish over an open fire until the skin turned black. The succulent flesh was the best I had ever tasted. The bread and eggs filled my stomach, and a can of condensed milk was a good dessert. I crawled into my sleeping bag and fell asleep. The sound of a thunderclap startled me awake at midnight, and the rain came drumming down. I rolled up the sleeping bag to keep it dry and huddled under the canvas. Within a short time, the stream was roaring and threatening to overflow its banks and sweep me along with it. I scrambled up a tree, and wedging the sleeping bag on a fork, sat back on a horizontal branch. I shivered in the cold and dozed fitfully.

The next morning dawned bright and clear, and I trudged back to the dorm, tired and soggy. However, the experience didn't put me off camping. I revelled in being out in the wilds.

Pear season arrived, and it was time to make wine. On my hikes to Bear Shola, I had monitored the state of the fruits in the orchards. Not long after they turned yellow, Dave, JP and I snuck out of the dorm late one night. We didn't need flashlights as the moon was almost full. Crawling through gaps in barbed-wire fences, we made our way into the gardens, avoiding the ones guarded by dogs. We took turns climbing the trees to knock down the biggest pears while the other two gathered the fallen fruits in a clean laundry bag. When we couldn't stuff in any more, we hauled the heavy sack back to the dorm.

Under a senior's supervision, we juiced the ripe pears by bashing the bag with a baseball bat and squeezing the resultant mush. We filled half a dozen empty Coke bottles with the juice, added two or three pellets of yeast to each, corked and hid them in our clothes closet. Several weeks later, we had a passable pear wine. Some turned into vinegar, and one bottle exploded and made a huge stink. We scrubbed and cleaned before the funky smell reached Mrs Gibbs's sharp nose.

We sipped our concoction with the school's old booze song, which we updated with the name of the current principal:

> Give a cheer, give a cheer,
> For the boys who make the beer,
> In the cellars of Highclerc School.
> They are young, they are bold,
> And the liquor they can hold,
> Is a story that's never been told.

And if Papa should appear,
Say 'Phelpsy have a beer',
In the cellars of Highclerc School.

Occasionally I scored a packet of Ganesh beedis for four annas and a matchbox for half an anna. Smoking on campus was a serious offence that could get the student expelled. While I enjoyed a puff out of sight behind the Brahmin hotel in the Budge, the true addicts smoked the harsh Charminar cigarettes, as cigarette filters were unheard of at that time. They popped peppermints to mask their breath and rubbed lime juice on their fingers to erase tell-tale nicotine stains. Despite the taboo around smoking, this ditty appeared surprisingly uncensored in the school yearbook, *Eucalyptus*:

Tobacco is a dirty weed,
I like it.
It satisfies my daily need,
I like it.
It makes me sick and turns me green,
And takes the hair right off my bean,
I like it.

Through all these shenanigans, I was still very much into hunting. I got permission to spend some weekends at Chris's house. After everyone had gone to sleep, the two of us snuck out of the back door with my shotgun.

The eerie moaning calls of flying squirrels from high in the eucalyptus trees rang through the valley. The eyes of these huge rodents reflected the light I shone into the branches. We marvelled at the creatures' ability to glide from tree to tree, looking like square frying pans against the moonlit sky.

One evening, we heard a thud and investigated. A flying squirrel lay quivering at the base of a tree. It had smashed its head from miscalculating its landing site. I noted the place so I could retrieve it later.

We followed the howls of a pack of jackals to the lake. I shone my flashlight along a tall hedge, and a jackal froze in the beam for a few seconds. Chris held the light over my shoulder while I took aim and fired. The SG cartridge's nine lead pellets hit the animal, but we couldn't find the body. We searched in the dark until we grew exhausted and called it a night. At dawn, we returned to find it lying dead in tall grass close to where I had shot it.

The jackals of the hills have long fur, and this one had a splendid coat. Rigor mortis had set in, which made the skinning easier. I removed the pelt of the flying squirrel as well. Rolling them up for salting and tanning later, we returned to Chris's house as everyone was stirring out of bed.

On my next visit to Shembaganur, Father Tanner helped me tan the skins. Robert Kasi gave me the cured pelt of a beautiful black Nilgiri langur. The animal-hide collection hanging on my dorm-room wall grew.

I learnt about birds and mammals, but my knowledge of snakes was limited to Ditmars's *Snakes of the World*, which had been my bible for many years. I wanted to learn more about Indian snakes, but I knew no one I could ask in India. I wrote to Ditmars, care of the Bronx Zoo, New York, seeking his guidance and expressing the hope of meeting him someday. Long after I had forgotten posting the letter in 1957, I received an envelope embossed with the zoo's emblem. The zoo curator, James Oliver, wrote, 'I'm happy to hear of your interest, but I regret to advise that Dr Ditmars passed away in 1942.' I was crestfallen, but my friends howled with laughter at my cluelessness.

On the dusty shelves of the school library was an old, tattered book, *A Popular Treatise on the Common Indian Snakes*, written in 1900 by Major Frank Wall, a medical doctor and British Army officer. It was just the book I needed. I borrowed it for the duration of the year, since there was no danger of anyone else wanting it. In later years, Wall would have an even greater impact on me, when I would read the hundreds of scientific papers he wrote about snakes in the *Journal of the Bombay Natural History Society* and elsewhere, describing at least thirty new species and making original observations on snake behaviour.

Also in the library was an issue of *Coronet* magazine, which had an article about William E. Haast at the Miami Serpentarium. He looked stern in his white scrubs, black hair swept back and thick-framed glasses obscuring his eyes. In one photo, he was feeding a snake through a tube. He kept hundreds of venomous snakes, including cobras, mambas and vipers, and milked their venom, which he sold to pharmaceutical companies for research and manufacture of antivenom. He sounded like the person to emulate. Until then, I had struggled to describe the career I imagined for myself.

I wrote to Haast of my deep feeling for snakes, of my experiences in India and, of course, my desire to visit his serpentarium. On receiving a reply several weeks later, I couldn't contain my excitement. In answer to my question about feeding snakes, he gave a detailed explanation. He blended eggs, ground meat and protein supplements, and fed the 'meatshake' with a converted caulking gun. The plastic tube had to be lubricated with water before gently inserting it down a snake's throat. He wrote of his interest in Indian species and invited me to call on him whenever I was in the States.

While I obsessed over all things wild, it was time for the annual dance. We dressed by taking cues from songs such as Marty Robbins's *A White Sport Coat*:

A white sport coat and a pink carnation,
I'm all dressed up for the dance.

We wore tailored shark-skin dinner jackets with round collars made to our exacting standards. But I was yet to ask a girl. By then, the girls I had my eyes on had already committed to others. Classmate Gwen agreed to be my date, which was a relief.

On the evening of the dance, I put on a brave demeanour to mask my nervousness. Gwen looked calm and lovely, with the orchid corsage I had made pinned to her long formal dress. The DJ's stack of 45 rpm vinyls included the top 40 hits from the States. We danced to slow songs such as Pat Boone's *Love Letters in the Sand* and Sam Cooke's *You Send Me*. When Elvis's *All Shook Up* or Chuck Berry's *School Days* started rocking the place, I gave up. Jitterbugging was beyond me. Gwen said she didn't know how to jitterbug, either. Liar! We stood on the sidelines, watching the others on the dance floor.

* * *

On one of my vacations in Bombay, I saw stray dogs harassing a black kite—the bird, not the paper contraption—in the Shangri-La car park. I scooped it up in my arms and took it to our flat. A wing was injured, likely by a cutting manja kite string. For two days I kept it under an upturned large basket and fed it pieces of meat. Once it stopped being skittish, I set a cane chair as a perch on our balcony, from where it could watch the other kites flying by. Within a few days, it tamely accepted pieces of meat from my hand, but jealously covered the prize with its wings and hissed if I approached. I bonded with the various cats and dogs Mom and other family members had as pets, but there was something fulfilling about befriending wild creatures, whether they were birds of prey, toddy cats or snakes. It took a lot more effort to get them to accept me, a human, as a non-threatening friend. That process also changed me. I began to see the world through their eyes.

When Amma came for a visit, she presented me with a big-format book, *The Decisive Moment* by Henri Cartier-Bresson, which the great photographer had inscribed to her. Inspired by his example, I borrowed film rolls from Mom and wandered everywhere with the camera hanging from my neck, taking photographs of everyday life.

At the lab, I shot the breeze with film technicians, and at the motorbike repair shops in Worli hung out with the mechanics, who had a miscellany of vintage German BMWs, the light, racy 90 cc Italian Ducatis and the 'dog-killer' Harley-Davidsons. Most of these machines were too far gone to roar back to life.

I accompanied Mom on her weekly shopping to Crawford Market, a chaotic jumble of shops, where everything from fish and chicken to dry goods and imported goodies such as Crosse & Blackwell grape jelly and stuffed olives were on sale. Not only was the place photogenic, but it also had a live animal market, which sold puppies and kittens as well as tropical fish and the occasional reptile. Star tortoises were often on sale. More than once I bought a skinny monitor lizard for ten bucks and let it go outside of town, hoping it would survive.

On one occasion, Ayo, Mom's Danish lady friend, accompanied us. We left Mom at the grocery store and wandered to the pet-market section. A six-foot python in perfect condition was for sale. She asked the seller how much he wanted.

'Hundred rupees,' he said. 'Is cheap. Very tame, no biting.'

But he covered his arm with a gunny sack to open the chicken mesh cage. The snake wasn't agitated when he picked it up, so I took it from him and let it run through my hands, keeping it well away from my face.

'Yes, he seems tame,' I told Ayo. 'But you have to be careful. Snakes have lots of teeth.'

'Do you want it?' she asked.

Without waiting for my answer, she handed a hundred-rupee note to the seller. Too stupefied to thank her for this fantastic gift, I hoisted the gunny bag on my shoulder and we made our way to where Mom was getting her purchases packed into boxes.

Typical of her style, Mom calmly took the news of a reptilian addition to the household.

'What happens when you go to school next month?' she asked after we arrived home and Ayo had left.

I hadn't thought of that yet.

'Make sure it doesn't eat Trichy.'

Besides Trichy the cat, Nina's pets, a rabbit and a palm squirrel, also ran around the apartment.

I rigged a makeshift box, placed a bowl of water inside it and transferred the python from the sack. Mukund, Mom's carpenter, promised to have a container complete with ventilation holes delivered in two days. I set rat traps downstairs in the garage, and one held a dead rodent the next morning. The hungry snake lunged, wrapped his coils around his meal and took his time swallowing. Although I had kept a sand boa, water snake and Russell's viper, this was the first large snake of my life. For as long as I had the python, trapping rats became part of my routine.

At the army and navy store at Flora Fountain, a pamphlet, *The Bomber's Handbook*, caught my eye. Produced in Britain during the Second World War and designed to teach ordinary citizens how to defend themselves against a German invasion, it provided recipes for making explosives with household materials or items available over the counter at a local pharmacy. I paid two rupees and looked forward with glee to experimenting in Kodai.

In the evenings, I let the python explore my room after closing the windows and doors. Once, I found the room's door ajar when I returned after dinner. *Who had left it open? Had the snake disappeared?* With no hope of finding him inside, I pushed the door open. A crouched Trichy slunk closer to the python, which had bunched up, ready to strike. I yanked the cat by the tail just as the snake lunged. The startled cat bit and scratched me before running out. Had it been the rabbit or squirrel, I would not have been able to save it. I slammed the door shut and washed my hands. The snake was restless from the excitement and wasn't ready to retire yet. It took many minutes to get him settled back inside his box. The next day, I fed him a whole dead chicken to make up for his disappointment.

In later years, Ma was fond of saying Trichy and the python were friends, and the cat often slept on the coils of the snake. I had a hard time believing her, especially after that incident. She wasn't given to exaggeration, so she may well have seen Trichy curled up on a well-fed scaly ball. I, however, never missed an opportunity to deflate her sweet story by telling her how I had snatched Trichy before she became python food. Ma was unfazed and repeated this anecdote until the end of her life.

Shangri-La was much closer to Breach Candy, a ten-minute drive away, on Warden Road, so Nina and I went there often. When four-year-old Neel wanted to join us, we promised Mom we'd take good care of him. But the man at the front desk of the club wouldn't let Neel enter. Breach Candy was only for Whites, he declared. Neel was several shades darker than the rest of the family.

'You are the black sheep of the family,' we teased him.

There was no way we could argue Neel was white, nor did we feel any outrage at the racist rule. I wasn't even aware of racism in those days. We felt bad for him, but the desire to swim was greater. We left him sitting in the car with the driver, Abdullah Jan, while we enjoyed ourselves. He still dredges up that memory to make us feel guilty.

During that vacation, I discovered the joys of fishing at Powai Lake. On a visit to Ramnord, I got chatting with Erik Schoder, a jovial German technician with a beer gut, who said he had caught an almost-ten-kilogram catla, a large species of carp, the previous Sunday. He invited me to go with him the following weekend, and I couldn't wait.

Early Saturday evening, Schoder picked me up in his old Willys Jeep. Driving to Powai was like going into the wilds. It would take another decade or more for the area to be concretized. He rented a boat, and we paddled for about twenty minutes to a floating machan, a cabin lashed to eight 44-gallon drums as floats and anchored offshore. It was equipped with two comfortable cane chairs and two stools. A machan was essential, since casting from the marshy shore meant that the hook would get tangled in the fringe of thick reeds and grasses.

Schoder had brought a picnic basket of sandwiches and cookies, a thermos of coffee and a spare rod for me. We got our casting reels with heavy line sorted out while it was still light and settled to wait for nightfall. Some scuffling in the grass along the nearby bank turned out to be a mongoose, with a checkered keelback water snake wrapped around its body. In the next few minutes, it overpowered the snake and crunched it up.

When it grew dark, Schoder pumped a reflector-shielded Petromax lamp and set it on a stool overlooking the water. His bait was a paste made by kneading spices and fresh bread to a consistency that stuck on the hook.

'This is how you float-fish for rohu,' he said as he threw his line in front of the machan, where the water was about eight feet deep.

Rohu is another carp, which grows to almost forty-five kilograms. I followed his example, shaping a ball of bait around the hook and chucking it in. Schoder had rigged both lines with stripped peacock-feather floats that bobbed straight up. Each feather shaft had three bands of coloured thread. These markers would tell us if there were even small nibbles.

While we waited for the fish to bite, Schoder said, 'Let me show you what ledgering is.'

Using a heavier rod and a larger hook with a dough ball, he heaved the weighted line far out to keep the bait at the bottom.

'This is how we can catch a nice big catla,' he explained.

He then taught me how to set the drag on the reel and to control how fast the fish could strip the line without burning our skin by pressing our thumbs on the pieces of leather attached to the spool.

It was a long wait before we got any action. Fruit bats skimmed the water surface as they drank, and we listened to nightjars, spotted owlets and other sounds of the night. Schoder upped the odds by throwing a few large balls of mud flavoured with aniseed and masala, which he was convinced would attract fish.

'This is called ground baiting,' he instructed.

German carp fishers, he said, threw in a sack of rotten potatoes, which he promised we'd try one day.

'Breecy,' he called my name in his thick accent. 'Watch the float.'

He lit another cigarette.

'It will tell you what the fish is doing,' he continued. 'Sometimes it will move back and forth, and that's when a big catla is waving its tail and fins over the bait. This way they break up the dough.'

When the heavy rod jerked, Schoder grabbed it and struck hard. The line spun from the reel. The fish fought for about fifteen minutes before it grew tired. As Schoder eased the catla close to the machan, I was amazed. The thrashing fish had been hooked by the tail! It must have been fanning the dough, as he had said, and knocked the line by mistake. I already knew the drill, and slipped the landing net under it. I could barely lift the fish on to the deck, where it lay with mouth and gills gasping for breath. We strung the eleven-kilogram catla on to a piece of nylon cord and lowered it into the water, where it would stay alive until it was time to go home.

After the excitement wore off, boredom set in. Within minutes, Schoder snored on his side of the machan while I struggled to stay alert, willing the float to move. The gleam of an orange eye approached from the lake bank. I swallowed hard and watched with fascination as the crocodile, eyes reflected by the Petromax, glided by. Its graceful tail propelled it into the darkness.

Now wide awake, I stared at my float, but nothing nibbled. Fish came up for air, opening their mouths at the surface. I dropped a hook into a gaping mouth and yanked at a two-kilogram rohu. Schoder woke up to assist me. I didn't tell him how I had hooked it, knowing it hadn't been sporting. I slipped the fish on the nylon line in the water and threw in another bait.

The next morning, we picked up the line with catla and rohu and paddled back. The actor Shammi Kapoor had leased a nearby machan, and we saw him hunched over his line. The two men, colleagues in the movie business, waved to each other.

At the boat landing, I talked to the fisheries department assistant about crocodiles. The department wanted to eradicate them as they were bad for fisheries and dangerous to humans. It offered a reward of ten rupees for a crocodile egg and fifty rupees for every crocodile killed. At that stage in my life, I didn't know better, so I didn't argue with him.

I went fishing with Schoder every weekend for the duration of the vacation and caught many rohu—no whoppers—using fair means. I aimed to catch a big fat catla, but didn't succeed.

I planned to spend two weeks in Bangalore (now Bengaluru) with Dave and JP before heading to Kodai. By this time, the kite had healed and flown short sorties. One day it didn't return, and I imagined it cruising the air with other wild kites. The python would travel with me to Bangalore and then Kodai. I didn't allow anyone to touch the extra knapsack throughout the trip.

In Bangalore, Dave and JP suggested storing the bag under my bed and not mentioning a word to their father. Since most students came from missionary families, I ought to have expected the brothers would be mish kids. Their irreverent humour, however, had beguiled me, and I was shocked their father was a preacher in an Assembly of God church. People in his congregation became possessed and spoke in tongues in the middle of Sunday service. Their dad declared they had a direct link with the Holy Spirit.

Except for these bizarre religious interludes, we had the time of our lives in the quiet cantonment town. I learnt to ride Dave and JP's new Lambretta scooter on the then-empty MG Road. Another milestone for this fifteen-year-old who imagined he was in the big league of motorbike-riding. At the end of the vacation, we caught the train to Madras and on to Kodai Road.

10

TRYST WITH EXPLOSIVES

Appetite for Destruction

AFTER SETTLING INTO THE dorm, I had one last job—to find accommodation for the python. The only option was the tin trunk in which I stored my stuff during vacations. I borrowed a manual drill from the school carpenter and punched holes in it for ventilation, lined the bottom with old newspapers and let the snake explore his digs.

Since no pets were allowed, I had to swear Chuck and the others to secrecy. I didn't want to find out what Mrs Gibbs would do if she discovered the python. She had overlooked my parakeets, perhaps because she had one herself. But an enormous snake was in a different league. I shoved the trunk under my bed with the other luggage and hoped for the best.

The next day, I set rat traps around the garbage pit near the science building. With a steady supply of mole rats, the python didn't starve. Despite my busy weekends, I soaked in the sun with him every Sunday afternoon. If anyone strolled by, I flipped the edge of the bedspread we were lying on over the snake. It was a relief no one wanted to keep me company. I established a routine of catching rats, feeding him and taking him out for warmth.

Following the instructions in *The Bomber's Handbook,* Chris and I made Molotov cocktails, adding tar to gasoline and filling the fuel into light bulbs. We lit the wicks and threw them against the granite wall of the science building, the only reasonably secluded place, where the smoky scars remained visible for decades.

In the chemistry lab, we experimented with chemicals, such as mixing ammonia water used to clean toilets with iodine crystals, easily available since they purified water for drinking. The black mixture was harmless as long as it was wet. As soon as it dried, it became volatile. Even a sneeze could blow it up in a puff of beautiful purple cloud. We harassed our math teacher by sneaking into his room and sprinkling this paste all over the floor. At the end of the day, when he returned, with every step, he would hear tiny explosions, like popping popcorn. Was he mystified or did he see through our stunt? We had no way of finding out, since he never made a scene.

However, I had my comeuppance after the deed. Before scraping out the dried paste encrusting the Petri dish in which I had mixed it, I should have moistened it. But I didn't. It exploded in my hands and singed my eyebrows and hair. I was lucky not to have been blinded. That God of Idiots still smiled upon me.

Chris and I spent months experimenting with explosives. We made rockets out of the hollow aluminium towel rack we ripped from the bathroom wall, and underwater bombs with waterproof lacquer-coated fuse we bought from our quarry buddies.

A friend declared *The Bomber's Handbook* was for wimps and wanted to concoct nothing less than nitroglycerine. We tried reasoning with him, but he paid us no attention. He mixed concentrated nitric and sulphuric acids. Since he had no access to ice to cool the acid blend, he stashed it in his cupboard. The next morning, when we returned to Block after breakfast to pick up our books, a chemical stench wafted throughout the dorm. And the source was that guy's room. We were all relieved it hadn't blown up the whole building or exploded at night when we were asleep. We waited until the last of the smoke leaking from the gaps around the doors drifted away and watched from the window as our friend cracked the wooden closet door open slowly. The noxious vapours sent him racing out, and in that sudden movement, his Sunday suit disintegrated and crumbled to a pile of powder. We told the cleaning ladies not to clean that room, and being shy women, they didn't ask questions. The four boys who shared that dorm slept in other rooms in sleeping bags spread on the floor until the smell dissipated, which took days.

My obsession with explosives may not have reached such extremes, although some of my escapades ranked as reckless. The school made enquiries for someone to remove an enormous rock beehive that hung low to the ground below Block. I volunteered my services, which were accepted. The administration's confidence in me to get the job done without killing myself must have been flattering. My friends were more anxious than the grown-ups.

'You don't know what you're doing,' warned a dorm mate.

'You could get killed,' said another. 'Better leave it to professionals.'

'It takes only twelve stings from these big bees to kill ya,' said a third.

'I know what to do,' I replied cockily.

I attached a firecracker to a stick before covering myself first with a jacket and a raincoat to protect my head and neck, tucking pant cuffs into sneakers, and donning three pairs of socks over my hands. My friends watched me with misgivings.

'They'll get your face.'

I wrapped another raincoat sideways over my head, using the sleeve as a peephole.

'You look like a boogeyman,' commented yet another.

Perhaps. But one who'd be impervious to bee stings.

Everyone disappeared into the dorm and closed the windows and doors. I lit the cracker tied to the end of the stick and shoved it into the hive. The blast blew part of it away. Before the angry bees found their way through the raincoat sleeve, I crimped it shut. They buzzed around but couldn't sting me. I stumbled blindly back to Block, daring to take an occasional glance down through my peephole.

'You ain't coming in this room, Breezy,' one guy called from behind his bolted door.

I waited on the verandah. Several minutes after the buzzing quietened, I removed the raincoat covering my head and examined my work. A few bees lay dead on the ground and some continued to stagger. The rest had fled as the branch was bare. I regretted not negotiating with the school to pay for the job.

Then Chris and I nearly got into trouble. I cut open several atom bomb firecrackers—which, as the name suggests, explode with a deafening bang—and wrapped the powder to make a ground-vibrating monster I labelled 'Breezy Brand Firecrackers'.

On a movie night at the gymnasium, we rigged a Breezy Brand behind the screen on the stage with a time fuse. *The Bomber's Handbook* suggested using a lit cigarette. This gave us ten minutes to saunter around and take our seats in the back row.

I glanced at my watch every few seconds. *Surely the cracker should have blown up by now.* Just when I was beginning to doubt whether the cigarette was aligned with the fuse, an almighty boom echoed through the auditorium. Students screamed and stampeded for the exits. Chris and I didn't expect the blast to be so tremendous. Shaken, we joined the exodus. We had gone too far, even in our estimation. Perhaps I had wrapped it too tightly. If the school administration caught us, we'd be expelled for causing the explosion and for smoking cigarettes. That night, I lay awake worrying about the consequences. *Would I be thrown out? Where would I go?* Although I hated to admit it, the leniency of Kodai school suited me well.

The next day at assembly, the principal announced, 'Whoever is responsible for this dangerous trick had better confess, or there is going to be trouble for everyone.'

Neither of us confessed. The other students may have suspected Chris and me, but the prankster who made nitroglycerine seemed a more likely culprit. We acted as if we knew nothing about it. The fear of being expelled outweighed the temptation to brag. We didn't confide in anyone. It was a matter of time before the teachers remembered my success in blasting the beehive. Regret wracked my thoughts. Movies were cancelled as punishment, but the school's investigations into the caper led nowhere. We lay low.

In the meantime, I attempted befriending girls, walking them to their dorm or inviting them to the formal dance. One evening, when I came out of the gym, Nancy, a pretty girl in tenth grade, walked by alone. She was tall, had shoulder-length brown hair and high cheekbones. *Has she broken up with her boyfriend?* Using the late hour as an excuse, I escorted her to Boyer. When the movies resumed, I asked if she'd go with me. I had been expecting a brush-off, but to my surprise, she agreed. I resolved not to blow this opportunity.

The successful Don Juans did much more than look cool and fashionable. They held doors open, pulled out chairs and made every effort to show the girls their interest. I copied their efforts and Nancy rewarded me with a dazzling smile. I asked her out more often.

Raja copied a chunky ring that a boy had brought from the States, setting a star sapphire in the centre. I wanted to ask Nancy to go steady with me and waited for the right moment. I came close to giving the new ring to her on many occasions, but my nervousness held me back. *Would she refuse to wear it? Was I being too forward? Should I wait a few more weeks?* Days went by. Unable to stand the tension any longer, I thrust it towards her one evening. Both of us blushed, but she accepted it. The rest of the date passed in a tizzy. She wore it on a silver chain around her neck and gave me her little gold ring with an inset pearl, which I slipped on my pinkie. It was now official: We were going steady.

Nancy's father, a doctor for an oil company in Palembang, Sumatra, was then posted to Bahrain. Before her folks relocated to the Middle East, they spent some months living in Kodai at Coaker's Walk, and she moved out of boarding to live with them. Walking her home meant spending an hour with her. We hid behind her house after dark, hugging, kissing and feeling each other, but we didn't do anything serious.

After a monsoon storm, on the way back from Nancy's, I found a large bird injured on the school campus. It had the long neck and beak of a pond heron, but its colours were unfamiliar. After keeping it overnight at the dorm in a cardboard box, I thumbed through bird books in the library and identified it as a Malay bittern, or Malayan night heron, as it's called now. But the species hadn't been recorded in Kodai before. I photographed it to show Father Tanner and let it go in

Bendy field. The day's rest seemed to have done it some good. It flew up over the trees and disappeared. Somehow the thought of killing and stuffing the bird didn't enter my head.

I still managed to find time on the occasional weekend to visit Father Tanner, who agreed with my identification.

'Next time you go home,' he said, 'go to the Bombay Natural History Society and speak to the curator about the bittern.'

I hadn't heard of this institution before.

Back in school, Nancy put me in a quandary when she asked to see the python. If girls were found entering Block, they and the boys responsible would get expelled from school. I figured the only place we could meet was behind the science building. I carried my pet in a knapsack, and she touched a snake for the first time.

'It feels wonderful,' she said. 'Everyone always says they are slimy.'

Then she got me to pose for a photograph with the snake.

Since learning to drive the scooter in Bangalore, I hankered for a motorbike. The problems were: No money or driver's licence. But this was India, and at fifteen years of age, I imagined I had steel basketballs. Chris and I badgered Raju to find us a cheap second-hand bike in working condition. That seemed like a tall order, considering the trashed ones we'd seen so far.

One song I heard on Merrick's radio was by The Cheers:

He wore black denim trousers and motorcycle boots,
And a black leather jacket with an eagle on the back.

I may not have a motorcycle, but I could at least look the part. When Mom made preparations to go to the States, I begged her to buy me a black leather jacket. She said she'd see about it. She wasn't happy with my report card, so I didn't hold any hope she'd indulge me.

Weeks later, Raju said a 'miltry model' 500 cc, single-cylinder 1941 Norton, belonging to the retired postmaster, was for sale. Excited, Chris and I followed him to the back of his garage, past the frames of bikes and cars that would never sputter into life again. Leaning against a post stood a decrepit motorcycle that looked no better than the ones gathering dust. My heart sank. *Would our dream of riding a motorbike remain just that?* I kept my thoughts to myself as I listened to the mechanic list its virtues—mechanical front forks, no rear shocks and heavy-duty springs in the seat. He seemed to think it had promise, and he made a deal. If we bought it, he would help to get it going. Chris and I haggled like stingy businessmen and got the bike for a song. But a serious song worth several months of pooled pocket money, the princely sum of two hundred rupees.

Sweating and huffing, we pushed our heavy acquisition uphill to Chris's cottage in the German Settlement. Over the following weeks, we dedicated every spare moment after school to working on the bike. With rags and a wire brush dipped in a can of kerosene, we scraped, scrubbed and brushed more than a decade's build-up of caked grease and grime. Chris's mother brought us a mug of hot chocolate and doughnuts, which kept us going until dinner. I disappointed Nancy sometimes by excusing myself from movies and dances. Chris and I lived to get that Norton roaring to life.

Since the clutch and brake cables were rusty and frayed, we scavenged in Raju's shop and the junkyard. We removed the carburettor, gave it a good petrol rinsing and reamed the jets. We cleaned the gas tank, drained the congealed oil from the gearbox and scraped together enough money for two litres of oil. After all these ministrations, the kick-starter turned over once the oil seeped in, and the big piston slid through the cylinder. We imagined the sound it would make once we fired it up. Working on the bike filled us with anticipation of the day we would jet around on it.

We finished the bodywork and much of the mechanical stuff. Now all we needed were tyres and tubes that would fit the rusty rims, which wasn't as easy as it sounds. India didn't make motorbike tyres and tubes of any kind in those days, and we had to do some serious scrounging. Dave and JP saved the day. In Bangalore for a long weekend, they found the right tyres and some patched-up tubes at a junkyard. What's more, they hauled them up to Kodai.

We rolled the bike back to Raju's garage for him to check the magneto, dynamo and the rest. At first, the prognosis wasn't good.

Raju tinkered and soldered loose wires, and we kicked the starter lever until our knees and thigh muscles ached. But no spark. The mechanic kept old cars going well beyond their lifespans, so if anyone could bring our bike to life, it was him.

One Friday evening, when Chris and I arrived at the garage, Raju flashed a toothy grin and said he had gotten a spark out of the plug.

'You give it a kick,' I said to Chris with elation, 'and I'll work the throttle.'

Chris pumped the starting lever to get a feel of the compression in the cylinder, and then on the count of three, he kicked, leaving the ground to put his full weight on it. I twisted the throttle to let the gas flow into the carburettor. *BAM!* A tremendous backfire blasted from the tailpipe. We grinned like idiots at each other.

'Timing too advanced,' Raju said. He removed the magneto cover and turned two tiny screws.

'Now,' he instructed Chris.

Chris gave it another mighty kick. This time, the engine caught, sputtered and then throbbed as I throttled it. Our hearts seemed to beat louder than that machine. I yelled, 'Yeeehahh!', and gave it an extra twist. The silencer hardly muffled the roar, which echoed out of the garage door to the surrounding hills. Dogs barked and people came to their windows. I savoured the glorious sound of the idling engine. This old clunker that had sat around for a decade or more in a mouldy garage was not only running, but sounded so smooth.

'Let's drive this beast down to the plains tomorrow,' Chris suggested.

We spent an hour greasing every moving part from wheel-bearing and chain to the brake pedal, topping the oil sump and pouring half a gallon of gas into the massive tank. This was like our moon rocket launch.

The next morning, I wriggled into my frayed blue jeans, slipped on a T-shirt and scruffy windbreaker with the collar turned up to look the part of a cool teenager. *If only Mom would buy me that black leather jacket.* I didn't have to wait at the corner for long before Chris zipped up on his moped, and I rode pillion to the workshop, where Raju had finished painting a bogus number on the licence plate. The bike hadn't been registered for at least a decade. We strapped a canteen of water on the back of the Norton, bought a packet of dosais from a nearby restaurant and stuffed it into my torn rucksack. We borrowed five rupees from the mechanic for another gallon of gas, which wasn't measured in litres in India yet. Chris kicked the bike into life and we puttered to the gas station, surprising the attendants with the monster of a bike.

And then we were on our way, with Chris driving the first leg. There was barely any traffic and no policemen patrolled the roads. We started down the ghat road, with the cool breeze whipping our hair. We didn't yet know about Che Guevara's epic tour of South America in 1951 on a 1939 500 cc Norton, but that's whom we'd be emulating if we did.

About halfway down to the plains, we stopped for a picnic near a stream. For the first time, I was in a lovely spot and didn't have pit vipers or, indeed, any snakes on my mind. It was my turn to drive. The powerful engine made it seem as if we were floating. More importantly, we felt invincible.

I took the last sweeping bend in the ghat road and let 'er rip on the straight flat road on the plains. The speedometer wasn't functional, but I reckoned we clocked 100 kmph on one long stretch, but it felt like 150. I felt like I had died and gone to heaven. Bullock carts, buffaloes and dogs reminded me to be careful. I would have driven to Trichy, but the tank didn't have enough gas. We frequently stopped to peer into it to make sure we weren't running low, since there was no gauge.

It had taken us two hours to go downhill, but the going would be much slower on our way back uphill. About noon, after a quick pit stop for vadai and coffee, Chris took the first stint, heading up the ghat. We had to get to Kodai before dark, since the bike's headlight was also kaput.

We must have crept no more than sixteen kilometres up the steep road, when smoke spewed from the engine and the Norton shuddered to a halt.

'Oh shit!' Chris exclaimed.

'*Shekal da ruksha!*' I swore in Abdullah Jan's words.

The stench of burnt metal indicated a serious problem. We stood by the roadside, staring at the motorbike, wondering what was wrong and how to get to Kodai. A friendly lorry driver hauling sacks of cement stopped and two guys riding with him helped us load the heavy Norton on to the back. We clambered aboard and made ourselves as comfortable as possible. Accepting beedis offered by the workers, we brooded over the setback as we puffed. We hoped the old grizzled motorcycle hadn't given up the ghost after that unforgettable ride.

It was dark when we arrived at Raju's closed shop, where we parked the bike. Throughout Sunday, we were as restless as a mother cat with newborn kittens. On Monday after school, we went to see Raju. He fiddled with the Norton while we prayed for him to work his magic. Finally, he confessed there were too many parts worn out that were unavailable in India. The bike returned to the spot where we had first seen it, at the back of Raju's garage. As memorable as that old Norton was, I kicked myself for not getting a photograph of it.

My weekends of messing with the motorbike hadn't gone over well with Nancy, and I had to make amends. We met outside the gym in the evenings after she played basketball, and the smell of her sweat was heady. On Sunday afternoons, we sat together in some secluded nook doing dorky things like holding a buttercup under her chin to see the yellow reflection on her skin or blowing dandelion seeds from a dry stem while she whispered 'he loves me, he loves me not', and then laughing when the final blow was for 'he loves me not'. We searched for four-leaf clovers for good luck.

After one evening dance, the school organized a hayride. Five or six bullock carts stood in a line at the gym, on which couples could sign up for a ride. Nancy and I, cosy under a blanket, leaned back on the straw pile and gazed up at the canopy as the cart rolled around the lake. A loud voice broke into our reveries, 'Well, hello.' We sat bolt upright as Nancy's uncle looked from one to the other.

'I wish I were in your place,' he said to me finally.

Disgust replaced my self-consciousness. But he left us alone and continued on his walk. Some evenings I took Nancy on boat rides at the lake.

One night after 'lights out', the dorm rang with raised voices. I peeked out the door to see other puzzled boys in their pyjamas emerging from their rooms. All the action centred on Dave and JP's room. *What did they get up to without me?* Mrs Gibbs shooed us back inside, so we didn't discover until morning what had happened.

The dining hall buzzed with the news. Two girls had knotted sheets together and climbed out of the window of their room after dark and crept into Dave and JP's. And all four had been caught. The rest of us jealous boys heatedly debated whether it had been worth the risk. *Would they be expelled?* The brothers were nowhere to be seen. Later that day came the news they had indeed been expelled. Weeks later, JP wrote to me from Bangalore to say they were going to Bishop Cotton School. We lost touch after that. I missed these two guys for the rest of my time in school.

By the end of that year, more friends left, including Chuck and Merrick, who graduated. Except for Merrick, who came back after college to work in India and Bangladesh, I wouldn't see any of the others again.

My letters home over the years were filled with news about hunting and apologies for bad grades. This is one example from a letter sent to Mom: 'There's a rogue elephant about twenty-four kilometres away, and there's a thousand rupees in shooting it. I'm trying to persuade a friend of mine who has a double-barrel .500 rifle to come after it with me. Next week on Sunday a guide is coming with me to hunt a pair of mountain goats (as Nilgiri tahr were called in those days), which come into someone's garden all the time.' I don't recall going after either the elephant or the tahr. Perhaps I failed to convince the friend, whoever he was, and the guide failed to show. But I certainly was acting the hero to deflect from my poor academic record.

The question of careers weighed on our minds. Mike wanted to become an airline pilot, and others talked about becoming engineers, going into business or joining a Christian ministry. I listened to their aspirations and anxieties about the future.

'You are silent, Breezy,' one commented. 'What are your plans?'

'I'm going to become a zoo curator or an extractor of snake venoms,' I replied.

All of them looked surprised.

'Never heard there were such jobs,' said another.

I told them about Ditmars's career at the Bronx Zoo and Haast's work with snake venom. Although it sounded weird to them, I insisted there was a career for me along these lines.

'If you don't get serious, you'll end up becoming a snake charmer,' teased yet another.

But I had made up my mind.

About this time, Mr Krause, the school principal, said guns would not be allowed from next year. I was devastated. I lobbied with him to make an exception. A surprising ally in my efforts was a teacher. Mr Krause remarked that if I showed a fraction of my hunting interest in studies, I'd be an excellent student. He had a point.

Before I left for Bombay on vacation with the python, I succeeded in getting permission to keep my airgun. Nancy and I shared a cosy train compartment to Bombay, and from there she departed for Bahrain, and we promised to be in touch until school reopened.

* * *

Mom had bought the leather jacket after all, and I felt like a film star. I hardly went anywhere without it, even in warm, humid Bombay. All I needed now was a motorcycle.

Taking Father Tanner's advice to heart, I visited the Bombay Natural History Society, then in a small building on Walkeshwar Road, before it moved to its current address next to the Prince of Wales Museum in the centre of the city. I showed the photograph of the bittern to Humayun Abdulali, the secretary of the society, who confirmed it was a first record for the Malayan bittern in the Palani Hills. He pulled drawers of stuffed birds out, many dated back a hundred years. But I was more interested in the shelves lined with jars of preserved snakes. Before he left me alone to examine them, I thanked him for his time.

'Come more often,' he urged. 'Make use of the library and the collection room. Become a member.'

However, I didn't return until a decade had passed, when the society would have a far-reaching influence on my career.

Amma visited Bombay for a few days, but we didn't talk much. Absorbed with fishing at Powai Lake and loitering in the markets, I regret not getting to know her better. But she was also busy.

Mom told me later my snake obsession offered Amma an easy excuse to avoid people she didn't want to see.

'Please come over,' Mom overheard her say on the phone more than once. 'You must come and see my grandson's python that lives with us ... Yes, it's a very big one ... Oh, you won't be able to come? What a shame.'

After a night of fishing with Schoder at Powai, I returned home to find the latch of the python box open and the snake nowhere to be seen. He wasn't under the bed or inside the bathroom. Nina and Neel helped me search every room. No luck. I had big trouble on my hands. Amma and Mom were worried, but they were also understanding. I feared the worst. He could be anywhere in the apartment complex. If someone else saw this big snake, they might kill him. In my preoccupation, I didn't consider the danger he posed to our neighbours' dogs and cats, or even their children. Mom worried we'd be thrown out of the apartment.

As I combed my hair and put on a clean shirt, Mom counselled me to say 'pet' and not 'snake'. I went from apartment to apartment, rang the doorbell and enquired if anyone had seen my pet. Most of them said no.

'Was it a cat or a dog?' a few friendly neighbours asked.

'Er ... it's a python,' I answered, beaming to hide my nervousness. 'He's absolutely tame ... If you see him, please call me, and I'll come and get him.'

The smile on a matronly neighbour's lips froze.

'Of course, I'll call you,' she mumbled.

But Mr Khan, who lived in an apartment above us, took it badly.

'You lost a snake?' he shouted. 'Is it poisonous? Have you informed the police? How can you have a pet snake? This is no joke! You better find it fast, or I'm calling the police!'

'Not to worry,' I replied, struggling to keep the panic from my voice. 'We'll find him today. He won't hurt anyone. He's a pet. I'm very sorry for any problem.'

He slammed the door in my face.

The snake better show up soon, or this could get out of hand. But no one in the apartment block had seen him. *Has he escaped into the Mahindra factory?* If he had, he was as good as gone. The fear of Mr Khan calling the police hung over my head. I snuck like a thief when going out and returning to avoid being waylaid by him. As days passed, I became convinced the python had found a wonderful life, feasting on rats in the neighbouring jungle.

I examined the box. *How did he get out?* The python had busted the latch, which had been too feeble to withstand his muscular pushing. Although I had little hope of seeing him again, I fitted the box with a bigger latch.

Almost a fortnight later, Mom asked me to fetch a suitcase from the storeroom, since Amma had to pack for her return to Delhi. I moved a stack of trunks, and tightly coiled underneath in the gap between the wooden runners was the python. He had the run of the entire place, but instead he had found the most secure spot to hide while shedding his skin. Relieved to see the familiar coils, I gave the snake a squeeze by way of a hug while carrying him back to his box.

'Glory be to Hannah's kittens!' Mom exclaimed as the stress of the missing python lifted.

I'm not sure of the origin of this delightful phrase, but the Norden sisters often used it when they found something after a long search.

At Breach Candy swimming pool, I met a pretty English girl my age named Jill. I hid Nancy's ring for the rest of the vacation, while Jill and I dated, going to Bombelli's for dessert, to the movies or meeting at each other's house. She sat on my lap and removed blackheads, then rampant on my teenage face. She knew her wriggling drove me crazy, but it was also pleasureful.

Vacation drew to an end all too soon, and it was time for the python and me to catch the train south again. The day before my departure, Mom sat me down for a talk, admonishing me about my abysmal grades and asking me to do better in school if I wanted to graduate that year. I promised to try my best.

11

THE FINAL YEAR

School's Out Forever

THAT YEAR, I GOT the job of bell ringer, a childhood wish come
true. To my immense disappointment, my tenure was cut short a
few months later with the installation of a modern electric contraption
that lacked the sonorous ring of the old brass gong.

Soon after the term began, the vice principal, Mr Root, called me for
a meeting. He stated the painfully obvious: I didn't have the requisite
number of class credits, having performed poorly in math and Latin
the previous grade. My heart sank. I was done for. My extracurricular
activities throughout my school life had taken precedence, and despite
my poor grades, the school had promoted me from one grade to the
next. I knew where this was headed: *I couldn't graduate that year. What
would I tell Ma? She would be so disappointed in me. At least I'd have Chris
and Nancy for company.* As my brain worked overtime taking stock of the
situation, I wasn't paying attention to Mr Root's suggestion. It took me
a moment to realize he was throwing me a lifeline. He advised I make
up the shortfall in credits by taking three additional classes. The ones he
chose were, as he kindly put it, fail-proof—typing, wood workshop and
general science. The last was a ninth-grade subject, which indicates how
bad a student I was. *Is Mr Root so eager to get rid of me he's even willing to
go out of his way to make my graduation that year possible?* I enthusiastically
agreed to the deal.

With a vigour I had not shown in any study-related activity, I banged on the keys of the typewriter, even dreaming of the letters A-S-D-F-G-F. No more frivolity and horseplay. I was determined not to blow this chance.

The question about higher studies hung in the air. My classmates pored over university brochures at the school library and debated the relative merits of various courses. Their seriousness about the subject was contagious, and for the first time, I gave it thoughtful consideration. One suggested it would be a lot cheaper and easier to get into a land-grant university. Before I could ask what that meant, another recommended Antioch College in Ohio for its alternative vision of education. The more I heard about it, the more the college appealed to me. Choosing the university was only part of the decision. What to major in was another. If I wanted to be a zoo curator or work with snake venom, zoology was obviously the avenue. I didn't want to do boring general zoology. Wildlife management seemed much more action-oriented, but few universities offered such a specific course. That ruled out Antioch. The flyer of the University of Wyoming, Laramie, caught my eye for two reasons: It had an undergraduate degree in wildlife management and the state advertised it had more deer than people. The college town was located on a mountain plateau 7,200 feet above sea level, the same elevation as Kodai, but I didn't appreciate the fact that winter temperatures plummeted to minus 35 degrees Celsius.

While I agonized over filling out application forms, my father said he'd pay my tuition fees. At least this worry was off my head. Having long since moved on from the family's pharmaceutical store business, he now worked for American Cyanamid, a large agrochemical company.

I applied to the University of Wyoming with my lacklustre school transcripts, convinced my chances of getting in were slim. But I hoped that by some miracle, it would accept me.

One evening, as I walked Nancy back to her dorm, she confessed she had become friends with a sailor at the American naval base in Bahrain during vacation. Fury hijacked my mind and body. Without a word to her, I turned on my heel and left. *Do I resent her dates with the sailor? Or do I object to her description of him as cute?* The ferocity of my jealousy took me aback. But I didn't for a moment think of the times I had spent with Jill in Bombay. Nancy had been the first girl to show an interest in me, doing wonders for my self-confidence. Now my insecurity overwhelmed me.

I refused to talk to her, and when she tried to catch my eye, I looked away. Not content with snubbing her, I befriended her cute, shy classmate, Alice, who had an alluring Southern accent. But I didn't keep this up for more than a few days. My heart melted on seeing the hurt on Nancy's face, and we became an item once again. But I remained friends with Alice.

While typing was boring, I had a blast at the carpentry workshop. The inspiration for the first thing I made came from *The Bomber's Handbook*—a wooden replica of a real hand grenade, complete with primer cap and fuse.

'Nice work,' said the teacher, even as he shook his head in resignation. 'Let's hope you don't go exploding it now.'

Does he know of my pyromaniacal exploits?

When I needed a breath of fresh air, I fished at the lake. Only occasionally, to remain sane, did I venture out hunting or solo camping. Chris and I became members of the Kodai Boat Club and convinced the secretary to let us hold races. Six of our friends enthusiastically helped in cutting and shaving off the branches from ten-foot wattle trees to use as masts. We rowed the larger four-man rowboats against the wind to Laughing Waters at the far end, where we rigged the cross pieces, tied double bedspreads to them for sails and coasted downwind. As long as it was windy, we had great fun racing against each other. But the moment it dropped, we had to put our arms to the oars again. All this rowing ought to have made my torso muscular. But to my disappointment, my biceps didn't develop and my shoulders remained narrow.

Our class camping trip to Kookal Caves was another welcome break from the tedium of school. We slogged our way through 'Leech Shola', named for the hoards of leeches that appeared like magic after a rain. The first-timers shrieked, cursed and hopped, and then made the cardinal mistake of stopping in their tracks to pluck off the offending bloodsucker and becoming standing ducks for several more, which crawled unnoticed up their legs. I pushed on without pausing to watch their amusing antics and emerged on to the grassland on the other side of the shola. A classmate tried to flick a leech off, while I stopped to catch my breath.

'This is like trying to get rid of a booger,' he complained.

A girl collapsed beside me and took her shoes off. It was this newcomer's first trek through a rainforest. She was distraught at the sight of an engorged leech caught between her toes. Although I let the bloodsuckers drop on their own, I pinched her leech and threw it away. She gave me a grateful smile.

'Will they give you malaria, like mosquitoes?' she asked.

I shook my head. Having spent so much time in these forests, I had forgotten my first encounter with these creatures. Mr Root, our chaperone, passed around a bag of salt.

'Watch what a little pinch of salt does to the leeches,' he said.

The others sprinkled it on the hitchhiking bloodsuckers, which dropped as if singed by fire. It seemed cruel to torment them, although it was the easiest way of getting rid of them.

By the time we arrived at our camping spot, our pants and socks were stained red and blood trickled to our feet. Some students pitched tents and others dug trenches surrounded by canvas, which were to be make-shift toilets, while I made the campfire, cutting dry wattle sticks into kindling with my good old Bowie knife.

That evening, we roasted potatoes under a clear, starry sky. A loud 'Kraak!' echoing from the nearby caves made everyone jump.

'Could be a leopard,' one suggested.

'It's barking,' someone else argued. 'It must be a wolf or hyena.'

'That's a barking deer,' I corrected them, ever the Mr Know-It-All. Then I added for good measure, 'It's probably spotted something dangerous like a big predator.'

'That'll be you, Breezy,' said Mr. Root.

Everyone laughed.

Soon, everyone started chanting in a low voice:

Way down south, not so very far off,
A hoopoe died of a whooping cough,
He whooped so long and he whooped so loud
He whooped his head and his tail right off.

Then they repeated the whole thing louder and faster until they were all shouting in unison. I despaired that the silence had been shattered and sent all the animals for miles around scurrying away.

When we returned from the weekend camp, Shadrach told me a cow had been killed the previous night by either a tiger or leopard on Observatory Hill. Chris and I went to see it. In a field near the edge of the forest, we circled the fly-covered, bloated and stinking carcass while pinching our noses closed. The hindquarters had been eaten. Deep wounds punctured the throat. I didn't know then that a frontal attack was the classic leopard strategy, while tigers attack from behind and sink their teeth into the nape of the neck. Still puzzled about the identity of the carnivore, we scouted around and found paw prints in a muddy spot. They weren't as huge as the plaster casts of tiger pugmarks at the Shembaganur museum, so I surmised it was a leopard.

About forty-five metres from the kill, a pot-bellied, moustachioed local hunter was tying palm leaves to a bamboo structure by a rhododendron tree. His ancient muzzle-loader stood propped up nearby. As tempting as it was to sit with him in the hide that night, there were credits to earn. The next day, after school, we climbed the hill to see if he had shot the animal. When we were halfway up, a villager told us the cat hadn't returned, so we trudged back, disappointed.

Summoned to the principal's room one day, I went warily, wondering what nightmare awaited. *Is Mr Krause going to object to Mr Root's plan and make me do math? Or worse, repeat twelfth grade?* I needn't have worried. My reputation as a snake boy had reached the Mother Superior of the girls' school Presentation Convent. Her pet Pomeranian was missing, and the gardener had reported finding a piece of shed skin of a 'very big snake'. Mr Krause asked me to go over and look for the snake. It would have taken me half an hour to hike to the convent, but Mother Superior had sent a car.

At the office, the agitated elderly lady poured tea and urged me to help myself to the convent's famous pastries arranged on a tray. I couldn't take my time scoffing the goodies when she was paranoid that the snake might attack a student. Stuffing a few into my pocket, I followed the gardener, who had been waiting for me.

The man led the way to a dense raspberry thicket and pointed. Rains had washed away most of the shed skin, but a few pieces clung to the plants. To my amazement, the width of the belly scales gave the impression of a fair-sized python, which I hazarded to be about ten feet long. I had been conscious that Kodai's weather might be too cool for my pet and made sure he got enough sun. But here, unexpectedly, was a thriving member of his kind. I examined the compound with the gardener, catching occasional glimpses of the pretty girls in their starched uniforms. But we didn't find any further sign of the snake even after two hours of searching.

Back in the office, I reassured Mother Superior that pythons were not venomous, and while this one may have swallowed a dog, it was unlikely to bite a student. About two weeks later, Robert Kasi said the workers had found the python in a storm-water drain, and he shot it with his shotgun.

'Why didn't they call me to catch it instead?' I ranted. 'Where's it now?'

They had thrown the carcass somewhere in a nearby forest. No one remembered where, so I was unable to measure and skin it. I grumbled at the wastefulness.

The rest of the year passed in keeping my head low and nose to the grindstone. When the university admitted me, I scarcely believed my luck. With my future charted, I concentrated on passing the school exams. All those weeks of work paid off, and I made it through.

Ma came for the graduation ceremony. Dressed in our formal best, my class of twelve received diplomas from the principal in an auditorium filled with high school students and our parents. We then filed into the church for the inevitable service, which ended with the *Happy Wanderer* song.

I love to go a-wandering,
Along the mountain track,
And as I go, I love to sing,
My knapsack on my back.

I was in a daze, and for once didn't try any of my usual pranks. Afterwards, when we emerged into the bright sunlight, we squinted at each other in disbelief. We had graduated.

That night, a group of us made our way to the ice-cream parlour on Bear Shola Road. What were the owners thinking when they let us use an unused room above the shop? I don't know. We had already bought rum and gin at the Budge, since Prohibition had been lifted the previous year. During that riotous evening of loud music, jokes and revelry, I lost track of the number of drinks, and they were a few too many. I woke up with a severe hangover and found a puddle of puke and an empty gin bottle beside me. *Had I polished off the whole thing?* The others had fared no better. After cleaning up, my wasted friends and I returned to the dorm. We went through the day like zombies. All I wanted to do was clutch my head and curl up in a dark corner. The smell and taste of gin put me off for decades.

That year the school yearbook, *Eucalyptus*, had this to say about me:

Have you ever seen a little green thing eating cookies on the dining room table? You must have, because Breezy's latest pet, his Mandapam parrot, comes to tea almost as many times as his owner. Animals and the outdoors are just as much a part of Breezy as revolutions and bullfights are of 'Papa' Hemingway. Just about every Saturday he heads for Tope, Rat Tail or some other far-flung spot where he can 'get away from it all', and, in his wanderings around Kodai, he has found the enjoyment which he seems to find lacking in most Highclerc social activities. The fauna which he brings back from these treks are a source of interest, consternation and amusement, be they parrots or pythons.

A quote from Walt Whitman's poem *Song of Myself* printed alongside summed it up: 'I think I could turn and live with animals, they are so placid and self-contain'd.'

Before I left Kodai, there were lots of goodbyes to say to everyone, from my fishermen pals to Brother Daniel at Sacred Heart College. But most of all, leaving my closest friends was tough.

'Chris, someday we'll take a motorcycle trip around India together,' I said when we gave each other a bear hug.

Nancy and I became teary-eyed, and we promised to write and try to meet somewhere, sometime. I never saw either of them again.

Looking back, I learnt much about the natural world during my seven years in those gorgeous hills of the Western Ghats. Although I was a dunce academically and rebelled against the school's overt religiosity, the freedom Highclerc afforded me to get into the wilds set me on my future path.

Ironically, the now-renamed Kodaikanal International School invited me to give the commencement address for the graduating class of 2010 on my birthday, exactly fifty years to the day since I graduated. I didn't tell the gathering of a hundred students and their parents about our misdemeanours. I still raised a few knowing grins with some of my stories.

But in May 1960, I turned seventeen, ready to start my real life, even if it was for more studies.

12

MYSORE
The Horn of the Hunter

I HAD ENTERED INDIA AS an eight-year-old on Ma's passport. In Bombay, I applied to the US consulate for a passport and sorted through my possessions, piles of books and clothes, animal skins and stuffed birds. I sold the Diana rifle to the same shop from where I had bought it. The question of what to do with the python occupied my thoughts. I didn't know anyone who knew how to care for him. With many misgivings, I gave him to Asmeth, the snake charmer.

'When you come back from the States, you can have your python back,' he said with a grin.

I hoped he would make good on his promise. I wrote to Dad about my plans and enclosed the photograph Nancy had taken of the python draped around my shoulders.

One evening over dinner, Ma made a dramatic suggestion.

'You're too young to go to the States, Breezy,' she said.

My fork froze in the air as I struggled to follow her train of thought.

'Why don't you spend a year in India?' she asked.

Rama seconded her. I liked the idea too. But would the university agree?

'What would you like to do for a year?' Ma asked.

'Taxidermy,' I blurted. 'I want to learn to stuff large animals.'

She grimaced, perhaps hoping I would apprentice with a photographer.

'Who'd teach you?'

'Mysore is famous for taxidermy.'

Amma, as the head of the All India Handicrafts Board, sponsored a wooden toy factory that was conveniently next door to the South India Taxidermy Studio in Mysore (now Mysuru). She organized an apprenticeship under the owner, the venerable V. Pradhania, who had learnt the skill from the more famous Van Ingen & Van Ingen. In the heyday of hunting, when lions, tigers and leopards were termed 'vermin' by the British colonial government, Van Ingen tanned skins and stuffed animals from all over India and even Africa. In 1960, hunting continued to be fashionable enough to keep at least two large taxidermy studios in business. Major and minor royalty, and certainly several tea and coffee planters, knocked off the occasional tiger and sent the skin to taxidermists for mounting.

The Wyoming University admissions office accepted my request to defer my admission by a year, and I bought my train tickets. Ma was concerned the jungles around Mysore had snakes.

'Snakes I can handle,' I teased her. 'But what about elephants, tigers and leopards?'

My reply did nothing to lift her worries.

Amma had also arranged for me to stay at Vanivilas Mohalla with the kind, hospitable family of a toymaker, Veerappa. But they were vegetarian, which didn't suit me at all. Wandering about the laid-back town, I found the Bahá'í-owned Golden Age Café, where I'd stuff myself with meat dishes in the days to come.

Pradhania, a lean middle-aged man dressed in shorts and a sleeveless undershirt, opened the door when I presented myself at his house. He led the way to a large workshop in his backyard, cluttered with moulds of animal heads, boxes of nails, hammers, paint cans and assorted things. I didn't know Kannada, the state's language, so we communicated in broken Hindi and English with much laughter. Pradhania's chief assistant was his elder son, Neelakantiah, who was already a professional. A handyman did all the rough work.

I spent the first week learning the basics of preparing skins and constructing papier-mâché moulds of tiger, leopard, deer and antelope heads. Pradhania and Neelakantiah rarely mounted whole animals. Big cats were usually reduced to a rug with a snarling head. They patched bullet holes with a piece of skin taken from elsewhere in the body, taking care to match the stripes or spots, and sewed on with tiny stitches on the inside. Tongues made of plaster of Paris were painted red. On the rare occasion they stuffed the whole creature, it was modelled in a standing pose. Pradhania inserted rolled pieces of cardboard into the nostrils to give them shape. A bowl of cats' claws sat on a stool, but were rarely used since the models didn't display them. Another container held hundreds of half-cut marbles of varying sizes with hand-painted pupils—yellow ones with elliptical black slits for cats, orange ones with dots for elephants and black for ungulates. Despite the attention to detail, many trophies looked shoddy.

At a loose end in the sleepy town over the weekend, I dropped in at the zoo and chatted with the keepers in a patois of Hindi and Tamil. I took to spending the end of every week there, gazing at the animals and helping the keepers.

An adult male leopard that had come to the zoo as a cub came closest to being a friend in those first lonely days in Mysore. I arrived early on Saturday mornings and snuck up to his cage. No matter how stealthy I was, I could never surprise him. He always spotted me and hid behind his water trough, with only his ears and eyes peeping above the top. When I climbed over the short fence and leaned against the enclosure, he bounded up like a large puppy and crashed against me. Had there been no steel bars between us, the force of his greeting would have knocked me down. I put my arms through the gaps and scratched his head and neck, while he rubbed the full length of his body against the cage, his powerful purrs reverberating through my body. The living, pulsating animal was very different from the dead leopard ages ago at Lawrence School. In later years, I learnt that reaching through the bars of a leopard cage was stupid. He could have torn my arm off, or worse. But I didn't know any better then.

My first solo job at the taxidermy studio was mounting an albino crow that had died at the zoo. Peeling the skin off was no problem, since I had learnt the skill well at Shembaganur. But to mount the bird in a lifelike pose took many hours of moistening the legs to straighten them and setting the claws to hold on to a small branch. The toughest part was finding a glass piece of the right colour for its eyes. I rummaged in the box that contained the marbles, but none were appropriate. I bought a pink marble, broke it and slipped two shards into the softened eye sockets. The white crow looked pretty realistic when finished, and local townspeople dropped in to see it.

'White boy stuffs a white crow,' commented one.

Between the studio and zoo, my week was spent with dead and live animals.

Just as I had been the 'snake boy' in Bombay and Kodai, it wasn't long before people brought orphaned creatures such as a jackal, jungle cat and even a leopard cub to me. Housing these creatures at the Veerappas, was not an option. I turned a kennel into a cage in the ample studio, aided by Pradhania's younger son, Someswara, a studious schoolboy. He wanted to learn English and came over to the workshop to chat with me every evening. Both of us shared the same love of animals, so he helped me care for them until they grew older. We felt sad handing them to the zoo, but letting tame animals go in the wild was out of the question. They'd run to the first person and get clobbered. One pet I doted on was a fledgling black kite that flew sorties and returned to my shoulder, digging its claws painfully into my flesh while I ripped a piece of chapatti or dosai and rewarded it.

I walked everywhere—to the studio and the restaurant on weekdays and to the zoo on weekends. With the money from the sale of the Diana air rifle, I was ready to buy my own set of wheels. The Pradhanias directed me to Gandhi Square Gujri Market, a place for trade in second-hand goods. Motorcycle mechanic shops stood side by side at one end of the alley. My Hindi was adequate for the Dakhni the mechanics spoke, and I put the word out for a used motorcycle.

A few days later, mechanic Baba Sait took me to see a bike. The rusty and decrepit two-wheeler seemed destined for the junkyard rather than the streets of Mysore. It was a 1943 (the same year I was born) single-cylinder, 350 cc Triumph, one of the thousands brought over to India by the Brits during the Second World War. Despite its appearance, the seller started it with the first kick. On hearing the magic *thop, thop, thop* of a four-stroke engine, I was smitten. It reminded me of the Norton back in Kodai, but this one was in much better shape. The mechanical fork in front and the lack of a rear suspension other than two big springs below the seat made me feel like I was riding a bucking horse. But I didn't care. It needed some work, a new chain and a paint job. I paid all the money I had, one thousand and fifty rupees.

Baba painted the bike a metallic peacock blue and chrome-plated the curved exhaust pipe and silencer. The repairs cost another two hundred and fifty rupees, which I begged from Rama. Once the Triumph was all fixed up, what a proud young sonuvabitch I was! I drove everywhere and fancied myself the sharpest boy on the road. Sometimes, I even stuck a cigar in the corner of my mouth for effect. In the early mornings, I cruised through the empty streets with the black kite perched on the handlebars, where it hunkered low with partly outstretched wings. It loved these rides.

In the weeks ahead of the ten-day Dasara celebrations, the town shook off its lethargy. For the grand parade, the organizers asked Pradhania to prepare a float displaying stuffed animals. He and Neelakantiah debated which of their trophies to display. Perhaps tigers, leopards and gaur in a forest tableau. Or maybe an African savanna with lions, zebras and a kudu.

A pair of rheas, ostrich-like birds from South America, died at the zoo. I drove to Pradhania's house with the exciting news, and he hired a Jeep with a trailer to cart them to the studio. These were the biggest birds I had ever seen, much less stuffed. The meticulous job of skinning took hours. Unlike small birds, these were more like big mammals with thick, tough skins, which I rubbed with boric acid powder to preserve. I carved out two kilograms of the tempting red meat and the cook at Golden Age Café made an outstanding curry.

The following Monday, Pradhania and Neelakantiah crafted wire frames supported by central iron rods of the approximate height and shape of the rheas. On these structures they slapped bits of cardboard dipped in rice paste to create papier mâché mannequins on which to fit the skins. The process took several days before the models began to take a lifelike appearance. The plans for the float now included these peculiar-looking creatures.

One weekend, a pretty blonde woman wandered through the zoo. Foreigners were an unusual sight in Mysore. I introduced myself and chatted with her. Within a few minutes, Vera became distraught as she described the difficult situation she was in. She had come to the city for Dasara and through her family connections had been invited to stay as the house guest of an elderly Dutch man who lived there. He took every opportunity to touch her inappropriately, and each day was becoming more unbearable. The previous evening had been a nightmare as he had chased her around her bed, attempting to grab her. She had run out and bolted the door. He had yelled and screamed, demanding to be let out, while she huddled in the living room. She desperately wanted to move out, but didn't know anyone else in the city.

That afternoon, I picked up Vera from the Dutchman's house. He wasn't anywhere to be seen, much to my relief. I took her to a hotel in the heart of the city.

Just when we thought all the elements of the tableau for Dasara had come together, a pair of king cobras, ten and twelve feet long, died in their cramped cage at the zoo. After skinning the snakes, I boiled the meat off the larger skull in Pradhania's kitchen while his wife was away visiting relatives, and glued the fragile bones together. Mounting snakes was a first for the studio, and Pradhania and Neelakantiah approached the job with diligence. As a finishing touch, they coiled the serpents over a large model of a termite mound. They may have been experts in preparing mammals and birds for display, but they didn't know these reptiles at all. Although snakes have a simple tubular body structure, the stuffed ones looked like badly stuffed sausages to my critical eye. The rheas and king cobras took pride of place on the Dasara float.

On the big day, the palace was lit with millions of decorative lights, and barricades made of casuarina poles prevented the throngs of people from coming on to the well-adorned main road for a better glimpse.

After days of anticipation, the atmosphere was electric. Pradhania got special seats among ministers and other dignitaries for the grand parade. I accompanied his family and took photographs. The Maharaja, sitting on the howdah on the back of his elephant, led the procession of a dozen caparisoned elephants. All day long, troupes of performers—musicians, jugglers, acrobats—entertained to cheers from the crowds. Vendors sold fried snacks, boiled peanuts, roasted channa and sweets. The assault on the senses was overwhelming. When the floats rolled along, I couldn't wait to see the one we had worked on for weeks. Despite the strangeness of the rheas and the drama of snarling tigers, the snakes drew the most attention from tourists, who ooh-ed and aah-ed at their size. It won the best tableau prize at the festival. I returned exhausted late that evening to the Veerappas', who had also been at the parade.

Now with Dasara behind us, we were back to the routine job of fulfilling orders from clients. Around that time, two Europeans arrived at the zoo. Albert Meems, whom I assumed was German, sourced Indian animals for clients in Europe. It was only while writing this book that I discovered that he was a Dutch spy for Nazi Germany during the Second World War, but by all accounts, the overweight gentleman was inept at espionage. According to a fellow spy captured by the Allied forces, Meems was to report on military matters, but knew too little about the subject to be effective. In Mysore, however, he was very much the animal dealer, negotiating deals for European zoos. I became friends with the younger guy, Dieter Rinkel, who was an elephant keeper at Hanover Zoo, owned by Herman Ruhe, a German animal dealer who operated several zoos in Europe and had a long association with the Mysore Zoo. Dieter had two months to train six young elephants before taking them by ship on a seven-week voyage to Germany.

After my affectionate romps with the leopard on weekend mornings, I arrived at the elephant paddock to greet Dieter and help Chinniah, the head keeper, feed the five calves. The sixth would join the group later. By that time, Chinniah and his assistants had kneaded ragi (finger millet) flour mixed with chunks of brown sugar and laced with vitamin powder into cantaloupe-sized balls. After feeding, I helped the mahouts bathe the calves and walk them around the grounds. The young elephants loved these sessions, since they were cooped up in small, boring stalls for most of the day. I picked up a few words of Kannada from hobnobbing with the keepers.

Although the elephant calves were tame, I learnt an important lesson. I was squeezing past Chintu, a chest-high calf, when she leaned, pinning me to the wall. My few strangled 'ugh, ugh' sounds weren't loud enough to attract attention. I couldn't push her, and my chest hurt. If she didn't ease off, I could be in serious trouble. Dieter came by then and pushed the elephant back with the ankush, a bullhook for elephants.

'You dummkopf, Rom!' he scolded. 'She doesn't know her own strength, and could have crushed you. That's why you shouldn't get between an elephant and a wall.'

That experience taught me never to lower my guard around any wild animal, even if it was tame.

In the meantime, my efforts at wooing Vera didn't go anywhere. After her recent experiences, she probably didn't want to have anything to do with men. But we remained friends. When I heard the Dalai Lama was visiting, I drove, with her riding pillion, to a newly established settlement for Tibetan refugees. People wearing traditional chubas even in the heat of peninsular India stood in a line to greet the bald-pated young monk. Many cried as they bowed deeply before him. His smile and murmured words offered solace to the traumatized displaced people. When he came to us, Vera and I bent our heads to receive his blessings. He wouldn't have remembered meeting a thirteen-year-old me at a dinner in Bombay, where he had been captivated by the cherubic, golden-haired Nina. There wasn't any time to reminisce as he moved on to greet others. Soon after, Vera left Mysore.

I accompanied Dieter to the forest department's elephant camp in Bandipur to pick up a male calf to make the total of six. What sounded like a simple operation turned into a heart-rending scene. The mahouts restrained the mother with leg chains, but separating the two-year-old calf from her was a tough job. She wailed, and the youngster screamed as he dodged the men and tried to crawl under her belly. Finally, they bundled him into the back of the truck.

I rode with the elephant calf, stroking his head and ears to calm him, but he slapped my hand away with his trunk. I was another hated human responsible for his sad situation. At the zoo, he drew some consolation from the other calves and, in a few days, became part of the boisterous gang.

On my daily commute, I often passed a pretty light-eyed Anglo-Indian girl. She wore knee-length dresses, unlike the other girls her age in Mysore, who dressed in saris. One day, she was struggling with her bicycle by the roadside near the Mysore Palace gate, and I pulled over to offer help. She mumbled that the chain had come off. Despite fumbling, I fixed it back on the sprockets. Before I could ask her name, she flashed a guarded smile, flipped her long braid over her shoulder, said a shy 'thanks' and pedalled away.

Over the following weeks, I learnt the route this lovely girl took to her place of work, a dress shop near Ganesh Talkies, one of two theatres in Mysore that showed English movies on weekends. At the nearby Golden Age Café, the waiters said the girl's name was Irene, who often had a snack at the restaurant with her friends after work. I waited at the eatery one afternoon, hoping to chat with her. When she arrived alone before her friends, I saw my chance.

'Hi, I'm Rom.'

Since arriving in Mysore, I had used my formal name as it added gravitas. She wasn't as nervous as the other day.

'I'm Irene. I know you work for Pradhania.'

She was interested in me enough to find out where I worked. That was promising. I described my work at the studio and my weekends at the zoo helping with the young elephants, and she listened with interest.

'Would you like to come on Saturday and help me feed the animals?' I asked.

She nodded. When her friends arrived, I made myself scarce.

I spent the rest of the week in anticipation of my date. That Saturday morning, I waited for her at the main gate of the zoo. The poor leopard may have been expecting me, but my thoughts were on Irene. I didn't have long to wait, and she arrived, looking pretty in a bright dress.

I introduced her to my special friend, the leopard, and then we headed to the elephant paddock, where Chinniah had the basket of ragi balls ready. First in line was a waist-high two-year-old named Megha. She knew the routine, lifting her head and opening her mouth on my approach. I tucked a ball all the way into the back. Her tongue was silky smooth and slimy with saliva.

'Come on, she wants another one,' I said to Irene.

She shoved a ball into Megha's mouth, her hand disappearing behind the tongue.

'Good, now let's feed the others,' I said.

After feeding the other five elephant calves, we wandered around the zoo, and Irene seemed to enjoy the animals. The hour was up, time for her to leave. She had told her parents she was visiting a friend near the Palace, and she wanted to hurry back before they discovered her lie. I looked forward to spending the following weekend with her.

When I saw her on the sidewalk the next day, I slowed.

'Good morning, lovely Irene,' I greeted, no longer bashful.

To my shock, instead of smiling, she scowled at me.

'You better not talk to me again,' she muttered. 'My father found out about my visit to the zoo, and he was furious. So go away.'

She seemed scared, and I wondered if her folks had beaten her. I protested, but she turned her face away and kept walking. I was heartbroken. *I'm not ever going to have a girlfriend.* The Weavers song came to mind:

Goodnight, Irene,
Goodnight, Irene,
I'll see you in my dreams,
Sometimes I live in the country,
Sometimes I live in town,
Sometimes I take a great notion,
To jump into the river and drown.

When we passed each other, I never failed to beep, and she'd give me a quick, nervous smile, which did my heart good.

For a change of scene, I went fishing in the Cauvery River in Srirangapatna. After parking my motorbike on an embankment, I slid down the slope to cast in the water. I was excited after catching a feisty freshwater catfish called wallago, when I heard a shout and a loud racket. Another motorcyclist had seen my parked bike and tried riding on the narrow bund. But he had lost his balance and tumbled down the side. I gave the White guy, a coffee estate manager from Coorg, a hand, and he invited me to have a beer with him at the nearby KR Sagar dam. While regaling each other with our fishing tales, he warned me of man-eating crocodiles that infested the Cauvery. After he left, I wandered into a small museum nearby. Among the jars with preserved monkey foetuses, snakes and other creatures, I stopped short on seeing a human foot taken from the belly of a crocodile. The manager wasn't kidding.

On a following trip, the fishing spoon got caught among reeds on the opposite bank. I tugged and yanked, but it wouldn't give. That was my last one, and I couldn't afford to lose it. *Should I swim across the river and retrieve it? But there are big crocodiles that ate human feet. If I don't get it, there would be no more fishing.* I tucked my gaff hook into my belt and waded in. *If any croc was bold enough to attack, I'd gouge it.* I survived despite being stupid.

The Triumph had literally been through the war and needed tinkering from time to time. I spent a lot of time with the mechanics, sometimes sharing a lunch of paratha and chilli hot kurma. I learnt the fine art of tuning the bike, getting the correct mixture of air and petrol through the carburettor, setting the timing so it sparked at the right moment to create the explosion in the cylinder that propelled the bike forward, and taking a link or two out of the drive chain to tighten it. When it stalled and refused to move, which was often, I picked up small tricks to make it flare to life, such as cleaning the jets in the carb, rubbing the points in the magneto and scraping the spark plug.

For weeks, I thought about driving up to Kodai, seeing Chris, Nancy and other friends, and of course, showing off my motorbike. Confident it could handle the 350-kilometre ride and my ability to fix mechanical problems should they arise, I started one early Friday morning with a full gas tank and my knapsack with a change of clothes. I had charted the route straight south on an old, tattered map of Madras State.

The long stretch of concrete road to Chamarajanagar was smooth and empty. On some stretches, the iron-rimmed bullock cart wheels had made deep ruts, risky for motorcyclists. Near Talavadi, a herd of elephants stood beside the road. They may have been minding their own business, but other motorcyclists at the mechanics' had traded stories of scary encounters. The gigantic animals didn't like the sound of motorcycles and chased many a biker. I gave them a respectfully wide berth, going off the road and bouncing back after I had gone past.

At Bhavanisagar that evening, a Muslim hotel served a good mutton curry and paratha. It was past harvest season and stacks of rice straw were piled in field after field. Unrolling my bedsheet on a springy pile of hay, I drifted into a deep sleep after the bone-jarring ride. I loved being on the road, watching the changing scenery, stopping to chat with road workers and sleeping rough. Around six the next evening, I reached the bottom of the Kodaikanal ghat road. I pulled into an empty construction site rather than drive at night.

The ride up the ghat early in the morning was exhilarating. I remembered the misadventure with the Norton and passed the spot where JP had crashed off the road on his bicycle. At the viewpoint overlooking one of my old haunts, Rat-Tail Falls, I bought tea and several fresh hot vadais from a stall. The cool air and the familiar calls of barbets, hill mynas and the cackling call of a grey hornbill brought waves of memories of those seven years. I had missed Kodai.

By late Sunday morning, I arrived in Kodai and parked on the side of the road near the school gate. A group of white kids dressed in their Sunday best walked up.

'Come to steal our girlfriends, huh, Breezy?' one teased. 'You with a fancy motorbike and all.'

We walked to the Budge to eat at the Brahmin hotel. They said Nancy hadn't returned to school for her senior year and was studying in Bahrain. Chris and his family had left for Germany. I was disappointed and sad not to see them. But it put me in a quandary. I had planned to spend the night at Chris's home. The idea of being out in the cold didn't appeal to me one bit. One of the boys said there was an empty room in Block, if Mrs Gibbs would let me stay.

Mrs Gibbs hadn't changed. I was happy to see the stern but good-natured old lady and her parakeet again.

'I hope you don't smoke now that you're out of school,' she warned. 'Remember, no smoking in the dorm.'

'What! Me? Smoke?' I pretended to be scandalized by the idea.

She swatted me away playfully. Although my attempts to teach her parakeet foul words hadn't gone anywhere, I regretted them. She had been kind to us.

That evening at Block, I listened to the latest records a kid had brought back from the States: *Walkin' to New Orleans* by Fats Domino, *Cathy's Clown* by the Everly Brothers and *Only the Lonely* by Roy Orbison. Hanging out with these guys made me nostalgic, but I was free and seventeen, and they were still stuck in school. After saying my goodbyes, I got a good night's sleep and headed out at daybreak on the long drive back to Mysore.

It was back to the routine of working at the studio and the zoo. While shooting the breeze one afternoon with mechanic Akhter, I learnt that he often went hunting to Gumtapuram, about a hundred kilometres away, with a single-barrel 12-gauge shotgun. He invited me to go with him the following weekend.

Early on Saturday morning, I picked him up and headed to Chamarajanagar. South of the town, we got on to the Talavadi Road and turned towards some low hills. We crossed the Mysore State border into Tamil Nadu and drove through the forests to Gumtapuram. At a roadside shop, Akhter greeted a small, wizened man of indeterminate age.

'Raghava, we've come for deer,' he said. 'Can we find some tonight?'

'Have I ever failed?' the other replied with a paan-stained smile.

Leaving the motorbike at the shop, I followed the two men. Akhter carried the shotgun and a long, heavy, five-cell torch. We squatted under a tamarind tree and leaned against its trunk, smoking beedis and watching the last light in the sky fade. When it grew dark, Akhter slipped batteries into his torch, tested it and patted it affectionately.

'It will find the shining eyes of a fat deer and you will shoot it,' he said, handing me the shotgun.

This was an exciting prospect. I was finally after big game.

We walked in single file on the bunds separating fields of ripening sesame. When Raghava stopped, Akhter perched the big torch on his shoulder and swept the light beam from one side to the other.

'Nothing,' he said softly, and we trudged on to the next field.

As soon as the torch went on this time, we saw the bright reflective eyes of four spotted deer about a hundred metres away.

'We must get closer,' Akhter whispered. 'Take off your shoes.'

Both of them were barefoot. I hadn't expected this, but he was right. I couldn't make any noise to spook them.

As we approached the deer, Akhter played the torch first to one side, then the other, up and down, and then, just for an instant, directly at the alert animals. They were entranced by the bright light and froze for seconds, becoming easy targets. Americans call this 'jacklighting'. The buck faced us, ears forward and alert. We were close enough to discern that it didn't have a big set of antlers, but that didn't matter since we weren't after a trophy. It was meat we wanted. Akhter pushed me in front of him. He shone the torch over my shoulder and on top of the gun barrel so I could see the sight.

The sight on a shotgun is rudimentary. I aligned the tip of a shiny brass knob at the front with the top of the barrel above the trigger. The deer jumped the moment I pulled the trigger. Four of the six balls of lead in the LG cartridge slammed into its chest, and it collapsed. The others scattered in panic.

By the time we stood over the buck, Akhter already had his knife unsheathed and performed halal before it died. Akhter gave a leg to Raghava and butchered the rest to fit into the two gunny sacks he had brought along. I would take a leg and he would share the remaining meat with his family and friends.

We spent what was left of the night trying to sleep on a cement wall on the roadside next to the shop. The hard surface was uncomfortable and mosquitoes wouldn't leave us alone. At dawn, I gave up on sleep and walked along the forest edge, watching the stirrings of birds and listening to the distant rumble of an elephant. Being next to the forest made me feel alive and energized as pure air filled my lungs.

Akhter suggested we meet a European padre who lived on a farm a few hundred feet away. After parking the bike at the gate, we walked in hesitantly, calling, 'Hello, hello.' A gruff voice asked, 'Who is it?' A bearded Franciscan brother in a brown cassock reclined in a cane chair on the porch, sipping from a cup. I introduced myself while shaking his hand, 'Romulus, but please call me Rom.' He chuckled. *What is so amusing about me?* Then he introduced himself as Brother Romulus. Then it was my turn to chuckle.

'Not too many people named Romulus in this village,' he said.

I told him to call me Breezy and gave him my share of the buck.

Brother Romulus didn't have any priestly responsibilities. Instead, he taught villagers new farming techniques and distributed seed stock and fertilizer. He was a beer-quaffing German with a great sense of humour. His bushy moustache and full beard were streaked from exhaling beedi and cigar smoke. He also had an armoury, comprising a double-barrelled shotgun, a single-shot Winchester .22 rifle and a monster of a .500 Nitro Express.

'Next time come alone and stay here at the farm,' he said in his thick German accent, out of Akhter's earshot. 'There's always a spare room. I'm getting too old and overweight to hunt. We need someone like you to get us some meat now and then. It would also be great if you could sit at the ragi field at night before harvest time. Otherwise elephants and deer will finish it off.'

That sounded like I had a job.

13

GUMTAPURAM

Living in Elephant Country

A WEEK LATER, I HEADED alone for Gumtapuram along the cool, shady forest road. I banked a corner, singing Elvis's '*Blue moon, keep a-shinin' bright*'. Not even thirty metres away stood a big tusker. I jammed on the brakes, skidded to a halt and almost fell over. He had been crossing the road, and on hearing the Triumph's roar, swung towards me. For a moment, we stared at each other. When he took the first steps forward, I spun around. Gunning the motorbike, I didn't stop to check if his charge was half-hearted or full-on business. Had the bike stalled, it would have been a different story.

My heart was still racing when I reached the forest checkpost at the state border and told the guard about the elephant.

'That tusker even stopped the morning bus for an hour,' he said. 'It will be getting dark soon. Rest here tonight and go tomorrow.'

It was a sensible suggestion until he showed me where to sleep, the lock-up for illicit woodcutters and poachers. Luckily, it was empty. I covered the concrete bench that passed for a cot with my lungi and lay down. Only then did the strong odour of dried piss hit me. Mosquitoes looking for a blood meal made the night even more uncomfortable. I whipped the sarong from under me and covered myself, but it wasn't long enough to cover my feet. The guard was asleep outside, and his snores reverberated through the walls. I was tempted to join him, where the breeze would ward off the insects, but then I'd have to contend with the guard's rhythmic grunts and growls. Envying his facility for deep slumber, I glanced through the open window at the darkness, wishing the sun would hurry up.

When the first glimmer of light brightened up the sky, I got up, unable to bear another second in that miserable room. Not waiting to hang around to thank the sleeping guard, I rolled the motorbike down the road before kicking it to life. At a crossroads, about one-and-a-half kilometres before the site of the elephant encounter, I killed the engine and waited for a vehicle to come along. I didn't want to take a chance and run into that tusker if he was still in the neighbourhood. When an old truck came wheezing under the weight of its cargo, I tagged behind, enveloped by the black exhaust it farted. Two girls, perched on top of its load of firewood, giggled at this choking and coughing white guy. The elephant had spent some time on the road yesterday after I sped away. Broken bamboo stems littered the place, but now he wasn't anywhere in sight.

At the farm, Brother Romulus showed me to my room. Since he was busy through the day, I wandered around, poking in the bushes and exploring a dry stream bed. At dusk, he settled into his reclining cane chair on the porch and handed me a cigar, 'Java Whiffs', made in Trichinopoly, the same Trichy of Persian cat fame. How he lit the cigar without setting his long whiskers on fire amazed me. Then he launched into stories of years spent living next to the jungle.

When a bold panther, as everyone used to call leopards in those days, had killed a dozen sheep and goats in the village, Brother Romulus waited for it on a machan built above a carcass. At a crunch in the dark, he flicked his dim torchlight on, and reflected in its beam were the cat's bright eyes. Instead of getting it in the heart, he gut-shot the poor animal, and its intestines spilt on to the ground. It picked itself up, slashed its entrails and staggered away before Brother Romulus could get a clear aim with the second barrel. He spent the rest of the night on the machan, intending to go after it at daybreak.

When he climbed down at dawn, Charles, his handyman, rushed up to him.

'Doraisami, something terrible has happened,' he said.

Two children out for their morning ablutions had seen a leopard lying in lantana bushes and pelted it with stones. It leapt up and scratched one of them.

'It is still hiding in the same spot,' Charles continued.

The men rushed to the other side of the cultivated fields. When they approached the place, Charles warned, 'Be ready, dorai,' and did exactly what the poor boys had done—threw rocks at the dense bushes. The leopard growled. Charles chucked more stones, and it bolted out into the open. The monk aimed the shotgun at the limping cat, which was only fifty feet away, and pulled the trigger. By the time the smoke from the black powder cartridge cleared, the collapsed leopard was in its last convulsions.

I felt uneasy. Although no one taught me the ethics of hunting, I knew a hunter should kill an animal with a clean shot without making it suffer. A gut shot was despicable. I hoped never to make that mistake myself. But the firearms I had seen so far, with the exception of Nadudorai's, were held together with wire, the sights inaccurate and the cartridges unreliable. Brother Romulus's firearms, however, were well maintained and in good shape, so he didn't have that excuse. Lost in these thoughts, I realized he was waiting for me to respond to a question. He wanted me to sit up awake that night and guard the ripening ragi from elephants. I gulped. *Did I have to kill them if they appeared?* As if reading my mind, he said all I had to do was pepper any visiting elephant with a shotgun blast of Number 8 birdshot.

'It will run away,' he declared. 'In the forest, an elephant is sure of itself. It will go after you. But in the openness of ragi fields, it is nervous and easy to chase.'

Unless, of course, it was a tusker in musth, a breeding condition in male elephants, when they became dangerous at any time or place.

Then Brother Romulus launched into another story of shooting crop-raiding elephants back in the early 1950s. Few people owned a rifle big enough to bring elephants down, but his .500 Express could kill them with a shot through the brain or heart. He fired at a makhna, a tuskless male, which was causing havoc, but the bullet pierced its lungs. I imagined what torment that must have caused the pachyderm and forced myself to listen to the rest of his ghastly saga. The elephant bolted from the ragi field into the forest, where it spent the night roaring in agony until it finally succumbed in the morning. It wasn't his poor aim, as I thought. If the animal had died on his land, he would have hell to pay. This was my first lesson in how a system meant to protect animals led to excruciating suffering.

Although these tales were macabre and revolting, they also fascinated me. I had read plenty of books on hunting, of course, but Brother Romulus's stories seemed much more vivid because we sat not far from where the action had occurred.

More stories followed. Ivory poachers with puny muzzle-loaders smeared themselves with elephant dung before approaching tuskers. They kneecapped the giants by shooting the front leg at knee height, and then delivered the coup de grâce shots to the brain or the heart at point-blank range. Even this wasn't clean. They pinged the elephants for hours before they succumbed. Cruelty on this scale was par for the course in those days.

That night, with the stories still fresh in my mind, I reclined in a comfortable cane chair on the edge of the ragi field, the double-barrelled shotgun loaded with birdshot across my knees, a big five-cell torch in my hand, and Jimmy, the resident black Labrador retriever-mongrel, tied to the chair. I was torn between two conflicting emotions—the anticipation of encountering an elephant and the fear of facing one.

A spotted deer's sharp alarm call jolted me awake. The answering cry was closer. A predator, probably a leopard, was about. My fingers itched to switch on the big torch, but I waited, giving the animal time to approach. Alert and tense, Jimmy stared into the darkness, seeing, hearing and smelling better than me. I tracked the predator's movement by the deer calls. When they sounded from the edge of the ragi field, I estimated the cat to be within range. Resting the long torch on my shoulder, I turned it towards the sound. Half a dozen pairs of red eyes glittered for a moment before the deer bolted into the forest. I had sabotaged the predator's hunt.

The rest of the night was uneventful. I drifted in and out of sleep, relying on Jimmy to warn me of any unwanted visitors. In the kitchen in the morning, I told the monk about the alarm-calling deer. He, too, thought a leopard had likely set them off and narrated a recent incident.

He had been kneeling in the garden, training some tomato plants, when a leopard, half-hidden among the foliage, stared at a transfixed Jimmy. The cat sinuously rolled over on its back, waving its legs in the air and twitching its tail. Without uttering a bark, the hypnotized dog walked towards the predator. Although Brother Romulus was fascinated by the panther's behaviour, he couldn't let Jimmy get any closer. He shouted, 'Shoo!', and waved his arms at the cat, which disappeared so fast the poor dog didn't know what happened. At least it wasn't another gut-shot story. I didn't have the stomach for any more of those.

After breakfast, as I walked to my room to catch some sleep, I ran into a young girl coming from the cowshed. I greeted her with 'Namaste', expecting her to be coy. Instead, she smiled warmly and returned my greeting. Hiding my surprise, I continued on my way. Like the girls in Munnar, she didn't wear a blouse. *How the hell could Brother Romulus remain a celibate monk surrounded by such beautiful women?*

Later that afternoon, after learning from the cook that the girl's name was Shanti, I sought her out in the cowshed. I tried to converse in a hotchpotch of Kannada and Tamil, while she replied in Kannada. By the end of the evening, when it was time for her to go home and for me to get ready for another night of ragi watch, we had become friends.

On Monday morning, I returned to Mysore and my routine at the studio. By then, Albert and Dieter had taken the young elephants to Germany, and Gumtapuram was more interesting than the zoo. I spent every weekend at the farm, hiking in the nearby jungle during the day, sitting up at night watching the ragi, listening to Brother Romulus's stories in the evenings and flirting with Shanti whenever I could. She taught me the Kannada names of trees and birds, laughing when I goofed up the pronunciations, which was often and sometimes deliberate.

Eventually, my interest in taxidermy waned. I had learnt how to skin an animal without tearing holes, and fashion earless papier-mâché models of deer and antelope heads. Pulling the damp, tanned skin over the mould was tricky, as was sewing it in place with the stitches hidden from view. It was an art that required skills in sewing, moulding and painting, and I was still a novice. But I had the time of my life at Gumtapuram and played truant from the studio more often. Nobody seemed to miss me, and neither was I yearning for their company.

After the ragi was harvested, there was no more reason to watch the crop after dark. I could keep normal hours. On the first night, I lay awake bathed in sweat in my stuffy room. The thought of leopards prowling in the garden stopped me from dragging the charpoy on to the verandah. At a strange sound from the forest, I stilled my breathing to listen. An animal was moaning in pain with each breath. Grabbing the torch and shotgun, I followed the sound down the steps towards the forest. The farther I walked by the pale moonlight, the fainter the moans became. The animal was moving away. I returned to the house, and no sooner had I lain down than the sound started in full volume again. A wounded tiger or leopard was holed up on the other side of the building. I crept to the corner and peeked around. Nothing. I edged along the wall and passed below the window of Brother Romulus's room, and almost burst out laughing. His snores sounded like an animal in pain.

One evening, Brother Romulus asked me to accompany his workers into the forest to collect several logs they had cut a few days ago. Since felling trees without a permit was illegal, it was to be a nocturnal operation. Loading the contraband needed many hands, and even Shanti and her sister were enlisted. As on every nocturnal excursion, I shouldered the heavy .500 Express double-barrel in case an elephant attacked the work party. Carrying the weapon night after night for weeks permanently changed my gait. I still walk with one shoulder raised, bearing an imaginary rifle. Charles perched on the bullock cart and made a racket, whacking a sheet of roofing tin with a club. There was no fear of running into a forest guard at that time of the night, so we could make as much noise as needed to scare the elephants.

An ear-splitting scream about fifty feet to the right froze our blood. Scared, Shanti huddled next to me, and for a few lovely seconds, I felt her warmth and inhaled the smell of the coconut oil she had massaged into her hair. Even before I raised the rifle, a startled elephant crashed through bushes and trees in the opposite direction. We stood still, listening to its progress through the forest before resuming our way. It didn't take long to load the cart, and we returned to the farm without any further excitement. As she walked away, I gave Shanti a fond goodnight squeeze of her hand. She responded with a firm handclasp. *Or is it my imagination?*

My heart leapt when Shanti smiled at me the next day. I conspired to work with her at every opportunity. If I couldn't find anything to do, I used the pretext of learning Kannada to be with her. She also taught me how to rip the tough purple skin of a sugarcane stem with my teeth and then bite into the juicy fibrous core. After working my way through a whole stem, my mouth and tongue were sore, but the sweetness of the sugarcane and Shanti's proximity made it worthwhile.

My favourite times always began with Brother Romulus saying, 'Take the shotgun and go with Charles and bring us back a deer or blackbuck.'

Charles and I rode along village dirt roads. When we spotted blackbuck grazing in a field, we stalked them. Hiding behind bushes and trees, we would try to creep within sixty feet of the antelope before taking a shot.

One time, the air burst with the loud calls of red-wattled lapwings, 'Didyadoit, Didyadoit.' The suddenness of their warning startled me, and before I could collect my wits and aim, the alert blackbuck sprinted away. I cursed the birds, as I would in later years when they prevented me from getting close to crocodiles and gharials to take pictures. But these plovers worked in my favour once when a pair screamed and dive-bombed a beautiful ten-foot python in tall grass that I wouldn't have spotted on my own.

Sometimes, Charles and I hitched rides on bullock carts. Not only did they save us from the exertion of walking, but they also hid our approach from the antelopes. Since the animals saw and heard the noisy wagons with huge wooden wheels every day, they continued grazing unperturbed.

Hiding behind a cart, we edged towards a small group of blackbuck feeding in a fallow field one afternoon. When we were within sixty feet,

I tapped the driver's leg to stop, held the shotgun tight, clicked off the safety and fired at the shoulder of a big male with a magnificent set of spiral horns. The animal dropped where he stood, kicked up the dirt and then lay still as the females scattered. We picked up the dead animal and convinced the cart driver to take us back to the parked motorcycle in exchange for a leg. Draping the rest of the carcass over the bike's fuel tank, we drove to the farm. It was after dusk and I was sorry Shanti wasn't there to see my triumphant return.

In the backyard, Charles wasted no time butchering the blackbuck with his sharp hunting knife. After he finished with it, I removed the skin from the head, the way Pradhania had taught me, salted and wrapped it in a banana leaf. On my next visit to the studio, I mounted the head as a trophy. The following year, in the States, I hung it in the living room at Hoosick.

We didn't have much luck most of the time. Charles pointed to vultures circling, and he beckoned to me to look for the kill. The carcass of a cow was too far gone. But I held my nose and walked around, looking for the spoor on the dust and bite wounds. A leopard.

Another time, we had walked twenty kilometres and were wiped out when we heard voices coming from a farmer's machan. Three guys were butchering the carcass of a big sambhar stag that they had shot with a muzzle-loader. They offered us a leg. At least we had some meat to take back to Gumtapuram.

Since the wary ungulates didn't allow me to approach within range during the day, we took to hunting after dark. I learnt to distinguish between the eye-shines of different nocturnal animals—the bright glow of deer and blackbuck, the bouncing reflection of civet cats, and the dull single glimmer of elephants, which was easy to confuse with that of a nightjar sitting on a tree branch.

Elephants were the only animals Charles and I considered dangerous. They trampled, fatally kicked or flung scores of people who guarded crops or squatted behind bushes to take care of bodily business. We kept both ears open for the sound of a stomach rumble or the crack of a breaking stick. That was our cue to stop and check the location of the pachyderm and in which direction the wind was blowing.

Despite its size, an elephant can outrun a man, and Charles had some hair-raising stories. Once, when a tusker in musth had chased him, he climbed a banyan tree. Just when he thought he was out of reach, the pachyderm curled its trunk around his leg. He yanked his foot away, but before he could claw his way higher, the giant tugged off his lungi. It took its fury out on the human-scented cloth, ripping it to shreds and pounding it into the dirt while poor Charles, clad only in a shirt, clung to the tree. Long after the tusker had left and Charles's jangling nerves had calmed down, he descended. Covering his modesty with his shirt, he returned to the farm. His appearance became the foil for the other farmhands' jokes. These tales kept me alert on our walks.

I sought out Shanti every morning. While she cut grass in the fields for the cows, I squatted on a bund nearby and regaled her with exaggerated stories of my adventures. She listened with rapt attention, gratifying me by sounding awed or sympathetic. I hoped Brother Romulus would send us together on another errand in the dark. Sadly, there were no more night-time trips to the jungle with her.

When there was nothing to do, I trekked alone in the neighbouring jungles, enjoying the solitude, listening to the sounds, smelling the forest air, and observing birds and insects. If someone else, like Charles, was with me, we talked more than paid attention to the surroundings. I learnt the species living in these lowland deciduous forests. Most of the large mammals were the same ones as in the wet hills of Kodai, but here they seemed to be in much larger numbers.

One evening, as usual, we two Romuluses sat on the porch smoking, when Jimmy started barking from the backyard. Brother Romulus shouted at him many times to shut up, but the dog yapped even more furiously.

'Something must be the matter,' I said, rising to my feet.

Tangled up in a rope, he was hopping and nipping at it at the same time. His behaviour was odd. *How did he get enmeshed in the cord?* Only when I approached did I see that the rope was a big rat snake. I unravelled its coils without being bitten by the agitated reptile or the panicked dog, and released the snake into the garden. This incident brought home to me the kernel of truth in a story I had heard many times in Kodai and Bombay.

People complained rat snakes sucked milk from cows' udders.

'Snakes don't drink milk,' I'd declare with derision.

But now, seeing what had happened to Jimmy, I realized what gave rise to the belief. When stepped on, the legless reptiles defensively intertwine around the animal's legs, whether cow, bull or mule. Prior to milking, people tie their cows' hind legs with a rope so they don't kick, and sometimes, when stressed, the cows don't yield milk. Therefore farmers who witnessed rat snakes wrapped like ropes around their animals' legs jumped to the conclusion that the snakes drank the milk of their panicked cows. The next time someone brought up this story, I knew how to debunk it.

In the meantime, I had confessed in a letter to Ma that I wasn't spending time with Pradhania any more, while describing my life at Brother Romulus's farm. When she replied she was bringing Nina and Neel for a visit, I put in a request for cartridges, asking her to seek the advice of Thakur, an employee at the lab, who was a hunter.

'If there are any .500 Express black powder cartridges available, get two—they're very expensive (four rupees each),' I wrote. 'It's very important. There's a man-eating leopard that we are going to go after as soon as there's no moon.'

I threw in the mention of a leopard to add urgency to my request. Although Brother Romulus had good cartridges for the shotgun, the ones for the .500 Express needed a machine for reloading, which we didn't have.

On the day of the family's arrival, I returned to Mysore. When they stepped down from the train following Ma, I couldn't believe how much Neel and Nina had grown. After loading their luggage into a taxi, I followed them to the government rest house where they would be staying. I listened to the kids' stories while Ma unpacked. Besides the all-important cartridges, she had brought chocolate and cheese, knowing my cravings too well.

Over two days of sightseeing, which included a visit to the taxidermy studio and the zoo, I took my siblings on joy rides. At six, Neel was small enough to sit on the tank in front of me, and Nina, riding pillion, wrapped her hands around my belly and clung like the young primate she was. We cruised along the empty jungle roads of Bandipur and the adjoining Mudumalai sanctuaries to see elephants, deer and gaur. How our mother allowed these trips into the forests with young children I don't know. At bedtime, I made up scary stories of being chased by elephants and tigers without realizing they would keep the kids awake at night.

Amma joined us two days later, and we piled into a car for a trip to Kodai. At the closest point to the Tope, I asked the driver to stop and alighted, saying I was going camping.

'Are you heading off from here?' asked a concerned Amma. 'What protection do you have?'

'I know this place very well,' I replied with a chuckle. 'Besides wild boar, there's nothing dangerous here.'

Later on, Ma said Amma had been close to tears after I left.

After a long silence, Amma had asked, 'What are wild boars?'

'Wild pigs,' replied Ma. 'They have tusks that can do a lot of damage.'

They drove on to Kodai while I trekked to my old haunt. It was great to soak in the sights, smells and sounds of the familiar forest. I slipped into the cool pool and drank my fill of the clear water, which you wouldn't even think of doing these days.

As evening approached, I ate my picnic by the stream, deafened by the cicadas' song. Clouds rolled in and thunderclaps suggested it would be a wet night. I picked my way through the boulders to a huge overhanging slab of rock, which would keep me dry. The rain came in a heavy downpour, lightning struck the hill slope above and thunder crashed. Despite the dramatic weather, I slept like a log, with my jacket protecting me from the chill. The next morning, the deep imprints of a leopard's paws edged around the entrance. Maybe it had hoped to shelter under the same overhang but thought better of it.

Refreshed by the few hours in the forest, I walked to the Periyakulam Road and caught a bus to Kodai, where I joined the family. Amma and Ma were relieved the wild boar had left me alone and I had made it back in one piece. I took Nina and Neel on boat rides and walks, while the ladies did their own thing. Since none of my old friends were at the school any more, I didn't drop in for a visit. Then it was time to return to Mysore.

The Maharaja of Mysore had invited Amma to see a khedda operation, a traditional method of capturing elephants, at Kakanakote, on the banks of the Kabini River. We went with her. About a hundred spectators had gathered to see the action. The forest department had built bleachers overlooking the river, and the stockade was made of massive logs and bamboo. Ma's Rolleicord camera hung from my neck as we waited for the drive to come into view.

Distant shouts and drumbeats, punctuated by screams of frightened elephants, reached us. Soon the first elephants came splashing through the shallow river, guided by the river banks and log fences. Mahouts on trained elephants, called kumkis, along with hordes of beaters with drums and bamboo clappers, shouted as they herded the terrified creatures towards the stockade. The noise was deafening and the scene chaotic. We craned our necks to see the herd milling around the trap. Ma pointed out an elephant calf and mouthed, 'The poor thing!' We worried for its safety in that confused milieu of massive legs and trunks.

Through this commotion and excitement, I struggled to take photographs. The camera's viewfinder protruded from the top, and I had to look down to peer through it. Since everyone was standing on tiptoe and obstructing the view, I couldn't get a line of sight. Another spectator held his Rolleicord upside down above his head and framed pictures by looking up into the viewfinder. I copied him and took several photographs.

After the kumkis guided the wild elephants into the stockade, they slotted heavy logs across the entrance, trapping the hapless creatures. Although it was exciting, we couldn't help but feel sorry for the imprisoned animals, especially the distressed calves.

Over the following weeks, the mahouts would become elephant trainers, singling out healthy ones for training. They'd tie the elephants' legs with ropes and chains, and use the old carrot-and-stick technique to break their spirit. The captives would then learn to respect humans and obey commands. We didn't stay to witness this long process, but I had seen it play out at the zoo.

We headed back to Mysore and Amma left for Delhi. I took Ma, Nina and Neel to Gumtapuram to meet Brother Romulus. While the adults chatted, I led the kids for a wander around the farm, and Shanti greeted us with her dazzling smile. At lunch, the monk placed a plate of steak in front of them and said, 'Elephant steak. I shot a rogue last night.' The kids' eyes grew wide with amazement. He was pulling their leg and I played along. When Shanti brought another plate, he declared, 'Bison steak.' 'Venison' followed.

After the family left for Mysore, Brother Romulus told me about an encounter he had with dholes while I was away. He had been picking ripe ears from the cornfield when he heard the distinctive whistling of a pack of these wild dogs on the hunt. A half-grown spotted deer came charging up to him, sides heaving from breathing hard and saliva frothing at its mouth. The proximity of the human forced the six dholes to give up the chase. The deer stayed some minutes longer after the predators disappeared and then wobbled off in the opposite direction without a glance back at its saviour. I had missed the opportunity of seeing a species I hadn't met yet.

I had a few more months left before my year was up, and I made the most of them, going into the jungle every day. One morning, I startled a wild boar that had been wallowing in the drying stream bed, which we called the Pallam (meaning 'depression'). We stood still, facing each other, neither daring to move a muscle. As we stared at each other, my thoughts zoomed into the future: What would Ma and Amma feel when they received the news that I had been ripped by this beast? I had been joking earlier on the way to Kodai, but was it about to become a reality? I imagined bleeding to death on the bullock cart taking me to hospital. After what seemed to be a lifetime, the wild boar took a step backwards, snorted once and trotted away. I exhaled with relief and continued on my way.

Later in the day, when crossing the spot on my return, I found leopard tracks superimposed over my footprints from earlier. I realized with a shiver that it might have been stalking me. What an inept hunter to be unaware of a predator on my trail. *Had it been a man-eating leopard, I would have been dead meat.* It had perhaps witnessed my face-off with the wild boar. *Was the leopard the reason the pig ran away?* I'd never know.

I followed the track of paw prints all the way to the cowshed. When I alerted Brother Romulus, he had the workers pile thorns on the roof. But he remained worried that the cunning cat would break into the shed and take a calf. He called Charles to bring a dog from the village to use as bait. *Is he going to kill the leopard?* My heart sank. Then I realized with a shiver of excitement that he wanted me to get it. Within moments, my earlier misgivings disappeared as the thought of hunting a leopard gripped me. Bagging one would be a rite of passage. I could call myself a real hunter.

That evening, Charles tied a half-grown village dog to a tree stump near the cowshed. It snarfed up the cooked rice he offered. But its happiness didn't last. It started whining when we walked away. Soon its wails turned to full-throated howls.

Brother Romulus had a few original Eley Kynoch cartridges, which were more reliable than my home-made reloaded ones. I loaded the right barrel of the shotgun with a ball cartridge, a fifty-gram lead bullet, rifled so it would spin for accuracy, since shotgun barrels are smooth. This was sufficient to hit a leopard in its chest or head. The left barrel, which was choked for birdshot, took an LG cartridge as a back-up, in case a wounded cat charged, I thought with a mixture of excitement and trepidation.

We ate dinner and lounged outside with our Java Whiffs cigars, listening to the non-stop canine wailing a few hundred feet away. Suddenly the dog fell silent. Brother Romulus and I looked at each other. He jerked his chin in the dog's direction. Snuffing out my cigar, I grabbed the shotgun and torch, slipped out of my sandals and crept towards the cowshed. Except for a nightjar's monotonous, repetitive call, the evening was still.

At the corner of the shed, I switched on the light. The beam reflected the dog's eyes and nearby was the brightest eyeshine I had ever seen. A leopard. My heart hammered as I cautiously moved forward, shining the torch up and down, from one side to the other, never fixing it on the cat, as Akhter had played the deer. About sixty feet from it, I turned off the light, raised the shotgun to my shoulder and held the torch against the barrel to see over the front sight. I took a deep breath and turned on the light. The leopard was still sitting in the same spot, looking at me. I aimed at its white chest and pulled the front trigger. The noise was tremendous on that silent night.

When the smoke cleared, there was no sign of the leopard. The dog crouched and trembled with fear. I walked forward, shining the torch all around. The cat had vanished, not leaving any spots of blood. I had missed! I had already imagined showing off the beautiful pelt to my family and glowing in the adulation that would follow. Of course now, sixty years later, I'm happy I failed. That was the closest I ever came to shooting a big cat. It must have got the message it wasn't welcome, since it didn't return.

A group of army men arrived one evening in a roaring truck. They sipped tea until nightfall, when they asked me to go hunting deer with them. It made me proud that these grown men were relying on me to take them, but that feeling didn't last long. As if their vehicle wasn't noisy enough, the men banged the side *clang, clang* to get the driver to stop when they saw an eyeshine. Every animal in a 150-kilometre radius would have fled, thanks to the racket. I despaired of seeing anything at all. Some animals froze in the headlights—jungle cats, jackals, hares— and the guys shot them all. This indiscriminate killing turned my stomach. Until then, I had thought of hunting as a noble endeavour, as a way of feeding people or eliminating a dangerous predator. This slaughter was unconscionable. For the first time, it occurred to me that jacklighting was unsporting and didn't give animals a fair chance. Deer and blackbuck vanished before we could draw close, and I cheered silently at their escape. We returned to the farm at dawn and the men left after breakfast.

On one of my last solo forays into the forest with the .22 rifle, I hoped to bag a hare or maybe a barking deer. About halfway up a nearby 1,000-foot hill, I heard a loud snuffling sound ahead and peeped from behind an enormous boulder. A big black-furred object was half buried inside a termite mound, and now and then, it blew a cloud of dust. A sloth bear was feasting on termites, oblivious to the world around it.

Charles had warned me that sloth bears were the second-most dangerous animals, next only to elephants. Being short-sighted and noisy, they often didn't hear people approaching until too late. A villager had lost a nose and his face was disfigured with huge scars. A woman had her breast ripped off and one boy had been completely scalped, but survived. The bears' explosive violence may seem over the top for the mistake of not adequately announcing oneself. According to one theory, their attack-first-ask-questions-later reaction was their fear of being killed by tigers.

I watched the bear for some time and took a circuitous route to the peak. By then, the heat of the midday was oppressive and my throat was parched. I had forgotten to bring my canteen of water. Deer and boar tracks circled a puddle of rainwater. Kneeling beside it, I cleared the floating algae and quenched my thirst.

Back at the farm, I fell violently sick. Rice kanji and charcoal pills were the only remedies available, and I learnt an important lesson about carrying water in the bush. I rued every day of the two weeks that dysentery put me out of action.

Before I knew it, the exciting year was up. Ma wanted me to return to Bombay for my eighteenth birthday. It was time to prepare for college and depart for the States, a decade after I had arrived in India.

I sold the Triumph for a thousand rupees to a friend of Baba Sait in Mysore. In hindsight, I regret not having saved it in a coffin of grease. What a fine machine that was and what that vintage classic bike would be worth today. I bade farewell to Brother Romulus, Charles and Shanti, with the promise of coming back to visit after my college graduation.

SECTION 2

FINDING MY FEET

14

ARRIVAL IN AMERICA

A Legal Alien

IN JULY 1961, I flew out of Bombay via Cairo and Rome. I don't remember any details of the journey itself, but the trepidation and uncertainty that filled my being as I disembarked from the plane at LaGuardia Airport in New York are a stark memory. I spoke with an American accent from years of growing up with American kids in Kodai and held an American passport. I didn't stand out among the hordes of White people thronging the terminal. Nobody gave me a second glance, but I felt as if I belonged to a breed apart. The States may have been my country of birth, but it was foreign. I was more an Indian at heart than a Whitey. This cognitive dissonance has lasted all my life.

A bored immigration officer stamped my passport, and I was relieved at passing what had seemed like a test. I headed outside the terminal, to the kerb where cars and taxis were lined up. I looked at every slowing vehicle, hoping it was Dad come to pick me up. Before leaving India, I had seen a few old black-and-white photographs that Ma had, but I wouldn't be able to spot him in a crowd. I couldn't imagine how he'd recognize me either. *What if he's forgotten when I'm arriving?* I shifted from one leg to the other, wondering what to do. *Should I call him from a pay phone?* Wrangling with a contraption I had never used before made me even more nervous. A car pulled up in front of me, but to my disappointment, it wasn't a middle-aged man who hopped out, but a stylish, pretty girl. She walked up to me and put out her hand.

'Hi, Breezy, welcome home!' she said. 'I'm Carol, your stepsister. And this is my boyfriend, Val.'

My jaw might have hung open with astonishment. I didn't know I had a stepsister.

In his infrequent letters over the years, Dad had mentioned marrying for a third time after his wife, Sara, died. But he hadn't said a word about Carol or even Penny, my half-sister. Carol had recognized me from the photograph I had sent to my father a year ago. She seemed older than me, perhaps by a year or two, and studied fashion design. Val was self-assured and of obvious Italian descent. Both of them were warm, friendly and made me feel welcome. On the way, they had a lot of questions about India.

At his house in Glen Head, Long Island, Dad, a tall, handsome man, greeted me with a bear hug and introduced me to his German wife, Ingrid. My stepmother. It was strange not only to meet him after so many years, but to have this entire side of the family about whom I knew nothing. Ingrid was a secretary for the Swiss pharmaceutical giant Ciba-Geigy. Dad had quit his job at Cyanamid and become a qualified chiropractor.

Over dinner, Carol and Val plied me with more questions. Dad, however, didn't ask me anything at all about my years in India. In fact, he wasn't even listening to our chatter. His lack of interest took me aback. *Does he find our conversation boring?* Ingrid was standoffish too. Perhaps the son of an ex-wife made her insecure. I struggled to be as natural as possible, which was difficult in the strained atmosphere. When the meal ended, Carol and Val left, and I escaped to my room. *How am I going to stay here for three days?*

The next day, Dad took me to lunch at the Veterans of Foreign Wars bar and grill to meet his buddies. Although hanging out with a group of older men didn't appeal to me, it was an opportunity to bond with my father. The variety of draught beer taps was astounding, and I couldn't decide on what to choose. Back in India, I had known only one brand—Golden Eagle. I opted for the familiar Budweiser, having seen it advertised in magazines. Carrying my first legal pint, I followed my father to a table occupied by four of his friends, to whom he introduced me as his long-lost son. One asked what I planned to study. When I mentioned wildlife management, that inscrutable look reappeared on Dad's face. *Did I read his expression correctly?* I had no time to dwell on it, since the waiter arrived to take our orders. The moment passed, and I forgot about it.

That evening, over dinner at his house, he talked about opening a private practice.

'Wouldn't it be great if you studied medicine?' he asked. 'Then we can be partners.'

I didn't want to study medicine, nor did I fancy living in a big city. Working with wildlife in remote forests was my sole goal. Carol saved me from a reply by asking me to pass the butter. Months later, what Dad's plans meant for my future would become clearer.

No matter how hard I tried to find some common ground with Dad, I didn't make headway. I regaled him with fishing and hunting stories from India, thinking he'd be interested. But they fell flat. After that I avoided being in a room alone with him. When others were present, I trod warily around any conversation about my future.

Without Carol's help, I'd probably have fallen out with Dad. Perhaps sensing the tension in the house, she took me out to meet her gregarious friends. But I was a social misfit, unable to converse with these worldly wise girls or understand their slang and cultural references. They seemed to be speaking another language.

Carol thought little of my fashion sense. I was behind the times, she said, and insisted on taking me shopping. I wanted to fit in and didn't protest as she led me into a department store. She pulled several drainpipe pants from the racks and sent me to the fitting room to try them on. They were tight in the crotch and hard to put on and take off. When I self-consciously stepped out, she eyed me up and down and rejected them all. I despaired of finding anything that would meet her approval. Eventually, she chose enough to make a small pile. Wanting to humour her, I caved, even though the outfits were uncomfortable. I wore those clothes only that one time.

When my visit ended, I hopped into Carol's car with relief. She drove me into the city to Aunt Elly and Uncle Razzack's apartment overlooking Washington Square in Greenwich Village, the art, music and hip centre of this part of the world. They had moved from 248 several years ago. Carol and I hugged on the kerb and promised to be in touch, but that was the last time I saw my stepsister.

Elly was as lovely as ever and continued to be New York's famous commercial artist. But Razzack looked ravaged. A heavy smoker, he had been diagnosed with lung cancer and surgeons had already removed a lung. His coughing fits left him weak, and I massaged his surgery-scarred back to relieve the pain while narrating stories of my experiences in India, especially my last year at Mysore and Gumtapuram.

When I planned to visit Hoosick, where Gail was to be married in a few days, Elly gave me detailed instructions on how to reach the subway and buy a token. Razzack's health prevented them from driving up. I had travelled by train and bus in India, but here the system was different. I was nervous despite Elly's coaching and watched other passengers get their tokens and pass through the turnstiles before mimicking them. I arrived at the Port Authority Bus Terminal and caught a Greyhound to Albany. Although I took care to appear as nonchalant as every other person, I had to think my way through each step. Unlike India, no one here paid any attention to anyone else, so my fumbling escaped notice. Everyone appeared to be living inside their own bubble.

I sank into my cushioned window seat on the bus. The passing scenery didn't seem familiar at all. *Am I on the right bus?* We were headed north in the right direction, so the brief moment of confusion and panic passed. The country had probably changed a lot in the last decade, or I had forgotten the way. *Would I recognize the house?* At Albany, I boarded a bus for Bennington, Vermont, since Hoosick was along the way. I dozed off and woke up with a start, paranoid about missing my stop. My watch showed it was still ahead. Finally, the bus pulled into Hoosick village. I remembered the gas station, turned into the side road, and walked a kilometre. There it was, the impressive old mansion.

No one lived in the house, and the grounds were overgrown. The Babsons came occasionally to make sure everything was okay.

The key was under the flowerpot on the back porch as Elly had told me, and I let myself in. The rooms looked haunted with creaking floorboards, and bats created merry hell in the attic. I was sad to return to a place of many fond memories to find it deserted. Tidying and stocking the kitchen kept me busy for two days.

I walked down to the cellar, remembering how petrified we kids used to be of going alone into the dark, dank space. Standing propped up in a corner was an old fishing rod, which gave me an idea. I turned over rocks in the yard, looking for worms, but instead uncovered a milk snake, probably a descendant of the ones I had caught years ago under the same rocks. I released the snake and put the rock back gently without squashing it. After collecting worms under other stones, I ducked between the lines of the electric fence, crossed the railroad tracks, where homeless people had set up camps, and trekked to the pond. To my delight, the path was so familiar that I could have found my way blindfolded. Perch were biting, but for the first time, I wasn't concentrating on hooking a fish. It felt good to be in the States, on the verge of adulthood with all the excitement ahead. Sitting on the grassy bank of the stream with my shirt off, listening to the birds and frogs, and feeling the warmth of the sun, I was lost in the cusp of the past and present. Memories of childhood summers spent at this place assailed my mind while I savoured the shimmer of dragonfly wings in sunlight. The village kids had called the insects darning needles, saying, 'You gotta be careful; they'll sew up your lips.' *Were any of my old playmates like Sonny and Billy Peckham still around?* Later, I enquired at the post office, but their families had moved away.

Gail arrived with her fiancé, John Wynne, another Syracuse graduate. He looked serious with thick-framed spectacles, and his deadpan demeanour belied his incredible sense of humour. He reminded me of Clark Kent, the comic-book alter ego of Superman. I don't have a clear memory of the small ceremony where I gave away the bride. Ma couldn't make it to the country for the wedding, but my father, who could have come, didn't.

I returned to New York and packed my things in the elegant trunk Razzack gifted me. I said a fond goodbye to my aunt and uncle, and took a taxi to the Port Authority Bus Terminal, where I boarded a Greyhound bound for California. The other low-budget, long-distance travellers included students, folks on holiday and people hoping for work out west.

We slept on the reclining seats, and unlike buses in India, there was a toilet on board. At a stop, I stood in front of a big, red vending machine, the only way to buy a Coke, reading the instructions. Even then, I was uncertain about how to do it. This was one thing I had forgotten to ask Elly. A girl behind me patiently waited her turn.

'I've never used these machines before,' I confessed, hoping she'd help me.

She thought I was joking until she saw me fumbling.

'Give me a dime and I'll get it for you,' she said.

'That's my problem. I only have a quarter.'

'Not to worry. The machine will give you change.'

She put my quarter in, pulled the lever and an ice-cold can tumbled down into the pickup window. I couldn't believe it when the balance fell into the coin-return slot.

'So where are you from?' she asked.

'India. I just got here two weeks ago, and I'm heading to Laramie to go to college.'

'Wow! India! I'm headed to California to visit my dad. He's in the navy there.'

At every stop for the rest of the way, I chatted with the girl.

* * *

I arrived in Wyoming forty-two hours later, the longest bus ride of my life and one I hoped never to repeat. Laramie was disappointing at first sight. The mountains were far away, and the land was flat and featureless. The small college town buzzed with thousands of students. It was 'rush week', with fraternities and sororities vying to attract members. I wanted no part of the social life.

After staying in a dorm on campus for a while, I scoured the ads on the university bulletin board for alternative accommodation. A tall, skinny chap beside me was also scanning them. We were classmates in the wildlife management course. Neither of us liked our living arrangements, but the advertised rentals were beyond our means. If we joined forces, however, we could afford to rent a half-decent house. Ken and I looked through the rental ads in *The Laramie Daily Boomerang* and found a run-down furnished house with two small bedrooms on the edge of town, where Arapaho Indians and Mexicans lived. We stocked the functional kitchen with cans of soup, canned tuna, jars of peanut butter and jelly, cheeses and plenty of bread. We didn't know how to cook.

The coursework was tedious, and the boring classes made me fidget. The zoology textbook dated to the Middle Ages. Math was unavoidable and flunking was certain. I was under the mistaken belief that college would be different from school. Although sociology seemed far removed from wildlife management, I picked it as an elective, thinking I could breeze through it without breaking into a sweat. To my surprise, the only interesting subject was geology. The professor, palaeontologist Paul McGrew, spiced up the lessons by talking about his recent finds on dinosaur digs. In all, not a great academic line-up of subjects. Socially I did as well as I always had. I left people alone and they, in turn, left me alone.

The sociology professor gave the class an assignment, to present a ten-minute talk on a controversial topic. I agonized over it, thinking up ideas and rejecting them. Either they were not contentious enough, or I didn't know much about them. As the deadline loomed, my mind blanked. The Berlin Wall dominated the newspaper headlines, and that sparked a brainwave.

When it was my turn, I extolled the success of the Marxist Communist government in the Indian state of Kerala in achieving the highest literacy rate in the country, as well as providing a better standard of living for its citizens than the other states. The rest of the class glared and murmured, 'commie', and none applauded when I finished. But the professor seemed pleased, and this was the only subject in which I eventually got a good grade.

What was the point of arriving in the Wild West and not having guns? At a pawnshop, I bought a used 12-gauge pump-action six-cartridge shotgun, a Remington single-shot .22 calibre rifle with no fancy stock or scope, just iron sights, and a snub-nosed .22 revolver. All for under a hundred dollars. I wanted a big-game rifle, a .30-06, but didn't have the money for it. Then a stop at the 7-Eleven corner store to get some boxes of ammo, and I was set. After living under India's tight gun laws, I delighted in the ease with which I could buy firearms and ammunition. I was itching to try them out, but the opportunity didn't arise until some days later.

Ken invited me to his ranch near Torrington on the Nebraska border one weekend. I took the .22 rifle along. After he showed me around, we arrived at the stables. He suggested we go for a ride, and I confessed to being uncomfortable with horses since Lovedale, nearly ten years ago. He had just the horse for me, he said, and helped me saddle up a docile-looking mare. As soon as I mounted, she started bucking as if she were possessed. I clung to the saddle horn for fear of falling and being trampled. Instead of controlling the demonic beast, the bastard couldn't stop laughing. After what seemed like a lifetime, he grabbed the reins and calmed her. This experience sure didn't help me get used to horses.

We set up cans and bottles as targets in the backyard. My complaints about not having ready access to guns in India had made him think I was a novice at shooting. I inserted a tiny .22 bullet into the bolt-action Remington, which was amazingly accurate. There was no point in having a whole clip and going tat-tat-tat. If I had to kill a mule deer, I had to do it with one shot. I could also use a long-rifle, hollow-point bullet, which had a lot of power. Ken was surprised when my shots found their mark.

That weekend, Ken taught me to drive his Chevy pickup on the dirt roads around the ranch. Back at Laramie, I practised driving his truck in the afternoons after classes for two more weeks before passing the test. I tucked the driver's licence, a rectangular piece of cardboard, into my wallet, one more marker that I was well on my way to becoming an all-American teenager.

I made friends with another Wyoming boy in zoology class. Dean was short, stocky and taciturn, with a gruff voice. His dad worked at the huge oil refinery in Sinclair, and whenever he got free time, father and son fished or hunted. Like me, he didn't find college inspiring or even interesting. Both of us wanted to work with wildlife, and we talked about jobs such as wildlife biologist, wildlife technician, wildlife ranger and fisheries biologist. They all required at least a bachelor's degree.

'Why can't we make a living hunting and fishing?' Dean asked rhetorically. 'I'm already a top-notch scientist, goddammit.'

I agreed.

Since arriving in the country, I hadn't ventured out to hunt or fish, and I was desperate to try my hand.

'Where are the best places for fishing?' I asked Dean.

'I know a good spot for brook trout nearby,' he replied. 'They don't get big, but it's fun catching them and even more fun eating them.'

In preparation for the trip, Dean took me to a pawnshop, where I spent five dollars on a fibreglass fishing rod and a Garcia spinning reel, which were both in decent shape.

On the following Saturday, we climbed into his old Studebaker as daylight brightened the sky and drove to Lone Tree Creek, about sixteen kilometres out of town. Dean was proud of his state's fall colours.

'I never get tired of how beautiful this season is,' he said.

I agreed it was pretty.

'That tree looks spectacular, doesn't it?' he asked.

It looked like every other tree.

'What's special about it?'

'Are you blind or what? All its leaves are red.'

'I'm colour-blind, man. They're all just brown to me.'

He didn't say another word about the gorgeous colours for the rest of the trip.

When he turned on to a dirt road, I saw a snake and yelled, 'STOP!' Dean slammed on the brakes and looked at me, dumbfounded.

'What for?' he asked.

He had not seen the small creature lying motionless as a strip of tyre. Without explaining, I jerked the door open and ran in front of the car, where the snake had bunched into a coil and was buzzing like a hive of bees.

'It's a rattlesnake!' I hollered. 'The first one I've ever seen.'

I had dreamt of finding one since childhood. I kneeled to get a closer look at the rattler, which was quiet now and had tucked its head close to its coiled body. Rough scales gave it a velvety appearance, and large circular blotches separated by bright bands ran down the length of its back. The two-foot-long creature was a Northern Pacific rattlesnake, one of Wyoming's two rattlesnake species. Dean stood by the car, watching as the snake started crawling. Using a ballpoint pen I carried in my shirt pocket, I pinned its head to the ground and gripped its neck. Even though it was still sluggish from the cold, that was a stupid thing to do.

'You be damn careful, Rom,' he advised. 'You do not want to get bit.'

I used the pen to pry its mouth open.

'Look at those fangs,' I said with wonder. 'Sharper than needles.'

Although I didn't take my eyes off the snake, I saw Dean shake his head in resignation.

'I've never seen anyone actually admire one of these bastards,' he commented. 'My dad kills every one he finds.'

I regretted not bringing my camera to record the event. *Should I take the snake home?* I hadn't brought a bag and vetoed the idea. I set it down on the ground beside the road and jerked my hand away. The rattler bunched up and started buzzing again as my heart went pitter-patter.

We continued on our way. My thoughts were on the rattlesnake while Dean chattered on about fishing. I committed every feature to memory and replayed every move it had made. He must have realized I wasn't paying any attention, because he stopped talking. He parked where the road came to an abrupt end. We grabbed our gear and walked on a steep trail lined with pine trees beside a bubbling stream. Where the path levelled on a plateau, there was a series of pools with half-submerged logs, signs of beaver activity.

I clipped a spinner on my line and stalked the pond in a crouch, without giving the game away to any wary lunker trout. For the first time since coming to the States, I was in my element and didn't need anyone else to tell me what to do or how to do it. I cast in the middle of the water and reeled, avoiding a log. A big trout grabbed the spinner and tore line off the reel.

'That ain't no brookie!' I exclaimed.

The fish took off to the other side, where it was deeper. I let it go as far as it wanted, as I didn't want the line to snap or the hook to straighten. My heart sang at the sound of zinging reel, and my knees trembled with excitement. No fish I had caught so far in my life was this gamey.

Instead of casting, Dean watched me play it, curious to see what I had. When it stopped pulling, I eased it towards our shore. Halfway across, it surfaced to shake the hook off.

'A rainbow,' he murmured. 'Never would have thought to find one here in brookie country. I guess they can jump those waterfalls too.'

As I pulled the tired trout ashore and unhooked it, Dean commented it was double the size of a large brookie. We estimated it was close to twenty-five inches long, a monster compared to the little ones I had caught in India. As I put it into the sack tucked into my belt, he hunched over and cast his spinner where the stream entered the pond. As soon as it hit the water, he hooked one.

'This is a brookie,' he said.

I wondered how he knew without looking at it. He must have heard my unasked question.

'You can tell by the way they dart back and forth when they are hooked.'

Dean brought the fish ashore and held it up for me to look at. It had the classic trout face, and yellow spots peppered its sides. Since I couldn't see the red colour of its belly, I didn't appreciate how beautiful it was until he pointed it out.

'They don't grow enormous,' he said. 'But boy, are they tasty!'

We spent the rest of the day reeling in a mess of brookies. Before heading back to Laramie, we cleaned them beside the stream, leaving the heads and guts for the scavengers.

At the house, Ken helped us fry the lot in breadcrumbs and butter. It had been a most satisfying day, catching my first rattlesnake and the largest rainbow trout of my life. Dean and I fished almost every weekend after that successful trip.

Larry, Ken's studious and meticulously dressed friend from the nearby town of Rawlins, suggested Ken and I enrol in the Reserve Officers' Training Corps, or ROTC (pronounced rot-cee). Although now optional, it had been compulsory for all male students at state universities not so long ago. Many still joined to avoid being drafted into the army in case another war broke out. The experience of their fathers' draft during the Second World War influenced Ken and Larry's decision, and I followed them. The advantage was if we were ever drafted, we'd be officers instead of enlisted men. After we signed up for the air force branch of ROTC, we got uniforms and attended weekly classes on aeronautics and military history, which put me to sleep. I wrote to Ma, 'ROTC, of course, is the lousiest waste of time, dressing up neatly in Mickey Mouse uniforms with a tie, of all things—it's enough to kill me.'

Larry invited me to his home next to the Snowy Mountains Refuge for a weekend.

'My folks would love us to get them some cottontail rabbits,' he said, 'and I have a deer tag, in case we see a muley.'

That was an invitation I couldn't resist.

We arrived in the afternoon to a sumptuous lunch of chicken and dumplings. With our stomachs full, we drove to the nearby forested hills in Larry's pickup. Besides his revolver, Larry had his 30.06 rifle slung on his shoulder, and I carried my .22 nine-shot pistol in a holster.

'Let's walk separately along that embankment,' he said after parking the truck. 'Cottontails will be close-range action. So be careful.'

I pulled out the gun and stalked one side of the slope while Larry disappeared to the other side. When a cottontail burst across my path towards the bank, I shot. The bullet hit a burrow and all hell broke loose. About six cottontails exploded out of that tunnel and ran in every direction. One came straight for me. Without thinking, I fired four or five shots, aiming ahead of it as it dove between my legs. My ears rang from the sound of the firing and a sharp pain erupted in my leg.

My jeans had a tattered hole above my left knee and a dark colour spread across the denim. In the sub-zero temperature, the blood steamed, making my pants look like they were on fire. And fire was indeed what I felt where the .22 long-rifle hollow-point bullet had torn through the flesh. *My knee must be in smithereens.* Hollow points create maximum internal damage. I was nauseous and dazed. I always prided myself on my sense of gun safety, and I couldn't explain how this had happened. One moment I was squeezing off shots as the cottontails ran past me to get to their burrow, and in the next, I was looking at the blood spreading through my jeans.

'Hey man, I fucked up big time!' I called to Larry, limping towards him.

'Holy shit, you fuckin' shot yourself in the fuckin' leg!' he exclaimed.

I hobbled along the snow-covered path to the pickup, which, to my relief, was only fifty feet away. Somehow I climbed into the seat, even though my leg was stiff and the pain excruciating. Larry tore down the road to Rawlins.

'What does it feel like?' Larry asked.

'Feels like I fucking shot myself,' I replied, with a mixture of embarrassment and sarcasm. 'I hope the bullet missed my kneecap. There's a hole going in, but there ain't one coming out. Guess they'll have to dig it out.'

Larry had a worried look, perhaps hoping I wasn't bleeding to death in his truck.

'Should I tie a tourniquet?' he asked.

'Nope, don't think so,' I replied.

The dark bloodstain on my jeans wasn't spreading and my boot wasn't filling with blood, so I figured no artery or vein had been hit.

The ride seemed a lot longer than the hour it took us to get to the emergency room at the Carbon County Memorial Hospital. With Larry's help, I limped in and slumped into a chair while he explained the situation to a nurse. As she unlaced and removed my boots, she told Larry to wait outside. She reached for a pair of large scissors to slice through the jeans and the thermal long johns.

'No, please,' I protested. 'I'm a poor college student and I can't afford to buy another pair of pants. Let me remove them. Don't worry, I've got undies on.'

'Suit yourself, but let's be quick,' she replied and put the scissors down. 'We have to stop the bleeding and see what's happened.'

She helped me tug the soggy jeans off, and I grit my teeth to keep from yelping in pain. With a metallic clink, the bullet fell on the floor. She examined it and looked at my leg. There was a neat hole in the middle of my thigh and a longer gash below my knee on the left side, where the bullet had come out, not even penetrating the long johns. It had travelled through seven inches of flesh without shattering bones.

'You're one lucky boy,' she commented.

She handed me the bullet, which was flattened on one side where it must have grazed the tibia. I was relieved to have an intact leg.

'Keep it as a good-luck charm,' she said. 'We're going to give you a tetanus shot and a course of antibiotics.'

She then spent a long time cleaning and bandaging the wounds.

'You're good to go,' she said. 'You're the third gunshot-wound patient we've had this week. There are two others in the hospital right now. They weren't as lucky as you.'

Another college boy at the hospital had pulled the trigger of his brand-new .44 Magnum revolver too early while practising quick draw. The high-powered bullet blasted his ankle, and he was on crutches. He'd limp for the rest of his life, the nurse said. A ten-year-old kid got a face full of birdshot when his brother had mistaken him for a sage chicken on the other side of a thick bush. Luckily, none of the shots hit his eyes. I didn't feel so bad about my stupidity after hearing these other stories. I sent my silent thanks to the God of Idiots for keeping my limbs intact.

Larry, who was in the waiting room, looked surprised to see me hobbling out.

'That's it?' he asked. 'Are they not going to keep you here?'

'It was a flesh wound,' I said, quoting a typical line from a western movie while holding up the bullet. 'Went straight through my leg.'

The next day, Larry and I headed back to Laramie. I was too ashamed to tell anyone except Dean and Ken what had happened. When others asked about my limp, I replied with a bland 'Hurt my leg'. I had scrubbed the jeans clean of bloodstains. *Would someone recognize the bullet hole in the pants?* No one did. The wounds healed and left barely discernible scars. I kept that bullet for a long while, but lost it sometime over the course of my life.

* * *

It was tough getting a beer, since the drinking age in Wyoming was twenty-one. I depended on Ken to buy me the occasional six-pack with his fudged driving licence. But I didn't want to rely on him all the time, so he offered to falsify my licence too. With a scalpel blade he had filched from the biology lab, he scraped the 3 off my year of birth, 1943. Then, using a very fine pen nib dipped in black ink, he wrote 0. He blew it dry and then threw the piece of cardboard on the floor and stomped on it with his shoe while I watched in horror.

'Don't worry,' he said with a chuckle. 'The dirt will hide the minor alteration.'

He admired his work before handing it to me. 'Congratulations. You are now twenty-one.'

I had to admit he had done an excellent job.

'Don't smile when you show it,' he advised. 'Make yourself look older and sterner. Button up your shirt. Use your deepest voice when you say, "Two six-packs of Coors."'

The ID worked for as long as I was in Wyoming. The young clerk at the liquor store saw through our game, but didn't give a damn.

15

CUT ADRIFT

Ending Academics

K EN GAVE ME A ride to college every day in his pickup truck, and Dean took me fishing in his. I couldn't depend on them to take me places all the time. I scanned the classifieds looking for old cars and spotted a tiny ad: 'British Motorcycle for Sale—AJS, 500 cc single, in running condition, only $175.' The seller was in Casper, a good 240 kilometres away, but my mouth watered. Never mind all the signs of the coming season, icy roads, cold air and the formidable wind, I had decided. Forget a car—I wanted the bike.

'A motorcycle!' exclaimed Ken. 'You're out of your fuckin' mind. It's gonna get fifty below zero here in a few weeks, and you'll freeze your nuts. No one rides a motorcycle in winter in Wyoming. Nobody!'

He spat out 'nobody' with vehemence, but I didn't listen. Weaned on a 1943 Triumph, I adored the sound, power and clean looks of British bikes. Ken refused to take me to Casper, perhaps hoping to discourage me.

Dean also thought I was loony, but agreed to go with me. Early on a frosty October morning, the next-door neighbour gave us a lift in his delivery truck. I had 175 dollars in cash, plus another fifty bucks for gas, coffee and food for the trip. We had packed our knapsacks with extra layers of clothes for the ride back.

Chad, a tall, full-bellied and bemused man, wrenched open the garage door where the AJS leaned, smothered by everything from garden rakes to black rubber hose pipes and even a good-looking dusty saddle.

'I've had this bike sitting here for close to five years,' he said, as we helped him clear the junk. 'I'm gittin' too old for bikes.'

When we uncovered it, I gazed at the chrome-plated tank with the big emblazoned letters 'A J S'. It was like meeting an old friend.

'She started up real good back in the warm weather,' he said, pre-empting my question.

He grabbed a broom and a rag, and we cleaned most of the dust and caked grease, but the wheels and chain were gummy and gritty.

'Go ahead and crank 'er up,' invited Chad. 'There oughta be half a gallon of gas in the tank.'

On one kick of the starter lever, it sputtered to life, and the steady bass beats of a healthy old British machine reverberated through the garage. I revved the engine a few more times and listened for any mechanical rattling or timing problem. It ran for several minutes without a quiver or a missed beat. Chad accepted the cash and shook our hands.

We stripped in the garage and donned long johns, two pairs of jeans, a sweatshirt, wool sweater, hooded parka, balaclava, arctic gloves, a pair of scratched goggles I had found in the attic at Hoosick, thermal socks, hunting boots and canvas mukluks.

'You're nuts,' offered Chad. 'The real Wyoming winter will be here soon.'

Resembling Abominable Snowmen, we mounted the bike and were ready to set off.

'Go easy on that front brake when the road is slippery,' Chad reminded me. 'Don't do anything sudden on icy roads—braking, accelerating, cornering. And no wheelies. That's for sure.'

It started snowing as we turned on to Highway 487 to Laramie. I avoided the icy asphalt and drove on the gravelly verge. We made slow but steady progress until a highway patrol car pulled up. Two boys wearing huge overcoats chugging along on a motorcycle during whiteouts and gentle blizzards confused the guys. Following their orders, we got into their toasty warm squad car, leaking caked snow and ice over the back seat and floor. One of them knew our classmate, and as we complained about the futility of our coursework, they thawed and let us off. We made it back to Laramie in the early evening, half-frozen, but without incident.

A few days later, I took a corner without realizing the icy conditions and fell. A pickup stopped and a couple ran over to help me up. My knees hurt, but otherwise there was no damage to me or the bike. But I learnt to be much more careful and drove on the gravel edge of the road, even though it was a pain.

Every night, after returning home, I removed the spark plug and kept it in my heated bedroom. The next morning, I warmed it on the stove while making coffee and headed for another boring day of classes. Ken couldn't start his Chevy in the freezing temperature, but refused my offer of a ride to college, fearing I might fall again. Occasionally, he took me up when he had to get there in a hurry. He then got around his problem by filling his radiator with antifreeze and taking the spark plugs inside as I did.

As in Mysore, I realized a motorbike mechanic would be my best friend. Through word of mouth, I heard of Jim McQuatters's mobike repair shop. I visited him after classes one afternoon to make his acquaintance. I liked his easy-going smile and irreverent humour as he cleaned the carburettor. My bike and I were in expert hands.

Despite making three good friends, I was lonely and unhappy. Although my father covered my tuition and rent, I had to scrape by for my living expenses. Instead of washing dishes in a restaurant, Ken and I hunted rabbits along country roads. He drove while I shone a spotlight over the snow-laden prairie. When I spotted an eyeshine, I yelled 'Stop!', and he braked hard. I drew a bead on it and brought it down. A dog-food company paid us a dollar apiece for the hefty jackrabbits and we shot the little cottontails for meat. Although we knew jacklighting was a cruel way to hunt, we were desperate to earn every dollar.

'You gotta be careful,' said Ken, when I got my first cottontail. 'These guys sometimes get tularaemia, "rabbit fever".'

He held the limp, warm carcass by the scruff of its back with both hands and ripped in opposite directions, leaving the cottontail skinned. In the pickup's headlights, we examined the inside of the skin for any lesions.

'If you see a lesion, throw it away,' he said.

Ken's mother instructed him over the phone how to batter-fry rabbit, and we had a good dinner. The money from hunting saw me through the winter, and we never bought meat to eat.

We picked up road-killed coyotes, deer and antelope, as they brought five bucks as long as we couldn't pull the hair out—meaning the carcass hadn't decomposed.

On one occasion, Ken invited two guys to go hunting with us. The deal was they would bring the beer and we would pay for gas, but the rabbits belonged to us. I didn't like the idea of mixing beer and hunting at all. It wasn't my truck, nor were they my friends, so I didn't say anything. Ken drove while his buddies sat in the back, drinking. When I spotted a jack, I yelled at him to stop and yanked the door open to get a shot. I had lined up my sights when a deafening bang blasted close to my ear. One of Ken's idiot friends had fired his 12-gauge shotgun from the other side of the Chevy, over the roof and past my head. And he had missed. Both the rabbit and I were lucky to be alive.

'That was dumb,' said Ken while his friend looked sheepish.

I was furious but kept silent. Later that evening, when Ken and I were back at our house, I insisted that we not take anyone else along on our hunts, especially anyone drinking, and he agreed.

We rented a meat-freezer locker for five dollars a month. The facility had rolls of wax paper, grease pencils, knives and even an electric bone saw, everything we needed to carve a large animal like an elk. Although we hadn't yet gone after anything big, we had enough cottontails to need the storage space. We became outright carnivores, eating meat for lunch and dinner every day.

The longing for home in India began to grow like a tumour. This came as a surprise. I remembered being homesick for Hoosick when we had moved to India ages ago. Without realizing it, my sense of belonging had switched continents. A small tin of Madras curry powder I found in the local store flavoured a rabbit curry that resembled something Kumar would have made with chicken back in Bombay. Ken and Dean enjoyed it, so I cooked that whenever the fancy took me.

Ken and I drove to a forested hill west of town one Saturday afternoon. He parked the car and we split, promising to meet before nightfall. I had my .22 rifle for rabbits or sage grouse. While I was trudging through the knee-deep snow, a basset hound came bounding to me. I rubbed his drooping, satiny ears and swivelled around, looking for his owner. No other human was in sight. He put his nose to the ground and started pursuing a scent, looking back to see if I was following. A hunting dog. I plodded after him as he led the way from the road to where the snow was deeper. I huffed and puffed to keep up with the hound, whom I thought of as Old Yeller, of Walt Disney movie fame.

At the tree line, he shoved his nose deep into the tracks of a deer, ate the snow and pushed on. When he stopped stock-still, I stared through the trees and caught sight of the bobbing rear ends of a herd of fleeing mule deer. *They live so close to Laramie!* The dog looked at me with his doleful eyes, perhaps wondering why I didn't shoot. How was I to tell him I didn't have a high-powered rifle for the job? He reluctantly abandoned the deer and set off again.

Before long, Old Yeller had snuffed and snorted a trail of tracks headed uphill into a deep canyon lined with tall ponderosa pines. I might have been new to these parts, but I recognized the footprints of a big cat. They were the size of a leopard's paws and could only mean one thing—a mountain lion. I wasn't prepared for that encounter with a piddly little .22 rifle, nor did I have a licence to kill a puma.

'Old Yeller,' I called out. 'I'm heading back to town, and you follow it all by your lonesome.'

The disappointed dog looked at me as I headed to the pickup and hesitantly followed. When we got to the Chevy, I opened the rear door and he hopped in. Ken showed up before long and was surprised by the dozing canine in the back seat.

Old Yeller had been with us a week when an ad appeared in *The Laramie Daily Boomerang*: 'Basset hound missing, answers to the name Sammy. If you see him, please call the below number.'

'Sammy!' I called, and the dog came trotting from the kitchen.

I rang the number for the address, and Ken and I delivered the basset hound to his owner and her two overjoyed kids.

'Sammy will follow anyone who's carrying a rifle,' the lady said. 'He lives to hunt.'

I'd miss Sammy.

In early December, I received devastating news from Elly. Razzack had died. He had been a wonderful, generous uncle. Elly said he had suffered from pain during the end stages, and death was a relief. She urged me to continue with my studies instead of coming to New York for the funeral. If she only knew what kind of education I was getting.

Christmas arrived, and Ken, Dean and Larry went home. This was the first year I'd be far from my family for this normally feast-and-fun-filled holiday. I spent the festive day treating myself to a six-pack of Colt 45 malt liquor and roasting two thick elk steaks a hunter we met at the freezer locker had given us. Radio stations played Del Shannon's *Runaway*, Elvis Presley's *Marie's the Name* and Ray Charles's *Hit the Road Jack*. Neither the booze, food, nor the music helped me shake the homesickness that smothered my insides. It became a constant companion even after the others returned from vacation.

We didn't buy meat, nor did we suffer from the lack of it. Ken had brought back a mule deer from home one weekend, and other hunters gave us what they couldn't stuff in their lockers. But now hunting season was over.

On a Saturday morning following New Year, I checked the thermometer on the windowsill. It was sunny, but the temperature was twenty degrees below zero. Ken had gone home and Dean was staying with me. He was too broke to pay for the college dorm and had already sold his car. I didn't want to go out into the cold, but there was no choice. The freezer was empty, and both of us were poor and hungry.

'Let's head out on Roger Canyon Road,' I said. 'A dog once showed me a place with muleys.'

We dressed for motorcycling this time of year, and I donned an old aviator's leather helmet and the goggles from Hoosick. I looked like a First World War bomber pilot, but I was really a poacher.

The Remington single-shot rifle was in two pieces in my knapsack. Dean did the same with his. No point advertising we were going hunting out of season.

I heated the motorbike spark plug on the stove and, with clumsy gloved hands, tightened it with a wrench into the top of the cylinder. The old bike sputtered and started in three kicks. The frigid breeze froze my cheeks, but the goggles prevented my eyes from tearing. I sang aloud Del Shannon's *Runaway*:

> *And I wonder,*
> *I wah-wah-wah-wah-wonder,*
> *Why, why, why, why, why, why,*
> *She ran away,*
> *And I wonder where she will stay-yay,*
> *My little runaway.*

Dean huddled behind me, using me as a windbreak. No one else was on the road, which suited us fine. We headed to the place where Sammy had pointed to mule deer recently. I pulled on to a trail with loose snow, which made it hard to balance. Using my feet to steady the bike, we reached the forest edge. We'd have to walk from here.

I leaned the AJS against a tree. After I put together the Remington and Dean assembled his .222, which had a much better range than my .22, we were ready.

'You head to the left of that stand of trees and I'll go on around the right side of the hill,' he said. 'One of us is bound to find a deer. They seem to know it ain't hunting season, so you can get good and close to them, which is what you need to do to get a shot with that little peashooter of yours.'

I scowled and trudged the gentle slope to the shelter of the first trees. I hadn't ploughed through two hundred feet before a movement in the forest caught my eye. A spike-antlered buck deer was pawing the snow to uncover some edible bush. With the tree branches weighted low by snow hiding my approach, I got close. The stag was still intent on finding forage. I clicked the safety off, raised the rifle and waited for him to raise his head. When he looked straight at me, I squeezed the trigger. The hollow-point bullet smashed into his brain. He flopped down and died without much more than a twitch or two. Dean was out of earshot, as there was no sign of him. That's when I realized we had forgotten to bring a cleaver for butchering.

My trusty Swiss Army knife would have to do. I field-dressed the buck right there, slicing the carcass open and spilling the steaming guts on to the white snow. For the next hour, I carved it into pieces to fit under my coat and into the two side boxes of the motorbike, severing the tendons in the joints of the fore and hind legs, and using a rock to smash the pelvic bone. I scraped the gore from my icy hands with pine needles and snow before donning my gloves. I had finished when Dean arrived, empty-handed.

We stuffed the liver, heart and ribs into the panniers, and tucked the hind legs under Dean's big overcoat and the front limbs under mine. Our shirts became wet and sticky from the blood, but we were more worried about hiding the carcass. We both looked stouter than usual as we put-putted straight to the freezer. After ensuring no one was around, we cut the meat into manageable chunks, wrapped each in wax paper, taped the packages, labelled them with grease pencils and packed the lot into our locker.

That evening, after we had washed and changed, we were in the kitchen cooking dinner when there was a loud knock.

'Open up, this is the Game Warden,' called a deep voice.

Busted! In a panic, I looked at Dean, who stared back at me. My mind was blank. *How are we to defend ourselves?* I opened the door with my heart hammering. It was Ken, laughing like a hyena.

'How the hell did you figure out we had got a deer?' I asked.

'You doofus! Look at the blood under the motorbike in the garage. Either you had a near-fatal accident or you shot a deer. I decided it was the latter.'

Since I couldn't see red, I didn't even notice it, and Dean had ignored the puddle. It was our sheer luck that a game warden hadn't stopped us. Our goose would have been cooked if he had noticed blood dripping from the side boxes. I cleaned it before it began to stink.

Except for the splurges on firearms and the motorbike, I lived frugally. The income from selling jackrabbits and coyotes couldn't pay my bills. I had to get a job. I pored over the newspaper classifieds looking for part-time employment, but the competition for low-skilled work was high. Although I called right away, they had already given the job to someone else. That's when I spotted a notice on the bulletin board. Geology professor McGrew was offering the minimum wage of one dollar twenty-five an hour to help him at the museum. I applied immediately, and to my utter delight, he hired me. In the prep room, while tapping tiny pieces of shale from a forty-foot-long fossil of a mosasaur, a marine predator and the ancestor of snakes that ate smaller dinosaurs, I listened to him speculate on the habits of this monster of the Jurassic era. This beat washing dishes any day.

'Makes you think people like us were born millions of years too late,' he said at one time.

I nodded.

A few weeks later, Jim, the mechanic, called with a job offer. He needed help to dig a cellar space under his shop and was paying two bucks an hour, which was better than the minimum-wage work at the museum. He had hired three other men as well, and we chatted as we dug. The four of them planned to drive their motorbikes up the snowdrifts in Medicine Bow National Forest.

'Rom, you gotta come with us on Saturday,' Jim said. 'You'll love it, and you'll get to see what your AJS can do on steep slopes with a cheater sprocket.'

I hadn't a clue what he was talking about. He took me to the back of his shop, where his BSA twin-cylinder bike stood, and pointed to the enormous sprocket on the rear wheel.

'You put one of these cheaters on your old bike, and it'll zip up hills like a mountain goat,' he said.

My heavy AJS didn't seem to be built for that kind of excitement. Jim must have seen a flicker of scepticism cross my face.

'Come over on Saturday morning,' he said. 'I'll fix it up for you.'

I packed a stack of sandwiches into my knapsack early Saturday morning and drove to Jim's shop, where four bikes were already parked.

They were smaller machines than mine, and all of them had knobby tyres for hill climbing.

Jim took the rear wheel and chain off my bike, and bolted a cheater sprocket on the regular sprocket.

'We're going to have to add several links to your chain too,' he explained as he worked. 'You gotta take out that silencer. It'll hit for sure.'

While he fixed the chain, I unscrewed the silencer. In forty-five minutes, the bike was off-road ready. The last thing he did was remove the stand as well. By then, the others were getting impatient. When we started our bikes, all with straight pipes and no silencers, the chorus of deafening roars shattered the quiet of the early morning. There should have been a law against it.

'Fooorward ho!' Jim yelled as he waved his gloved hand in the direction we were about to go in. The motorbikes roared as they leapt forward. We drove the eighty kilometres along Highway 230 to reach the wildlands. With Jim leading the pack, we turned off the highway on to a thin trail and climbed the lower hills near Medicine Bow. He revved his throttle a few times and headed straight up a steep slope. One by one, the other bikers followed, their wheels kicking up clods of mud and snow. I copied their example and throttled like hell, shifted my foot gear into first, released the clutch enough to get moving, and then released it all the way to feel the full strength of the engine. The huge sprocket on the back wheel gave the motorbike phenomenal pulling and climbing power. I tore after the rest of the gang, but couldn't keep up with them because my bike didn't have knobby tyres. I was so excited I let out a rebel yell, which was, of course, drowned in the roar.

When we crested the top of a pass, Jim pointed to an undulating downward slope to our right, gave us a thumbs-up and gunned his machine. He exploded through the first snowdrifts, the white powder arching through the air on either side. The other three dudes smashed through after him. I twisted the accelerator, gunning the motorbike for a section of the still-intact drift. I burst through, with the snow hitting me in the face and sliding down my neck. There was no time to pause and savour the feeling. The men kept going, and I tagged behind. It was as much fun watching them as doing it myself.

Cresting over a steep rise, Jim beckoned. We braked alongside him. In the distance, a big black bear bounded away, looking over his shoulder at us as he ran. After about an hour of hitting drift after drift, we arrived at a shed used by fire-watchers.

We leaned our bikes against trees and ate our sandwiches.

'It's good that Jim bursts through the drifts first,' said one between mouth fulls. 'Could be a log in there.'

I hadn't thought of that. Crashing into a log at that speed could kill. Another glassed the hill slopes with his binoculars as he chomped.

'There's a herd of muleys,' he said. 'A big eight-point buck and five or six does.'

He handed me the binoculars to have a look and raised his hands as if aiming with a rifle. The stag with a big rack of antlers stood on a ridge, silhouetted against the sky. It was stunning. I regretted not having a long lens on my camera. After a cigarette, it was time to return.

'Let's go back by a different route,' Jim said. 'Rom, you're gonna get some sudden experience going downhill. Remember to keep your cool and ride your gears, not your brakes.'

I didn't understand then, but I understood what he meant when we started descending.

Steering and balancing while driving uphill was easy because of the momentum and traction. But heading down, especially in the wake of the other guys, who made the trail mushy, it was hard to use the brakes just enough to slow down but not enough to slide to the side and fall. I fell with my leg pinned under the bike. Before any of the others noticed, I got up with a supreme effort. The engine was still running, so I raced after them, slipping and sliding the entire way down. I smelt the brake shoes burning from the strain and wisps of smoke rose from the back wheel. That downhill ride tuckered me out.

We didn't have far to go before the trail met the highway, where we stopped for a cigarette.

'So, how was that?' Jim asked.

'Everything you said it would be and more,' I replied.

'Everyone gets a kick out of hill climbing. But let's tighten your brakes, which you probably wore down to a nub.'

He unpacked a bag of tools and adjusted the brakes on all the bikes. We thundered into Laramie, tired and happy. Jim removed the cheater sprocket and screwed on the silencer pipe before I went home. Although the day had been fun, I was too busy hunting and making some money to go off-road biking again.

By this time, I had lost all interest in the wildlife course. It took willpower to drag myself to classes when the temptation to fish and hunt was stronger. In a letter, my father reiterated he wanted me to study medicine. After years of being allowed to do whatever I pleased, I didn't react well to his demand. When I couldn't sit through the classes I had opted for, expecting me to plough through a medical course in which I had zero interest was asking too much. In my reply, I evaded his expectations.

With the melting snow and flowing streams beckoning one weekend, Dean and I festooned the motorbike with sleeping bags, a pot and pan, and our fishing rods. We drove through Saratoga to a wild stretch of the North Platte River. Since he had been a kid, Dean had come fishing here with his dad. Off the highway, we followed a rutted timber trail until it ended. My heart sank when I saw the rushing muddy river.

'How are we gonna catch trout when it's so murky?' I grumbled. 'No fly-fishing, that's for sure. Even a spinner would be invisible.'

'Wait and see,' Dean said with a smile. 'We're gonna get some lunkers.'

We set up camp, stretching a tarp between some pine tree branches, though snow or rain wasn't likely, and scrounged along the riverbank for deadwood to make a fire. On hearing the distinctive honking of geese in the distance, Dean rammed a shell into his short-barrelled .22 rifle with iron sights. He followed the birds when they flew overhead and squeezed the trigger. The last goose in the formation fell to the ground stone dead about a hundred feet away.

'Good shooting,' I complimented.

'It's too big for us to finish,' he said with a broad grin. 'Let's clean it and take it back to Laramie. We've got some trout to catch.'

Dean rigged a rod with a round lead weight and two treble hooks, and cast into the quiet water near shore. *What kind of fishing used treble hooks?* He jerked the rod sharply, reeled in some line and yanked again. After a few minutes, the rod bent.

'Got one,' he said as he pulled the thrashing fish. 'This here is a long-nose sucker. You can catch it only by foul hooking.'

He showed me its tiny mouth with sucker lips and how the hook had snagged the fish in the side. He chopped off the fish's head, and filleted and sliced the body into a dozen small squares.

'Now let me show you how us Wyoming boys catch trout when the water is too murky for the fish to see anything and they gotta use their superior sense of smell.'

Dean snipped off the treble hooks, attached a single hook on the weighted line and skewered a piece of the sucker meat.

'Now look there, see that boulder under the fast water? I reckon there's a big rainbow trout hungry for a chunk of sucker meat in that riffle.'

Even though he seemed to be a pro fisherman, I was sceptical. The bait landed with a plop in the current. I didn't have time to count to ten before his rod bent and reel started whining as the line zipped out. Dean struck the fish.

'Whatdiditellya,' he said, grinning with triumph.

He played the fish, tiring it before he brought it close to the bank, where I was ready with the landing net. It was a good twenty-inch-long rainbow trout with a beautiful sheen.

I walked upriver and started casting at the first riffles. On my second cast, I caught a trout. That familiar tingle of excitement at hooking a gamey fish ran through me. It made several spectacular leaps, trying to spit out the hook, and then swam against the current. The line spooled out from the reel until a third of it was gone. When the fish was spent, I reeled it in.

Two hours later, when Dean and I met at the camp, we had six fine trout. At dusk, we started the fire, baking some biscuits wrapped in tin foil while whole potatoes roasted in their jackets. After we had cleaned the fish, we barbecued two until the skin was burnt to a crisp. A dash of salt and pepper made it a gourmet dish.

As the temperature dipped to freezing at midnight, I snuggled in my sleeping bag. At sunrise, my face felt damp. It was gently snowing and a light breeze blew the flakes over us. It was a new experience for me. I didn't want to stir out and deal with the cold, but we had to get going. We stirred the smouldering fire to boil coffee and make biscuits, which we ate with reheated leftover fish. At Laramie, we stopped first at the meat locker to stash the goose and extra trout. Tomorrow was another day at college, ho-hum!

My father's demands became more and more insistent. When I didn't confirm switching my course to medicine, in a fit of pique he refused to pay for my studies. Little did I know this was a life-changing moment as my formal education ended.

When April 1962 arrived, it was time to cram for the final exams. A lot was at stake for any freshman aspiring to become a sophomore. I worked as hard as the last year of school, but there was no Mr Root to find shortcuts for me.

My transcript showed I had flunked math and had squeaked through in zoology. To pursue this wildlife management course, I'd have to get a tutor and make up adequate credits in summer school. I had no appetite for any of it. Besides, I had to earn a living and pay tuition fees for the next semester.

Some guys made a packet of cash during the summer as salesmen. If I earned enough money during the vacation, I could continue college. An ad pinned on the bulletin board on campus sought salesmen for Future Homes Incorporated, a company specializing in cookware, china and crystal. Another student, Joe, was in the same boat, so both of us applied.

Ken and Dean headed to their homes and promised to keep in touch. I needed the house for two weeks longer, so Joe moved in and helped with the rent. We attended a three-day training course run by experienced senior students who had worked their way through college with Future Homes Incorporated.

The products we were to sell dovetailed with the aspirations of girls throughout Middle America. In anticipation of marriage, many of these young ladies maintained the European tradition of a hope chest, which held everything they needed, such as cookware, silverware and bed linen, to establish a home.

With a big heavy satchel of china, crystal, cookware and silverware samples, I was ready to visit the homes of marriageable girls and impress their mothers by cooking them a gourmet meal. And then with precise timing, I would clinch a sale. My commission was 15 per cent of every sale, a pretty good incentive.

I sold my rifles to a pawnshop, since there would be no time for hunting and no place to stash them. Little did I realize that my hunting days were over. I would never shoot an animal again.

This enterprise needed a car, not a motorbike. I bought a cheap '53 Chevy in great condition, my first car, for 125 dollars, from an old lady who said she couldn't drive any more.

After stashing the AJS at Jim's bike shop, I set off on my new career as a travelling salesman, hoping to become a millionaire soon.

16

ODD JOBS
Travelling Salesman Joke

I STARTED BY VISITING GIRLS in the towns of Rawlins, Medicine Bow and Chugwater, who had bought our company's cleverly designed raffle tickets. The prize was a beautiful big cedar hope chest. For every address of a friend each girl gave me, she received a raffle ticket. This allowed me to knock on those friends' doors and ask, 'Is Carol home? Her friend Susan suggested she might be interested in adding to her hope chest.'

On a keychain, I carried a sample ring that showed the cross-section of the cookware, brass sandwiched between layers of stainless steel. As part of my sales pitch, I asked a prospective buyer to hold it while I heated the other end with a cigarette lighter, so she could feel for herself how the heat spread quickly and uniformly. To show the quality of crystal, I wet my forefinger and rubbed the rim round and round until it hummed. I couldn't tell the difference in tone between crystal and plain glass, but I made a point of noting, 'See how real crystal hums eerily?' There was nothing unique about the china except that it was made in Japan.

'Nowadays Japanese china is the best in the world,' I said knowingly.

If my customers bought a lot, I threw in a complete set of stainless steel cutlery for free.

In house after house, I gave my spiel about the marvels of the new kitchenware. If the family expressed a desire to see other options on the market, a professional would take them around to the local stores and persist until they bought something. But I lacked the killer instinct. If the girl declined to make a purchase, I asked her out for ice cream instead.

The few initial sales made me dream of a promising future as a salesman. But the going grew tougher and tougher. The senior students who trained us had dinned it into our heads that the key to success was introductions. I visited towns where I had university friends, who introduced me to girls they knew from school. But there was stiff competition from other marketers, selling everything from encyclopaedias to bathing suits and wedding dresses. After a while, I ran dry of names and addresses in that part of the state. Then I improvised by asking a girl for her high school annual book and visiting her classmates. This led to some sales, but not for long. Then I took to knocking on every door along a street, but was often told to 'get outta here' in no uncertain terms. Door-to-door salesmen had a rotten reputation even then.

The job wasn't as simple as it had appeared at first. I ran into Joe at a friend's house, and he had the same bad luck. If we teamed up, we could save on expenses. He sold his car and we took turns driving. Upon reaching a town, we targeted different addresses before moving on.

We had exhausted our contacts in towns near Laramie, so we drove west to Green River, Wyoming. Travelling salesmen were declared illegal in many places, and Green River was The Place where the law, the Green River Ordinance, was enacted. Marketers couldn't solicit by knocking on any door. The clueless souls that we were, Joe and I didn't know this. We were within the law as long as we visited the addresses of girls who had bought the raffle tickets. But we didn't stick to those houses alone. We solicited by going door to door, which was prohibited. One girl took offence when I rang her doorbell, and though I was polite, she slammed the door in my face.

I was walking out of another house on that street when the deputy sheriff pulled up and asked me what I was doing. I replied I was selling china and cookware for Future Homes Inc.

'I'm afraid that's against the law here and I may have to arrest you,' he said.

'I ... I'm on my way to the next town,' I stuttered.

He dropped me at the gas station where we had parked the car.

'You better go along now,' he said.

On seeing me get into the car and turn on the ignition, the sheriff left. I switched off the engine and waited for Joe.

We drove around the countryside, unsure of our next destination, when we fell behind a loaded pickup truck. It sped over a bump, sending a box flying out of the bed. We screeched to a halt, grabbed it and tried flagging the truck. But he was long gone, and there was no way we could catch up with him in our old jalopy. Since we were stuck with the box, we opened it to find two complete sets of fly-fishing equipment—collapsible rods, reels, fly tying kits, the works. We couldn't believe our eyes. *Why slog at the unpleasant job when we can fish in the beautiful Green River?* We caught cutthroat trout and cooked them on a frying pan that I pulled from my sample kit. This happy phase lasted a few days until we ran low on cash and couldn't delay returning to work any longer.

Taking a break didn't energize us, and our lack of interest showed in our sales pitch. While we burnt gas driving from town to town, we weren't making enough to fill the fuel tank. At one gas station, we offered a fantastic set of cutlery worth fifteen dollars in barter for five dollars worth of gas. The suspicious clerk didn't bite at first, but the quality of the stainless steel convinced him. We slept in the car since we couldn't afford a motel, freshening up in rest areas and gas stations. One night, exhausted from driving the whole day, we parked in an open lot and went to sleep. The sounds of heavy machinery woke us, and we found ourselves in the middle of a vast construction site. We got out of there pronto.

We continued westward to Salt Lake City, Utah, since we had the names and addresses of two girls who lived there. I made a big sale to a mother and daughter, who bought cookware, plates, soup bowls and crystal.

'Let me make you a meal,' I offered.

I shopped for ingredients to cook chicken curry. They seemed to like it, but they were more impressed with the cookware. If only every sale were as good.

Soon, we were desperate and couldn't buy even a burger. After starving for a day, we resorted to filching money. One trick I had heard from a college friend was to fold a strip of cardboard from a pack of matches like an accordion. Then, while pretending to call at a public phone booth, I shoved the folded cardboard into the coin-return slot of the payphone, trapping the change. We stuffed about ten telephones that stood in a line outside a supermarket, and returned the next day to unplug the slots. The pile of coins was enough for two cans of sardines, which we stretched to last a whole loaf of bread. We were so hungry that we soaked the bread with leftover oil and devoured it.

After defrauding callers that one time, we got cold feet. It seemed stupid to risk twenty years in prison for tampering with federal property. But then we didn't have money to eat, so we asked for old bread from bakeries. The staff took pity on us and often sold day-old loaves for ten cents and sometimes added a coffee cake past its use-by date. We dipped the dry, stale bread in hot, sweet coffee for a meal.

Running the Chevy became unaffordable. When the appraiser at a used car lot offered seventy-five dollars, I laughed in his face. I was about to stomp out when he suggested a hundred bucks. I took it and we bought ourselves a steak dinner, the first good meal in days. The car was not only our means of getting around but also our home. Without it, we were homeless, sleeping in gyms and parks.

When that money disappeared, we lived on dog food, the cheapest available snack. Hobos probably knew this trick. There was no point in putting off the inevitable. We dumped the remaining samples into a roadside garbage can. After the last of them landed with a crash, we looked at each other and laughed.

'We sure weren't cut out for this,' he said. 'There's gotta be a better way to make a buck.'

Neither of us had any idea how. He decided to hitchhike to Jersey while I planned on returning to Laramie. We promised to meet in New Jersey someday and went our separate ways.

I got a lift to Jim's repair shop. He still owed me a hundred dollars for the work I'd done for him. One of his customers suggested summer jobs were available during the tourist season in Mount Rushmore.

The next morning, I headed north-east on my motorbike, making the mistake of riding in the updraft behind a big semi-truck. My old AJS was reliable at 80 to 95 kmph, but I held my speed to 110 to stay with the semi. More than 160 kilometres from Custer, South Dakota, the bike made a terrible clanking. The engine sputtered and abruptly stopped, almost throwing me over the handlebars. The driver of a passing pickup truck saw my predicament and pulled over to help. We hoisted the bike on to his vehicle, and in two hours we were in Custer, where he dropped me at the first repair shop. The mechanic wanted two days to fix it, although it seemed beyond redemption.

I brushed my hair, straightened my clothes in the restroom and stood on Route 16 with my thumb stuck out. Getting a lift to Mount Rushmore wasn't hard. A couple on holiday gave me a ride. The huge profiles of the four former Presidents, Washington, Jefferson, Roosevelt and Lincoln, carved on the stone cliff, overlooked the whole town. They were much more dramatic than photographs.

I ambled down the main drag, looking for help-wanted posters in shop windows. A restaurant, with a spectacular view of the sculptures, required a carpenter's assistant to work on a lodge under construction. I lied to the owner about having plenty of experience and got the job. Accommodation was rent-free in a dorm at the back of the property, there was free food at the restaurant and the pay was ten dollars a day.

The head carpenter understood I didn't know anything about carpentry and assigned me to driving a dump truck. A special driving licence to drive an eighteen-tonner might have been necessary, but no one asked me about it. I was jittery at the wheel of the enormous, fully loaded vehicle as I drove out of the site and on to a narrow mountain road. Cars lined up behind as the truck grunted its way uphill. At the next available shoulder space, I pulled over to let the cars pass me. But several drivers honked their displeasure and one even gave me the finger. At the dumping site, I parked and looked over the brink, gulping at the 1,000-foot drop. The slope below was an unsightly mess, where the entire township unloaded its trash. Looking in the rear-view mirror, I backed up inch by inch up to the edge and pulled the lever to raise the trailer. When the last of the junk had rumbled off, I jumped out, only to find the massive pile of scrap lay between the truck and the rim. I had no choice but to shove the whole pile over with my bare hands. I became better at judging the distance, but it was a nerve-racking job.

The first weekend, tourists dropped me at Custer's motorbike mechanic shop. To my utter amazement, he had fixed it, and it sounded as good as before, and I drove it back.

I had a job and a motorbike. Now all I needed was a companion. Finding a girl to take on a date was impossible. A beautiful waitress, a runner-up in the Miss South Dakota contest, worked at a hamburger joint between the construction site and dump yard. But though she smiled and was friendly, she had many suitors and I didn't get to first base.

One weekend, for a change of scene, I caught a Greyhound to Scottsbluff, Nebraska, to see a guy I knew from the university. He introduced me to two of his basketball-playing friends, an African-American and an Indian. They wanted to go to dinner, and I suggested a steakhouse. They exchanged glances, but when they nodded, I didn't think much of it.

We walked into one and the whole place went silent. The diners, all of whom were White, stared at us. I didn't know what was going on.

'We can't serve you here,' said the waitress.

I became indignant and argued.

'Don't sweat it,' said the Indian. 'It happens all the time. Let's go someplace else.'

This was the first incident that made the racial tensions in the country clear to me. I had no Black friends in Laramie and hadn't been aware of racism. With a pang, I remembered Neel being denied entry to Breach Candy swimming pool. My lack of outrage at that episode rankled. I hadn't defended my own kid brother.

'Let's go to a soul food joint,' said the Black guy, with a laugh when we were outside.

We had dinner at a roadside fried chicken restaurant.

At Mount Rushmore, I had one friend. George, a full-time gold panner and a well-known fishing and hunting guide, lived in a slapdash cabin nearby and was always dressed in frayed army fatigues. He occasionally arrived at the carpentry shop looking for work when he was down and out. In the evenings, he regaled me with stories of the Wild West and the history of the Gold Rush days as we sipped beer at his shack.

'It took me two years to pan this much gold,' he said as he shook a heavy Mason jar half full of gold dust.

'How much is it worth?' I asked, excited by the prospect of making some easy money.

'A cool 2,000 dollars.'

'Can I go panning with you?'

'Let's go next weekend.'

We drove deep into the Black Hills in his 4WD and parked beside a stream.

'Watch the way the water flows,' George instructed. 'If it is rushing too fast, the gold is gone.'

I imitated him as he scooped a handful of sand in a pan and sloshed it around. We bent over the water and swirled our pans for what seemed like hours. After a day of back-breaking work, he had collected two pinches of gold dust while I had a couple of grains. Not much to show for the effort. My gold-panning career was over even before it began.

Summer ended and the town emptied of tourists. All of us temporary employees received a small bonus, and I said so long to George. I didn't need the AJS any more and sold it to one of the carpenters for 250 dollars. Parting from the bike felt as if I were losing a faithful pet dog. The prospect of returning to studies was daunting. I hadn't made enough money to pay the tuition fees, the winter was too bitter and the course boring. I was done with getting an education. Packing my remaining possessions into a knapsack, I wrote 'New York' in big black letters on a piece of cardboard and stood on the highway with my thumb out.

A Volkswagen Beetle with three guys my age, who were going to Chicago, stopped. We took turns driving, stopping only to refuel the car and our bodies. At traffic lights, we waved our arms, so the car looked like an overturned bug. 'Hey, a bug! Stomp on it!' exclaimed people. A few called it a 'kraut can'. It was the end of the day when I got down at an exit outside Chicago, since it was illegal to hitchhike within town limits and on major highways. It was still daylight, so I tried my luck in getting another ride.

A few minutes later it started drizzling, and I ran to shelter under the awning of the toll booth leading on to the highway.

'Move on, you can't wait here!' the attendant shouted.

I scowled and gave her the finger before stepping into the pouring rain. Within minutes, a highway patrol car pulled up.

'Were you giving the lady a hard time?' asked the officer. 'I could arrest you for hitchhiking.'

'No sir, I'm not hitchhiking. I was just getting out of the rain.'

He told me to keep walking. The key to hitching a ride was to appear clean, shaven and respectable. Looking like a drowned rat would not get me anywhere but even more misery. With my last paycheque still intact in my pocket, I could afford a room at a cheap motel. After spreading out the contents of my bag to dry, I had a good night's sleep and woke refreshed. With my half-dried New York sign, I thumbed a ride all the way to Buffalo early the next morning. Outside Buffalo, I stood on an exit, hoping I wouldn't have to wait all day, when a highway patrol car pulled up. I cursed under my breath, tucked the cardboard sign under my arm and started walking before the officer accused me of hitchhiking. He drew level with me, and I expected the worst. Instead, he leaned out of his window and asked if I wanted a ride to Albany. I swallowed my surprise and scrambled into his car. It was late at night when we reached and I got myself another cheap motel room.

After breakfast, I walked across town to the eastern outskirts. Exhausted, I was sitting on a half-wall when two teenage girls in a convertible, playing loud music, slowed down.

'Need a ride?' one of them shouted.

'How far are you going?' I asked after getting into the car.

'How far do you want to go?'

'Hoosick.'

They seemed to be aimlessly driving around and were happy to take me. I pretended to be a roadie for a rock 'n' roll band, and we bantered the entire way. The trip ended too soon, and I was sad when they disappeared down the road.

Elly was at the mansion with her new husband, Dugald MacLachlan. She was delighted to see me and a flicker of disappointment crossed her face when she learnt I had quit college. Elly and Dugald had known each other for a long time, since his deceased wife had been Elly's friend. Over the following days, I got to know more about this new member of the family.

As a kid, Dugald had run away from his home in Connecticut during winter. He was nearly dead from exposure when rescuers found him, and his frostbitten feet had to be amputated. He walked so well no one could tell he had wooden prosthetics. When I helped him move a huge heavy table, he dropped it on his foot. Elly and I freaked out, but his unperturbed smile reminded us he couldn't be hurt.

Dugald was modernizing the house with a burglar alarm system, central heating and the works. He had removed much of the junk Gail and I had played with as children in the attic. The smell of bats brought some happy childhood memories.

I worked outdoors to get the place in shape, cutting stands of invasive sumac bushes and trimming branches. Elly planned to hire a contractor to cut the huge elms infected with Dutch elm disease on the driveway. Several dead ones posed a risk to the house. Back in Kodai, I had watched tree cutters fell gigantic eucalyptus trees and was familiar with the technique. I offered to do the job for 600 dollars, half of the contractor's estimate, and she gave it to me.

I called brother-in-law John Wynne for help. He arrived with his cousin John Clauser, and we set to work with two rented chainsaws. The store also loaned wooden wedges, a sledgehammer and coils of thick rope. After we cut halfway through one side of the trunk at a forty-five-degree angle, we hammered in a wedge. Clauser tied a rope as high in the tree as he could climb and knotted the other end to the bumper of his Volkswagen, parked at a distance so the tree wouldn't land on it. We sawed the other side of the trunk until we were sure it was ready to topple. Clauser got into his car and stepped on the gas until the tree crashed. I was proud of our achievement. We brought down more trees, and I imagined we were pros at this.

We hurried to fell the last one, the closest to the mansion, before nightfall, and in our haste, didn't pound the wedge in far enough. As I was sawing through the other side, the tree leaned and the chainsaw got stuck. That meant a lot more work, and it was already dark. We had no choice but to leave it until the morning. Elly was anxious the wind might blow it on to the house. With the swagger of an experienced tree feller, I reassured her it would be fine. While we young men slept soundly, she stayed awake, worrying. Only she heard the huge old elm fall that night.

When we came down to the kitchen at dawn, she exclaimed, 'It's gone. It's gone.' We rushed outside and surveyed the scene. It had been a close call. Had it crashed a few feet to the wrong side, it would have smashed into the carriage house. We split the 600 dollars, and the two Johns left.

I spent an hour or two in the early mornings at my old fishing spots on the Hoosac River, nostalgic for my childhood days of fishing and snake-catching. I missed Ma, Nina, Neel and Rama, and wondered when I would return to India. The reason for coming to the States, getting an education, was shot, and I had to decide what to do next. The urgency of earning a living began gnawing at me. By the end of July 1962, I resolved to get a job in New York City. Before then, I thumbed a ride to Wollaston to see Mumma, Pappa and the Babsons.

I ought to have called ahead and warned them of my arrival, especially since I would reach at night. Cousin Joanie wouldn't let me in, refusing to believe it was me. The Boston Strangler had begun his murderous spree that summer, and paranoia was high. We hollered back and forth through the closed door.

'But it's me. Breezy! How could the Strangler know my name?'

'How do I know it's really Breezy?'

I racked my brains for the special details of events from our childhood to convince her.

'We had fun playing cowboys and Indians in the Hoosick barn.'

She wasn't convinced.

'Remember, I saved you from a hornet when we were both little kids?'

No dice.

'I caught you before you fell out of the upstairs window.'

She cracked the door open an inch to peek at me. We couldn't recognize each other, but she let me in.

'Breezy! It's really you!' she squealed with delight and hugged me.

I hung around with my cousins, catching up on their news and eating Mumma's cookies.

Two days later, I hitchhiked to the big city. Although Elly had given me a key to her apartment, I found a cheap two-room flat on Upper Broadway, wanting to stand on my own feet. I scanned the job listings in the newspaper every day and landed one as a retail salesperson at the attaché and briefcase counter in the big department store, Bloomingdale's.

Meredith, a young girl with an appealing thick Southern accent, also worked with me. Every morning, I tried to manoeuvre myself in the crowded lift so I could be close to her. We had little time to get acquainted. The store was busy all day long, and we crammed a hot dog or hamburger into our gullets for lunch.

After I sold an expensive attaché case to a quiet, good-looking Black guy, Meredith came over.

'Do you know who that was?' she demanded with a smile.

I looked puzzled.

'That was Johnny Mathis,' she said.

He was a popular singer of the time, but I hadn't heard of him. This was one of the frequent reminders of the cultural distance I felt from growing up in India.

I lasted only two weeks in this boring job. Not even charming Meredith could prevent the inevitable. With my paycheque, I took a break and caught a bus to New Jersey to meet Joe, my old travelling salesman buddy. I discovered his family was wealthy. Although we had been reduced to eating dog food and stealing, he didn't tell his folks how hard up he was. This was the very reason I refused to turn to my family for support either.

We talked about our plans. Joe's parents insisted he finish college and join his father's real estate business.

'At least you have a goal in sight,' I said. I guess he heard the irony in my voice.

'You let me know when you get your life figured out,' he said. 'Finishing university won't kill me.'

Back in New York, Schrafft's, the catering company, hired me to serve coffee and doughnuts to secretaries in a twenty-two-storey office building. On the first day, I realized there were two things difficult about the job—I could barely push the cart, as heavy as a Tamil temple car, on to the service elevator; and I had to serve hundreds of women.

'I brought y'all some fresh meat,' hollered a large Black woman, who had ridden the elevator with me on my first day.

Twenty heads turned around to stare at me with big grins. I felt a furious blush creeping from my neck to face, and I wanted to disappear under the carpet. That set the tone for my job thereafter.

I lasted about a week. It wasn't the women who drove me away. I was tired of earning a minimum wage for doing repetitive work like an automaton—commuting on crowded subways, the jammed elevators, clocking in and clocking out with my punch card, and pushing the cart up and down identical aisles. The indignity of it turned me off. The two experiences, at Bloomingdale's and Schrafft's, made me realize I wasn't cut out for a city job, no matter how exciting New York seemed to be.

I was a clueless nineteen-year-old. The lack of education didn't bother me. Homesick for India, I wanted to return home. But with no money in my pocket, how was I to buy a ticket? Swallowing my pride, I moved into Elly's swanky penthouse apartment to skimp and save what I had. The doorman handed me a pile of letters, and one of them was from Dean.

Dean had also quit university and become a merchant marine. It paid well and it was easy to save with nothing to spend it on while at sea. And the job took him around the world. His letter inspired me to become a seaman too. I could jump ship when it arrived in India. I wouldn't even have to pay for a ticket! The only catch was—I had to join a union.

My father Earl and mother Doris.
New York City. 1938.

Doris and my Swedish grandfather,
Samuel Norden, in Wollaston. 1930.

Mumma, Augusta Norden, at home in Wollaston.

Aunt Elly, the artist, in New York City. 1943.

My uncle, H.H.A. Razzack.
New York City. 1949.

Stepfather Rama Chattopadhyaya.
Massachusetts. 1945.

Doris, Breezy, Gail and
Tempest the dog. Sea
Cliff, Long Island. 1946.

First snake. Hoosick, New York. 1947.

A snakey family. Breezy, cousins Joanie and Johnny, and sister Gail. Hoosick. 1950.

Amma (Kamaladevi) at artist Beatrice Woods' studio in Ojai, California. 1961.

Prime Minister Jawaharlal Nehru and Granddaddy Harindranath. New Delhi. 1955.

Aunt Elly and Uncle Razzack's Hoosick mansion.

Gail, Doris, Breezy with Neel and Nina. Bombay. 1955.

Rama holding Neel's hand, with Doris and Breezy. Bombay. 1957.

Kodaikanal Lake, with Perumal Peak in the background.

Pet python. Kodai School. 1958.

Pet kite. Shangrila, Bombay. 1959.

Catfish and 1943 Triumph motorbike. Mysore. 1960.

Catch of the day. Veracruz, Mexico. 1962.

American crocodile. Miami Serpentarium. 1963.

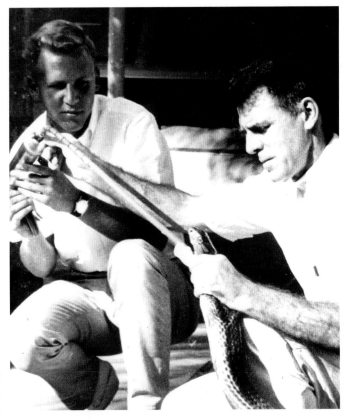

Assisting Bill Haast feeding
a king cobra. Miami
Serpentarium. 1963.

BSA
motorbike.
Miami. 1963.

Attila with an indigo snake. Florida
Everglades. 1963.

Yellow ratsnake.
Miami. 1964.

Schubert Lee.
Miami. 1964.

The Pakistani
cobra that bit
Schubert Lee.
Miami. 1964.

Big Mama, the six-foot eastern diamondback rattlesnake. Miami. 1964.

The Florida kingsnake that bit me on the nose. 1964.

Checking out the fangs of a water moccasin. Florida Everglades. 1964.

Guru Bill Haast extracts venom from a large king cobra. Miami Serpentarium. 1964.

Pet tarantula. El Paso. 1965.

The prairie rattler that bit me. El Paso. 1965.

Blacktail rattlesnake. Huachuca Mountains, Arizona.

Photo by Bob Ashley

Western diamondback rattlesnake. Common around El Paso, Texas.

406th Medical Lab, Camp Zama, with lab tech colleagues. Japan. 1966.

With Claire. El Paso. 1966.

Heyward with the gila monster I brought from El Paso. 1967.

Photo by Bob Ashley

Timber rattlesnake. Northern New York State.

Photo by Trent Adamson

Green rock rattlesnake. Arizona.

Willard's rattlesnake. Arizona.

17

SEASICK SEAMAN

The North Atlantic in Winter

I WAS CLEANING RAZZACK'S .22 rifle in the apartment when Elly rang to check on me. I mentioned my plan to become a seaman and the stumbling block. She thought about it for a moment before asking me to come to Hoosick to attend a house party. I decided to take the rifle along to hunt rabbits, but couldn't dismantle it as I would a shotgun or disguise it. It looked like what it was. Since being armed on subways was prohibited, I took a taxi to the northern edge of the city and thumbed a ride. It astonishes me now to think people were trusting enough to stop for a guy with a rifle.

I realized why my aunt wanted me to come when she introduced me to a guest, a Greek shipping tycoon. Intrigued I had grown up in India, his gorgeous wife asked me to show her how to wear a sari. She stripped to her bra and slip while Elly brought a silk sari. I became flustered and fumbled with the metres of slippery cloth. Elly saved me from embarrassment by taking over. I'll never know why the tycoon's wife didn't first ask my aunt to drape the sari.

Meanwhile, Elly had briefed the magnate of my plans and asked for his help. In the study, he scribbled a letter of introduction to the Seafarers International Union (SIU) of North America.

After the party, I travelled to the union's office in Brooklyn and signed up as a member, on the condition that I undergo two months of training at the Andrew Furuseth Training School in Philadelphia. They wouldn't pay me for the time, but they would give me free room and board. And the school was free.

I hitchhiked to Philly and presented myself at the South 4th Street Union Hall. The receptionist showed me a dorm, which I was to share with three other trainees. After I reported for duty, Joe, the Italian foreman, handed me a mop to swab the hall. If I thought I was going to learn the ropes, I was mistaken. We, the so-called trainees, saved the union the expense of hiring maids.

Up to forty seamen waited in the hall throughout the day, smoking, and watching TV and a big display with the names of inbound and outbound ships, their next destinations, and the number of crew members needed and their designations. I had smoked the occasional beedi in school, but now, hanging around in a smoky room with men who smoked all day long, I became addicted to cigarettes. Marlboro filter tips were my choice. I learnt about being a seaman by overhearing talk while I emptied the ashtrays, cleaned the windows, and waxed and buffed the floor.

Many of the ships were old rust buckets, the seamen grumbled. But, they advised, never board a Liberty ship. Nearly 3,000 of them had been built during the Second World War to send supplies and troops to Europe. They weren't made to last, and the Germans sank a lot of them. Those that survived were bought as war surplus and registered in Panama and Liberia. The men swapped war stories of rescuing people from ships that had been torpedoed, of friends they had lost to sharks and so on.

After our shift ended in the evening, the trainees grabbed a beer each and Joe regaled us with tales. He doubled as the chief cook at the canteen and chatted non-stop as he dished out Sloppy Joes and double cheeseburgers with trimmings. When he began, 'Can you imagine it,' we knew he would launch into his favourite topic—the large Black prostitute called Mama Sis. 'She was the only one-legged whore I ever met.'

'Aw, shaddup Joe,' an old-timer would retort. 'Do we have to hear that story for the hundredth time?'

That didn't discourage Joe, who carried on with his story.

Besides cleaning the hall daily, I ran errands for the honchos since I was a 'college boy'. I chauffeured the boss, a snazzily suited Black dude named Leon, in his big black Cadillac Fleetwood, to rough sections of the city and out of town, where he collected money. Someone said it was the numbers racket, sometimes called the Italian lottery.

In those days before scratch cards, a bettor picked three digits with a bookie and if it matched a randomly drawn number the next day, he won a windfall. I never understood how the scam operated and could only guess that Leon was collecting money from the bookies. I asked no questions, and he liked that. There must have been some risk, because he carried a .38 Special under his jacket, which he didn't bother to hide. He also stashed a sawed-off 12-gauge shotgun under the front seat, which I stumbled upon while searching for a rag to clean the windshield.

If that made me uneasy, there was more. When the seamen weren't talking about jobs and ships, they discussed our rival, the National Maritime Union (NMU), which was under the Teamsters Union, headed by the legendary Jimmy Hoffa. The old-timers called it 'Niggers, Mexicans and Undesirables'. This wasn't a casual, name-calling rivalry. They were expecting an imminent attack from their rivals. Ever since the Teamsters had driven a pickup through the hall's plate glass door the year before, the SIU members had stockpiled Molotov cocktails, sticks lashed with bicycle chains and other weapons on the roof, ready for future attacks. I wanted no part in any of this. All I wished for was to keep my head down and get on an India-bound ship at the earliest opportunity. I thanked my stars that nothing violent happened before I received a C card two months later, in November 1962. It's the first card a union member receives, which is used in place of a passport in foreign ports.

The other three trainees became angry when they were informed their cards would be delayed. Maybe my claim of being a college boy or the letter from the tycoon quickened the process for me. I didn't question my good luck. I could now sign on for menial jobs such as an ordinary seaman or crew messman. I could also be a wiper in the engine room, but I didn't fancy working below deck. I had little hope of going to sea soon, as I was one of many vying for a job.

In the normal course, I would have to put in two years as a C-card holder before I qualified for the next level of union seniority, a B card, which would make me eligible for an able-bodied seaman (AB for short) posting. I would also get a big pay rise. Specialists, such as an engineer, had no dearth of jobs, but all I had learnt was polishing floors and dumping cigarette butts, not skills of any use on the high seas.

I joined the throngs of idle smoking seamen in the union hall. There were no vacancies for the following few weeks, and I was tired of dirty Philadelphia. As I grew despondent, I saw my chance one evening. An old steam-powered freighter, the SS *John C*, was heading across the Atlantic to Europe and lacked a deck maintenance man (DMM). Ships could only sail if they had a full crew. Although I needed to have a B card for the job, it was a 'pier-head jump', meaning the ship was sailing at midnight and they wanted someone that very minute. Before anyone else raised their hand, I signed on for it.

'Fuckin-meejetly pack your shit up and get your ass over to the harbour!' yelled the duty officer.

This was an opportunity to earn some money until I could find a vessel bound for India. I packed my worldly possessions into a canvas duffle bag, bid my pals a quick 'see you guys sometime', got dirty looks in return and hailed a yellow cab.

The docks echoed with clanking and occasional shouts as the work of loading and unloading carried on in the dark. Lit only by a searchlight, the empty *John C* looked gigantic. I climbed the steep gangway and reported to the bosun, the chief seaman. I had just dumped my gear in my allotted fo'c's'le, living quarters, when the ship's horn sounded three blasts. Scrambling to the deck, I joined the crew, hauling the massive lines that tied us to shore and coiling the huge ropes around the capstan heads. As the vessel swung from the moorings, the lights of Philadelphia receded, and the swells lifted and swayed the ship as we steamed out of the Delaware River.

As the DMM, I felt self-important until a sea dog commented, 'Scrapin' n Paintin' Man is more like it, har har.' I knew nothing about what the job entailed, and I was to learn the veteran was spot on.

The bosun called me Whitey for my blond hair. He shipped with a different crew on every trip and couldn't keep everyone's names straight. So he gave us nicknames. The guy with dark hair was Blackie, a Cherokee Indian Cherry, and the radio operator was Sparks. A taciturn Hawaiian, the other DMM, with whom I shared a fo'c's'le, was Pineapple. It was racist, but the good-natured teasing masked it well.

Pineapple had the dreary task of teaching me the work—taking bilge soundings, operating the cranes, or 'booms', as they were called, cargo handling, battening down the hatches, the risks and the 'holidays', which referred to the bits you could neglect to paint because they were out of sight. He taught me the difference between a spring line and a heaving line, a bowline hitch and a dog's prick. I learnt to fold a knot at the end of a rope to keep it from unravelling, splice a rope and operate the winch that hauled in the big lines and cables.

'Don't get too religious when you're using the hammer,' the bosun chimed in. 'Tap the rust blister off and dab the spot with red oxide. Don't fucking chip through the goddamn railing or the fuckin' thing will fall off. And for fuck's sake, don't hammer a hole in the hull. Remember, the hammer taps are for rust blisters, the scraper for scaling paint and the chipping gun for the seriously rusted shit you can't scrape or hammer off.'

The information came at me thick and fast, and the bosun swore at me when I bungled.

As the only young blond boy on board, I was the target of horny men.

'How about visiting my fo'c's'le, Whitey?' one propositioned.

I made it clear I wanted none of it. One pot-bellied AB patted my ass when I walked by him.

'Look, motherfucker,' I growled while indignantly puffing myself up. 'I may be smaller than you, but I'll kick you in the balls if you try that again.'

'Sorry, honey,' he replied with a chuckle. 'It's always worth a try.'

On the weekly fire and boat drill, we couldn't lower the lifeboats, since the winches were frozen with rust. We freaked out.

'If this ship were to go down, we are all fucked,' an AB said.

For two days, we overhauled the lifeboat winches, greased the cables and got the rigs working.

Every morning, my first job was to drop the plumb line into the bilges to check for leaks. I spent the rest of the day chipping and scraping the deck, capstans, railings, blocks and tackle, mast bases, the whole topside except the masts. Then I painted a coat of red oxide primer and two coats of black deck paint. Besides the scraping and painting, I opened the big block and tackle rigs, and smeared them with grease. The job of keeping the salt air from returning an ageing ship back to earth in the form of rust never ended.

While working with the mind-numbing electric chipping gun, which we called the 'hurdy-gurdy', I saw daylight through the hull. I stared at the hole, unsure of what to do.

'Better slap some white lead on that hole, Whitey,' I heard the bosun's raspy voice behind me.

'Tomorrow you can paint it with red oxide primer. We're gonna run into heavy winter weather.'

It didn't occur to me we could be in trouble while crossing this vast ocean in a rust bucket.

Riding the ocean was a special feeling. On deck alone at night in the mid-Atlantic during winter, I watched the waves and glowing white caps. I felt fear and exhilaration as I romanticized being the man at sea from *The Cruel Sea*, *Moby Dick* and other sea classics.

When the sea turned rough, I promptly became seasick. The mere thought of food made me puke.

'Go into the kitchen and get yourself a piece of raw bacon with a string attached to it,' advised an older seaman in earnestness, and I listened attentively. 'Swallow it and then yank it out.'

As I rushed out to puke, although there was nothing left in me, they guffawed behind my back. Their banter irritated me then, but it had a purpose. I was over being sick by the next day when I stood on a pitching and rolling deck on the high seas. I was getting my sea legs. Sometimes the sea was so rough that if you were standing on the deck talking to somebody with your body swaying and keeping balance, you'd be talking to his bellybutton one moment and in the next, he'd be talking to yours.

Sparks chose this time, when the waves battered the hull, to tell us that a Liberty ship off the coast of Nova Scotia was radioing distress calls. Its single engine had died, and it was in danger of capsizing. The next morning, he announced, the vessel had indeed sunk during the night, but everyone scrambled into lifeboats and was rescued by another Liberty that was luckily close by and responded to their SOS. This was cheery news compared to the other stories the old seamen narrated.

'Those fuckin' Liberties!' the bosun said as he shook his head. 'Wouldn't sail on one if they paid me double overtime.'

These stories of ships going under made me fear for our own safety. *Would the cargo ship's fragile rust-pocked skin last the voyage?*

One night I dreamt of being aboard a ship of fools abandoned at sea. When I woke, the waves boomed as they smashed against the bulkhead, and the four life jackets I had wedged between me and the sides of the bunk to keep me from rolling over the edge had loosened. The jerk-off curtain that afforded privacy when pulled across fluttered with each starboard roll. Seconds later, the massive copper propellers chopped through the air, sending a scary shudder from stern to stem. The ship lurched, and two of the jackets popped from the bunk and slid across the crazily tilted floor.

I muttered profanities under my breath, careful not to wake up Pineapple asleep in the next bunk. I needn't have bothered, since he could sleep through a typhoon. The radium dial of my cheap watch read quarter-to-six. Another two hours before my shift started. Neither could I doze, nor could I stay in my bunk.

I went to the head and took a leak without watering my feet. It's a question of rhythm, but sometimes the sea likes to play jokes on you. After splashing cool water on my face from the spring-loaded faucet over the round steel sink, I staggered out. Steadying myself with both hands on the railings lining the companionway and climbing the ladder to the upper deck was fun. Take a step, stop and hang on; another step, stop and hold on. No one was in the galley at that hour. The cooks had cooked nothing for the second day in a row. It was impossible to keep a pot steady on the stove in this weather. I slipped off the fridge clamp and took a salami, which the seamen called 'horse-cock', and a cheese sandwich wrapped in wax paper. After sloshing a cup of the strong black brew from the thermos rattling in its secure holder, I drank without scalding my lips.

I sat alone in the brightly lit crew messroom, where the lights were never switched off. Guys were always on duty on the bridge and in the engine room. I asked myself for the umpteenth time: *What the fuck am I doing here on this tin can in the middle of an insane sea?*

I'd clear 1,000 dollars at the end of this four-week trip, after dues to the SIU, Social Security and taxes. A lot of money. I wouldn't have to ship out again or do any work for a few months. I could even buy a ticket home to India. That is, if we didn't sink into Davy Jones's Locker. I planned my future while listening to the eerie keening of wild wind through the cracks in the door, the intense rhythm of the waves and the pounding of the screws.

After I had slurped the coffee, I made my way to the bridge. The AB's job of steering was much easier with the hydraulics, gears and bearings, compared to wrestling the wheel in the old-time ships, but Cherry still struggled to maintain course in this blow.

'What's up, Whitey?' Cherry asked, his voice loud over the howl of the wind. 'It's so rough you couldn't jerk off?'

I grinned in reply, used to the vulgar talk. The sky was getting brighter and the ocean a mass of whitecaps. I zipped my fleece to the neck as the winter air seeped through old, straining panels.

'Imagine if a supertanker was coming towards us on this same heading,' he said, with a lopsided grin and glanced at the compass. 'Fourteen degrees north-east. Neither we nor they can see fuck-all in the storm, and the radar doesn't work worth a shit. It'll all be over with a big crash, and we don't even have time to get the lifeboats out. And what would be the point in this fuckin' rough sea anyway?'

The weather played on our worst fears, but we derided such talk with sarcastic looks.

'You're one sick puppy,' I commented, while wondering if he spent the whole of his four-hour watch with these morbid thoughts. I gave him a mock salute and stepped out.

It was almost daylight now. When the ship crested another forty-foot swell, the deck swung down. The vessel shuddered as it slid on the trough of the massive wave. I never knew a ship could take such a beating. A big pod of pilot whales breached from the wall of the wave. I yelled, 'Thar she fuckin' blows!' Four guys tottered up the ladder as the boat crested another swell, and the five of us stood on the pitching deck, holding on to the railing and drinking in the sight of these sleek whales cruising alongside our wallowing hulk in the light of the dawn. After they sped away, I went below to get ready for my shift.

Steaming along at a measly twelve knots, we still had nine days and nights to reach Southampton. Sometimes, it appeared as if we were going backwards. The vast ocean liner, *Queen Elizabeth II*, sailed past on her outward trip from England to New York. Six days later, we were in the grip of howling winds and pounding waves, sometimes making only sixteen kilometres in a whole day, when *Queen Elizabeth* passed us again, this time on her return journey. As no doubt the others did, I fantasized about travelling on a fancy ship with good food, booze, women and white sheets on a springy mattress.

The engines throbbed through the deck plates and a cold sun lit the rigging, the capstan heads and the rusty railing. Being a sailor was fun at first, but now I had enough of endless expanses of ocean and monotonous work. Memories of fishing in Hoosick and hunting in Wyoming kept me going as we rolled with the swells. I sang loudly whatever took my fancy, maybe a Presley or Dylan song, The Beatles or even The Kingston Trio.

I come on the sloop John B,
My grandfather and me,
' round Nassau town we did roam,
Drinkin' all night,
Got into a fight,
I feel so broke up,
I want to go home ...

After work, I re-read my Steinbeck or Hemingway books or watched the inevitable game of five-card stud poker in the messroom. I wasn't tempted to play, as there was no doubt I'd have been skunked. The second mate had a stash of booze, which he sold for a profit. But the non-stop tossing and dipping of the ship wasn't conducive to getting even woozier.

Conversations were predictable. Women featured a lot in them. One guy brought up the subject of women officers and crew serving on Swedish and Norwegian ships, and wondered why American, French and Spanish ships didn't allow women.

'There'd be chaos,' replied another.

The others nodded in agreement. Then came tales about the infamous mythical Joe de Grinder, that smooth-talking sonofabitch back home who seduced wives and lovers of seamen while they were away. Howlin' Wolf's *Back Door Man*, released a year earlier, referred to this Joe. The other topics were union politics and how to avoid paying union dues.

'Tell them you're saving for college, Whitey,' advised one chap. 'That sometimes works for you young cunts.'

I tucked this information to use when the time came.

When we finally berthed at Southampton, I accompanied the others ashore. The security guard barely glanced at our ID cards and waved us into the country. It was a relief to walk on solid ground, watch girls and sit in a warm pub. I even appreciated the room-temperature beer that the English of the day preferred. Anything was better than chipping and painting and rolling with the sea. The good-time girls followed us with their eyes. We were in the harbour part of town, where no 'decent' woman could have ventured without being propositioned. As the youngest, I got extra attention and the old sea dogs made oblique jokes at my expense, questioning my virginity. I blushed with embarrassment. To tell the truth, I was indeed an ageing nineteen-year-old virgin.

The pubs closed at 10 p.m. A few shipmates and their girls had wangled their way into a private club. With nothing else to do, the rest of us returned to the ship, which was being loaded with bales of cloth bound for New York. The vessel undocked in the morning and headed into the misty English Channel to cross over to France to pick up our next cargo—wine.

Le Havre had the prettiest prostitutes. For some strange reason, prices for these girls were identical as in Southampton, and I'd later learn, it was the same everywhere—fifteen dollars for all night and seven dollars fifty for a short time.

I watched the others at the bar choose their girls. They looked at the lady of choice and asked, 'OK?', and she replied, 'OK.' That was the most communication they could manage. Or the girl made the first move by looking at you and seductively sucking her finger. When a man and woman paired up, she took a 'short-time towel' from a cupboard next to a stairway, draped it over her arm and led the way up the stairs.

I didn't have the courage to follow my shipmates' example. Instead, I fell in drunken love with the dark-eyed waitress. Sometime later, I woke up and my head spun. *Where am I?* Startled by the gentle breathing on the bed next to me, I was relieved to feel a woman and sank back into a stupor, only to wake up to the din of someone pounding on the door.

'Whitey!' the voice yelled. 'Get the fuck up. We gotta make it back to the ship, NOW!'

The woman sleepily bid me au revoir as I struggled to put my pants on while my head throbbed. We stumbled to the port.

'Didya get any?' one asked with a sly grin.

'Yeah, she was fine!' I said, nodding as if I were experienced. *But was I? Did anything happen last night? Who was the woman? Had I blown the opportunity?* I couldn't remember a goddamn thing.

We steamed into the North Sea to Bremerhaven, Germany, to take a load of stainless steel nuts and bolts for factories back in the States. After the vessel docked, I followed my shipmates to a crowded, noisy saloon. I complimented a girl, who introduced herself as the 'Anita Ekberg of Bremerhaven', on her magnificent tits without being shy and hot around the gills. After experiencing two ports, I felt like a veteran, not pondering any more why the rates were the same everywhere. It was as if these wonderful women belonged to a sex workers' international union.

Our stay in Germany was brief, as we had to report for duty by nightfall. When we berthed at Rotterdam, Holland, the bosun said to me, 'Whitey, you better make sure you watch the mooring lines.

There'll be hell to pay if you don't loosen and tighten the lines with the tide and current.' This meant I was on gangway watch, not only checking the ropes tied to the berth but also the papers of any stranger who boarded the ship. The Dutch longshoremen loaded the holds with Heineken beer. A few seamen colluded with them and reported several crates as 'damaged'. We stashed them under a pile of tarp to enjoy later, without paying the second mate's extortionist price.

That night, when my watch was over, a group of us visited The Hague. After three hours of hitting the bars and gaping at the sexy girls on display in the windows, I settled on a cosy bar stool, listening to rock 'n' roll music playing on the jukebox while following the young lady bartender with attentive but zonked eyes.

My buddies had disappeared and I was alone. When *Ahab the Arab* by Ray Stevens came on, this girl's hips swayed.

'This is a crazy song, huh?' I asked her and winked.

She nodded and smiled as she cleaned the counter.

Once business slowed at midnight, the girl asked if I'd come behind the bar and help her tap a new keg of beer. Crouching next to her and inhaling her wonderful smell, I almost keeled over. I caught her eyes and hoped mine were overflowing with meaning.

'Will you join me for a drink?' I asked.

She winked at me, filling both our glasses from the keg with foamy brew. Ray Charles was singing *I Can't Stop Loving You*. Perfect timing.

Elena spoke English with a lilting accent. She was hoping to start college with the salary and tips she was earning, and her boyfriend was working on an oil rig somewhere far away. It wasn't fun for a country girl to be stuck in the city in winter, she said. I told her about Hoosick and Wyoming. She liked my stories, and I insisted on buying her another drink.

When she locked up, Elena took me to her apartment. She giggled at my clumsiness and turned it into a crazy tickling match. We ended up on the floor, tearing at each other's clothes. With a magician's flourish and a cute grin, she produced a rubber. 'Zee French Leather,' she called it. That wondrous night in Holland, I became one of the boys. The next morning, I swaggered aboard and joked like a sea dog.

Our European jaunt was over and the loaded ship headed west. It was back to scraping and painting with cold and numb fingers. When the weather eased and the ocean was flat, I swung on a bosun's chair, a strip of wood with two strands of heavy rope, over the water, and scrubbed and repainted the name SS JOHN C across the stern. By the time we docked in Brooklyn two weeks later, I had scraped and painted the entire 400-foot-long steel-plated deck.

Onshore, I went through the union rigmarole, pleading my case about being a poor student who needed all the money he could get to rejoin college. The group of dues collectors looked at each other, and one gave a subtle nod.

'OK, Whitey,' another said. 'We'll let you off easy this time.'

I received my pay in cash, having no bank account, and headed to Elly's apartment. After being poor for so long, I felt rich to have a stash again.

I was the centre of attention, regaling Elly, Dugald and their dinner guests with my adventures as a seaman, minus the part about women, of course. It felt great to be within the warm family fold again.

With money to burn, I lost sight of my goal of returning to India. Instead, I sought the good things in life. I wandered through book and record stores in Greenwich Village by day, and grooved on folk and protest songs by Dylan and Baez wannabes in coffee houses by evening. I caught a bus to Atlantic City in Jersey to meet Phil, a school friend who ran a fitness club. Every morning, his class met on the beach to exercise. I hadn't worked out until that day. Between the huffing and puffing, I became acquainted with two of his students, Connie and Beth. I bought a 1956 Ford for 250 dollars from a used-car dealer, and a record player and a stack of records in the neighbourhood music store. I convinced my new friends to travel with me to Hoosick.

After the girls got over their astonishment at the immense size of the house, they helped me clean the twenty-two rooms. We baked bread and collected raspberries to make a pie. At the village-store-cum-post-office, we were buying ice cream when we ran into a neighbour, who remembered me as the little snake boy. He gifted us a jar of honey from his hives, complete with chunks of honeycomb.

The girls and I fished in the Hoosac River, but the neighbours told us not to eat the fish because an upstream tannery polluted the water, one of my first personal encounters with the world being ruined. In the evenings we drank cider, ate home-made goodies and listened to the pile of records. And then it was time to drop Connie and Beth at the Greyhound bus stop, so they could return to Atlantic City.

In March 1963, after selling the car in the nearby town of Hoosick Falls, I caught a Greyhound to Wollaston to bid adieu to the family, and from there to New York to see Elly and Dugald one last time. Back in Philly, I returned to the union hall looking for a job.

18

SEASONED SEAMAN

That Romance Run—Phew!

'I F YOU NEED A job, come early tomorrow morning,' said Joe softly to me before closing up one evening.

After spending the night at a seedy motel nearby, I showed up at the union hall earlier than anyone else. The *Alcoa Pilgrim*, a cargo carrier belonging to an aluminium company, was taking heavy machinery and used cars to Iran and then, they told me, to India. What a stroke of luck! I signed on as an ordinary seaman, which paid less than my previous job as a deck maintenance man, but the work was the same—chipping and painting the ship.

Spring in the Atlantic wasn't as turbulent as the winter crossing. I was happy singing and working on the deck, even though the voyage was monotonous. The seascape was always the same, day in and day out, from horizon to horizon. The occasional booby offered a diversion, but otherwise, I entertained myself. Gibraltar brought memories of being with my mother and two sisters on the SS *Independence* a dozen years ago. We steamed through the calm Mediterranean waters for twenty-four hours and arrived at Port Said, Egypt. A pilot came aboard not only to guide us through the Suez Canal but also to navigate through the many shallow reefs and submerged islands across the Red Sea. We sailed close to land, passing sand dunes, date palms, camels, sailboats and fishermen along the banks. I luxuriated in the heat and took off my shirt while working. The pilot disembarked at Djibouti and the ship entered the Arabian Sea. We chugged north-east, hugging the coasts of Yemen and Oman, and turned into the Persian Gulf, heading for Bandar Shahpur, now known as Bandar Imam Khomeini, Iran.

We approached the Iranian port, a sleepy village with most of the action at the harbour. No whorehouses and bars, not even speakeasies in this backwater, said the experienced seamen. After many days of being ship-bound, my body had become used to the unsteadiness of the sea. I took a few wobbly steps on solid ground when we docked. The tropical heat reminded me of India, and the thought of arriving home soon added lightness to my step. A group of us sailors made for a small café on stilts over the water that advertised cold beer. A dented jukebox filled with 45 rpm records from the '50s took American quarters, and I selected a few soppy ones such as *Only You* by The Platters and the sole Jerry Lee Lewis song, *Great Balls of Fire*. I felt contentment in the simple pleasures of sipping beer, listening to music and watching mudskippers with gorgeous dorsal fins demonstrating to each other on the mudbanks below.

The mid-afternoon heat peaked at fifty degrees Celsius, unlike anything we had experienced. Back on the *Pilgrim*, we turned on the fire hoses and sprayed each other with seawater. The respite was brief as the hot air wicked the skin dry within seconds. A consignment of open trailers for monster earth-moving machines stood on the deck. Since they were to be unloaded days later in Karachi, Pakistan, we plugged the holes in one and filled it with water, turning it into a swimming pool. We would have soaked through the worst of the heat, but the worries of sunburn and dehydration drove us out.

The longshoremen took two days to remove the cars that were tightly arranged in the holds below the decks. We'd have helped them and sped up the process so we could leave this furnace of a port soon, but union rules forbade us. With nowhere to go and nothing else to do, I watched the unloading from the deck, when the sound of a car ignition followed by a scream reverberated from the hold. A local longshoreman had foolishly started a vehicle and crushed a fellow worker against the bulkhead. A cacophony of shouts and yells rang between the stevedores in the hold and the seamen on the deck. The bosun winched a cot down, on which they placed the injured man. His shirt was soaked with blood, and he moaned in agony as they carried him down the gangway. We never learnt if he survived. The unfortunate accident and the heat made for a miserable stop.

The fo'c'sles were like ovens. Lying bare-bodied on the deck after dark offered no relief. I overheard my shipmates chat about air-conditioned European ships and, predictably, one started talking about the women crew.

'There'd be chaos!' was the chorused rejoinder.

I imagined every crew on every ship had the same conversation.

We were impatient to leave, but our departure was delayed further. An AB suffered a heat stroke and had to be evacuated to a hospital. Later, we heard he had been flown back home. As we left the port and chugged into the Arabian Sea, the cool breeze was a blessing. Our next stop at Karachi, Pakistan, had no beer joints where we could kill time. The others might have felt the lack keenly, but I was buoyant with a rising tide of anticipation. Bombay was a short skip away. In my rusty Hindi, I asked for directions to a mithai shop, where I bought a box of sweets as a gift for the family.

I was confused when a shipmate said we were returning to the States.

'Aren't we going to Bombay?' I enquired.

'Karachi is the last stop,' he replied. 'We now steam straight back to Philly.'

The display board at the union hall said the *Pilgrim* was 'going to India', but whoever had typed it didn't know the difference between Pakistan and India. I considered jumping ship and travelling overland, but I knew no one in Karachi who'd help me. I was despondent for three days until I consoled myself that there would be other opportunities. The box of sweets helped to raise my spirits too.

The vessel retraced the outward voyage back to Philly. I didn't take a break in New York or Hoosick but waited for the display board in the union hall to list a ship to India.

I was chatting with another seaman when an engineer slapped my back.

'Whitey, take the *Pilgrim*. It's going on the Romance Run.'

The vessel I had just been on wanted a crew messman for a South American trip.

'I don't want to be a messman.'

'You don't know what you are missing. Sweet women, good rum.'

Another older guy listening to our conversation joined in, 'Yeah, Whitey, sign up. If I were you, I wouldn't be standing around with my thumb up my ass.'

I preferred being alone on deck, even if it was only to scrape and paint. The galleys were hot and claustrophobic, while the pervasive smell of food hung heavy in the air. It was a brief trip and not a transoceanic voyage. A messman would have plenty of free time between meals, so working a few hours below deck wouldn't kill me. Besides, no ships were bound for India. This was a chance to earn money and sample the attractions.

I caught the *Pilgrim* at Baltimore harbour and joined the ordinary seaman on bow watch as we wended our way through the Chesapeake Bay at night. The ship manoeuvred around boats, sounding the horn often to warn other watercraft. The receding city lights made for a pretty sight. Once we swung south along the east coast of the States, my work as a messman began.

I set the dining tables for the twenty crew members three times a day, dampening the tablecloth to keep the plates and silverware from sliding across the table. Memorizing the orders was a particular challenge at breakfast, with its choice of eggs or pancakes, bacon or sausage. Once the cooks readied the dishes, I served one or two men at a time in the beginning, much to their irritation. Balancing plates piled with food while the vessel tilted and swayed seemed an impossible task at first. Before the end of the trip, I carried four at once. The job was no different from a waiter's at a restaurant, except for the rolling seas.

The crew members ate and left within half an hour with a few stragglers, usually the black gang from the engine room. Besides the frantic activity at mealtimes, being the messman wasn't hard work.

I was up on deck a lot, smoking, enjoying the warm breeze and getting a tan. I was glad not to be the pantryman with the never-ending job of doing the dishes.

After sailing around the Florida Keys and Dry Tortugas, we crossed the Caribbean Sea, arriving in Veracruz, Mexico, to take a shipment of asbestos pipes for an oil line in Venezuela. The longshoremen would spend fourteen days, an unusually long stopover in port for these merchant ships, to load the fragile cargo. The chief mate sent word through the bosun that we could stay ashore.

'Make sure you get back here in ten days,' said the bosun.

It was that simple. Heeding the old-timers' warnings of syphilis and gonorrhoea, I collected a supply of rubbers from the ship's dispensary and split. With two voyages under my belt, I was more self-assured and did my own thing instead of being part of a group.

The noise, smells and chaos of Mexico contrasted sharply with the States. I passed a souvenir shop where a pretty saleswoman was arranging the window display. When she glanced at me, I winked and walked on until I heard a soft whistle. The dark-eyed lady crooked her finger.

'*Senorita*, ¿cómo se llama?' I asked with a smile.

She looked surprised.

'Josefina,' she replied and unleashed a torrent of words.

A look at my uncomprehending face made her giggle. I had exhausted my knowledge of the language.

'I'm Rom,' I said in English. 'Do you know a place where I can get a room?'

I formed a peak with my hands, expecting a hotel recommendation.

'You stay with me.'

I was surprised by her offer, but gladly accepted. It was three in the afternoon. She gestured at her watch and asked me to return at five, when she closed. I wandered the streets in the neighbourhood, whiling away the time. After she locked the shop, I followed her to her first-floor apartment, which she shared with her mother. The older lady returned my greeting and made herself scarce. When Josefina showed me to her room, I was taken aback. I had assumed she had a spare room to rent. It hadn't occurred to me she might be a whore.

That evening, we sat on the beach, sipping a beer and eating seafood like two lovers. She told me about herself with actions more than words. She and her mother had fled Cuba in 1959, four years earlier, when Fidel Castro and Che Guevara had ousted the America-supported dictator Fulgencio Batista. Josefina's description of the horrific events during the revolution made me wonder how, as ignorant kids, we had been so enamoured of these machismo heroes, thinking they were Robin Hoods.

I became Josefina's Spanish teaching project. Putting two sexually attracted people together who can't communicate with words is the best way to learn a language. An entrepreneur could give the staid old Berlitz language school stiff competition with 'Learn Spanish with the senorita of your dreams.'

While Josefina was at work, I sauntered through the by-lanes near the port, where I met Jaime, a friendly young fisherman, mending his net. As with Josefina, using a combination of my little Spanish, their little English and sign language, I arranged to fish with him and his dad. The following morning, we set off in their wooden skiff with a stuttering old Evinrude outboard motor. They crossed themselves, muttered a brief prayer and spat on the mullet baits before chucking their hand lines over the side. I used a casting rod that Jaime lent, but I couldn't compete with the guys. They pulled in twice as many kingfish and bonito. I reeled in a big flopping fish, which sent my heart racing. Sometimes only a head, neatly cut off and still snapping, was left on the hook.

'Tiburon [shark],' Jaime said with a shrug.

When I returned to Josefina's apartment in the evening, her polite mother took the fish to the kitchen, while Josefina, holding her nose, led me into the bathroom. She made me shower fully dressed. 'I'm not going to wash your stinky clothes,' she gestured. Then she stripped me and gave me a loofah scrubbing that turned my skin a high pink. The first time she tried to douse me with some cloying, sweet-smelling eau de toilette, I said in my broken Spanish I didn't want to smell like a senorita. She giggled and sprinkled it anyway. She blasted fast Cubano music at top volume on her plastic transistor radio, which covered the sounds of our lovemaking. On especially good fishing days, I carried big king mackerel to the *Pilgrim* and hung them up in the walk-in reefer box.

Then this sweet time in Veracruz was over. Josefina and I had tears in our eyes when she walked me to the dock. I gifted her a silk scarf bought on my solo wanderings and gave her a last hug as the seamen hooted from the bow of the ship.

'Bring her along, Whitey,' one shouted, and another added, 'And her seester too.'

They defused the tanginess of the moment. I winked, tucked a wad of cash in her hand, and said, '*Hasta luego* [See you later].' Josefina grinned in response.

The sea was calm, and the weather hot and wonderful on the run to Venezuela. A messman's job wasn't so bad, after all. I was on deck every chance I got, watching flying fish skimming over the glassy water surface. Dolphins cruised on the bow wave and cavorted like kids on a playground. At Puerto Cabello, Venezuela, a customs agent came aboard with two young soldiers armed with submachine guns. They remained on duty at the gangway, preventing anybody other than the ship's crew or longshoremen from entering the ship. I noticed graffiti all over the wharf, declaring 'Viva Romulo'. The Venezuelan President was a namesake, Rómulo Betancourt. Since unloading the pipes would take as long as loading them had, the first mate told the crew to go ashore.

I found a homely place called the Mar y Sol, built on stilts over the lapping waves of the Caribbean. But I couldn't possibly stay there alone, and prostitution was illegal within city limits. A rattling taxi drove me to La Paradisi, a well-known dance hall at the edge of town, which my shipmates had talked about.

Nursing a bottle of chilled Cerveza Polar, I watched girls dancing with each other in the almost empty room. To my utter amazement, one had a red-tailed boa constrictor around her slender neck, and my eyes stayed glued to her graceful, swaying hips, brown arms and lovely breasts. I tried to catch her eye, but she didn't look my way, lost as she was in the rhythm. After draining the beer, I joined her on the dance floor.

'*Buenas tardes* [Good afternoon], *senorita* ,' I said. 'I, too, like snakes.'

'It's my baby,' she replied in English with a smile. 'Dance with me.'

She draped a coil of the boa around my neck as her body swayed to the music. I needed no invitation.

'¿*Cómo se llama*?' I asked.

'Carmelita, I'm from Colombia,' she replied in English.

Careful not to squash the snake, which stayed immobile around our necks, we danced close, and Carmelita's gorgeous eyes, glistening red lips and the sweet frangipani perfume intoxicated me. After the dance, while sharing a beer with her, she agreed to keep me company during my stay.

We walked to her apartment, settled the boa in its box and took a taxi to my room over the water. Over the following days, we hiked through the beautiful countryside and picnicked on tortillas, enchiladas and fish or chicken burritos we bought from a café next door to Mar y Sol. I continued to learn Spanish, but Carmelita was more interested in learning English as she had plans to travel to Estados Unidos (the States), a mecca for many South Americans.

On my last day in Puerto Cabello, I paid her for those wonderful days and nights, and gifted her a silver necklace I had bought in Veracruz. It had a pre-Columbian lapis lazuli bead carved in the shape of a half-bird-half-reptile creature. We knew we'd never see each other again, and I was sorry to leave her.

As the now-empty ship made its way to San Juan, Puerto Rico, to take on a consignment of sugar, we sealed the cracks and holes in the wooden plank-lined holds. Even though I was only a messman, the chief mate offered time-and-a-half overtime if I worked with the crew from dawn until late into the night, between mealtimes, for two days.

I went ashore in San Juan wondering how to celebrate my twentieth birthday.

'*Una Cerveza Corona por favor* [A Corona beer, please].' I ordered at a bar on the main drag.

The bartender set an opened cold bottle on the counter.

As I lifted it to my mouth, I heard, '*Salud. Usted habla español* [Cheers. Do you speak Spanish]?' A beautiful young Black woman with mesmerizing light green eyes seated nearby raised her drink and smiled.

'*Un poquito* [A little],' I replied, grinning.

I took that as an invitation and went over to her table.

'Will you help me celebrate my birthday?' I asked.

'Of course ... At my place.'

Unfortunately, I had to report to work early the next morning. It didn't take long for a huge vacuum cleaner-like device to fill the holds with sugar. Waking up beside this smooth, dark-skinned girl tempted me to jump ship. But I dragged myself to port, and we returned to the States to Mobile, Alabama. My Romance Run had ended.

The crew got air tickets to Baltimore, since we had boarded the *Pilgrim* there. I caught a shuttle bus from the pier to the Mobile airport, where I was shaken by the signs on bathroom doors—Men, Women, Coloured. Once again, the racism in my country of birth disgusted me.

At the counter, I re-routed my ticket via Lexington, Kentucky, to see Alice, whom I had dated briefly in Kodai. She was a university student and invited me to the house she shared with three other girls. All my sexual experiences had been with prostitutes, and I had to learn how to flirt with a college girl. At a drive-in movie, we made out passionately in her car. The rest of the time we hung out with her friends. Later, she said a roommate had asked her, 'Who's that hunk?' Or she knew how to fan a man's ego. Hearing a young woman refer to me as a 'hunk' was a tremendous confidence booster. I felt older and wiser than my years.

I returned to the Philly union hall every day looking for an India-bound ship. This time I confided in some veteran seamen of my plans.

'Go to Port Everglades in Florida,' advised one. 'Ships carrying wheat frequently leave for India from there.'

'All you gotta do to jump ship,' another counselled, 'is furnish a doctor's certificate saying you are in no condition to work.'

It would be a cinch to get that piece of paper in Bombay.

As I learned later, a grand US aid scheme called PL-480, or Food for Peace, sold surplus grain to poor countries. India, suffering from severe food shortages and unstable prices, paid for the imports in rupees, money that the States then gave to the Indian government as loans. The rice-eating nation began to eat more wheat, since it was now readily available through the countrywide network of subsidized ration shops.

But the programme was not without controversy, with accusations of government reliance on imports rather than encouraging domestic production.

At that time, however, all I cared about was that one of those grain ships would carry another import—me. Grabbing my old canvas duffle bag of possessions, I headed for the highway. It took eight different uneventful rides and two full days of hitchhiking to cover the nearly 2,100 kilometres to Miami. I looked like a college student going home, so people were helpful.

Before setting off halfway around the world, I had to do one last thing. I had to make good on a promise to myself—meet the world's most famous snakeman, Bill Haast, at the Miami Serpentarium.

19

MIAMI SERPENTARIUM

Working for the Man

O N MY SECOND DAY on the road, a salesman picked me up in
   Georgia on his way to Key West. South of Miami, a gigantic
white concrete cobra came into view. As we drew closer, we gawked
at its dramatic size, towering over US 1 with its forked tongue pointed
at the roaring traffic. The salesman dropped me right below the hooded
snake, at the entrance of the Miami Serpentarium.

On that weekday, the serpentarium's gift shop was empty. I paid for
a ticket and chatted with Bruce, the young man behind the counter,
telling him of my interest in snakes.

'Could I meet Bill Haast, please?' I asked.

'Bill is very busy,' he replied. 'He doesn't meet anyone without an
appointment.'

My heart sank.

'I don't suppose he would remember inviting me to visit,' I pleaded.
'I'm from India, and I'm on my way to catch a ship home.'

Bruce wouldn't budge.

I wandered around the spic-and-span grounds, gazing at the captive
crocodiles and alligators, snakes and tortoises. Iguanas free-ranged across
the paths and on the hedges. Through hidden speakers, a woman's
voice announced that the venom extraction demonstration was about to

begin. I hurried over to join the visitors, who materialized from other parts of the park.

In front of the laboratory, Bill arranged several boxes of snakes on a table-high wall. In white slacks and a bush shirt, the immediately recognizable figure was shorter and more intimidating than I had imagined. Thick-framed glasses obscured his eyes. An elegantly dressed lady, who I guessed was Clarita Haast, introduced the show as Bill deposited a golden African Cape cobra on a board. It stood tall and beautiful with its hood spread, staring at him. He waved his right hand to focus its attention and jerked his hand away when it struck. The crowd inhaled as Clarita's voice grew louder, building the tension as the snake lunged again. It was a thrilling performance. Through it all, Bill concentrated on the cobra and remained calm, seemingly unaware of his wife or the crowd.

'Mr Haast, aren't you afraid it might bite?' shouted someone from the audience.

'Of course not,' replied Clarita. 'He's done this thousands of times.'

'Mr Haast, which is the most dangerous snake?' asked another.

'The taipan is the most venomous, but the cobra kills the most people,' Clarita replied.

Bill showed no sign of having heard the questions or replies. He kept his head bowed and had eyes only for the snake.

'Is he deaf?' asked a man standing next to me.

'He isn't. He has to concentrate on what he's doing.'

At the finale, while the cobra stared at his moving hand, Bill slowly reached with his left hand behind its head and swiftly grabbed it around the neck. Everyone in the audience gasped in unison. He tucked the front part of its long body under his arm. For the first time, I noticed his assistant, a young man also dressed in white, who stepped forward to hold the writhing sinuous body. When Bill brought the now-open-mouthed snake to a wine-glass-shaped beaker fixed to a stand, it latched on with a vengeance to the elastic material covering the container, and thick, yellowish venom trickled from both fangs.

'Golden drops of death,' said Clarita. 'That's enough venom to kill all of us.'

After the demonstration, Bill returned the cobra to its box and strode into his lab before I could catch his eye. With hundreds of visitors thronging the serpentarium every day, he knew how to avoid people.

At the gift shop, I badgered Bruce once more about meeting Bill.

'Do you want a job?' he asked in reply. 'The guy who does the tours quit yesterday.'

'Yes, I'm interested,' I stuttered.

He informed Clarita on the intercom and directed me to her office. Luckily, I was presentable, my shoes and T-shirt were new, and the frayed jeans were clean.

Clarita was even more glamorous indoors. Her honey-coloured hair was coiffed in layers, and her dress looked expensive. She had been a model after becoming Miss Guatemala and was voted one of Miami's 'Ten Best-Dressed Women'. I told her of my lifelong interest in snakes, my willingness to work hard and mentioned the exchange of letters with Bill.

'We'll try you out,' she said. 'If you do well, your salary will be sixty-two dollars fifty a week.'

I swallowed. That was a steep pay cut from what I made as a seaman. But this—working with snakes and Bill—was the chance of a lifetime.

'Sure,' I replied feebly, unable to believe my luck.

The plan of catching a ship to India was now on hold. That night, after I checked in to the Mariner Motel, a cheap place close to the serpentarium, I feasted on a sirloin steak with a side order of mushrooms and mashed potatoes. It had been days since I had a proper meal, and I felt like celebrating.

I walked to work at seven the next morning. Automobiles zipped down the highway and the tropical sun reminded me of Bombay. The prospect of finally working in my chosen profession was exciting. I wouldn't miss the sea, but the low salary concerned me. I was lost in my thoughts when a jogger overtook me. It was my new boss, the fifty-three-year-old Bill, running to work, while Clarita drove a Cadillac. At the serpentarium, I met the two other employees who were my age—Rick Anderson and Heyward Clamp—and they briefed me on the daily routine. Besides giving the guided tour, I would feed the animals and clean the grounds.

We cleaned the outdoor enclosures and paths of cigarette butts, candy wrappers and reptile poop, and I got an up-close look at rhinoceros iguanas, alligators, and the big Nile and American crocodiles. From the way Bill conducted himself, I knew he expected us to work hard and keep the place spic and span. Then we moved indoors to clean the snake cages, which held fifty species, from African puff adders and Australian tiger snakes to Indian cobras, Japanese habus and European vipers. This was the first time I saw most of them in the flesh.

Bill used a hook to remove each snake from its cage, after which we scooped up the old sawdust and spread a fresh layer of bedding. Ditmars's book had pictures of snake-handling tools with large L-shaped hooks at the end. Until then, I had made do with sticks and by bending wire coat hangers. As an apprentice snakeman, I resolved to procure a professional snake hook for myself as soon as possible.

I accompanied Rick to the local supermarket for baskets of overripe tomatoes and bruised lettuce. We also bought chicken necks for juvenile gators and whole frozen chickens, feathers and all, for the big crocs.

'You'd better get yourself some whites to wear,' said Rick. 'The boss likes that. We even use white shoe polish on our sneakers.'

A white uniform seemed impractical for the job. But if that was the way Bill liked it, I wasn't going to quibble. On our return, we chopped the produce into bite-sized pieces for the giant Aldabra and Galapagos tortoises and rhinoceros and green iguanas.

'Leave some tomatoes whole,' Rick said. 'The giant tortoises like to squash them in their big mouths.'

The gates of the serpentarium opened at 9 o'clock. I followed Rick as he led the first group of visitors on a tour around the enclosures. In two days, I was to conduct tours by myself, so I memorized his script—iguanas were called 'bamboo chicken' in Central America, reticulated pythons grew to nearly thirty feet and occasionally ate people, alligators were found only in the States and China. It wasn't hard, since I knew most of it from years of reading. He finished half an hour later by letting the tourists hold a beautiful six-foot black indigo snake. I loved its calm, gentle nature. I would learn that even wild indigos had a similar temperament. Clarita took over the end of the tour when her husband extracted venom from snakes.

Since kraits, vipers and rattlesnakes don't raise their heads like cobras, Bill pinned their heads with a hook and gripped their necks without much ado. But with cobras, and even king cobras, he performed the sleight-of-hand manoeuvre I had witnessed the previous day, and it never failed to excite the audience.

Bill had formulated a mixture of eggs, ground meat and vitamins as snake feed, a recipe that hadn't changed since he replied to my letter six years ago, which he loaded into a converted caulking gun. After the extractions, he inserted the feeding gun's plastic tube, lubricated with water, down the snake's throat, and Heyward squeezed the handle half a dozen times. That provided enough nutrition to last a week until the next extraction.

I got carried away watching them feed snakes when Clarita's voice came through the speakers.

'Rom, there's iguana BM [bowel movement] all over the path here.'

Mortified, I searched for the offensive turds and wiped the tiles clean with a piece of old newspaper.

After work that evening, Clarita called me to her office.

'Rom, you seem like a hard-working guy,' she said. 'Keep it up, and we'll give you the job.'

I was relieved she didn't hold the wayward iguana poop against me.

After a dozen tours a day for a week, I could deliver the talk while sleepwalking. Only a pretty girl or an intelligent question snapped me awake.

I loved feeding Cookie, the fourteen-foot overweight Nile crocodile. Not only was his size impressive, but so was the gleam in his eye when he knew food was on its way. He tracked my progress around his enclosure wall with, I imagined, the alertness of his wild relatives in the Mara River, Kenya. When I leaned over the barrier and dangled a frozen rock-solid chicken, he rose dramatically from the water to snatch it and crunch it like popcorn. Tourists' cameras clicked in chorus. Heyward and I had a fleeting thought that Cookie might attack a tourist stupid enough to lean over and wave a hand. But we didn't change the routine.

About fifteen years later, long after I had left the serpentarium, a visitor balanced his toddler son on Cookie's wall and turned away for a moment when the boy fell into the water. The crocodile, primed to grab chickens, snapped and killed the child in an instant. The father leapt into the enclosure and hit the crocodile's head with his fists to force him to drop the lifeless, mangled body. By then, employees had jumped in and tapped the animal's snout with a stick. Cookie dropped the child, and they escorted the bereaved man away. Heyward said a distraught Bill emptied his 9 mm Mauser into Cookie's head. For no fault of his, the crocodile paid with his life. This incident was always at the back of my mind when I worked with my own captive crocodiles years later. I didn't want to create a stupid situation that put tourist lives at risk.

With the meagre paycheque, I couldn't afford to stay at the motel any longer. I scanned the classifieds in the newspapers and scouted for places to rent, but either the neighbourhood was rough, the place filthy or the price outside my modest means. Both Rick and Bruce lived with their folks in Coral Gables, so I discussed my options with Heyward, who rented a one-bedroom apartment at the back of the serp. The Haasts had lived there years ago while the facility was being built and had since moved to more palatial digs about a mile away. Heyward suggested I move in with him and pay half the monthly rent of one hundred dollars. The living room became my bedroom and the couch my bed. This was the start of my lifelong friendship with this soft-spoken snakeman from South Carolina. His library of books included *Venomous Animals and Their Venoms* edited by Wolfgang Bücherl and Eleanor E. Buckley, and *Bibliography of Snake Venoms and Venomous Snakes* by Findlay Ewing Russell. After work every evening, I opened a can of beer and settled down with a book from his library. I had a lot to learn.

If I was to become a professional snakeman, I needed professional tools. Bill's snake hooks didn't have a manufacturer's address, so I sought Heyward's help in buying one.

'We make our own, Rom,' he replied. 'Bill's are made from golf clubs. Buy a grass whip and bring it to me.'

Later, I watched him unscrew the blade and bend the tapered end of the shaft to form an L. For decades afterwards, I used converted grass whips and golf clubs as snake hooks. It was only in the 2000s that I bought my first off-the-shelf hook.

Clarita gave me a permanent position, but I had still not exchanged more than a word or two with Bill. He had the uncanny ability to tell when we were taking it easy. When one of us leaned on the rake or took a smoke break, he appeared out of nowhere to ask if all our work was done. Heyward and I began reverentially referring to him as God. The best days were when there were few tourists and we worked with Bill getting cages ready for new arrivals or shifting snakes around to his specifications. Watching him in action was fascinating but also frustrating, since he was a man of few words.

Once, Bill's skin turned a shade of orange. Even I could see his unusual colour despite my colour blindness. Heyward somehow ferreted out the cause. Bill was on a special diet—drinking carrot juice and eating boiled carrots three times a day. This fad lasted a few days before another, a protein-only diet, took hold. I became conscious of the extreme lengths he went to stay healthy. He worked out, practised yoga, and as I discovered on my first day on the job, jogged to and from work daily. He never drank or smoked. We envied his health and energy, but weren't tempted to emulate him.

By the time I started working for him, Bill had already survived at least eighty venomous snakebites. He claimed the secret of his survival was immunity. He had been injecting himself with a diluted mixture of the venoms from the Indian cobra and American coral snake, from as far back as the early 1950s, ignoring doctors' warnings that his kidneys and liver could get damaged. Academic and medical experts had nicknamed him 'Wild Bill' because of his experiments. He also touted the use of snake venom in treating multiple sclerosis and other muscle-degenerating diseases, which the Food and Drug Administration disavowed.

Though he generally took the precaution of getting to a hospital after a bite, he was sure he'd be fine, since he thought his blood had a high antibody titre against neurotoxic snake venom. Not only did he survive these bites, but his blood was also used several times to save snakebite victims in the absence of antivenom.

Venomous snakes have a hypodermic-syringe-like apparatus, glands filled with venom in their cheeks and needle-sharp hollow fangs to deliver the lethal fluid. They don't add venom to every bite. In fact, they control the muscles around the glands to adjust the quantity of venom flowing into the victim's body. They can give a fatal dose, none at all or anywhere in between. When a snake doesn't inject any venom, it's called a 'dry bite'.

Of course, when snakes bite, we have no way of knowing how much venom they have injected. But Bill received wide publicity for these cases. If the reptiles had given a sublethal dose or no venom at all, the victims would have survived even without the blood transfusion.

After I had left the serpentarium, there was a dramatic effort to save the life of a snakebite victim. The police closed US 1 to traffic so a chopper could land in front of the serp and pick up Bill. At Homestead Air Force Base (now known as Homestead Air Reserve Base), a waiting fighter jet flew him to an airport in Peru, where a boy had been bitten by a coral snake, against which there was no antivenom. A transfusion of Bill's blood was said to have saved the kid. It earned the States a lot of goodwill at a time of turmoil in Latin America.

Our daily routine was broken occasionally when Bill sent us to the Miami Airport cargo office to collect containers of snakes arriving from around the world. It was not as exciting as it sounds, as we were allowed to only do the paperwork and pick up the consignment. By no means were we to open the boxes.

Once, Heyward and I had to clear a shipment from the famous east African snake hunter C.J.P. Ionides. A large tin box with its lid soldered shut and punched full of holes had a warning label pasted on its side: DANGER! BLACK MAMBAS! DO NOT OPEN! The suspicious customs officers wanted us to prove the consignment didn't have contraband.

'You guys could be smuggling diamonds from Africa,' they sneered.

Heyward invited them, in his South Carolinian drawl, to open the container and see for themselves.

They declined and cleared the shipment.

At the serp, Bill cut the top of the tin with a can opener and bent the lid. A slaty grey snake shot up from the dark interior. Startled, we jumped back, but Bill was unflappable. The black mamba stood three feet high and spread a slight hood. No wonder he didn't allow us inexperienced kids to open these shipments with venomous snakes. He slid the seven-foot snake from the box with a hook on to the ground as we admired its sleek magnificence.

'Keep an eye on the tin,' commanded Bill, as he transferred the mamba to its new cage. 'Could be others out of their bags.'

Reluctantly, we tore our eyes from the snake to watch the container, but no other snakes slithered out. He lifted two bulging bags, each holding a six-foot-long black mamba. The escapee's empty bag was at the bottom.

On another occasion, we returned from the customs office with two large wooden boxes that had arrived from Thailand. On opening them, we discovered an unholy mess. The consignment of a hundred Thai cobras, luckily not the spitting kind, fifty in each box, had been packed in fishnet bags. The holes were wide enough for the smaller cobras to stick their heads and necks through, and many were stuck as firmly as fish in a gill net. A few had died, and stank. Bill reached past the gasping heads to cut the strings without getting bitten. Perhaps the poor snakes were too exhausted to bother.

The serpentarium, being a popular tourist spot, attracted people from all walks of life, from tourists looking for entertainment to celebrities. One visitor was Scott McVay, who worked with the famous dolphin man John Lilly and would later record the songs of male humpback whales. We had a good chat about cetaceans and reptiles.

'You don't like people much, do you, Rom?' McVay asked during a lull in the conversation.

I was taken aback and didn't know how to react. Perhaps I was becoming like Bill, which explained my continuing lack of success in dating girls.

Tongue-tied Heyward was worse than me, so I sought the advice of Bruce, who was a veritable Casanova in comparison. He confessed to masquerading as a photographer for *Playboy* magazine.

'You do some heroic stuff like hand-feeding the big crocs,' he advised. 'When they go "ooh" and "aah", that's when to strike.'

When a pretty young tourist visited on a weekday, I acted on Bruce's advice. While I showed her around the empty serp, she introduced herself as Suzanne Pleshette. I didn't recognize the movie star's name, so if she had been putting me on, she failed. We came to Cookie's enclosure, where he lay like a bloated walrus on the bank of his pond. Since it wasn't feeding time, he was soaking in the sun and daydreaming. I threw a garfish at him, thinking he'd be roused to action and show his toothy jaws. He made no move to pick it up. Either he was lazy or didn't see it. I jumped over the wall to retrieve it for another try. We often leapt into the pen to clean, but at that moment I wasn't thinking about what I was doing. In my eagerness to impress the lady, I got too close to the croc. He may have looked fat and slow, but he moved lightning-fast.

'*Carajo cojones, pinga caballo* [Fuck balls, horse prick]*!*' I swore under my breath.

He whacked my leg with his bony head, and as I skittered in reverse, he grabbed the cuff of my white trousers, which ripped loudly. I rejoined Suzanne, whose face had frozen in an expression of horror. My heart pounded at the narrow escape, but I plastered a stupid grin and pretended this was an everyday routine.

'Are you sure you're not hurt?' she asked.

'Of course. This is how we exercise Cookie.'

Suzanne didn't seem convinced at first, but I continued giving the impression it had been nothing. All that effort earned me a dinner date. That night, in her motel room, she examined the bruise on my shin, and I shamefacedly admitted to my stupidity. She left the next day. Although Bruce's advice had worked, I quit trying any more idiotic tricks with Cookie.

One wet evening, I was reading a book when Heyward suggested we go road cruising. I didn't know what he meant and climbed into his flashy red '63 Ford with anticipation. We headed on the rain-drenched highway south to Florida City. He explained that the coolness after a downpour brings the snakes out on to the warm tarmac, and we merely had to hop out of the car to catch them. We could cover much more ground and grab many more snakes. I was excited by this novel method of hunting, which seemed easier compared to turning over rocks and logs and looking in crevices, as I had done in Hoosick and Kodai.

As soon as we were on the less-travelled roads off the highway, we saw water snakes everywhere, but they weren't what we were after.

'There's a yellow rat snake, near the edge there,' Heyward said as he slowed to a stop.

I got out, scooped it up and bagged it in a second. That was simple.

Then Heyward turned on to a deserted dirt road with fields of tomatoes and potatoes stretching for thousands of acres on either side.

'For this kind of hunting, you gotta sit on the hood of the car,' he said, braking to a stop. 'Don't worry. I'll drive slow. You won't fall off. And if you see a snake, tap the hood. Rats infest these farms, and we'll find indigos, yellow rat snakes and eastern diamondback rattlesnakes.'

I took my precarious seat on the wet hood, ready to jump on snakes before they could escape. The car tyres crunched the gravel while we scanned the road lit by the headlights. In a couple of minutes, I saw my first red rat snake and thumped the hood. As Heyward slowed down, I jumped off, lifted the beautiful snake and stowed it in an empty bag. There were no moccasins or rattlers about that night, but we caught half a dozen rat snakes. I could see the promise of road cruising on this, the first snake-catching trip of my career.

On another day, Heyward took me to the Everglades. The overgrown levees provided a perfect habitat for snakes. He dropped me at the start of one embankment, parked the car a mile down and walked farther along the levee. I hunted my way to the Ford, drove it past Heyward, parked it and continued hunting. Then it was Heyward's turn to hunt up to the car and park it farther down. We searched the dikes by relay.

I parted the ferns and tall sawgrass with my hook as I padded between them. I loved snake hunting, not only for the snakes but for the experience of being alone in the wilderness with plenty of time to take everything in, breathing the clean air, and the possibility of going from calmness one second to an adrenaline rush the next. A spooked quail fluttering past my face sounded like a rattler and made me jump.

Even before my racing heart could calm down, I spotted the tail of a rattlesnake disappearing into a clump of ferns. I stepped around the other side to head it off. The eastern diamondback froze. I didn't expect to come across the largest species of venomous snake in North America. I pressed the hook on its broad striped head and grabbed its neck as I had seen Bill do. It rattled and squirmed as I yanked the flour sack from my belt with my free hand and shook it open. I put it tail first into the bag, and when it pulled away from me, I let go of its neck and dropped it inside in one movement. I twisted the mouth of the sack closed and knotted it. Eastern diamondbacks, one of the heaviest venomous snakes in the world, are said to weigh as much as fourteen kilograms, but this four-footer was only about two kilograms. Still, the excitement of catching the first one of my career made me beam like an idiot. All Heyward had got was a Florida kingsnake. Bill bought the rattlesnake from us for its venom.

After watching Bill give himself his weekly venom shots, we discussed whether we should immunize ourselves. Since we handled rattlesnakes more frequently, it made sense to build immunity to their venom. Unlike cobra, coral snake and krait venoms, viper venom destroys tissue. So we abandoned the idea.

Although I enjoyed working for Bill, learning about snakes, their husbandry and the venom business, I looked forward to my off days. After tasting success, I couldn't wait to go hunting in the wild again. Heyward and I had different days off during the week, so I borrowed his car.

In my frequent outings, I learnt snakes' preferences for habitat and when they liked to be out, and their temperament and the smell of their musk and shit. For instance, indigos are early risers and the best places to find them were farm roads around Florida City. Yellow rat snakes, red rat snakes, kingsnakes, black racers, coachwhips, water snakes, garter snakes and many more were active later in the day when it became warm. Heyward said we could sell any snake, so I kept them in knotted bags at the apartment.

On a productive solo hunt, I filled five pillowcases with rat snakes and moccasins. I had no more empty bags, but there was still daylight and it was too soon to call it a day. I kneeled beside the edge of the canal bank and leaned over to peer underneath. Before I could react, a kingsnake latched on to my nose. *It could have been a moccasin, idiot!* I pried it off my face. Blood and tears streamed down to my mouth. If I put the snake with the others, this snake-eater would have a feast. I removed my pants, tied the cuffs with a string and dropped it down one leg. A few minutes later, I caught another kingsnake far less dramatically, which I slid into the other pant leg. Shirts can't contain snakes, and besides, the sun was setting. I drove back after dark in my underwear, wondering how I'd explain my half-nakedness to the cops if they stopped me. *Would I be booked for indecent exposure?* To my relief, the situation didn't arise, and I reached home pleased with my day.

One afternoon, the 7-Eleven I frequented was empty, so I dithered at the till, making small talk with Bobbie, an attractive new hire.

'I work at the serpentarium,' I said. 'Come when you're free and I'll give you a special tour.'

'Do you catch snakes?' she asked.

'Of course. Mostly rattlesnakes and water moccasins.'

'Would you take me sometime?'

'Are you free on Monday?'

Early Monday morning, I cleaned Heyward's car and went to pick up Bobbie.

'Is this what a snake hunter's car smells like?' she asked, wrinkling her nose.

I spent too much of my time around reptiles to notice any odour.

'It gets even better once we have a few snakes in the back seat,' I replied with a grin.

When we reached the fallow weed-choked tomato fields near Homestead, I asked Bobbie to take the wheel.

'I'm going to sit on the hood,' I instructed. 'When I spot a snake, I'll tap and you stop. Don't slam on the brakes. Got it?'

Bobbie looked nervous as we did a few practice stops. I hoped she wouldn't send me sprawling face-first on the gravel, and we set off.

Within minutes, I saw a large indigo edging from the road and yelled, 'Stop!' In my excitement, I banged my hand on the hood. Bobbie slammed the brakes, and only the angels saved my face and knees. I hit the dirt running, arms flailing to keep my balance, and dove headlong on the disappearing black tail. On being grabbed, the frightened indigo squirted a healthy cloaca load of shit on my arms. I sat upright, cradling its six-foot length with both my hands until it calmed down and inquisitively tongued at my nose.

The indigo is the most aristocratic of America's non-venomous snakes, and I loved its elegance and good temperament. It's not an especially fast snake, but once it makes it into the dense undergrowth, it's hard to find.

Bobbie turned off the engine and came over. I handed the indigo to her while I wiped the shit off my pants and dusted myself. She was apprehensive at first, but her demeanour changed with every minute of holding it. I showed her how gorgeous its belly was, with its iridescent blue-black colour. She became an enthusiastic snake-hunting chauffeuse whenever we could both get off work on the same day, which wasn't often.

When bags filled with snakes covered all corners of our apartment, Heyward drove me to an airplane-hangar-sized warehouse. Screeches, growls and roars resonated across the parking lot, and when we approached, the stink of animals hit us in the face. Inside, it had everything from jaguars and sun bears to snakes and macaws. Heyward introduced me to Bill Chase, the middle-aged owner of the biggest animal dealership in south Florida. Chase opened one of our bags and pulled out the indigo.

'Six feet,' he called, without bothering to put a tape measure to it. 'Twelve dollars.'

He peered into a bag with six water snakes.

'Twenty-five cents each.'

Red rat snakes and kingsnakes were fifty cents a foot, yellow rat snakes thirty-five cents a foot and the uncommon scarlet kingsnakes were five bucks each. He bought everything we brought.

On the way to the car, I asked Heyward what Chase did with those snakes.

'He sells the indigos to exotic dancers, circuses and carnival shows,' he replied. 'Some people also buy them as pets. He sells some to zoos. But I don't really know who he sells the rest to.'

Although we were ignorant of the details of the business, we were content to have a buyer. With our meagre salaries, we needed every dollar we could get. Any venomous snakes Bill didn't buy, we sold to venom producers such as Gordon Johnstone in New Jersey, Ross Allen in Silver Springs, Florida, or Ralph Curtis, who also sold books on snakes. I started building my own library. The day I bought *Snakes and Snake Hunting* by Carl Kauffeld, who was the curator at Staten Island Zoo, I was impatient to return to the apartment and start reading it. He wrote about where to find each species, the habitats they preferred and how to care for them in captivity. To my frustration, the species in his book were not found in Florida. I would have to learn what I could from Heyward, Bill, and by going out into the swamps and fields.

Rick borrowed Heyward's car on his day off and drove full speed down a farm road. The Ford spun out of control and landed in a ditch when he slammed the brakes to avoid squashing a yellow rat snake. A towing truck pulled it out and he washed the muck off. But a huge dent marred its fender. I didn't blame Heyward when he seemed reluctant to let either of us use his car again. I needed to get my own set of wheels. A motorbike.

I gazed at the tempting line of used ones for sale at 'B and B— House of Wheels' down the road from the serpentarium. I took a 1955 BSA 350 cc single on a trial spin. Its low beat made me nostalgic for the AJS in Laramie and the Triumph in Mysore. But its price tag of 450 dollars was more than I could afford even in two instalments. Since I worked nearby and the salesman knew Bill's son, Bill Jr., a well-known motorcycle racer, he agreed to let me pay for it at a hundred bucks a month.

On my next day off, I roared to my favourite spot near Florida City, where I had caught my first eastern diamondback. After parking beside the road, I tucked a few tall flour sacks into my belt and picked my way through the thick bushes along a palmetto-and-fern-overgrown levee. Insects hummed, butterflies flashed their wings and birdsong filled the warm, humid air. A dark, sinuous shape shot out from under my feet and slid into the weed-choked canal with a splash. I cursed myself for missing the first water moccasin of the day.

I inched forward, stopping to peer through the reeds at the water's edge. On the other side of a clump of sawgrass was a fat moccasin, America's only venomous water snake. I leaned over to look straight at the black triangular head. The snake reacted immediately, opening its mouth and flashing the white interior as a warning. The behaviour had earned it the nicknames of 'cottonmouth' and 'trap-jaw'. Just as I had pinned and bagged the eastern diamondback before, I caught the moccasin. A few steps later, a smaller one lay half-concealed in a pile of dry water weeds that an alligator had brought with it while hauling out to bask. Since my quarry was the eastern diamondback and I already had a larger moccasin, I passed up this one.

I descended from the levee and entered a stand of pine and palmetto trees growing on the rough ground that had been a coral reef millennia ago. This was a paradise for quail and swamp rabbits, the main prey of big diamondbacks. I listened to the sounds and watched the play of sunlight on the leaves. Contemplative and at peace with the world, I stepped along the margin of the woods. A long black snake gleaming like wet tar brought me up short. It poked its head into the pine needles, perhaps searching for rodents. The indigo hadn't seen me yet, and I leapt on it before it could react. It swelled its throat in alarm and struggled in my hands as I admired its glistening iridescence in the morning sun. Since indigos brought a pretty penny, I slipped the seven-foot snake into one of the large flour sacks. Almost all the indigos we caught were big adults, six or seven feet long. *Where do the small ones hide?* I never found out. Someone brought an eight-footer to the serpentarium, the biggest I ever saw.

Every dappled sunlit patch looked like a diamondback. Then I did a double take. Deep inside a hollow formed by the bushes, a sunbeam spotlit a perfect diamond. *Am I hallucinating?* I parted the plants with the snake hook and stared in disbelief at the massive coils of the biggest eastern diamondback I'd ever imagined. She retracted her head and hissed as loudly as a young alligator. When I eased my snake hook under a coil, the huge rattler tensed at the shock of being touched.

I hoisted her on the hook and estimated she was six feet long. She was not only heavy with young but also two large lumps in her stomach bore the outline of a pair of swamp rabbits. I set the rattler gently down in the open. Her neck was poised and her black tongue waved slowly up and down. I pinned her head and gripped her by the neck with my left hand. Dropping the hook, I supported her mid-body with my right hand. She stiffened, but she was too incapacitated with food and babies to struggle much. The head, bulging at the sides with great muscles and swollen venom glands, was almost as wide as my palm.

I yanked an empty flour sack from my belt, kept one end of the open mouth tucked in and eased her tail-first into it. Then I dropped the rest of her body while releasing my hold on her neck simultaneously. She snapped the air, flexing a pair of inch-long fangs. It was a stupidly dangerous way of catching a snake of these proportions. After I knotted the bag, I sat for a few minutes until the adrenaline rush passed. She had an impressive rattle, but she hadn't shaken it once.

I wiped my sweaty face with an empty sack and became aware of the insect and bird noises around me. Although it wasn't yet afternoon, I decided to return, unwilling to risk leaving the enormous snake in a bag unattended.

The sacks with the moccasin and indigo fit in the bike's carrier, but the one with the mammoth rattler did not. I kick-started the bike, made a cushion with three empty flour bags by draping them over my crotch and thighs, and placed the seven-kilogram-heavy bag carefully on the gas tank. The snake hissed again. This was my second complicated and dumb manoeuvre of the day.

I drove cautiously along the highway, aware those massive fangs could pierce through the several layers of cloth. When I reached the serpentarium parking lot around lunchtime, I was relieved she had been calm through the entire ride and not restless, like some freshly caught rattlers. When Heyward came over, I lifted the bag from the tank and the snake hissed.

'What did you get, a gator?' he asked.

'No, a big fat diamondback.'

'You carried it on your lap, you crazy sombitch?' he said, shaking his head in disbelief. 'Show it to me.'

At the apartment, when I took her out, Heyward whistled and agreed she was over six feet long.

'Not a world record, but that's the size you see only once in a coon's age,' he declared in his typical turn of phrase.

We kept Big Mama in a box and fed her road-killed marsh rabbits.

A month later, she delivered twenty-four babies, which we released in the Everglades. Instead of selling her to Bill, I agreed to let Heyward's brother Teddy, who was visiting then, take her. He operated The Snake Pit, a snake exhibition, in Salley, South Carolina, and wrote to say visitors were wowed by her size. She'd become a star attraction.

On 22 November 1963, a strange scene greeted me when I went to the nearby Burger King for lunch. The servers stood frozen in place; the customers had stopped eating; and everyone was staring at the television, some with their mouths open.

'What's going on?' I asked the cashier.

'JFK has been shot,' he muttered without taking his eyes off the screen. 'Looks like he might die.'

It was my turn to join the tableau. I struggled to make sense of the chaos on television, and the news took a long time to sink in. John F. Kennedy was the only familiar American President. The previous Presidents were vague figures who came up in conversations at home in India. The afternoon passed in a blur, and a pall of gloom affected everything for the weeks following his death.

When Bill wanted gators for display, Heyward and I eagerly headed into the Everglades at dusk on my motorbike, since Heyward's car was at the repair shop. This was three years before alligators became a protected species. After parking at a levee, we walked in the dark past water snakes and a big moccasin, which dove into the water. We held our flashlights to our temples and scanned the canal. A red eye glowed at me.

'Gator,' I whispered, and indicated the spot by drawing a circle around it with my light.

Heyward had explained that a foot-long head on the water surface meant a seven-foot body lurked below. This one seemed to be a three- or four-footer, just the size Bill wanted. I waded through the shallows, keeping my flashlight aimed at it, while Heyward waited on the bank. It was either transfixed by the light or confident of its invisibility, and stayed still. Only when I got close did I realize we had underestimated its size. The gator was almost five feet long and required a two-hand catch. With the torch clenched between my teeth, I lunged and grabbed its neck. Its sharp scutes cut my arms, and I dropped the light.

'Good catch,' said Heyward, wading over with his flashlight and retrieving mine, which had gone out. 'Now how the hell are we gonna get it back to the serp?'

We closed the gator's mouth and tied its hind legs together with two thick rubber bands, specially made for the purpose by slicing car inner tubes. But we had no snake bag large enough to hold more than half the reptile, so we left the tail hanging out. I kicked the bike alive, and Heyward clumsily climbed on, holding the gator firmly so it didn't clobber either of us with its bony, round, shovel-shaped head. In India, people transport all kinds of livestock on motorbikes, but I suspect this was unusual, probably even illegal, for the States. None of the other motorists could have spotted a black tail draped over our legs in the dark. It kept still most of the way, and as we approached Miami, perhaps the lights and sounds of the traffic spooked it. It struggled and gave Heyward a good, sharp slap with its tail to the side of his head. He yelped, but somehow kept a firm grip on the reptile, while I balanced the bike against the sudden movements. Back at the serp, it joined six others in their enclosure.

But Heyward and I weren't done with gator-catching. Bill wanted more, preferably a seven-footer, perhaps because we had proved we could handle a five-footer. We had learnt our lesson about transporting struggling gators on motorbikes and waited until the mechanics returned Heyward's car. We threw some rope, bags and snake hooks on the back seat of the Ford and joined the lines of cars headed south to the Keys for the weekend.

Dave, a visitor to the serp who raised ducks, had mentioned facing gator problems. We drove towards Homestead, and when we spotted the landmark—an old army Jeep turned turtle—we left the highway and turned on to a dirt road. Our approaching headlights alerted Dave, who stood with a welcoming grin by the open gate.

'Howdy, if you can help me out with these goddamn gators, both I and my waterfowl will thank you kindly,' he said, by way of greeting.

He told us to drive straight on through to the duck ponds.

We walked around the perimeter of a pond, shining our powerful flashlights while making sure not to illuminate each other and give the game away. Almost immediately, two pairs of eyes glowed in the dark. We crept up to the closest of the gators. It was Heyward's turn to catch, and I switched off my torch as he waded into the marsh with a rope noose draped over his snake hook. From the bank, I watched his silhouette lasso the gator, which submerged unalarmed. But when he yanked the rope to tighten the knot, the water exploded as it twisted and splashed. It was caught like a fish on a hook. Its big, black, shiny tail emerged from the water as it fought to shake loose. Heyward tugged back.

Seconds later, he was being pulled towards deeper water, and I wondered who had who. Before joining him, I shone the flashlight along the shoreline and two more gators' eyes blinked back brightly at me. *Should I stay and keep an eye on them, or wade into the water and help Heyward?* When he gurgled, I swung the light back to him. He was up to his nose in water and trying to say something.

'What did ya say?' I shouted.

I couldn't hear his bubbled reply. The animal gave a mighty pull and the intrepid gator-nooser submerged, leaving his battered old hat floating on the surface. I waded into the black water to give him a hand when Heyward's head bobbed metres away across the pond. Still clenching the taut rope in his fists, he plodded ashore festooned with aquatic weeds, slime, frogs and crawdads. I couldn't be sure if a red-bellied mud snake or two fell from him. Worried about the other gators, I swam towards him.

'It's bigger than I thought,' he said, spitting out a gob of duckweed.

I bent over in a fit of laughter at the ludicrous situation, but he wasn't amused.

When I pulled myself together, we both hauled on the rope and the tired gator slid ashore. I threw a wet bag over its head, and Heyward sat on it and gripped its neck while I held the tail.

'It's eight feet and more,' he said as he snapped two rubber bands around its jaws.

We tied the hind legs and wrapped the gator in snake bags before carrying it to the car. We spread more snake bags on the back seat of the Ford so shit wouldn't soil the seat, and I climbed in with the gator. On the way home, its claws scraped my wet jeans as it struggled.

The next morning, when Bill saw the gator, he looked pleased.

'Was it an easy catch?' he asked.

'He didn't give us any trouble,' replied Heyward as I grinned.

I learnt new stuff every day from Heyward about catching snakes in the wilds, cruising the roads and hunting gators. I revelled in every experience—this was the life I had dreamt of as a schoolboy.

I had no doubt at all about what I wanted to do in life.

20

SNAKEMAN

If the Skeeters Don't Get You, the Gators Will

B ILL WANTED OUR APARTMENT to convert into extra holding space for snakes. We looked through the classified-ads section of *Miami Herald* and shortlisted the cheapest ones. We picked the best of the lot, a two-bedroom house at Shipping Avenue in Coconut Grove with a monthly rent of 175 dollars. We furnished it by salvaging old furniture from dumps and repairing them. A concrete Venus de Milo statue with some wear and tear added a touch of class to our front yard. We converted discarded TV cabinets into terrariums for keeping captive snakes. When we were home, we blasted the rock 'n' roll radio channels playing The Beatles' *I Want to Hold Your Hand*, Roy Orbison's *Oh, Pretty Woman* and The Drifters' *Under the Boardwalk*. The busy evening life in the Grove was in sharp contrast to the quiet vicinity of the serpentarium.

After a long day's work, Heyward and I headed to a coffee house. The Flick and Gaslight South were favourites. We sipped cappuccino sitting at rough tables in front of a makeshift stage while listening to musicians such as Tom Rush, Dave Crosby and Oz Bach, who sang blues, folk rock and protest songs. We made friends among the assorted funny-looking people who called themselves hippies. In 1964, we were too cool to clap at the end of a song. Instead, we snapped our fingers.

Only rednecks and football players drank booze. Being considered a redneck didn't stop me from drinking a can of suds. Hipsters preferred being stoned, but I hadn't toked yet.

Listening to the songs, poetry readings, and rants against the government and the looming Vietnam War, I became immersed in the issues rocking the country. The Cold War was at its coldest since the Cuban Missile Crisis two years earlier. The Grove was a hotbed of peaceniks, and the polarization of America's youth was one of the biggest subjects in the news.

Several commercial snake hunters we met at the serpentarium dropped by to visit our new pad. Arnie Newman, Gary Maas, Joe Laszlo, Wayne Tyson, Brad Bradford and Attila Beke grew from being acquaintances to good friends. Most had fingers deformed by snakebites. For the first time in my life, I had a like-minded peer group.

Bill Chase ordered twenty yellow rat snakes, which were popular in the pet trade because of their gorgeous colour and large size. Heyward and I consulted Attila, who had arrived in Florida as a kid from Hungary. He didn't have a regular job and made his living solely from catching and selling snakes. His knowledge of where to find different species was the best among our cohort.

'Lake Okeechobee, man,' he replied in his thick Eastern European accent. 'That's the place for yellows.'

The largest freshwater lake in the southern States was about a three-hour drive north of Miami, and Heyward and I somehow got the same day off.

Early that morning, we picked up Attila, who was already stoned. The wooden pump houses in the extensive sugarcane fields encircling the waterbody were painted with smelly black creosote. Even without flashlights, bunches of rodent-stuffed, brightly coloured yellows glowed against the dark rafters. But we couldn't pick them like bananas, as these fierce biters will leave your hands bloody.

'If one bites you, Rom,' Heyward had warned me, 'keep your cool. Don't yank your hand away. If you do, the teeth will break off and you'll have festering wounds.'

Despite our precautions, angry red slices and punctures marked our hands by the end of the day.

We headed back to Miami with bags of yellows.

'Pull over there near that culvert,' said Attila to Heyward. Then, turning to me, he instructed, 'There's a pile of old tyres at the bottom of the embankment. Just run your hand around inside, and you're sure to find one or two yellows.'

I slid down the slope, wondering what was special about the place.

'Watch out for yellow jackets!' yelled Attila. 'They're mean hornets.'

How could anyone sit in a car and conjure a snake several metres away? It's a fool's errand. But I followed his instructions and eased two good-sized yellows out of the tyres. *Son of a gun!* They were still sleepy, so I escaped without getting nailed. *How on earth could Attila be so accurate?*

We drove on with the two of them bantering while I, sitting in the back seat, tried to figure out how Attila knew about the yellows.

'Stop!' Attila yelled. 'Go to that casuarina tree and climb up to the second set of branches. You'll find a hole big enough to get your hand into. With luck, you'll fish out a red rat snake.'

As the understudy, I did his bidding, and there was a red rat snake, as he had predicted. *What magic is this?*

'I haven't checked these spots for weeks,' he said, smiling like a Cheshire cat. 'Time enough for snakes to climb in.'

He must remember the spots where he found snakes during his long career as a professional snake hunter. This was the only explanation for his uncanny predictions. We made about twenty-five bucks each that day. Heyward and I used our share to buy two Mexican cantils, a red-tailed boa and a pair of black Pakistani cobras to keep at home in our terrariums. If we only knew the tragic role these cobras were to play later.

Wyeth Laboratories, the antivenom manufacturers, placed an order for moccasin venom. But Bill didn't have enough snakes to fulfil it, so he called a snake catcher in Mississippi for western moccasins and a local hunter, Schubert Darmon Lee, for eastern ones.

The species seemed to have an undeserved reputation for being aggressive, as our captive specimens were shy, mild-mannered and reluctant to bite. But when the shipment from Mississippi arrived, we were in for a surprise. These western moccasins were feisty little beasts, far snappier than their Florida cousins.

I was assisting Bill in milking venom when he got bitten by one. He returned the snake to its cage and swung his arm round and round while grimacing in pain.

'Rom, put the equipment into the lab,' he said as he walked into his office.

He didn't resume until the swelling subsided two days later. Then Heyward got nailed and Bill gave him the day off. When I returned home that evening, he was rolling in bed, moaning in pain. Moccasin bites are rarely fatal, but victims have lost hands and feet because of gangrene. Neither bite was serious enough to warrant going to the emergency room.

Then Schubert brought in some good-sized moccasins. Older than us by a decade, he was gangly and taciturn, but friendly. Although we were curious to learn where he had collected this nice bunch, we avoided asking him. Hunters could be extremely cagey about divulging their special locations, and we didn't ask unless they were buddies. He extended an invitation to visit him on the Tamiami Trail, where he lived in a trailer. Like Attila, he earned his living by hunting snakes, and he would know the best places from years of wandering these south Florida swamps and farmlands.

I took Schubert up on his offer and arrived one early morning at the trailer he shared with his Cuban girlfriend, Florence Gutierrez. The diminutive woman was a veterinarian, and the local newspaper called her The Lizard Lady. Her iguanas, tegus and other South American lizards lay draped over the furniture. Schubert waved me to a vacant spot on the couch and put on the kettle. A large curious tegu climbed my leg, and its sharp claws dug through the jeans and into my calf.

'She likes to meet new people,' Florence said as she lifted it off me.

I accepted the cup of strong black coffee and we sat on the steps of the trailer. We listened to the warblers and starlings in the swaying cattails and watched the sun flashing from the last puddles of water in the roadside canal. It was not only the dry season, but we were in the middle of a severe drought. I was lost in my thoughts. *Would Schubert take me to his favourite snake spots today?*

'Anything with legs I don't trust,' he declared, apropos of nothing.

Winking at me, he set his cup down and walked in a crouch to a rusty pipe sticking up from the ground. I couldn't see what he was after. He froze. His right hand whipped out and grabbed something. He eased a brilliant four-foot-long red rat snake from the pipe and wiped the dirty water off its body with his already stained shirt. *How did he spot the snake's head from that distance?* I had much to learn.

We set out in his car, a two-door '50 Ford, bumping along the washboard ruts of Loop Road, a dirt track that would later become asphalted. When he pulled over to the side, we tucked several long flour sacks under our belts and lowered ourselves into the fetid muddy slush to which the canal had been reduced. He had no use for a fancy metal snake hook. Instead, a sturdy stick picked up from the ground was his tool of choice. The stench of rotting fish filled the air, and by day's end, our clothes reeked of it. White egrets, blue herons and black-headed ibises that had been feasting on the trapped fish flew away on our approach. Turkey vultures circled overhead. The brown, green and banded water snakes with engorged bellies moved sluggishly aside as two clumsy humans waded through the thick mud and clinging mats of water weeds.

The more I peered among the roots, the more they resembled snakes.

'Here's one,' Schubert called out.

He pulled the black tail of a moccasin hanging at eye level from a network of tunnels in the ancient coral substrate. The snake's head appeared out of another hole and before you could say 'sombitch', it nailed his hand. From where I stood, it looked like a good two-fang bite. *Oh shit! What do we do now?* We were far from the car. *How do I get him to a hospital if it is a nasty one?* He pinned the snake at an awkward angle and dropped it into the bag I held open for him. As I knotted it, he wiped the blood and mumbled 'Dumb shit!' under his breath.

'Let's have a smoke,' he said, lifting himself out of the sucking mud and on to the dry bank.

We sat cross-legged on the ground. Schubert dragged on his cigarette while I dreaded the outcome of the bite, imagining the venom seeping into his bloodstream and causing pain and rapid swelling. By the time he flicked away the smoked butt of his unfiltered Lucky Strike, his hand had shown no symptoms.

'Dry bite,' he announced with a grin. 'Let's go.'

We spent the better part of the morning wading through sticky mud and catching moccasins. I pulled myself up on the levee to avoid a choked section of the canal. Half hidden in the tall sawgrass was what looked like the thick coil of a diamondback. I crept close to it and was about to pin it when it flashed open its wide white mouth. As the big moccasin slid from the dike into the water, I grabbed its tail and pinned its head to the ground before securing a grip around its neck. Picking up its stout body with my other hand, I shouted with elation.

'Schubert!' I called. 'Come and see this monster.'

'That's the biggest goddamn moccasin I've seen,' he exclaimed.

I was chuffed to have caught one that even he considered humongous. After bagging it, we agreed it was over five feet long.

By noon, we had seen seventy to eighty water moccasins and bagged about thirty large ones. When Schubert called lunch break, I spotted a beautiful two-footer coiled on a half-submerged log.

'Too small,' he commented when he saw me eyeing it.

But I wanted to keep it in the terrarium at home. He shrugged as if to say, 'Suit yourself', and walked away.

I waded towards the gorgeous snake, which looked up as the snake hook came close. It seemed too torpid to make a getaway. I pinned the head and was about to grab the neck when the log submerged. It pulled itself free and sank two white needle fangs into my right thumb.

Stupid! Clumsy! Idiot! Shithead! Schubert's gonna be pissed. These thoughts flashed through my mind. It withdrew its fangs and closed its mouth, probably in a fraction of a second, but it seemed to happen in slow motion. I flipped the moccasin on to the bank and called Schubert.

'It bit me,' I said in a quivering voice.

'They'll do that sometimes,' he replied casually.

It would become one of our stock phrases, for anything from getting dumped by a girl to running out of gas or cigarettes. But at that moment, it didn't seem droll. I hauled myself up and bagged the snake before it escaped. My thumb burnt. It wasn't a dry bite. Schubert looked at the rapidly swelling hand and called it quits.

'Guess we better be getting these snakes to the serp,' he said. 'Mr Haast can tell you if you need to go to the hospital.'

I was too embarrassed about wrecking half a day of productive hunting to say anything. I didn't even dare moan when my arm throbbed. On the way, I began to think of my first venomous snakebite as a rite of passage. Now I was a professional snake hunter, one of the boys. I was no more the understudy.

If I thought Bill would commiserate, I was mistaken.

'It'll be okay in a day or two,' he said disparagingly. 'Take tomorrow off.'

Heyward showed no sympathy and called me dumb. Getting bitten by a snake is like shooting yourself in the foot. I reluctantly agreed that my ineptitude and clumsiness were to blame. The others, Attila, Wayne and Gary, didn't cut me any slack either. When a snake hunter gets bitten by a snake, it's his fault. A good lesson, unpleasantly learnt. The pain was excruciating, as if someone were trying to stub out his cigar into my thumb. Our friends crowded around when I settled the fellow in a terrarium, and cried 'ooh' and 'aah' over the gorgeous bastard.

That evening, I stood outside a coffee house smoking a cigarette between sets when a striking girl touched my swollen arm, which throbbed with dull pain. I flinched.

'What in hell's name happened to you?' she asked.

'Just a moccasin bite,' I muttered. 'No big thing. Want a smoke?'

She was Dorothy, like in *The Wizard of Oz*, but friends called her Dottie. With her long black hair and Italian features, she resembled Joan Baez. She worked as a sailmaker at the Dinner Key boatyard and lived at Stone House on SW 27th Avenue in the Grove, around the corner from mine. By then it was time for the next set, and we sat at the back of the crowded room.

That night, it was hard to sleep with the throbbing pain. I reported to work a day later, even though my hand was still tender and swollen. It took a week to heal, and Dottie and I spent every evening together.

Bill hired the stylish and attractive Nancy as his assistant. She wore plenty of make-up and teased her hair in a mass of curls. I tried hard to impress her by pretending to be a swashbuckling snake hunter. She surprised me by asking me to take her hunting. She didn't seem like a field person. On the appointed day, she was dressed as if she were going to the movies and not to muck about in the Everglades. At least she wasn't wearing heels. With some misgivings about how it would turn out, I told her to hop on the motorbike, and we set off.

We walked across baked mud covered with the tracks of turtles, alligators and snakes, to hummocks that still had some pools. We caught a dozen moccasins by midday when it became too hot to continue. Sweat plastered Nancy's hair to her scalp, and she was exhausted, but to her credit, she didn't complain. After I showed her how to pin a snake, she pinned several on her own. We drove back to the serp, and when Bill strode in to see what we'd brought, her eyes sparkled with excitement.

'Did you catch these?' he asked her with a frown.

'I helped Rom,' she replied proudly.

When Nancy was out of earshot, he chastised me.

'How can you let an inexperienced girl handle venomous snakes?' he demanded.

I confessed to having been foolish, and I didn't take her snake-hunting again. Years afterwards, Bill married her after his divorce from Clarita, and I wondered if he had been jealous. When Janaki and I visited them three decades later, Nancy and I reminisced about this episode while Bill nodded as he murmured, 'I remember.' I didn't wonder any more—I knew.

At Bill Chase's, Heyward and I befriended another animal dealer, Ben Johnson. Since he was confined to a wheelchair, we offered to lend him a hand anytime he needed to move big animals. He wasn't comfortable with venomous snakes, which he would ask us to hold until he found a buyer.

Once, we housed a fourteen-foot reticulated python for him, the first I'd ever handled. The young chap who worked for Ben had it at his house. While cleaning the cage, he turned around and the snake struck his back. The four rows of long, sharp teeth in its upper jaw and the two rows in the lower jaw left a perfect pattern. We were amazed it could open its mouth 180 degrees wide. His girlfriend refused to entertain it any longer, so we kept it. From a distance, it seemed calm, like my pet Indian python at Kodai, but it was quick to snap when we approached it. We treated the irascible snake with an abundance of caution.

One morning, I woke up on hearing a scraping sound. The python was shedding its skin as it crawled around the bed. Without waking Dottie, I tiptoed into the living room, where its box stood open. Merely latching it hadn't been enough. I ought to have known better since my Indian python, which had been much smaller, also escaped from his box. I set the container on the side, propped the lid open with a hook and draped a rug over it. I pondered what to do next. If I grabbed it, it would bite, and we'd wake up Dottie. I poked its body more than halfway down its length, standing away from its head so that it wasn't threatened, and it started making its way across the smooth floor. Whenever it paused, I prodded to keep it moving. The hassled snake made straight for the only dark corner in the living room—its box. Once it was inside, I closed the lid, and this time I locked it with a padlock. Dottie slept through this episode. Ben sold the snake soon afterwards.

The python's skin had sloughed in one long, intact piece. When I went to the Everglades next, as a prank, I draped it on some palmettos to freak out an unsuspecting snake hunter. I never heard if anyone came across it. Ironically, decades later, Burmese pythons would rule the wetland.

When Ben had a big consignment arrive from Bolivia, he called Rick, Heyward and me for help after hours. At the airport cargo terminal were two crates labelled 'LIVE REPTILES—KEEP OUT OF THE SUN'. We loaded them on to Ben's pickup truck and drove over to his animal shed. While Heyward and Rick worked on one crate, I pried the lid off another and peeked inside. A bag bulged as if it were stuffed with watermelons.

'Careful, Rom,' Ben said. 'I think a huge anaconda is in that one.'

I opened the sack and at the bottom was a huge snake with small, sleepy eyes at the top of its wide head. An anaconda this big must be a female. I reached in to secure a neck grip when she struck like a lightning bolt. A dozen razor-sharp teeth slashed my right hand. I wasn't about to lose face with my friends, so without reacting, I wiped the blood on the bag and continued with the job. This time I pressed her head down through the cloth with my left hand and then gripped her neck with my right. She reacted instantly—all twelve muscle-bound feet of her poured out of the sack. Her coils groped for a hold and found me. Wrapped up in anaconda, I staggered over to the enclosure where she was to live. My pals, meanwhile, stopped working and were beside themselves with laughter. Neither Rick nor Heyward offered to help.

'Will someone unwrap this goddamn snake?' I sputtered.

I unravelled the fat, muscular tail from my neck and felt a sudden rush of warm, sticky liquid. She had showered me with shit. I was a stinking mess from head to toe, with a few hairballs sticking to my shirt. After getting the monster into her box, I washed as best as I could, but my so-called buddies made me ride in the back of the pickup.

About ten months into my job, Bill finally allowed me to extract venom from moccasins in front of visitors on days he was away or preoccupied with other work. Until then, he refused to allow me to handle any venomous snakes, even though I was catching them in the wild every week. I must have passed some competence test and felt proud of myself.

Even though the visitors to the serp were scared of snakes, I could tell they were interested and enjoyed seeing them. Most of them didn't have a clue about reptiles and only came because their kids dragged them in. Once the older people saw what Bill was doing, they became fascinated. Bill put on a good show too. *If only I could do this in India!* An idea to set up a serpentarium in India began to take shape. The country was full of cobras. No one there was doing anything like Bill. The only people involved with snakes were snake charmers, who were a bunch of charlatans, sleight-of-hand experts. They played on people's fears and superstitions, and used snakes to attract crowds before performing their magic tricks and selling bogus snakebite remedies. Perhaps a serpentarium would be a hit. But I'd call it a 'snake park', as the word 'serpentarium' would be a mouthful for non-English speakers.

At home after a busy Sunday at the serp, I grabbed a beer and lit a cigarette while Dottie sipped a banana milkshake. She looked disapproving.

'Beer dulls the brain, and tobacco doesn't make you high,' she said.

I ignored her comment, as we had been over this a zillion times. She put a magazine in her lap and opened her Band-Aid box, in which she kept her stash of grass and Zig-Zag Wheat Straw rolling papers. I watched her as she discarded seeds and stems.

'Why don't you try weed?' she asked.

'Everyone in the world says it's addictive. And it gives your brain lesions.'

People I hobnobbed with at the coffee house talked about Ken Kesey and his Merry Pranksters driving the school bus, Further, across the country, distributing acid-soaked blotter paper and sugar cubes along the way. Eating a cube or a thumbnail-sized piece of the paper gave a hit of LSD. But like most folks, I lumped all the illegal drugs—ganja, hashish, opium, cocaine, heroin, morphine and speed—under one label: dangerous. She shook her head in disagreement.

She sang as she rolled a joint:

La cucaracha, la cucaracha, ya no puede caminar,
porque no tiene porque le falta marijuana pa fumar.
(The cockroach, the cockroach, cannot walk any more,
Because it doesn't have, because it's lacking, marijuana to smoke.)

I guess my concern showed in my face.

'Grass is not habit-forming,' she said in an admonishing tone. 'It enhances creativity, expands your consciousness, makes you accept things, be honest, be loving.'

'You mean I'm not honest and loving?'

She finished rolling the joint, and I lit it for her with my Zippo. She sucked on it, bent my head and kissed me. Taken by surprise, I inhaled as she gently blew thick smoke into my mouth. She didn't let me surface to the count of half a minute, then we fell apart and exhaled. She took another toke and passed the joint to me. I took a deep drag, and it was all I could do to keep from coughing as the smoke tickled my throat. Dottie put a vinyl record on the player, and Joan Baez's *Silver Dagger* filled the room.

My misgivings about marijuana evaporated as I grooved on my first high. It was different from getting tipsy on beer or hard liquor. It's difficult to explain the experience. How do you describe the physical texture of music? I became hyper-tuned to the sounds of the guitar and Joan's voice while gazing at Dottie as if seeing her for the first time. I loved the simultaneous sensation of intensity and peace. This marked the beginning of my affair with psychedelic drugs.

That evening, I got a call from Schubert asking if he could stay with us for a few days as he and Florence had fallen out. Although he talked little, I knew his troubles. The existing political tensions meant Florida refused to recognize Florence's Cuban veterinarian certificate, so she couldn't practise in the States. She worked a low-paying job at the Miami Seaquarium, looking after lizards instead of earning good money as a vet. The canals dried up in the drought and snakes had disappeared. Schubert wasn't making ends meet. Then, to top it off, he slugged a 7-Eleven cashier for not accepting a cheque and broke his jaw. The guy's lawyer-dad sued.

We cleared some space for him in our living room.

'You'll have to share the room with moccasins and cobras,' said Heyward with the concern of a gracious host.

'Been doing it all my life,' replied Schubert.

The next day, I walked into Dottie's house and found her sharing a joint with another man. They appeared to be familiar with each other, which made me furious. Assuming she was two-timing me, I spun on my heels and left. That old devil, jealousy, reared its ugly head. I gave the motorbike accelerator an extra rev, sped to a coffee shop and sulked over my mug. By late evening, I calmed down.

When Dottie invited me to celebrate her birthday that week, I couldn't refuse. Heyward had gone home for a few days and Schubert was brooding, with no plans of going anywhere. I told him to take it easy and left him with two quarts of Coors beer and a pack of Luckies. If only I had said more.

I drove to Stone House with my present, a cute Texas horned lizard with a box of ants for its first feed. Dottie was delighted with her new pet. I pecked her on the cheek and wished her for her birthday, but wouldn't meet her eyes.

'Look, if I share a joint with an old friend, there is no reason on earth for you to get uptight,' she said.

I was ashamed for jumping to conclusions, and we hugged.

Early the next morning, I rose without waking Dottie, gathered snake bags and my hook, and let myself out. It was my day off, and I planned to hunt in Florida City. But there was no sign of my motorbike. I looked up and down the lane. *Was I so stoned last night that I parked it somewhere else?* But I was certain of parking it in front of the house. There was no doubt it had been stolen.

After calling the cops, I walked along the road, peering into every yard. At the end of the street, I found it lying on its side in a ditch. I was relieved to find it whole and not even dented. The thief had obviously failed to start it and dumped it. A cop car slowed as I was pushing it on to the road. I gave the young officer the details of how I found the bike.

'I've never filled out a form on a missing vehicle that was recovered before the police showed up,' he said.

The rookie cop came inside for a cup of coffee. By this time, Dottie was awake. While the coffee brewed, the phone rang, which she answered. Something about her tone of voice made me look up. She looked pale and shaken.

'That was Rick,' she said as she replaced the receiver. 'Schubert's been bitten by a cobra at your house, and he's at Jackson Memorial Hospital. They don't think he's going to make it.'

Did a snake escape and bite him as he slept? I was sick to my stomach. Several thoughts whirled through my mind as I drove to Shipping Avenue. The front door was closed, but unlocked. The black cobras,

Mexican cantils and water moccasins were in their boxes. Nothing seemed amiss. *How could Schubert have been bitten?* I was mystified. I was about to start the motorbike and head for the hospital when a black car drew up. Two men got out and one pointed a drawn gun at the door.

'Federal marshals,' the other announced, pushing me aside. 'Is this where Schubert Lee lives? We gotta see the cobra.'

He made a mistake entering the house ahead of me. A life-size plaster replica of a bushmaster painted silver lay on the floor. With a startled yell, he staggered back, stumbled over his friend and both of them fell on the lawn. It was a miracle the one with the gun didn't shoot his partner. I calmed them down, explaining no snakes were loose. When they got up and brushed themselves off, I showed them the cobras, secure in their boxes. The feds seemed satisfied and left.

I headed over to Jackson Memorial and met Rick outside the intensive care unit. Bill had already been in to give Schubert a transfusion of his blood and brought fifty vials of cobra antivenom from his stock. But Schubert's heart had stopped beating several times, and a nurse told Rick that Schubert's brain may have been damaged. There was nothing to do but wait.

I found Florence in the waiting room, where we sipped black coffee. After I had left for Dottie's the previous evening, Schubert had been to visit her. They had fought and he stormed back to Shipping Avenue.

'I woke up in the middle of the night,' she said. 'I couldn't shake the feeling he needed me. Like he was calling to me. I rang your house, but no one answered.'

She had driven over and let herself in, since the door was unlatched. Schubert lay on the floor, blinking and struggling to breathe. His right wrist was bloody and swollen.

'Was it a moccasin?' she asked him.

He shook his head.

'Was it a cobra?'

He nodded and closed his eyes. She didn't call an ambulance, maybe because she didn't have the money to pay for one. Neither of them had health insurance. She somehow dragged his limp body down the front steps and into her station wagon. I couldn't imagine how she did it. Five-foot-tall Florence weighed no more than forty-five kilograms, while Schubert was a big-made six-foot-two and a hefty eighty-two kilograms at least. Adrenaline and desperation must have given her the strength.

'I drove as fast as I could, through all the red lights,' she said. 'A cop pulled alongside me. "Medical emergency," I shouted to him.'

Without asking any questions, he piloted her, lights blazing and siren wailing, the rest of the way to the hospital, where attendants loaded Schubert on a stretcher and rushed him in.

'I wonder what possessed this man to make the cobra bite him,' she said after a pause.

'What do you mean?' I asked in shock. 'Make the cobra bite him?'

Florence took a deep breath before replying, 'You know he and I have been having troubles about money and our future together. I guess he had too much to drink by himself last night, and then he must have decided to do himself in.'

Although she hadn't witnessed what happened, she was certain he pinned a black cobra and let it bite him in the wrist. She sobbed, and I put my arm around her thin shoulders. A nurse who was passing by came over.

'You are totally worn out,' she said. 'Come with me. There is a room where you can lie down and get some sleep.'

I hugged Florence, and she stumbled after the nurse.

I shuddered at what Schubert had done. It was not even mid-morning, and I was exhausted. I drove back to Stone House and gave Dottie the news. I lay down on the sofa, eyes closed, but wide awake. A helpless, unfathomable feeling of nothingness covered me like a suffocating blanket.

It took Schubert's tough body forty-eight hours to succumb. He died the day before I turned twenty-one.

Three days later, six of his buddies carried his heavy coffin from the hearse to the grave deep inside Caballero Rivero Woodlawn Cemetery. We borrowed suits, as none of us had anything better than jeans and T-shirts. Several friends didn't attend the funeral, but went snake hunting in the Everglades, the best way to remember and honour this quiet, private man and the legendary snake hunter that he was.

Over the following weeks, Schubert was often in my thoughts as I mechanically gave tours, fed the animals and cleaned the serpentarium.

In August 1964, when Hurricane Cleo roared through Miami, Rick, Heyward and I sat under the concrete overhang of an under-construction snake house, a secure place to watch winds howling at 160 kmph. We watched for hours as electric wires shorted in huge sprays of sparks, and palm fronds, boards and even roof sheets flew past. It was midnight by the time the storm moved inland. We headed out in Heyward's Ford to night-cruise for snakes.

There was little traffic, since the storm hadn't fully passed us yet. When Heyward turned on to the Tamiami Trail, every brown and green water snake seemed to have decided to cross the road at the same time. Rick and I ran ahead of the car, flinging them off the asphalt, but it was a hopeless task. There were hundreds, and Heyward wove all over the lane to avoid running over them.

'There's a good-sized moccasin,' he called as he braked.

I held my flashlight between my teeth, pinned it before it slid off the road and bagged it. The next snake wasn't a water snake but a red-bellied mud snake. A truly aquatic species that didn't bask and was therefore rarely seen. Its underwater lifestyle meant it couldn't crawl very well on the asphalt. I would have liked to take a moment to look at it, but there wasn't a second to lose. I heard a strange '*puch, puch, puch*' in the distance, then a gap of ten seconds and more '*puch, puch, puch*'.

'That's the sound of snakes getting squashed by a car,' said Rick.

We spent another hour flipping them into the undergrowth, but by then the traffic had picked up. Hundreds lay dead, and some writhed after being run over, dying slow, painful deaths. Many more waited on the edge, biding their time, and they'd be lucky if they made it across alive. As more vehicles roared by, we couldn't do anything. None of us said a word the entire way back, our hearts heavy at this massacre.

At our house, we discussed the scene we had witnessed. Heyward mentioned underpasses for snakes, toads and frogs at key breeding sites in England. We agreed Floridian reptiles could be saved from this senseless slaughter if they had some safe means of crossing roads. The pace of development was far too great and the public support for reptiles too low for the idea to take root.

On my day off, I followed a dirt road from Homestead towards the air force base, which Attila had told me about.

'There are plenty of canals and levees around the edges,' he had said. 'Good spot for diamondbacks. You can also hunt under the old wooden bridges for red rat snakes. You gotta be careful. They have mean dogs on patrol.'

There seemed no way of getting inside the razor wire fence. *Why didn't I ask Attila for more directions?* I was about to give up and turn back when I chanced upon a fallen palm tree pinning the wire to the ground. I was in. Spread out before me was a vast swamp criss-crossed with canals and levees. A sign posted on a wooden bridge warned, 'NO ENTRY—Department of Defense—Beware—Patrolled by Guard Dogs', with a sketch of a toothy German Shepherd.

I ducked under it and stepped along the creosote-coated beams, checking the joints and crevices for sleeping red and yellow rat snakes. I pried a four-foot red rat snake loose from its hiding place with the tip of my snake hook and bagged it. Several huge tarpons, a large fish sometimes called the silver king by fishermen, swam in the canal waters. *Next time I should bring a fishing rod.* There were rat snakes under every bridge. I crouched low under one when a fighter jet took off with a roar. When all was quiet, the voices of two guys on patrol reached me. They would have one or more dogs with them. With my heart banging against my ribs, I squatted, hoping the dogs wouldn't catch wind of me. Their chatter receded. Maybe the stench of creosote masked my scent.

I waited for several minutes before climbing out of my hiding place. The close call made me paranoid about getting caught. There would have been no point pleading ignorance, since warning signs were posted on every bridge. The penalty for trespassing on a top-secret Defense Department airbase wouldn't be light. I decided against hunting any further and retraced my way out of the base.

I was anguishing over Schubert's death while cleaning iguana poop when Bill called me to his office. *Had he seen me smoking dope behind the hedge that morning? Had he noticed I hadn't fed the yellow anaconda yet?* In that moment, I remembered with guilt the many things I was supposed to have done. If he fired me, at least half a dozen guys would sell their souls to take my place. I knocked on his door sheepishly, knowing I had no excuses to offer.

Bill told me to come in and introduced me to his visitor, Lawrence Hautz. The large, tanned gent was the owner of Salisbury Snake Park, in then Southern Rhodesia. Larry was looking for a young, experienced snakeman to manage his tourist attraction and asked if I was interested. Oh boy, was I! He offered 300 dollars a month.

'I know it sounds low,' he said. 'But it would go a long way in Rhodesia.'

It was the job I had been waiting for all my life. I'd get to work with mambas, boomslangs and gaboon vipers. On my days off, I'd fish and hunt. Africa! I agreed to continue working for Bill until he hired a replacement. I spent the day in a daze.

I was busy over the following week, writing home to India with the news, sorting through my meagre possessions and making a list of stuff needed for my new job and life. One afternoon, I grabbed a beer from the fridge and rifled through the pile of mail, tearing open an envelope addressed to me. In my hurry, I didn't notice the logo of the United States government on the long official-looking letter.

'Greetings,' the letter began. 'You are hereby ordered for induction into the Armed Forces of the United States, and to report at the Florida Armed Forces Induction Station, Miami, on January 12, 1965, at 0900 AM.' It stated in no uncertain terms that Lyndon B. Johnson wanted me to join the Army and defend the nation against communism by fighting the Viet Cong. I had been drafted.

Every time I remember this moment, I can't help but think of Frank Zappa's song:

I don't wanna get drafted,
I don't wanna go …
… I don't want nobody
To shoot me in the fox hole.

21

DRAFTED

One, Two, Three, What Are We Fighting for?

I DIDN'T WANT TO KILL people or be blown up in Vietnam. I had already experienced a bullet through my leg. *Shall I run away to India?* I'd be treated like a criminal and extradited to the States. At a coffee house, I talked with other young would-be conscripts, either working men or college dropouts, who had received draft notices.

Oz Bach, a folk musician who would make it big in a few years, sat at the other side of the table, listening to our conversation.

'Gents,' he said. 'What you want to do is research how to get a 4-F classification.'

4-F meant the candidate didn't meet the physical, mental or moral standards of the military.

'We could claim we're homosexuals,' said one.

'How will you prove it?' countered another fellow.

No one had an answer.

'We can behave like nuts and plead insanity,' offered someone else.

It would have been tried many times already and was unlikely to work any more.

'Get married and have a kid as soon as possible.'

Not enough time.

'Get our parents to pay for college.'

I hadn't called them when I didn't have money to eat. I would not ask them to bail me out now.

'Skip the country and go to Canada, Mexico or Sweden,' suggested Oz.

Sympathetic to draft dodgers, these neutral countries refused to extradite them to the States. We had a lot to think about, and there was silence for a while.

'Good dope in Mexico,' one offered with a lazy grin.

Dave Robinson—or Little Dave, as we called him because he was five feet tall—sat on the stage, picking at his twelve-string guitar.

'Hey Dave, play them the *Draft Dodger Rag*,' Oz yelled to him.

Dave strummed as he sang Phil Ochs's song in his croaky voice:

Sarge, I'm only eighteen, I got a ruptured spleen,
And I always carry a purse,
I got eyes like a bat, and my feet are flat, and my asthma's getting worse,
Yes, think of my career, my sweetheart dear, and my poor old invalid aunt,
Besides, I ain't no fool, I'm a-goin' to school,
And I'm working in a defence plant.

When Heyward joined us later, I asked him if he had received his draft notice.

'Not yet, Rom,' he replied. 'Teddy and I are thinking of signing up for the National Guard.'

If they joined it before the draft board called them, they would be on active duty for just one month a year, but they'd have to serve for seven years. This had been the logic of joining the ROTC when I was in college. If only I'd stayed in college, I'd still be in ROTC and wouldn't have been liable for the draft. All that had changed once I dropped out. Now I was draft bait. I had to think fast.

Since my registered address was Wollaston, I wrote to the nearest draft board in Boston the next day requesting a meeting, where I planned to plead my case. In the meantime, someone at a coffee house recommended a shady doctor who issued medical certificates to guys who wanted to avoid fighting in Vietnam. Five other men sat in his waiting room, all of us glancing out of the corner of our eyes at each other and assessing their ability to dodge serving. The doctor asked what my problem was.

'I have a bad back,' I replied. 'A lump in my foot prevents me from wearing boots, and a bad dust allergy, which makes me sneeze uncontrollably.'

He scribbled a medical certificate for ten dollars.

'To be honest,' he said. 'You don't look sick enough.'

I thanked him and left, resolving to put the acting skills learnt in school plays to good use at the meeting. Plus, I had the letter from Lawrence Hautz offering me the job of curator at the Salisbury Snake Park. *That ought to count for something.* I made the mistake of thinking what seemed important to me would appeal to the stodgy committee. At home, I rehearsed the talk I'd give about how valuable the work with snake venoms was and how we might even find a cure for cancer.

The board granted me an appointment for the following week, and Bill gave me time off. I couldn't make the journey on the BSA, so I sold it and bought a ten-year-old Oldsmobile Holiday, complete with a stereo radio system and electric windows, for 300 dollars. Only one window worked. I should have had a mechanic give the car a once over or at least checked the wheel lug nuts myself before embarking on such a long trip. But preoccupied with presenting a convincing argument, I didn't do either.

Two days later, I hit the road as sunrise tinged the world in rosy colours. I was driving through the suburbs of Fort Pierce when the front wheels started wobbling and the car seemed to be falling to pieces. I tried to pull over, but the wheels tugged so hard that the Oldsmobile slid down the embankment into the murky swamp. I switched off the engine and got out to look. The front wheels were buried in mud. This car wasn't going anywhere. But I still had more than 1,600 kilometres to go.

I stood on the road with my thumb out. A brand-new Chevy slowed.

'I'm heading to New York,' I told the young Black guy at the wheel. 'Could I get a ride as far north as you are going?'

The chap grinned at me.

'We're going to New York, and I could sure use some driving help to get us there.'

That's when I noticed the White couple sprawled asleep in the back seat. They hadn't stirred when he stopped, nor had they heard us yakking. The driver opened the trunk, and I threw my bag in.

'Those two are sleeping off a bender,' Jim said. 'The White cat has a crippled arm and can't drive, so they paid me to get them to New York.'

We drove through the day, only stopping for gas and a bite to eat. The couple in the back weren't surprised to see me driving when they stirred. Jim took over from me late night while I snatched some rest.

'Oh Lord!'

I woke up with a start. The car had fishtailed into the grassy median and come to a stop. Freshly cut grass stuck to the window on the driver's side. It was still dark. We had nearly flipped over, but even that hadn't roused the couple.

'I dozed off and almost killed our asses,' Jim said shakily. 'You better drive.'

We emerged from the Lincoln Tunnel into New York City at dawn. The couple's destination was midtown Manhattan, so I got off at Washington Square Park, where I waited on a bench until 7 o'clock, a decent time to knock on Elly's door. It felt good to lie on a soft bed and close my eyes after the marathon drive. The next day, I caught a Greyhound to Boston.

My heart sank when I entered the Selective Service System board office and faced six stern elderly gentlemen sitting around a cluttered table. One motioned me to the vacant chair. I presented the case I had rehearsed, of my work at the serpentarium, the job offer in Rhodesia and then the value of extracting snake venom for producing life-saving drugs to cure diseases. My spiel cut no ice.

'Son,' one man said, 'America is faced with the threat of communism taking over the world. We need every one of our able-bodied men to get out there and keep the world safe. I'm sorry your case doesn't meet the criteria for deferment. Thanks for coming.'

The rest nodded and shuffled the papers on the desk. I had been dismissed. As I left the room, I was dejected and then became furious.

I resolved to burn my draft card, join the hundreds of protesters and refuse to go to Vietnam. By the time I made it to the family home in Wollaston, my temper had cooled. The Babsons commiserated with me, as had Elly and Dugald. My only hope was the physical exam in Miami, when I'd have a chance to convince them of my unsuitability for military duty. With my preoccupations, I struggled to pay attention to the conversation around the dining table.

I hitched rides back to Florida and returned to work at the serp, where I waited with dread for the notice ordering me to appear at the US Army conscription medical centre for the physical test. On the appointed day, I joined a large group of forlorn men. No one smiled or joked. They made us strip to our underpants, hang our clothes on wall hooks and stand in a single file. A middle-aged army medic rudely stuffed a rubber-gloved finger up my scrotum and commanded, 'Cough.' When I did, he declared, 'No hernia', and checked a box on my chart. I showed him my doctor's certificate about dust allergy and bad back. Without glancing at the piece of paper, he took in my red eyes, stringy hair and belligerent pose for a silent moment.

'Look, shithead, hippy, rat shit, loser boy,' he said in a conversational tone. 'We see candy-ass draft dodgers every day here. We know what they fuckin' look like; we can even smell them. They all have fake medical certs like the one you have. Here's your choice—two years of serving your country or three years in prison. They do cherish young asses in the state penitentiary. Make up your simple shit-kickin' mind now.'

Intimidated and humiliated, I mumbled something incoherent. Before leaving, I had my orders to report for basic training on 15 February 1965.

Later that day at a coffee house, someone narrated the story of how one wise guy beat the draft. He had dropped 1,000 micrograms of LSD before his physical. He acted so strangely, the medic sent him for a psychological exam. He was so out of it that he couldn't remember a thing of what he had said to them. They gave him 4-F—unfit for military service—and sent him joyfully home with some tranquillizers and advice to seek psychiatric help. It was now too late to try that trick.

My things had already been sorted in preparation for Rhodesia. I didn't have the heart to go looking for snakes, and drifted through the evenings smoking dope with Dottie or listening to music at the coffee shops, with the draft weighing heavy as death row on my mind. Dottie and I spent our last night together on the beach at Coconut Grove. In the morning, both of us were teary-eyed as we hugged.

'Don't get sent to Vietnam, hear?' she said.

I bid my friends and the Haasts goodbye.

Those two years working for Bill Haast were my most formative. Several of us serp 'graduates', who had worked at the serpentarium over the years, were serious-minded enough to stick with the reptile obsession and put to use what we learnt from Bill. Heyward and his brother Teddy's Snake Pit evolved into the Edisto Island Serpentarium, South Carolina. George Van Horn set up his Reptile World Serpentarium in Saint Cloud, Florida. Jack Facente's Agritoxins Venom Lab, also in Saint Cloud, became the sole producer of coral snake venom in the States. Joe Wasilewski established Natural Selections in Princeton, Florida, a reptile-oriented operation providing animal support for films as well as controlling the spread of invasive Burmese pythons and South American green iguanas in the state. In 2016, George, Jack, Joe and I, along with other friends, joined Bill's daughters, Naia and Shantih, in setting up the King Cobra Conservancy, an NGO dedicated to king cobra conservation and research.

I boarded a green military bus bound for Fort Gordon, Georgia, filled with other scared recruits.

'Off the bus, off the fuckin' bus!' a loud voice jolted me awake. 'Come on, you shitheads, move it.'

I grabbed my bag and followed the others.

'Line up over there, ladies,' said the drill sergeant, pointing his swagger stick. 'Dump your shit on the table.'

We milled about like frightened animals at a slaughterhouse. The first recruit emptied his knapsack.

'You don't need that hairbrush,' the sergeant commented as he threw it into a garbage can. 'We're gonna take all your hair off.'

He whittled everyone's belongings to almost nothing. When my turn came, he picked up a book among my already meagre possessions.

'Omar Khayyam? Looks like pornography to me.'

The book flew into the trash can. Carl Kauffeld's *Snakes and Snake Hunting* escaped his eyes as just then another bus with recruits arrived and distracted him.

'You guys have some spare time 'til these recruits get processed,' said the sergeant. 'So spread out and police the area. Pick up every cigarette butt and scrap of trash you find. I want to see asses and elbows. Move it!'

We scurried obediently, picking the place clean. Within minutes, there was no litter left, and we bumped into each other in our anxiety to avoid being singled out for any punishment.

'Line up and get your fatigues there,' the sergeant ordered.

We hurried to another table.

'Move it, you lard-asses. You think we're here for pleasure? Your ass is sold to Company A, 1st Training Battalion, 1st Training Regiment. And remember, while you're here, there will be no smoking, no candy and no booze. I ain't joking.'

We had no idea then how much we'd crave cigarettes and chocolate bars. After getting our fatigues, we had our heads shorn, reducing us all to anonymous nobodies. Then we were shown to our bleak barracks. Our two-month basic training had begun.

Two hundred recruits woke up at 4 a.m. to the sound of the bugle playing: *You gotta get up, you gotta get up, you gotta get up in the morning.* Then we did an hour of callisthenics, including push-ups and chin-ups, followed by marching in the cold before breakfast, which we had to gobble down in three minutes. This was like being back in Lawrence School, only a lot worse.

Each of us got our own semi-automatic weapon, an M-14 with an ammo pack of 7.62 mm cartridges. I was pleased to get my hands on this high-powered rifle with its twenty-round box-type magazine. A recruit made the mistake of referring to it as a gun.

'You call that rifle a gun, you shithead?' the drill sergeant yelled, grabbing him by the collar and yelling in his ear. 'Hold your dick with your right hand and your M-14 with your left hand. Now repeat after me: "This is my rifle, and this is my gun. My rifle's for killing, my gun is for fun." Repeat that for the next half an hour. That way, you and the rest of the turds here will remember the difference.'

We marched up and down hillocks of sand with our eighteen-kilogram battle gear, which included an entrenching tool, a gas mask and a canteen. Our knapsacks held a partial tent called a shelter-half and a medical kit. Our five-kilogram rifles were slung from a shoulder. If anyone was out of step, he was pulled out and told, 'Drop! Give me twenty.' The poor sod would do twenty push-ups. It didn't take long before we were all expert marchers.

The only break from tedium was when the sarge made up a rhyme and cadence, and we sounded off and answered him.

Yer left, yer left, yer left, right left,
Sound off! One two,
One two three four,
You're right!
I don't know but I been told,
Northern pussy is mighty cold,
You're right!

With the mind-numbing drills, my brain was ready to atrophy from disuse.

The rest of the day, we attended lectures on the bleachers in the semi-wild forested grounds of the army base. Lessons included how to throw a grenade and duck behind sandbags before it exploded, and how to use the inside of the plastic bandage packet against a sucking chest wound, bringing the reality of the battlefield into the lesson. Classes in military terminology were especially boring and the training movies put us to sleep. The sadistic drill sergeants crept up to anyone who dozed off and blasted their whistles in their ear. By lunchtime, we were starving, but again we had only three minutes to eat.

Not smoking was tough. We snuck behind the barracks to smoke. One draftee unlucky enough to be caught was hauled up for public humiliation.

'Your mother was a buzzard, and she shat an egg,' the corporal yelled, his spittle spraying the poor sucker's face. 'That's where you came from, you piece of bird shit.'

We snickered into our hands while the recruit blinked and trembled.

'Drop and give me fifty,' ordered the corporal. 'When you are finished, you will go inside the boiler room and stack the coal into piles of fifty pieces each. It better be done before mess call. DO YOU HEAR ME? Now DROP.'

This was a lesson for the rest of us. I quit smoking immediately. The humiliation and punishment far outweighed the discomfort of nicotine withdrawal.

In the evenings, we had to polish our boots. Suddenly and randomly, we'd be told 'Inspection tomorrow AM!' and ordered to perform ridiculous chores such as scraping the wax off the barracks floor and then scrubbing it with toothbrushes. There was no free minute from dawn to dusk. We looked forward to resting our tired bodies at night, but often, even that was not to be. We were commanded to crawl on muddy ground under barbed wire while live tracers crackled as they zipped above our heads.

If anyone didn't hop to it and do it right, the sarge wrote DUD in chalk on his helmet. The draftee became his target for days on end. The point of it all was to make us obey like dogs, not even questioning the most ridiculous orders.

'It's what'll save your sorry asses once you cocksuckers are under fire, and the VC (Viet Cong) charge in to slit your throats and you are shitting your pants,' the sarge yelled. 'When I say move, you fuckin' MOVE, or you're dead.'

The first days were rough. Most were out of shape, and our flabby bodies were stiff from all the exertion. Exhaustion compounded by sleep deprivation made us weak and listless. We hated the drill sergeants for trying to break our wills. When we could finally hit the sack, there was quiet sobbing in the barracks. For these troubles, we earned eighty-three dollars a month. One conscript lost his mind. Within a week, he whimpered for his mother, and they discharged him from service.

Once I learnt what was expected, I settled in, becoming cheerful and even enjoying the sergeant's cussing. In a few weeks, my body toughened, although marching and running with our full eighteen-kilogram packs were still challenging.

Anything to do with firearms and explosives was fun. Carving a grenade out of wood for a school workshop was one thing, but feeling the weight of a real one in my hand, pulling the pin, chucking it and hearing the power of its explosive charge was in another league. To my disappointment, I was assigned to kitchen police (KP) duty for two boring days. My hands developed blisters from peeling potatoes to feed two hundred men and then washing huge steel sinks full of metal plates, cups and utensils while the rest received advanced instruction with machine guns. It was a relief to return to the training routine. Crawling on my belly in stinky mud was preferable to KP.

I was astounded we were all treated equally, even if it was no better than turds, with little or no discrimination between Whites and Blacks. I made friends with some cool Black guys, whom I'd rarely get to know in normal American society. I was amused and impressed by Southern White boys befriending Blacks, sharing jokes, learning hip jive banter and how to spit-polish boots till they shone like a mirror.

The Vietnam War escalated, and late at night in the barracks, we discussed the news of a large deployment of American ground troops. We were certainly bound for the front when we completed basic training.

Taking apart and assembling the M-14, cleaning and maintaining it, and shooting at targets were the next lessons. I loved loading and firing, feeling the kick of the rifle against my shoulder when I pulled the trigger. I scored an expert badge for marksmanship. This was followed by bayonet practice. After a brief demonstration, the sarge yelled, 'FIX BAYONETS!'

We fumbled but succeeded.

'CHARGE!' he barked, pointing to dummies stuffed with straw.

We ran towards them and, using our momentum, stabbed as hard as we could while yelling 'KILLLL!' at the top of our lungs. I had no doubt that if the mannequins were real people, we'd have charged at them

with the same gusto. I developed a grudging respect for how quickly
he had turned us into killing maniacs.

Halfway through training, the sarge announced that only those with
spotless M-14s would get a weekend pass. Several Southern boys and
I, who had shotguns or rifles as kids, knew to use an old toothbrush to
clean around the sights, bolt and trigger guard. We polished the rifling
inside the barrel with a ramrod until it glowed, using the reflection from
our thumbnail to check it. Rubbing shoe polish to fill the scratches
made it look brand new. It was no surprise we were the only ones to
receive passes to leave the base.

In the meantime, Heyward had quit the serpentarium and was back
in Salley, working with Teddy on The Snake Pit. I phoned Heyward
before boarding the camp bus to Augusta, where the brothers met me
with their old black '53 Chevy pickup. The town wasn't far from Fort
Garbage, as we recruits called Fort Gordon. I was delighted to see the
Clamps and looked forward to a weekend of snake hunting. As soon as
I got into the truck, I felt as if I had been released from prison.

The plan was to hunt the pine lands surrounding Okeetee Club,
prime eastern diamondback rattlesnake country, according to Kauffeld's
book. We stopped at a gas station, where I bought things I'd been
missing—a Hershey bar, Marlboro cigarettes and a six-pack of Colt 45
malt liquor. I savoured the taste of freedom, smoking, sipping a cold
brew, and watching the town and highway fade away as we turned on
to back roads.

We set up camp in a clearing in the forest. With no prospect of rain,
we didn't have to go to any great trouble. We stretched a tarp between
trees, swept the ground clean of pine needles to minimize ticks, made
a simple fireplace with rocks and our campsite was ready. As daylight
faded, we cooked hot dogs over the fire and traded stories of what we'd
been doing. It had only been a month in basic training, but a lifetime
seemed to have passed since I had last been in the wilderness. I was alert
to every sound and smell.

The Clamp brothers did snake shows at county fairs in the summer,
and always needed big diamondbacks, a canebrake rattler or two, and, of
course, a few moccasins. They also sold venomous snakes to Bill Haast.

'We got an order for as many diamondbacks as we can catch,' said Heyward. 'They gotta be over four feet long, and the pay is three dollars a foot.'

We knocked back a shot of smooth, clear corn whisky, moonshine that Heyward's cousin brewed, and called it a night.

Waking up at dawn in the forest anywhere, temperate or tropical, is like waking in a dream. I lost no time in squirming out of my sleeping bag, determined to make the most of every minute away from the base. I pushed the still-smouldering embers together to get the fire going. The other two rose to the aroma of brewing coffee. Nursing a mug each, we boiled eggs in a pan and baked instant biscuits. Heyward, as always, wore his Gokey moose-hide, snakebite-proof boots.

'You might have those fancy snake boots,' Teddy said, 'but wearing tennis shoes is gonna make us look harder for snakes, so we don't tread on them.'

It seemed like I had stepped into the middle of an unresolved argument between the brothers. I agreed with Teddy while pulling on my own sneakers. Heyward ignored us.

We spread out but within shouting distance of each other, checking every stump, peering into tree holes, and overturning logs and slabs of bark and replacing them. The sun streaming through the pines warmed the ground.

'Rom, over here!' Heyward shouted.

I followed his crooked finger, deformed by a snakebite, pointing at an old burnt stump lit by a shaft of sunlight. A beautiful stout eastern diamondback rattlesnake lay in a tight, symmetrical coil, tonguing at us but not rattling. I could have stood there forever gazing at its distinctive striped face and startling pattern. When Heyward pinned it, the snake started buzzing like a chainsaw, and he dropped it into the bag I held for him.

That weekend we found five good-sized diamondbacks, with the biggest half a foot shy of six feet. We also caught two large canebrake rattlers, a species we'd learn afterwards was possibly the most toxic of the thirty-two species of rattlers in America. A small one bit a friend of ours right there in Okeetee years later, and he died within forty-five minutes.

Sunday evening came too soon, and it was time to drag myself back to my prison. I had the fleeting thought of going AWOL and hiding in the woods.

'Anytime you can get away, Rom, let us know,' Heyward consoled me. 'We'll come and pick you up.'

His words made me feel better. I returned to stabbing dummies with my sharpened bayonet, and digging and filling trenches.

The day we learnt about gas was unforgettable. It wasn't used much in the Second World War. In the First World War, however, many thousands of soldiers had died horrible deaths or suffered scarred lungs. Obviously, the army thought we might face a gas attack in Vietnam.

'Today you pussies are gonna learn what gas is all about,' the sergeant said. 'If you hear the order "GAS", this is how you put your mask on.'

He demonstrated how to remove it from the canvas bag hanging from our belts and slip it over our heads.

'Now blow, to clear the air passage and then breathe normally,' he ordered. 'Any questions?'

The lecture lulled us into semi-consciousness, and no one piped up. With a loud hiss, clouds of fumes poured from under the bleachers. The two PFCs (Private First Class) standing at either end of the benches had donned their gas masks and were controlling some devices. The sarge yelled, 'GAS!' and whipped his mask on. As the cloud enveloped the front rows, some guys screamed in surprise and panic as they struggled to pull their masks out of the bags. I was way up in the last row and had enough time to put on my mask, do a test blowout breath and watch the chaos. A few abandoned their attempts, leapt from the bleachers and ran into the forest. The sarge shouted into a bullhorn, ordering them back. They trooped in sheepishly, and by then the gas had dissipated.

'You dickheads, that was plain old CS gas,' the sergeant continued with his lecture.

CS, commonly called tear gas, doesn't kill, but once it gets into your nose and eyes, you feel as if you are dying.

'Next thing you're gonna experience is chlorine gas, and that's a killer,' said the sarge. 'But if you stay calm and careful, you'll be fine. Line up near that bunker there. Put your mask on. Make sure it's cleared and secure. Go in, close the door, take a deep breath in your mask, remove it, salute the officer at the desk inside, and give your name, rank and serial number. Salute once more and get the fuck out of there before you take another breath. Got it?'

By the time my turn came, I had run through the scenario a dozen times in my mind. I followed the sequence of orders in the gas-filled room, where the masked officer sat as calmly as he would in an office, and stumbled out of the door. Outside, a few conscripts, who hadn't been careful and had inhaled before exiting the bunker, were bent over, puking.

Before the end of basic training, I got another weekend pass, and true to his word, Heyward came to pick me up in Augusta. He handed me a bottle of RC Cola, a big paper bag of hog cracklins, and a packet of moon pies, standard Southern comfort fare. Teddy was busy at home. As Heyward drove towards Okeetee, he said a research lab needed canebrake rattlers for some medical work and offered top dollar. I watched the passing countryside when I spotted her—red hair pulled in a loose ponytail, halter blouse tied in front, cut-off frayed jeans low on her hips, firm calves, trim ankles, feet clad in scuffed sneakers. She carried a bamboo fishing pole rigged with a red-and-white painted cork float and a can of worms.

'Stop,' I said to Heyward.

I stuck my head out the window and offered her a ride to the river. She climbed in and noticed the snake-hunting gear.

'Where ya'll headed?' she asked.

'We are going to catch canebrake rattlers,' I said with swagger.

The eighteen-year-old was intrigued. Her dad was a timberman and her mom worked at the county office.

'Can I go with you?' she asked.

'Of course,' I replied without hesitation.

Her sweet Southern accent floored me. Heyward didn't say a word as he turned off the main road and pulled up at a promising site on a rutted timber trail.

The air was warm, and the forest tall and quiet, except for a rat-tatting pileated woodpecker and the crunch of our footsteps. Lora Lou and I headed in a different direction from Heyward, and being the gentleman, I helped her step over a log. While Heyward's mind was on snake hunting, mine was not.

'I don't like spiders and snakes, so don't you go and scare me or anything, hear?' LL said.

If Jim Stafford had released his *Spiders and Snakes* track by then, I'd have sung in reply:

> *I don't like spiders and snakes,*
> *And that ain't what it takes to love me.*

Scaring her was not what I had in mind. When she stumbled, I grabbed her and then one thing led to another.

LL pushed me away when we heard a vehicle approaching. She pulled on her shorts in a hurry while I did the same with my pants. If it were her father or his timber boys, my ass was grass. A million thoughts ran through my head. *Should I run cross-country through the forest, jumping over stumps and hoping diamondbacks and canebrakes stay out of my way? But LL will be left to answer what she was doing so far from the river. Or we could hide, but the bushes aren't thick enough.* It was too late to act on any of them as the vehicle gained on us. I pretended to snake-hunt, earnestly looking under logs and peering into hollows. The snake hook added gravitas. The only false note was LL, who was too sexy to be out in the woods.

The battered pickup slowed as the driver was courteous not to cover us in dust.

'Howdy,' greeted the farmer. 'You kids all right?'

'We're helpin' a friend locate canebrake rattlers for a county fair,' I replied, doing my best to camouflage my Yankee accent. 'His car's down the way aways.'

'Snakes! I could tell you stories that'd curl your hair. Don't git bit, heah?'

And he left. *Phew!*

In the silence, LL and I gazed at each other, and we'd have gone back to what we had been doing had a 'Hoya!' not interrupted us. Heyward's voice came from the top of a hillock.

'You sorry-ass snake hunters,' he called. 'You hardly covered a mile.'

'We covered it carefully, stone by stone and stump by stump.'

'More likely hair by freckle,' he said. 'Help me get this rattler from this hole.'

I led the way, with LL following close behind me. The going was slippery on the mossy rocks, and I grabbed her hand before she slid down. We found Heyward on his hands and knees in a thick tangle of vines and broken branches. I joined him and peered into the dark hollow.

'You call it a hole?' I mumbled. 'This here's a cavern, man.'

When my eyes got used to the dull light, I saw a five-foot-long hefty canebrake, hidden by a bank of dry leaves with tree roots hanging over it. While LL craned her neck to look, Heyward climbed down under the feeble beam of the small flashlight that I held. After pinning and bagging the snake, a dirt-encrusted Heyward handed me the securely fastened bag and pulled himself out of the pit, puffing with happiness.

While he continued to hunt, I took his car to drop LL at her house on the highway before it became dark. I promised her I'd be back to see her once my training was over, but we knew that would not happen.

That night, as we lay in our sleeping bags gazing at the stars, Heyward gave me the news. The previous month, in March, an eighty-two-year-old peace activist, Alice Herz, had set herself on fire on a Detroit street corner in protest against the Vietnam War. More recently, a massive antiwar protest in Washington, DC, organized by the radical Students for a Democratic Society, had drawn thousands. I doubted these actions would change the course of the war and my destiny. My basic training was nearing its end, and I feared being sent to the front lines. This was perhaps the last time I would spend in a forest before shipping out. And then who knew what was in store? I had no wish to die fighting an unjust war, but my fate wasn't in my hands. I fell asleep feeling miserable and helpless.

When Heyward dropped me in Augusta on Sunday night to catch the bus to Fort Gordon, we didn't know when we'd meet again. Both of us were sad and promised to keep in touch.

I passed the basic training assessment with excellent scores, the kind I didn't get in school or college. A few days later, after the routine of roll call, the sarge read our orders:

Jim Barker. Staff driver, Pentagon, Washington, DC.

Charles Anderson. Infantry, Fort Bliss, Texas.

John Haines. Heavy armour, Fort Dix, New Jersey.

Romulus Whitaker. Medical pathology, William Beaumont Hospital, El Paso, Texas.

Although the immediate destination of Charles and John was elsewhere in the States, anyone assigned to infantry and heavy armour was most definitely bound for Vietnam. A moment's confusion later, it dawned on me that I would not be shooting Vietnamese people. At least not for now.

Two other guys and I were called for a meeting in an office next to the commanding officer's HQ. We met individually with a stranger dressed in civvies, obviously not part of the army.

'You grew up in India?' he asked. 'That's interesting. Would you like to work in the Military Intelligence Corps?'

I did not know what it meant.

'If you opt for MI, you won't have to wear a uniform,' he continued. 'You'll be posted in Washington at first, and likely overseas later. It's interesting work and it pays more.'

That sounded appealing.

'If you agree, you'll have to spend an extra year in the army,' he said.

That was a deal-breaker.

'No, thanks,' I replied.

Back in the barracks, I was still in a state of mild shock. I had bonded with the others, and now we would be scattered around the world. I was sorry for the guys who were to go to Vietnam while feeling relieved at my own good fortune.

22

A COLOUR-BLIND LAB TECH

Out in the West Texas Town of El Paso

THE 1,000-BED WILLIAM BEAUMONT General Hospital in El Paso was meant for military personnel and their dependants. I dropped my bag at the spot allocated to me in the barracks at the back of the grounds, freshened up and reported for duty. My colour blindness would be a handicap in the pathology lab, since I couldn't see blood. But I didn't want to own up to the affliction for fear of being sent to the battlefront. I had a lifetime's experience in coping with it, so that was not difficult.

All the doctors were officers, many of them draftees. None cared if GIs like me saluted them, had our caps on straight or our shirts buttoned to the top. This relaxed atmosphere suited me. There was no more marching, digging or peeling mountains of potatoes. With a salary of a little more than 200 dollars a month, my life was back to some semblance of normalcy. The Army PX was a tax-free supermarket. Cigarettes were only ten cents a pack. Freed from the restrictions of Fort Garbage, I resumed smoking. *How could I not when cigarettes were so cheap?*

At the Medical Pathology Department, ten of us privates, just out of boot camp, received on-the-job training (OJT) as technicians. First thing in the morning, we followed an experienced lab tech on ward rounds, observing him reassure nervous patients, finding veins and drawing blood. I had no trouble discerning its dark colour as it filled a syringe or collection tube. If anyone had played a prank by filling a vial with green liquid and told me it was blood, I'd have believed him. Thankfully for me, no one did. Every day, we learnt a new procedure in haematology, blood chemistry, bacteriology, urinalysis and blood banking.

Two days of observations later, it was our turn to draw blood. I pitied the patients who offered their arms, assuming we were pros. Dressed in hospital whites, we looked no different from the experienced technicians. Some patients even called us doctors. The ones whose veins were easy to find had it painless. But those with thin or squiggly veins underwent torture as we tried half a dozen times, causing ugly purple bruises, or haematomas, before getting a flow of blood into the vacuum tubes. With practice, we got better and took pride when patients asked for the 'good stickers' by name.

An army colonel from Fort Bliss was in the hospital with kidney failure and needed dialysis every two weeks. When the call went out for A-negative blood, I volunteered a donation. I showed off my expertise to other techs by shoving the fat twelve-gauge needle in my own vein and drained a unit. This became a regular practice for a few months until the officer was transferred.

I assessed the veins of everyone, especially the girls I passed on the street, for the relative ease of sticking. When we brought the specimens to the lab, senior technicians ran the tests while we observed. It would be a month before we could perform them ourselves.

We streaked an agar plate with a blood, spit or urine specimen and screened for bacteria. The bacteriology manual showed how to identify pathogens such as *E. coli* or *Staphylococcus*. A device punched tiny discs of different antibiotics into the culture, and after incubating them overnight, we could tell which antibiotics were most effective against the germ.

None of us wanted to work in the morgue, although we had to do a stint there as part of the training. Malaitis, the morgue tech, slid a cadaver out from a freezer box.

'This colonel donated his carcass for science,' he said. 'A lot of his body parts have already been taken out.'

Another understudy and I helped him load the corpse on to a stainless-steel stretcher trolley for a session with intern doctors.

'Let me give you a lesson to remember,' he said.

He flung away the rubber sheet covering the body, dug into the open chest cavity with his gloved hand and pulled out a lung.

'This guy was a heavy smoker. See what smoke did to his lungs? See these black specks? Now wait a minute and I'll show you what a healthy lung looks like.'

From a shelf, Malaitis removed a bottle containing a mass of tissue floating in formalin.

'This is the lung of a six-year-old who died in a car accident. Look how it is clear and pink as the day she was born.'

If anything could put me off smoking, that would be it. I went cold turkey once again.

Another time, he made thin slices of a human brain and offered it to us.

'Want some sliced meatloaf? Anybody for a sandwich?'

Our gallows' humour was nothing compared to Malaitis's sick brand.

On my first day in the paediatric lab, I watched an experienced tech deal with a five-year-old boy.

'Yours is the one-millionth blood sample collected today all over America,' he told the young patient.

'Really?' asked the gullible child.

'Really!' he lied as he stuck a needle into the kid's arm.

The boy's lips trembled, but he controlled his tears. I didn't have the heart to draw blood from a kid, nor was I confident of doing it expertly. It's the one thing they didn't teach us—how to tell stories to children while you stick a needle in them. I cajoled and coaxed the guys who managed the roster to keep me away from the paediatric and psychiatric wards.

We could enter Ward 30 for psychiatric patients only with an attendant. Even then, dealing with these inmates was as bad as handling children.

'What're you going to do with my blood?' asked one suspiciously. 'Drink it?'

'Take more blood,' pleaded another.

A third, who had to be cuffed since he wasn't cooperative, started screaming as soon as he saw the needle. Another slapped me. And so on. Each Ward 30 patient was a trial.

In the recreation room one evening, I was chatting with fellow lab tech trainees Jose, a Mexican from San Francisco, and Luther, a Black dude from Chicago, when a plant on the window sill looked familiar. Squinting at it, I asked, 'Is that marijuana?' Both of them stared at it before nodding.

'Sure looks like it,' said Jose.

'Are you guys contemplating smoking some of those plants?' asked a White guy with a smile as he approached our table. 'Don't you do it. It's plastic.'

He introduced himself as Jack. That banter solidified our camaraderie.

We nicknamed Jose 'Mex Mouse' on account of his height, despite his Salvador Dali moustache. Luther became 'Squeaky' for his habit of squeaking while inhaling the last tokes of a joint. Jack was 'Howdy', since he was always smiling. And I was 'Snake', for obvious reasons. Instead of the stiff army salute when we passed each other in the corridors, we performed a parody, raising a cupped hand in a cobra hood accompanied by a soft hiss.

On my first off day, I visited the El Paso Zoo to see the reptiles. An attractive young schoolteacher led a group of children into the room, talking knowledgeably about the animals, which was unusual for the time. The red-haired petite Nita said she, too, was a fan of Ditmars's reptile books. Two days later, she called me at the hospital, inviting me to dinner that evening.

I dressed with care and borrowed Howdy's car. Her directions led me to a tony neighbourhood. *How could she afford to live in a posh mansion on a schoolteacher's pay?* I knocked on the door, expecting to be told I had come to the wrong address. Instead, Nita answered, and she solved the mystery of the fancy digs. She was house-sitting for folks who were on holiday.

Music played through invisible speakers, and the smell of dinner made my stomach growl. She opened the bottle of wine I had brought, and we sank into the soft couch. I hadn't enjoyed a civilized evening in a long time, making me nostalgic for Elly's apartment in Washington Square. Nita and I became good friends, and I introduced her to Mex Mouse, Howdy and Squeaky. We often spent evenings together, talking and listening to music.

When the owners of the house returned, we missed having a place to unwind. Nita called me at the hospital one afternoon.

'Are you interested in a rental trailer?' she asked.

It was conveniently at a nearby trailer park.

That evening, Howdy and I met the owner and agreed to pay a rent of fifty dollars a month. With the trailer's keys in my pocket, we drove to a pawnbroker and bought a stereo set and a small used fridge, which we stocked with six-packs of Coors and Bud. Mex Mouse and Squeaky brought a stash of weed. Smoking joints and drinking beer in our own space felt good. We christened the trailer 'The Cube', and our code for a joint was 'cube steak'. All we needed was music, which we remedied at the PX over the following days by buying Dylan's *Bringing It All Back Home*, The Beatles' *Rubber Soul* and albums by The Yardbirds, The Rolling Stones and The Byrds.

When the food at the barracks' canteen grew boring, we grabbed a burger for lunch at a nearby café. A new waitress, overhearing our bitching and moaning about work, came to our table, arms akimbo, and asked, 'You know what you medical boys need?'

We looked at her in bewilderment.

'You need an optirectomy,' she declared.

We exchanged glances. None of us had heard of such a procedure.

'That's when they separate your optic nerve from your anal nerve to keep you from having such a shitty outlook on life,' she explained.

We burst out laughing, and I promptly fell in love with Estrella. I pretended to be living my karma with the Marty Robbins song:

Out in the west Texas town of El Paso,
I fell in love with a Mexican girl.

Estrella's shift ended at the same time as mine, and I took to walking her home near the railway tracks. At the corner of her street, she said bye, making it clear I wasn't to cross that line. One evening, I was returning alone after dropping her, when two tough Mexican guys accosted me. *Are they gonna mug me?*

'Hey, gringo!' one called.

'No fockin' GI is no fockin' good for my sister,' the older man growled with a snarl.

The handle of a switchblade stuck out of his fist. Estrella's brothers stepped towards me, and I put my hands up and backed off. In the following tense moment, we stared at each other.

'OK, OK,' I said. 'Take it easy. I'm gone.'

They spat and strolled away. I skulked back to the barracks, tail tucked between my legs. I avoided the café for several days, too embarrassed to see Estrella. When I returned, she gave me the cold shoulder. We never spoke a word to each other again.

After our three-month training period ended, we became full-fledged lab technicians, supposedly as adept as registered lab technicians who studied for two years.

Hour after hour of sitting on a bench doing tests was boring. A Black colleague blasted the Top 40 rock and roll tunes on his little radio. But our small gang had our own trip. Whenever we got a chance, we took a toke break. Being stoned vastly improved the experience of doing blood differential counts. We oohed and aahed over the shape and colour of lymphocytes, monocytes, neutrophils and basophils. Anyone could have busted us. Smoking grass made our eyes red, a dead giveaway of our toking habits. A friendly pharmacist, also a stoner, recognized kindred spirits and offered a bottle of Visine eye drops. Grass dried my mouth too. I had so many cavities that I was a frequent visitor to the dental clinic upstairs. The dentists commented on the lack of saliva, but didn't suspect the cause.

One afternoon, I was glued to the microscope when someone jabbed my side, and I banged my forehead against the eyepiece. Furious, I turned around.

'What the ...'

It was Mex Mouse, looking shifty and acting mysteriously. Curiosity replaced anger.

'Come to the Cube this evening,' he said. 'Fo' sure, OK?'

'What's going on?'

'Just be there,' he called over his shoulder as he left the room.

When we convened at the trailer, Mex Mouse pulled out a package from his mother, who had returned to San Francisco after a trip to Mexico. Under a development programme, the US government supplied Mexican farmers with mechanical adobe brick-pressing machines. One enterprising person had used the contraption to compress marijuana into bricks of Acapulco Gold. Wrapped in socks inside the box was half a block, which would last us for weeks, if not months. 'Socks' became a code word for grass.

I took the night shift as often as possible, happy to work alone. For every fourteen-hour night shift, I got two days off. That was the clincher. Besides, nights were usually slow. After finishing the routine lab tests, I smoked a spliff under the toxic fumes hood. With the music turned up, I read my snake books such as Charles Bogert's book on cobra fangs. Since I had a collection of teeth removed from dead snakes at the serpentarium, I studied them under the microscope, comparing the front-facing structure of spitting cobra fangs with the non-spitters' downward-pointing fangs. These venom-delivering teeth were astonishingly identical to the hypodermic needles I used every day in the lab. Another book I often turned to was Kauffeld's. His repeated mention of the Huachuca Mountains in southern Arizona made me want to head there.

My experiences looking for snakes in the desert surrounding El Paso until then had been disappointing. On my days off, I cruised the roads after dark in Howdy's car to look for reptiles. It was the wrong season—too dry and hot for anything to be out. When the first rains hit, I set off road cruising as Heyward and I had done in Miami. Instead of snakes, the sand crawled with tarantulas. This was my first encounter with these hefty arachnids. Although uncomfortable with smaller spiders, I scooped up a large, velvety black one in my hand, and it legged its way up my arm. With an upturned tile to hide under, a Petri dish as a water bowl and grasshoppers to feast on, it did well in a box hidden behind a curtain in the barracks. When I took it out, it explored my hand leisurely, making no attempt to scuttle away. It earned me the temporary nickname of 'Spiderman', or 'Spidey' for short. Before someone found the tarantula while cleaning or during inspection and killed it, I released it into the desert.

Occasionally, a night shift in the lab got hectic. Once, a stream of injured people involved in a shootout and car wreck near the Mexican border arrived at the ER entrance in screaming ambulances. The doctors scribbled STAT, STAT, SUPERSTAT (which meant IMMEDIATELY, IF NOT SOONER!) on the test slips that ward boys brought to the door with the tubes of blood. I worked non-stop until my shift ended.

On another terrible night, a small aircraft crashed at the airport. I was ready for the victims, but they were wheeled into the morgue in the basement. The smell of barbecue permeating the ground-floor lab made me nauseous. The next morning, a dental intern stood doubled up on the lawn, throwing up. He had been checking the teeth to identify the bodies, and he couldn't take it any more. But most nights were peaceful.

Colonel Lundberg, in charge of the daily operations, gave me the additional responsibility of blood banking, besides regular lab analysis work. Before giving a blood transfusion, it was my job to ascertain the patient's blood group and type, and then find matching donor blood. Even if they matched, some other components in the blood might not. I performed a cross-match, mixing a tiny quantity of patient and donor blood in a test tube and holding it up to the light. If the sample remained smooth, the donor blood could be transfused to the patient. But if the blended blood formed little clots, or agglutinations, the donor blood couldn't be given because the patient could die from extensive blood clots in the veins. Sometimes, a match needed confirmation under a microscope. Even a small oversight could kill a patient.

One June weekend, instead of goofing around with the others at the Cube, I hitch-hiked most of the day to reach Ramsey Canyon in southern Arizona. The golden evening light on the spectacular rocky slopes and forested valleys took my breath away. This was so unlike the desert around El Paso. I camped next to a gurgling stream and rose early the next morning to a screech owl's whistles. After a breakfast of my last bologna sandwich, I walked along a trail to a rock slide. For thousands of years, hillsides had collapsed, creating these slides and offering shelter to many small reptiles. Large sections of falling cliffs sounded like thunder, which is why the Apache Indians named them the Huachucas, or the Thunder Mountains.

I spotted my first mountain rattler, a green rock rattlesnake. It escaped between boulders before I could reach it. The snake hook, so versatile in other terrain, was useless among the rocks. After three hours of turning stones and poking into holes, I headed back to camp. The ground was thick with ladybugs. At specific spots high in the canyons, huge concentrations of the bright red insects covered whole tree trunks. I had only read about the migration and watched with wonder. But I had to hurry. It had taken longer than I had bargained for to arrive in the mountains, and I didn't know how long it would take me to return.

I made it back in time to report for my 8 a.m. shift. During a break, I searched through the big drawer of medical equipment for a tool to catch small snakes. A test tube holder seemed perfect, since it had a scissor-like grip. I straightened the stiff wires with a pair of pliers and wrapped some tape on the ends so snakes wouldn't get hurt. If I was going to be serious about snake hunting, I couldn't waste my time hitch-hiking. Howdy drove me to a used-car lot, where I paid 250 dollars for a '56 two-door Ford in reasonable shape. On the following weekend, I again headed west to the Huachucas.

I arrived at Ramsey Canyon by evening and camped at the same stream-side spot. The next morning, as the sun warmed the rocky walls, I began a careful search along the edges of the rock slides. A cold and slow green rock rattler emerged to bask, and I scooped the foot-long snake with the converted test tube holder. It was in the bag even before it could start rattling in alarm. Further down the trail, another green rock buzzed between two boulders. Before it disappeared into a crevice, I snagged it too.

On the other side of the canyon, I stopped at a house surrounded by apple trees where a heavyset, middle-aged lady was working in the garden. Nell Brown, the caretaker of the property, knew what I was up to without being told.

'Get any snakes yet?' she asked by way of greeting.

Several others who had been inspired by Kauffeld's book hunted in these mountains. While she got the coffee brewing, she showed me a ledger of visiting snake hunters who had filled in data on the species and numbers they caught. That archive, if it still exists, would be herpetological gold. One record showed twelve green rocks, four Willard's and six twin-spotted rattlesnakes.

'Some of these guys are really serious,' I exclaimed.

'You outta meet Dick. He comes here regularly.'

Her finger paused on a page against the name Richard Schubel from Tucson, and she gave me his phone number. When I rose to leave, she said, 'If you get tired of sleeping in the rough, the barn has an old spring bed. You are welcome to it.' And she invited me to dinner.

She lived alone and was starved for company.

I walked from Ramsey to Carr Canyon, paying attention to the sights, smells and sounds of the wilds. Fence lizards basked in the sun, and I picked up an ungainly Sonoran alligator lizard. Everything here was a first for me, and I had plenty of the West's reptile wealth to discover. I returned to Nell's house that evening, where we shared an early dinner of chilli con carne on rice, and I was pleased not to have to eat yet another sandwich.

In the course of our conversation, Nell revealed she saw people's faces in the windows of the cottage. Not any old faces, but of people who were going to die. While she didn't know many of them or what happened to them, she claimed the very recognizable mug of Adlai Stevenson appeared before he died. The politician had passed away just the previous week. The visage of the pastor of the Bisbee Baptist Church materialized a day or two before he succumbed to cancer. The glass panes were warped, and I could imagine a face peering at me if I squinted hard enough.

Spooked, I followed her in the dark to the barn. Besides seeing faces, her hobby was collecting old bottles, and the place was filled with thousands of them of all kinds, sizes and shapes. She handed me a bottle with swirls of blue.

'It's more beautiful in sunlight,' she said. 'When clear bottles lie exposed in the sun for a long time, they become solarized and develop these colours.'

Over the years, she had picked them up from the abandoned townships in the Huachucas, where miners had camped in the past. I thanked her for her hospitality and spread out my sleeping bag on a bed frame with pieces of cardboard covering the springs. I woke well before dawn and drove back to El Paso, where the director of the zoo was happy to have the two rattlers for display.

Ma wrote from New York saying she and Rama had divorced. The news came as a shock. She was visiting Elly, having left Nina and Neel with Sitamma in Bombay.

'If there's a chance you can come to see us, it would be wonderful,' she said in the letter. 'I fly back to India in a month.'

I applied for a four-day pass. An older lab technician told me I could go to any military airbase in the States and hitch a ride on a plane with my leave order. *Would it work? No harm in trying.* Nobody gave me, a uniformed soldier, a second glance at the high-security Biggs Air Force Base in El Paso. The duty officer suggested I board a C-130 Hercules cargo plane to the NORAD Strategic Air Command base in Nebraska, from where I might get a connecting flight.

The aircraft had no padded seats or hostesses. Besides me, five others sat on uncomfortable webbing slung along the side of the bulkhead. Big crates of machinery were lashed on to the deck in front of us. With a deafening roar, the plane shuddered as it raced on the runway. A warrant officer saw me exchange worried glances with the others.

'The C-130 Herk is one of the best aircraft ever made,' he shouted above the racket. 'It can fly even if three of the four engines conk out. Don't you worry, it'll get us there.'

When we were airborne, at least the shuddering stopped, if not the noise. I yawned for relief from the pressure in my ears. There was nothing to do but sleep for the two-hour trip.

I was lucky in Nebraska too. A pilot, two trainee navigators and their instructor were getting ready for a night training flight to Andrews Air Force Base in Maryland on a T-39 Sabreliner. The narrow confines of the small jet were intimate, and the controls were familiar from the classes at Air Force ROTC in college. In a large aircraft, the only movements you feel are the take-off, landing and the occasional bump when it hits an air pocket. The small plane, however, felt like a sports car with every slight shift sideways, up or down registering. The magic of the star-embedded sky and the distant lights of cities kept me awake. We landed at sunrise, and I caught a bus to New York City and arrived at Elly's apartment in time for lunch.

Seeing Ma after four long years was wonderful. She told me about how grown-up Nina and Neel were attending the Bombay International School, of which she was one of the founders. I described my work in the army, exaggerating what I had learnt about medicine and what fun I was having in the mountains of Arizona. When there was a pause in the conversation, she brought up the divorce. Rama had fallen for another woman. While that was difficult to deal with, she got anonymous calls of someone breathing heavily, sometimes in the middle of the night. She hoped the harassment would stop now that the papers had been signed. I assumed she would move to the States with the kids, but according to the terms of the divorce, she couldn't leave India with both of them at once. She seemed disappointed by this arrangement, but brushed it away. I was saddened by the divorce and hoped Ma would find happiness again. *Would I see Rama, Granddaddy and Amma, or would the break-up of the marriage sever my ties with them?* I didn't know the answer then.

Before I knew it, my leave time was up and I had to return. I caught a bus to Andrews Air Force Base, hoping to retrace my journey. An old cargo plane being fuelled was to fly to El Paso. The direct flight shaved many hours from the trip.

It was back to the routine of the hospital. On my way out of town one evening to cruise the roads, I spotted a boutique with fabric and symbols from India—the city's only head shop run by Wes and Jan Penn. A big sticker on the door read 'Legalize Pot'. *How can something so anti-establishment exist in conservative El Paso?* The psychedelic artwork, including abstract paintings and pottery, most of them the work of Wes the artist, left no doubt as to the radical leanings of this wonderful couple. Jan was a true hippie Mama. Although I, clean-shaven with my GI haircut, must have looked like a typical straight dude, she welcomed me into the shop.

While I browsed through the merchandise, Wes chatted with a group of young men, their voices audible through the open office door. I glimpsed a stoned man with wild hair and an infectious laugh. When they rose to leave, his parting advice was something straight out of Timothy Leary's mouth, 'Turn on, tune in and drop out.'

That was the beginning of a long friendship. I escaped the drudgery of Beaumont Hospital almost every weekend to listen to the latest hip music by Bob Dylan, Joan Baez and Jimi Hendrix. Toking a pipe on their back porch, I watched the comings and goings of students, artists and musicians. I read books, such as Aldous Huxley's *The Doors of Perception,* David Solomon's *The Marijuana Papers* and Bernard Roseman's *225,000 Indians Can't Be Wrong: The Peyote Story.* After reading them, I wanted to try psychedelics.

One lazy Saturday morning, I shared a pot of nauseously bitter peyote tea with Jan. I gazed at the treetops as everything began to swirl and take strange shapes. A hand touched my shoulder.

'Come, I want to read your I Ching,' said a lovely woman.

She flipped coins and read aloud from the *Book of Changes* while her sweet face mesmerized me. I didn't comprehend a word, but I wanted her to keep talking. I left my body and hovered above, seeing the back of my head. The need to be totally honest, to face myself pants down, no holds barred, was overpowering. The time was now to let all my inner tensions and evil thoughts spill out. I don't recall anything more than fragmentary thoughts, but I do remember experiencing a deep connection with the woman in front of me and others in the room. My first trip was interesting and mellow, but left me craving a more intense experience.

Nita called me at the lab one day.

'Do you want to try acid?' she asked.

A friend of hers had bought some from the local dealer. LSD got a lot of negative press, of bad trips supposedly leading to suicides or insanity. Wes had told me not to believe a word of it. I was curious to experience it, since that guy had dodged the draft by taking acid and babbling to the psych doc.

Squeaky and Howdy begged off. Mex Mouse and I arrived after dark at the posh house where Nita lived then. She unfolded a piece of paper with four little blue pills, 100 micrograms each, on the table.

'I was told it'll be a mild trip,' she said.

'Are you our guide?' I asked. 'Will you make sure we don't try something really stupid?'

'You mean something stupider than swallowing these pills?' she asked with mock seriousness.

Although she hung around with us, she didn't do drugs of any kind except wine. Mex and I swallowed a pill each.

We waited about twenty minutes for the trip to begin. When nothing happened, Mex lit a joint, took a deep toke and passed it to me. I was about to draw on it when he belched loudly, sending us both into a laughing fit until my aching stomach couldn't take it any more.

'Enough, enough,' I croaked while gasping for breath.

'Sorry, man. It was those chile relleno burritos we had for dinner,' he said.

The veins on the back of my hands bulged like coils of piping. The ride had begun. I leaned back on the couch and gazed through the window. It was dark, but small, fantastic creatures walked around.

Nita turned on the TV and *Ticket to Ride* burst forth. The Beatles were on *The Ed Sullivan Show*. Their nodding, puppet-like heads floated above their bodies and their grins were manic. I closed my eyes to stop the imagery, but they streamed behind my eyeballs, a never-ending torrent of consciousness. Endless rows of prickly pear cacti coasted below me and each thorn had a spool of coloured thread, which started spinning. Colours merged into a confusing cacophony. I had to open my eyes, or I would go insane. *What does it mean?* The sight of my friends comfortably seated under the dim light calmed me and I forgot what a mess I had been in moments earlier. To the soundtrack of songs we hadn't heard before, *Act Naturally*, *I Feel Fine* and *Yesterday*, I struggled to find the deep inner meaning of my vision. *Maybe it will make sense if I keep at it.* The guitar strumming vibrated through my brain.

It was a seductive feeling, that an incredible insight that could change my life was within reach. But it never materialized, like trying to remember a dream while being inside a dream that disappears in a microsecond. The frustration of not being able to latch on to this wisdom probably led to bad trips. Novices could be demoralized by thoughts such as 'I'm such a useless bugger' and 'I have so much potential but can't use it'. I was scratching the surface of a spiritual experience, although there was nothing religious about it. The brain seemed capable of a lot more than I'd imagined.

When I opened my eyes, a close-up of Ringo Starr filled the television screen, and he was pointing his finger straight at me.

'You know where it's at,' he said.

I was shaken. He was talking to me. *Where is what at? What does he mean?* After a moment's confusion, I realized I was one among millions of viewers of the programme.

After the show ended, Nita turned on a kaleidoscopic lamp, which changed colour as it rotated. It might ordinarily have been psychedelic, but it didn't impress me in my altered state. The reflections in the window were trippier. Nita's red hair, back-lit over her shoulders, swirled and grew until it took over the room. The effects lasted a few endless hours. When we came down, Mex stretched and yawned.

'Wow, thanks, Nita,' he said. 'Man, what a trip! Next time we gotta try a thousand mikes.'

I understood his desire to get deeper into his mind, as I felt the same way.

'I need some sleep,' he said. 'You drive, Snake.'

I rose shakily to my feet and kissed Nita goodnight.

A few days later, on a Sunday, Squeaky, Mex Mouse and I drove across the border into Juárez. We parked near the main market and poked around the stalls selling everything from agave rope to live chickens. Two Tigua Indian *brujos*, or healers, sold herbs, roots and seeds. A box contained small desiccated creatures, which could have been bats or rats. Another was filled with gnarled dried plants, which resembled collapsed grey tennis balls with long thick roots. Peyote.

Noticing my interest, the vendor said, '*Uno kilogram es cinco dollar* [One kilogram is five dollars].'

I slapped a ten-dollar bill in front of him.

'*Dos kilogram, por favor* [Two kilograms, please],' I said.

He weighed the cacti on an old hand scale, like the ones vegetable vendors used in India.

We were paranoid about crossing the American border with the contraband. At the checkpoint, we held up Bacardi bottles to show the customs officers. They waved us through, and the peyote remained hidden under my seat.

A week later, four of us arrived in the morning at Marie's house on the western edge of the city, overlooking the open Chihuahuan Desert. Marie, Nita's friend and colleague, had wanted to experiment with peyote too. After cutting and discarding the roots, we ground the cacti in a blender. Chewing the extraordinarily bitter plants raw, the Mexican Indian way, was out of the question. We sat at the dining table, painstakingly stuffing the powder into 125 empty gelatin capsules, which we had scrounged from the med lab. Then we each swallowed twenty-five pills with gulps of water, and relaxed, waiting for the trip to begin. At first, the queasiness was mild, but with every passing minute, it turned to nausea. We tried hard not to throw up, figuring the longer we held it in, the higher the euphoria. I used all my willpower to quell the rising tide within. Later, I read the Indians ate peyote and puked their guts out.

In about an hour, the nausea faded and the day started developing a strange glow. Everything had a silver, sometimes gold, edge. *Could the others see the same thing?* From their responses, it wasn't clear whether they saw the bright edges only because I mentioned it. In this state of mind, I could neither analyse nor think straight. I went with the flow.

I sprawled on the couch, gazing through the window at the empty sunlit desert that pulsated with light. The yuccas swayed and tumbleweeds rocked before a gust sent them bouncing along. A roadrunner ambled stealthily, looking for a luckless lizard, grasshopper or little snake. I became the bird, sharp-eyed, wary and predatory. Without warning, I had a clear but unusual view of the back and top of my head and shoulders. It felt normal to be out of my body, seeing myself as an outsider. My mind then zipped over the desert, inhabiting a beetle and then becoming lost in a swirl of colours.

I read aloud Allen Ginsberg's epic poem 'Howl' from his collection *Howl and Other Poems*:

> *I saw the best minds of my generation destroyed by madness, starving hysterical naked/Dragging themselves through the negro streets at dawn looking for an angry fix/Angelheaded hipsters burning for the ancient heavenly connection to the starry dynamo in the machinery of night/ Who poverty and tatters and hollow-eyed and high sat up smoking in the supernatural darkness of cold-water flats floating across the tops of cities contemplating jazz.*[4]

We laughed hysterically as our minds conjured up weird images that I had to give up reading.

Ordinary objects became fascinating. I stared at a chair, taking in every detail—the screws that held it together, the grain of the wood and the angle of the backrest. Time warped, expanding one minute and contracting the next. Thoughts flooded my brain faster than I could express verbally, leaving my sentences incomplete. Waves of multicoloured images tumbled one after the other. The breathless imagery reached a crescendo and then abated for a few restful moments. Sometimes, I flew with my friends and felt one with them. Then I ripped away and caught a wave of my own.

My friends wandered in their own realms. Something as subtle as an eye movement made us simultaneously sigh and 'descend' back to earth, or 'come down' as we put it. We felt normal or 'straight' for a short while, when we sipped soda or water before going off again on our personal tangents of kaleidoscopic visions. Even though colour-blind, I was dazzled by the colours of ordinary objects around me and their incredible expansions and contractions.

As the day wore on, I was lost in an alternative reality that was at times hysterically funny and at others, dark and deep when everything was tinged with negativity, like an inexplicable nightmare. I struggled to extricate myself from the depths of despair. It's for this reason that you

---

4 Allen Ginsberg, *Howl and Other Poems* (San Francisco, US: City Lights Books, 1956).

need a guide on the first trip. I wrestled with my harrowing thoughts, and eventually, the whirlpool of my mind spat me out, and I soared with euphoria. When Squeaky whimpered, I wrapped my arms around his shoulders and whispered calming words as if to a crying child or frightened animal, until he emerged from his tormented hallucination.

The doorbell rang at about 2 p.m. Earth time, and I dragged myself off the couch. Marie had somehow ordered pizza in a lucid moment. I expected a delivery boy, but encountered the deeply lined face of an ancient personage. Trying not to stare at him, I took the pizza, gave him some dollar bills and mumbled, 'Keep the change.' Delighted by the windfall, he sprinted to his motor scooter.

The others gathered around the table as I opened the box.

'I can't eat that montage,' Mex Mouse said with revulsion. 'It's fuckin' alive.'

I understood what he meant—the cheese strips resembled yellow worms burrowing through the heaving multicoloured layers of dried tomatoes, anchovies and green peppers. Marie pushed us aside.

'I'm hungry,' she said. 'And I'll eat it alive.'

We watched her eating the writhing slice of pizza in horror. Somehow that broke the spell, and everything became normal. The pizza had been 'killed', and I ate a piece.

Even after twelve hours of tripping, there was no letting up. We were tired, but the mescaline wouldn't let us rest or sleep.

'Maybe we took too much,' Mex Mouse groaned. 'Maybe we shouldn't have eaten peyote on an empty stomach.'

In the cool of the evening, we walked into the desert and watched the full moon rise. None of us said a word as we entered a meditative stage, sitting cross-legged on a sand dune. The world turned from red and gold into silver and ghostly white. Birds stopped singing and bats swooped and swirled. It was dark when we stumbled indoors.

Sleep overcame us sometime during the night, and when I woke in the morning, my mind had drifted back to earth. The trip had ended, but we were exhausted.

'I never knew anything could be so intense,' said Mex Mouse. 'It's so hard to even imagine where my head has been to and back.'

Nothing we can say in words truly captured our experience. I returned to work at the lab with a new sense of peace. Tendrils of the trip lingered for days and weeks.

Even now, many decades later, my jaws clench when a stray shadow of that peyote experience flits by my peripheral vision. Something had shifted permanently in my mind and the way I understood the world.

23

SNAKES, DRUGS AND
ROCK 'N' ROLL

Lost in the Rain in Juárez

T HE 1970S' TELEVISION SERIES *M*A*S*H,* about a medical unit during the Korean War, captures the weird morbid humour of wartime. Our comic spirit was fuelled by the use, or misuse, of booze, grass and pills. After that half brick of grass went up in smoke, Mex Mouse's mother sent another. The PX sold cheap beer, and Bacardi Añejo rum was inexpensive in Juárez. The others popped tablets such as speed and phenobarbital, which they scored from the same pharmacist who gave us the eye drops.

The first time I tried one of these drugs was on night duty. A regular user of the diet drug Dexedrine, a powerful amphetamine also called 'speed', gave me four tablets. I made the mistake of swallowing them all. Within minutes, my heart felt as if it would burst as it raced at 160 beats per minute. Unlike the calmness of being stoned, this trip made me anxious and agitated. To distract myself, I sang along to the hits of that year playing on the radio, The Rolling Stones' *(I Can't Get No) Satisfaction* and The Animals' *We Gotta Get Out of This Place*. After an hour, my pulse slowed and I stopped being fidgety. Pills weren't for me.

The paternalism of the army encouraged our juvenile sense of humour. Since the four-man blood banking crew was called 'the Vampire Squad', we had to live up to our name. A prosthodontist at the dental clinic was only too happy to make vampire fangs. The pointy canine teeth extensions fit into our palates, making us look like Dracula. During blood-collection drives, we pranked the soldier donors by flashing our evil smiles as we shoved needles into their veins. The nervous ones freaked out, but the others laughed.

Each evening, before knocking off work, we would sterilize the equipment in an autoclave. But first, the test tubes had to be cleaned of blood clots. Once, a technician shook a tube again and again to dislodge a coagulated clump. When he gave it one mighty flick, it flew across the room and landed on my chest, the deep red smearing the starched white lab smock. I retaliated, flinging a fat one from a big test tube, which caught him in the middle of his back. Someone yelled, 'Clot fight', and in no time, bloody slugs sailed in every direction. We didn't think how deadly some of those patients' clots might be. Even for the pre-AIDS era, this was reckless, not to mention the almighty mess we had to clean up.

As lab techs, we knew more about our specialized fields than medical interns. A young doctor held up a test tube of mixed donor and patient blood, and certified it compatible. But the sample looked clumped. I insisted he examine a smear under the microscope. The sample had agglutinated. A tragedy had been averted.

I played a prank on every new batch of residents by making a slide and staining the blood of a horned lizard. I gave them an obvious clue by labelling the patient's name on the results slip as A. Lee Zard and slipped it in with other slides of human blood. They went into a tizzy. Unlike adult human red blood cells (RBCs), lizard RBCs have nuclei.

'Nucleated RBCs!' exclaimed a young doctor.

'What's wrong with this guy?' murmured another.

The others crowded around the microscope while I continued working in my corner. If none of them could figure it out, I intervened before they called a senior physician and escalated it to a serious event. Once they realized the joke was on them, they laughed it off. I liked to think it was educational.

Despite these silly moments, I had my share of sobering medical experiences. I was on duty after lunch and toking on grass at the Cube when the emergency room summoned me. A local rancher had been kicked in the face by his horse and wouldn't stop bleeding. I collected his blood sample, stained a smear and peered at it through the microscope. It was packed with lymphocytes, way more than I had ever seen. The haematology manual said it was an indicator of acute lymphocytic leukaemia. I slumped in my seat. Being stoned exaggerated my feeling of sorrow for the poor man. *How must doctors feel when they have to give tragic news to a patient?*

Squeaky and I were constantly looking for ways to make extra money. We heard of a part-time job opportunity from the sergeant. An ex-army doctor, Colonel Smiley, ran a blood plasma collection centre.

'His lab needs technicians,' said the sarge. 'If you guys are interested, here's his number.'

Both of us jumped at the chance.

A steady line of poor folks, many of them Mexicans and Native Americans, came to Colonel Smiley's lab to earn a quick ten dollars by donating blood. We were to collect a pint, spin it in a centrifuge and skim the plasma into another sterile bag. The blood cells would be reconstituted with saline and then transfused back to the same donor in less than an hour. The collected plasma was needed to prepare gamma globulin against hepatitis and other deadly tropical diseases in Vietnam. The work was not different from our army job, but it paid more.

On a slow day at the hospital, Colonel Lundberg summoned lab techs who were on morning duty to his office to rearrange his furniture. We shuffled to the adjoining administrative building, expecting hours of boredom moving cupboards with files, desks and chairs. Our slouched backs straightened on seeing his new gorgeous blonde secretary, Claire. To our disappointment, the job got done in a few minutes, and we ran out of excuses to hang around near her.

On the following days, I didn't miss a chance to stop by Claire's desk to shoot the breeze before finally asking her out on a night drive into the desert. Besides the work at Smiley's 'Plasma Bar', as we sarcastically referred to the lab, I caught snakes for sale to zoos and venom centres.

Since the weather cooled in October, I had better luck finding them by road cruising than in the heat of the summer.

'Are you going to catch rattlesnakes?' Claire asked.

'Only if we see one,' I replied with a grin.

That evening, she picked me up in her red MG sports car and we headed out of town. When we turned into a side road off Anthony Gap, I instructed her to creep along with the dims on. Sitting on the steeply curved hood wasn't an option, as I'd slip right off.

'When I tell you to stop, that means I've spotted a snake,' I said. 'Please don't run over it.'

She nodded.

Within a few minutes, we came upon a good-sized western diamondback stretched out on the road. As we approached on foot, the rattler bunched up its coils and rattled with fear.

'Listen to it sing,' she commented. 'It doesn't seem to like you very much.'

I held its head and asked her to cut a piece of electrical tape from a roll in my knapsack and wrap it around the rattle.

'What on earth for?'

'I gotta take it into the barracks. If it buzzes, everyone will find out about it.'

After bagging it and putting it on the back seat, we continued on our way.

Further down the road, a medium-sized bull snake lay soaking up the warmth. Although I was after rattlers, we stopped so Claire could touch it, a first time for her. I picked it up and showed her how to hold it so it didn't feel threatened. She admired it by the car's light.

'It's beautiful,' she said, her eyes sparkling. 'I never imagined I'd get this friendly with a snake.'

After she released it by the side of the road, we slid into the car and rolled forward. We saw no more snakes for the next hour.

When she dropped me at the barracks, she said, 'That was definitely the most unique first date I've ever been on.'

'Not many girls would have found it romantic,' I replied.

She was hooked. So was I, and not only on snakes.

At night, we cruised the desert roads outside El Paso, such as White Sands Drive, Alabama Street and Gas Road. Sometimes, when Claire couldn't get a babysitter, her three-year-old daughter, Elaine, came along, sleeping curled up in the back seat. She was awake for the excitement when I jumped out to bag a scared and buzzing western diamondback, prairie or blacktail rattler.

I had to be careful about stashing my snakes. Since I returned to the barracks after lights out, they stayed in individual pillowcases within my knapsack inside the locker. A friendly PFC in the hospital's carpentry shop made wooden boxes, in which I packed the snakes. At the airport, I booked the containers to their destinations in Miami, New Jersey or New York. None of the airlines' booking staff batted an eyelid when they handled packages labelled, 'VENOMOUS SNAKES—KEEP OUT OF SUN.'

One afternoon, I reported for my two-hour shift at the Plasma Bar after catching snakes that morning. I piled five bags with a western diamondback in each into a large supermarket brown paper bag. If left in the car, they would die from overheating. The top of the tall air conditioner behind the building seemed a safe spot as it was in the shade and out of the way. Or so I thought.

An hour later, there was a big commotion at the back. I peeked outside and froze on seeing the ghastly scene. The five rattlesnakes lay dead on the ground with their heads and rattles chopped off. A group of men stood nearby.

'Who killed my snakes?' I yelled in fury as I rushed out.

'We did,' said one, holding a bloody rattle in his hand. 'How can you bring these snakes here into town?'

He had a point, but my anger took a long while to abate. They had stolen my bag and got a nasty surprise when they realized it didn't contain groceries.

'Thieves,' I muttered under my breath.

Gathering the empty snake bags, I stomped inside with a heavy heart. I somehow pulled myself through another hour of work, but my mind wasn't on it. As I calmed down, my anger turned on myself. I cursed myself for being stupid enough to leave the snakes unattended. It was a hard and bitter lesson.

Claire couldn't go with me on every snake hunt. One night, I drove out of El Paso with the radio blaring rock 'n' roll from XERF-AM in Del Rio, Texas.

'This is Wolfman Jack,' announced the gravelly voice of the disc jockey, who started his session with a howl. 'I'm here to keep you awake on the road with the latest and the greatest.'

The Coasters' *Poison Ivy* was playing when a prairie rattler slid off the tarmac and headed for a thick clump of thorny cholla cactus. I braked to a quick stop and ran to get it before it disappeared. In my hurry, I forgot to grab the snake hook. So I restrained it by the tail and tried pinning its head with my flashlight. With the car's headlights in my eyes, for a moment I couldn't see what I was doing and the snake nailed my right forefinger. A deep burning pain shot through my hand, but I bagged it and got behind the wheel.

I drove the thirty-two kilometres back to the city with a pounding pain and my brain repeating, 'Oh shit, oh shit, oh shit.' I cursed myself for my ineptitude. By the time I reached the Beaumont Hospital gate, my arm was swelling and my nose was clogged. If it didn't worsen, I could manage without medical help. I went into the coffee shop outside the entrance to wait before deciding what to do.

'Boy, are you crazy?' exclaimed the waitress on noticing my swollen hand. 'Get yourself into the hospital right now, hear?'

'Let me finish my coffee, willya,' I sheepishly replied.

'Crazy effin' GI,' she muttered.

Ten minutes later, the swelling reached my armpit. No point putting it off any more, and I walked into the emergency room.

A nurse helped me climb up on a bed and the doctor instructed her to start an IV and infuse five vials of antivenom, which made me think I was in expert hands. Within minutes, I was overcome by intense itching and non-stop sneezing. *What's happening to me?* The nurse ran out to summon the doctor.

'He's reacting to the antivenom,' he said. 'Give him .5 ml of epinephrine and let's start him on hydrocortisone.'

'Are you choking?' he asked me.

I shook my head between sneezes. The adrenaline and antihistamine calmed the intensity of the allergic reaction, but hives had broken out on my face and chest. I dozed but woke up when two nurses put my arm into a basin of ice. I was perplexed.

'Doctor's orders are to freeze your hand,' one replied. 'He's trying a new snakebite treatment protocol.'

Later, I discovered this experimental and unproven theory was advocated by toxinologist Dr Herbert Stahnke, who suggested cryotherapy could retard the spread of venom. I protested being treated like a guinea pig, but I was a GI, which amounted to the same thing. My arm became numb and stiff as frozen steak.

Sixty-one hours later, they removed the ice. I had always prided myself on my high pain threshold, but the agony was excruciating as my arm thawed. I clenched my teeth to keep from screaming. They gave me Demerol, and I floated above the bed, aware of the agony but unbothered by it. It felt like being on a permanent grass high. When I woke up in a drugged stupor, my sense of reality wobbled when a pretty nurse felt my pulse.

'Did I die?' I asked her. 'Are you an angel?'

'You're very much alive,' she replied sternly. 'I'm Amy, the night duty nurse.'

I drifted in and out of sleep. During one bout of semi-wakefulness, I was aware Howdy had come to draw blood.

'If the doc gives you "LoD no", you is fucked, man,' he said.

I hadn't thought about that. 'LoD no' meant I was doing something dangerous that wasn't in the Line of Duty, and I'd have to pay my hospital bill. I couldn't afford the antivenom, let alone the rest of the medical facilities. Besides, I might also have to work extra weeks to repay the recovery time. I freaked out, and even the Demerol lost some of its effect. I swore at Howdy for scaring the daylights out of me and was furious with myself for getting into this mess.

When the doctor came on his rounds, I asked him in my most pitiful voice, 'Hey, doc, is this snakebite considered LoD no?'

'Don't sweat it,' he said. 'It was clearly an accident.'

I breathed a sigh of relief.

I recovered and could return to duty, but the doctors kept me for another week. The venom had eaten the tissue around the site of the bite, a condition called necrosis, or dry gangrene. The nurses cleaned the dead flesh before dressing the wound. Lab technicians doing their morning hospital rounds visited me in the recovery ward to keep me company, but couldn't stay for long. Not only was I bored out of my wits, I also missed the wilds. By reading Kauffeld's book on snake hunting countless times, I memorized where he had found every species. I wrote to him in a shaky hand, praising his book and describing my own efforts at catching snakes. After asking Squeaky to mail the letter, I was at a loose end again.

Claire came to my rescue and took me, still dressed in my hospital pyjamas, on a drive to McKelligon Canyon, where we made out after a picnic. The memory of that day got me through my convalescence. She bought a card for Ma's birthday, and I scribbled a note: 'They kind of over-treated me—but it's a nice vacation from the lab. I have almost full use of my hand now, although the forefinger is still swollen and without feeling. A few more weeks, and it will be okay again.'

I was at first excited to receive a reply from the great Carl Kauffeld, but it left me sombre. He regretted advertising his favourite spots. He felt responsible for the unsustainable number of snakes being caught by hunters in places such as the Huachucas and the Ajo Road in Arizona, and Okeetee in South Carolina. In the same letter, he asked if I could supply him with the smaller, lesser-known species from the Huachuca Mountains, for which he offered an attractive payment.

Eventually, the open wound healed, but my finger was crooked and couldn't bend. At my discharge from hospital, the doctor prescribed physiotherapy and said to give it time as nerves regenerate at about a millimetre a month. I returned to active duty, relearning how to stick needles without using my forefinger. After work, I visited the pretty physiotherapy nurse, who put my hand into a whirlpool bath for an hour and gave me a rubber ball to squeeze.

'You gotta keep doing this every day for two months,' she said.

I followed her advice, waiting patiently for my finger to regain movement. In the meantime, I wrote about my snakebite experience and sent it to the editor of *HERP*, the Bulletin of the New York Herpetological Society. Back at the serp, I used to rummage through old publications, *HERP* among them, that Bill had piled up in the storeroom. The amateur notes about snakes, lizards, turtles and frogs in the bulletin had been fun to read. I had noted the mailing address with the idea of subscribing to the newsletter later.

I didn't hear back for weeks, and then, in January 1966, I got a copy of Volume 2, Number 4 and was excited to see 'A Case of Snakebite of Crotalus viridis viridis' by Romulus E. Whitaker III. It was my first publication of any kind and I couldn't resist showing off to Claire and my pals in the lab.

The director of the El Paso Zoo placed an order for a hundred fence lizards. I bought a cheap collapsible fly-fishing rod at a pawnshop, and dental floss, with which to fashion nooses. The itch to get out into the wilds grew stronger by the minute. Even though the finger wasn't normal yet and many weeks of physiotherapy remained, I applied for four days' leave. I packed my sleeping bag and snake bags, and set a cage for lizards on the back seat of the car. At Nick's Place, a café and bar in Nicksville, the last stop before I turned into Miller Canyon in the Huachucas, a helpful local introduced me to a man sitting at another table as his buddy, Ace Reynolds, the fire-watcher for the area.

On hearing I was there to find rattlers, Ace related stories of his work. He often fell asleep, trusting his horse to plod up the hours-long ride to Miller Peak. But sometimes, the animal also went to sleep and once bumped into a tree, sending him flying off the saddle. Neither mare nor man was hurt. This sleep-walking horse was petrified of rattlesnakes, and the tiny twin-spotted rattlesnake was common on the mountain path. The buzz of the rattle was enough to make it skittish, and Ace feared plummeting down a steep slope.

'Where do you stay at the peak?' I asked.

'There's a forest service cabin up there,' he said, slamming the key on the bar counter. 'If a storm rolls in, make sure you are not on the exposed hillsides. Those rocks are full of iron. You'll see the scars from all the forest fires set by lightning up there.'

'Where should I shelter then?'

'Not under a tree, that's for sure. Hunker down next to a fallen tree if its roots aren't grounded.'

I camped by the stream that night and hiked to Carr Canyon in the morning. An exquisite gold-and-black snake, the blacktail rattler, glided across the stones, which Kauffeld called the most beautiful of rattlesnakes. I could see why. After taking a few photographs, I clumsily manoeuvred the four-foot snake into a bag. It remained calm, and I would later discover blacktails are the least excitable of rattlesnakes. They buzz twice or thrice during capture, rarely strike and are more intent on escaping. The next snake I caught was a five-foot Mojave rattler, which is almost identical to the western diamondback. This one was on the opposite extreme of the nervous spectrum, possibly the most aggressively defensive rattlesnake.

I hiked from Carr Canyon into Ramsey Canyon, catching fence lizards with my modified fishing rod. Tying nooses took me ages as my bum finger got in the way. It would be a long time before I could become adept at using my hand again. I focused on the large beautiful males with metallic blue throats, as they had more appeal in the pet trade. Strange, civet-like animals called coatimundis, deer and javelinas skipped and snuffled through the valleys. Butterflies drifted past and jewel-like hummingbirds hovered over blossoms. I savoured the pleasure of kneeling at a spring and gulping the cold water. At midday, I found a green rock rattler on the trail, and another coiled under a cactus buzzed a few metres farther down. Both went into separate bags in my knapsack. Nell wasn't home, and I collapsed, exhausted, on the bed in the barn that evening.

The next day, I walked over sixteen kilometres from Ramsey to Miller Peak along Crest Trail. On the way, I caught a twin-spotted rattlesnake and many more lizards. I was absorbed in looking at the ground when the sound of a crack made me glance up. A big black bear had ripped into a worm-eaten log and was sniffing the debris. Perhaps he had snorted an ant or a grain of wood, since he started sneezing.

I hesitated, wondering what to do, since he was smack in the middle of the path. I coughed and cleared my throat. He whipped around, saw me and took off. It was late in the afternoon when I arrived at the watchtower, at 9,400 feet elevation, and I kicked myself for not bringing more sandwiches. Trekking had made me ravenous. In the cabin's kitchenette, I found some rice, powdered milk and butterscotch pudding, which I cooked into some sort of mess. It wasn't great, but would have to do.

In the cool evening, I walked the Montezuma Trail, the name evoking the Native Americans, miners, *bandidos* and mercenaries of old. As the sun set, the shadow of the mountain crept across the border into Mexico. I retraced my steps to the cabin as the clouds smothered other peaks from view.

An electric storm swept in during the night, and one bolt struck the lightning rod at the top of the watchtower with a bang that almost threw me off the cot. I wasn't prepared for the cold, so I covered myself with the only available thing, a filthy sleeping bag. And I paid the price the next day.

I left the shack's key for Ace at the Nicksville café and headed back to El Paso. Halfway, my crotch started to itch, and once I began to scratch, I couldn't stop. The rest of the way seemed endless. In the brightly lit barracks bathroom, I stripped and examined myself. Lice crawled through my pubic hair. By then, the vehement scratching had peeled the skin off in spots. A hot shower and changing into clean clothes didn't bring relief. The itching became intense at night, and scraping the open sores made matters worse.

I consulted the parasitologist, who wouldn't believe the crabs came from a dirty sleeping bag. She assumed I was too shy to admit to cavorting with the 'goodtime girls' in Juárez. Grim-faced, she wrote a prescription for Ascabiol, a topical lotion.

'Next time, be more careful!' she said as she handed me the piece of paper.

My friends thought my predicament was hilarious.

'To get rid of those crabs, Snake,' Squeaky advised, 'first, you shave half the hair off your crotch, then you arm yourself with an ice pick, set the other half of your hair on fire, and as the little mothers run out, you stab 'em to death, one by one.'

Everyone howled with laughter. I had to admit it was funny. My embarrassing problem took a week to cure.

In the meantime, I shipped the snakes to Kauffeld, who was happy that they arrived in good shape. He placed an order for more, and I made plans to head out west again. I sold the fifty lizards to the zoo director for half a buck apiece. By then, I got in touch with Richard Schubel, the snake hunter from Tucson that Nell had mentioned, and arranged to meet with him and his wife Nan at Ramsey Canyon. I wanted to learn from him since he was knowledgeable about this area.

I was at the lab examining a blood smear under the microscope when two policemen strode in.

'Where is Romulus Whitaker?' they asked loudly, at no one in particular.

On hearing my name, I swung around.

'That's me,' I answered. 'What's the matter?'

They wouldn't say what it was about and insisted I go with them. My mind swirled with a hundred thoughts as I climbed into the squad car. *Have I been busted? Has someone snitched that I smoke dope?* At least they hadn't handcuffed me. I didn't show my nervousness as we raced with siren blaring, not to the station but to the airport. Perhaps a case of mistaken identity. Only when we reached the cargo terminal did I realize what it was about.

A box of snakes dispatched by Heyward from South Carolina had broken open in transit. I had been expecting this shipment for a while. The zoo director had wanted a bunch of snakes from the east, and I had sent the order to Heyward. The airport staff was frantically searching an entire plane for the escapees. I looked inside the box and was puzzled, since everything seemed to be in order.

'All the snakes are safely in their bags,' I said. 'What are you looking for?'

'There are a bunch of empty bags,' one cop said, pointing to a pile of snake bags Heyward's mother had tailored for me.

'But they are folded,' I replied, by now cocky with relief. 'Do you think snakes would do that before escaping?'

They gave me dirty looks, but let me go.

The following weekend, Claire and I drove west with camping gear. At the stream bank, we spread out our double sleeping bag under the starlit sky, watching with wonder as clouds took form as we drifted to sleep. A thunderclap woke us, and we dashed to the car in time before the rain came down in sheets. We dozed on and off, listening to the downpour drumming on the car as if trying to beat it into the ground.

The next morning, after the sun warmed the stones, I scanned every sunlit spot on a slippery rock slide for a coiled rattlesnake. My ears were alert for the tell-tale sound of castanets. Claire walked on the trail below me.

'Rom, come quick,' she called. 'Snake.'

She stood beside the stream, holding an empty canteen. I scampered across the loose rocks to where she was pointing.

'An Arizona mountain kingsnake!' I exclaimed.

I picked up the three-foot beauty with its alternating bands of red, white and black. It is a serious contender for the title of the most beautiful snake in the world.

'Look at the colour pattern,' I urged. 'Red on black, it's okay, Jack. That's the kingsnake here. But if it's red on white, it's gonna bite. And that's a deadly coral snake.'

'Rom, you are so smart,' she said sarcastically.

I could get twenty-five bucks for it, a fantastic start to the weekend.

At noon, we drove to Nell's place to meet Dick and Nan. He was a young bearded PhD student of herpetology, and she was an enthusiastic outdoors woman. We spent the afternoon hiking through a maze of steep canyons through which the perennial Ramsey stream winds. The two ladies walked down the trail while Dick and I scoured the hill slopes. I marvelled at the dark columns of giant pines, which kept the canyon cool.

We reached our destination, the Hamburg silver mine, which had been deserted since the turn of the century. It was one of two locations in the States where the rarest rattlesnake, Willard's rattler, lived. Working our way slowly through the scattered remains of dwellings, neither of us was hopeful of finding one. Just poking around made me feel like a kid again. I entered the sturdier quarry shafts where outcrops of gorgeous quartz crystals, some a foot long, glimmered in the light. But there were no snakes. At the ruins of a crumbling settlement, I rummaged through the trash heap for bottles to add to Nell's collection.

We continued onward beyond Hamburg, past the remains of a corral in a spacious grassy opening. Down at Bear Spring, while filling my canteen, I spotted a rattlesnake unlike any other. An adult Willard's crawled unhurriedly on the cool pine needles. I lifted it on the snake hook and yelled over my shoulder to Dick. Setting the rusty-hued beauty in the centre of the trail, I photographed it while he made sure it didn't disappear. I became emotional finding this rare creature in such beautiful surroundings. And then we found two gorgeous juvenile Willard's rattlers that were too young to keep. Everything about that day seemed magical. By evening, we had also caught five twin-spotted rattlers. Before dark, Dick and Nan headed home to Tucson, asking us to drop by to see them soon. Nell admired our contribution to her collection of bottles while dinner cooked.

When there was no sign of my snake-bitten finger improving, I wrote to the well-known specialist Dr Findlay Russell at Loma Linda University in California. He replied cryotherapy was not recommended for treating snakebite. His letter made me furious. The doctors had used a discredited remedy despite my protests, and now I was left to pay the price. I sought the advice of the sergeant about filing a compensation claim for medical malpractice. After all, my trigger finger was disfigured, affecting my ability to shoot. He dismissed the idea, saying the army might counter-sue me for endangering my life while on active duty.

I shared a joint with the others at the Cube while staring at the crooked finger. Perhaps being unable to fire a gun was a good thing. They couldn't send me to Vietnam, a danger that was ever-present until my discharge. Or could they?

Dr Russell had added a note of caution in his letter—the clogged nose was a tell-tale reaction. Besides being hypersensitive to antivenom, I was also allergic to snake venom.

24

WAR DUTY IN JAPAN

5,000 Pints of Blood a Week

WE TUNED INTO THE counterculture, with musicians fanning the flames of rebellion. Bob Dylan had already released his accusatory *Masters of War* and *Blowin' in the Wind* two years earlier, in 1963. In September 1965, Barry McGuire singing the antiwar song *Eve of Destruction* made it to number 1 on the US Billboard Hot 100. Then came Tom Paxton's *Lyndon Johnson Told the Nation*. The hippie antiwar movement was going full tilt, especially in San Francisco. But we were stuck in the war machine.

By the end of 1965, America took its gloves off, moving from an advisory role for the Army of the Republic of Vietnam (ARVN) to engaging in active combat in Vietnam. The news in the weekly armed forces newspaper *Stars and Stripes* was ominous. A typical headline went something like, 'Over 500 Viet Cong Fighters Killed and 20 US Servicemen Lose Their Lives.' This was the beginning. Tens of thousands of young American soldiers and at least a million north Vietnamese civilians and Viet Cong combatants would die before the war was over. The maimed weren't even counted.

Circulars tacked on the bulletin board often asked for technicians to volunteer in Vietnam. None did. In January 1966, a notice sought lab techs to go to Japan to run a blood banking operation, and I signed up.

I looked forward to the six-month TDY (temporary duty) in the 406th Medical General Laboratory at Camp Zama, where a new central blood bank supplied fresh whole blood to the front lines, a first for any war.

I spent a week's leave in New York before heading for Japan. Elly and Dugald were in Hoosick, but the doorman had a key to their apartment. I rode on an air force cargo plane to McGuire Air Force Base, New Jersey, and then on a bus to New York City.

At the Gaslight Café, a Greenwich Village coffeehouse, I caught up on the news. The antiwar movement had gained intensity and momentum. Norman Morrison had immolated himself outside the Pentagon, beneath the office window of Defense Secretary Robert McNamara. The following week, another activist, Roger Allen LaPorte, did the same in front of the United Nations building. Then thousands marched in New York and Washington D.C. to protest what they called an illegal war.

The reports, especially of America torching entire villages with napalm, horrified me, and I sympathized with the protesters. At the coffeehouse, I couldn't be part of the peacenik group or join in the conversation as my GI haircut gave me away.

This brief interlude of civilian life ended too soon. The duty officer back at the hospital had my tickets to Los Angeles and the connecting flight to Tokyo's Haneda Airport. After riding on no-frills cargo planes, I enjoyed the plush seats, the silence of the cabin and the drinks the stewardess served on the commercial flights. At the other end of the thirteen-hour trip across the Pacific, an olive-green US Army bus waited to transport me and a group of newly recruited nurses to the 406th Med Lab.

On the way, the Japanese driver pulled over to the side of the highway and got out. We craned our necks to see why we had stopped. Without concealing himself, he unzipped and took a leak. The arch of urine backlit by the morning sun scandalized the nurses, who looked at each other. But I was transported back home to India, where pissing in public was an everyday sight. *How long before I can go home?*

Camp Zama, an enormous military complex with a hospital, research laboratories and administrative buildings, was located midway between

Tokyo and Yokohama. Two huge gymnasiums had been converted into barracks, which twenty lab techs shared with hundreds of wounded soldiers. Each of us had a bed and a footlocker separated by flimsy partitions.

On my second day, I was sitting on the toilet doing my business when the entire row of metal stalls rattled furiously. Even the commode shook beneath me. *Are we under attack? Should I shit or should I run?* It took several long seconds to understand what was happening. An earthquake. There had been no briefing on what to do. I hurriedly zipped up and exited the stall. Other GIs walked by with their toothbrushes and towels as if nothing had happened.

'What should we do now?' I asked one of them.

'It happens all the time,' he replied. 'You'll get used to it. If it is hard, run outside.'

Indeed, we'd stop sticking needles or doing any work when the overhead lights swung crazily or the bottles clinked together, and resume once it was over.

We were to supply 5,000 units of blood to Vietnam each week. The easiest way to fulfil this quota was on board aircraft carriers, which came from the South China Sea into the Sasebo Naval Base near Nagasaki. As soon as a warship docked, we installed a row of camp beds on one of the hangar decks while the commanding officer announced on the squawk box, 'Men, you all want to support our brave soldiers fighting on the ground. You will donate a pint of your blood before going ashore for your well-earned R&R. Please line up on the hangar deck, where the team of blood technicians is waiting and ready. Thanks and God bless.'

Each technician could simultaneously draw blood from eight marines or sailors as a counterweight cut the flow when the bag became full. A pint took about fifteen minutes to bleed, so ten of us vampires could do about 2,500 guys on an eight-hour shift.

A few fainted when the needle pierced their arm; one crashed with a thud after a finger stick; and another shat his pants. That these tough sailors and marines reacted so dramatically to a little jab flummoxed us. We rewarded every donor with a shot of whisky.

After packaging the blood into big cardboard boxes with dry-ice packs, we wandered around these gigantic ships, peering at the sleek fighter planes, A-4 Skyhawks and F-4 Phantoms. Aboard the 1,000-foot USS *Enterprise*, the first nuclear aircraft carrier and the largest warship ever built until then, a pilot let us climb into the cockpit of his Phantom. Sitting in the moulded seat facing the gauges and the control yoke, equivalent to a steering wheel, made me as excited as a ten-year-old.

'Press the button on that handle, and you unleash a ton of explosive steel in one minute of firing,' he said with pride. 'You got a choice—fire your cannon or launch a Sidewinder missile.'

I didn't miss the reference to the sidewinder, one of my favourite rattlesnakes. He made it sound thrilling, but how scary must it be at the receiving end of this ultimate supersonic weapon.

When there were no ships in port, we visited the half a dozen American air force and navy bases up and down the country, drawing blood from American expats, servicemen and their families. Since Japan was neutral, we didn't touch its citizens. The wives of soldiers and officers showed up with cases of wine and booze, and it became a party. Instead of the vampire squad treating everyone to whisky, we were plied like guests. By the end of the day, the blood was packed with ice and we were zonked.

At the lab, we typed blood groups, labelled the bags and covered them in dry ice for dispatch by plane to Da Nang Air Base in Vietnam. In all, the programme collected two million units of blood, which saved the lives of wounded GIs who would have otherwise succumbed to haemorrhagic shock. I was a cog in a greased war machine.

Sleeping wasn't easy, since the soldiers talked long into the night. This was the first time most of them poor Whites and Blacks from the hinterlands of America had been outside their hometown. While their experiences traumatized many, others relished being on the battlefield. To them, shooting Viet Cong was more exciting than shooting squirrels at home. 'When I get back to the Nam' was a common start to every dreamy story. I had avoided being sent to the front because of that one year of college education. Whether or not it was true, at least that was my belief. But if I had remained in college, I might have dodged the draft. *Which is a worse fate: studying dull subjects while struggling to make a living or being in the army with the constant threat of the front lines?* I was unsure.

I became friends with another lab tech, Jim Anderson, a tall Black man from Louisiana with an easy-going sense of humour. Every Sunday, we caught a train into Tokyo and wandered around Shinjuku, gawking at young women called ojousans. Jim was fascinated by the matronly kimono-clad mama-sans who shuffled down the street. He made them laugh by mimicking their walk. Before heading to the base, we stopped by a bar to have Kirin or Asahi Gold beer.

On a trip to Hakone, the resort town near Mount Fuji, we had a traditional Japanese meal served by a geisha, who was most amused by our inability to use chopsticks. Jim pretended to be clumsier than he really was, making us laugh with his antics.

'Back home in Pearl River,' he said in a reflective tone of voice, 'I wouldn't be seen dead with a White honky motherfucker like you.'

I held up my cup of warm sake and told him I was honoured to be the exception.

One Sunday, Jim reluctantly accompanied me to the Japan Snake Centre near the Yabuzuka train stop. The institute was financed by the Old Mam Wine Company, which made so-called medicinal wine with a whole mamushi, a small Japanese pit viper, pickled in each bottle. The curator introduced us to the head of research, Dr Yoshio Sawai, who showed us around the enclosures of the country's venomous species, such as the mamushi and the huge Okinawan habu. Since habus caused many deaths and injuries on the Amami Islands, the doctor and his team immunized thousands of farmers from 1961 onwards with tiny doses of venom over a period of time similar to Bill Haast self-injecting cobra and coral snake venoms. But the habu is a pit viper, as are rattlesnakes, whose toxins destroy tissue. Sawai's lab detoxified the venom with formalin before jabbing people. Although this unique experiment produced initial encouraging results, they abandoned it in later years. This was likely because the islanders needed booster shots at regular intervals to maintain effective immunity.

On another Sunday, Jim didn't get the day off, and I tried my luck at a Tokyo casino's slot machine. A lovely young Japanese lady next to me hit the jackpot, sending a cascade of coins tumbling and rolling on the floor. I helped her gather them, and she flashed a brilliant smile while thanking me in English. I pulled the handle repeatedly and wasted twenty bucks before giving up. Convinced my fortunes would not change, I rose to leave. The lady also headed for the door. She introduced herself as Masako, and I asked her out to lunch.

In a tiny restaurant, we ordered bowls of Okinawa soba soup and chatted about our lives as best we could with our limited language skills. She had been a college administrator and was now a private tutor. When she called me Lom for the third time, I corrected her. No matter how hard she tried, she couldn't pronounce my name, which sent us both into hysterics. She teased my ridiculous rendition of Japanese phrases.

'You real *gaijin*,' she said. 'You neva learn Japanese.'

We wandered hand in hand, looking into fancy, upmarket shops at Ginza. Then she surprised me by inviting me to her apartment. We became an item.

I grew tired of urban distractions and would have gone hunting for snakes, but it was too cold for that. Perhaps there was a fishing spot nearby.

'When I was a little girl, my father used to take me to this place,' Masako said. 'Maybe you'll like it.'

She took me to a shop in Shinjuku, a far cry from what I had imagined. We rented fishing poles at the door and bought a few pieces of rolled bread for bait. Inside, I saw elderly Japanese men with their poles leaning over a murky pool surrounded by a four-foot wall. While we baited our hooks, a man caught a big carp. The excitement of the catch was infectious.

We threw our lines in, and before long, Masako hooked one. She squealed with delight as the rod bent and she struggled to hold on. A helper scooped the fish from the water with a landing net. Shop assistants cleaned and packed the carp for us to take home to her tiny apartment, where she turned it into a soup with sticky rice wrapped in salty seaweed. She made eating with chopsticks seem so easy while my clumsiness resulted in a stained shirt. It took a few meals before I could wield a pair with dexterity.

But fishing in a tub didn't appeal to me. Sawai had told me about Richard Goris, an American herpetologist in Japan. When I called Dick, he invited me to visit him in Tokyo on an early weekend morning at the college where he taught. As an ordained Jesuit priest, he wore a cassock. That was unexpected. Before we headed out in his old 4WD, he changed into field clothes and brought an extra pair of rubber boots for me. We were going to look for fire-bellied newts he needed for his laboratory studies.

It was early spring, but the weather was still chilly. The growing season hadn't begun yet, and there was no one in the open countryside. I followed him through the fallow paddy fields. Where a stream opened into a tree-lined pool, Dick ran a small hand net through the water along the bank. Among the dead leaves squiggled a newt. I was surprised any amphibian could be out and about in the icy water.

'It's a fire belly newt,' he said.

With gloved hands, he picked up the dull brown five-inch creature and showed me the brilliant crimson abdomen dotted with black spots.

'Beautiful, huh? These guys have a neurotoxic secretion on their skins.'

In two hours, we netted six newts, which Dick stashed in a plastic box half filled with water to take back with him. Throughout the outing, he answered my questions about Japanese herps. No wonder he wrote the definitive *Guide to the Amphibians and Reptiles of Japan*[5] years later.

Before my TDY ended, I visited Dr Sawai, who gifted me four mamushis. I said my farewells to Jim and my other new friends, and spent one last night with the lovely Masako.

Onboard the American Airlines flight from Tokyo to Los Angeles, I cradled a brown paper bag containing the mamushis in individual

---

5 Richard C. Goris and Norio Maeda, *Guide to the Amphibians and Reptiles of Japan* (Malabar, US: Krieger Publishing Company, 2004).

cloth bags. They'd have been too cold in the cargo hold. I didn't worry about security personnel confiscating them, since there were none. In those simpler times, passengers showed their boarding passes and got on the plane.

'How cute,' said an elderly American lady, glancing at the bag on my lap while taking the seat beside me. 'You brought your own lunch.'

I smiled politely and stashed the mamushis on the floor in front of me after the flight took off. *How am I to answer to her inevitable follow-up question: Why aren't you eating your meal?* I needn't have worried, because she forgot about it. Once back in El Paso, I planned to send the snakes to Heyward for his Snake Pit.

I was on my way to report for duty at William Beaumont Hospital when Claire, a vision in a lemon-yellow dress, called my name as she ran towards me. She threw herself into my arms, and in my exuberance, I lifted her off the ground. It was good to be back.

I received a promotion to Spec 4 (Specialist 4) with higher rank and pay, but the work was the same. At the PX, I flipped through a stack of records, stopping at one with a surreal cover of hairy musicians in infrared, called *Freak Out!*. It was the debut double album of Frank Zappa and The Mothers of Invention.

At the Cube that evening, we toked while listening to psychedelic tunes such as *Hungry Freaks, Daddy*; *Who Are the Brain Police?*; and *It Can't Happen Here*. The lyrics were so subversive, we couldn't believe the PX had stocked the record.

My old Laramie pal Dean wrote from the thick of war in Vietnam, describing how he woke up one night in the middle of a gun battle. They were caught in a crossfire and hunkered down while praying none of the bullets flying through the thin walls of the barracks had their names on them. He talked of walking around Saigon and admiring beautiful Vietnamese girls in their flowing white dresses cycling past. While opposed to the war, I had a morbid fascination for it, wondering what it was like. Between the lines of Dean's matter-of-fact account, I detected misery and homesickness. My posting was a holiday compared to his, and I felt sorry for him.

My military career was coming to an end, or as we put it, 'I'm getting short, man. I'm so short, I'm going to disappear.'

One Friday evening, Nita and I drove to the town of Chihuahua to visit Dona Luz Corral, the widow of Pancho Villa, the most famous of the Mexican revolutionaries. During the five-hour drive through the Sonoran Desert, she shook me when I dozed off at the wheel.

'Pull over and get some sleep before you kill us,' she scolded.

I parked on the brush-and-tumbleweed-covered shoulder. We opened our doors to step out, and I cautioned her to watch for snakes. Then we made ourselves as comfortable as we could in the back seat for a snooze. When the sky brightened, I got out to take a leak and swore loud enough to jolt her upright. While pulling off the road, I had run over a large western diamondback rattlesnake. It would have still been alive when I had set foot out of the car at night and could have been bitten. I was saddened at crushing the beautiful creature and shaken by the close call.

At Chihuahua's town centre, a postman directed us to Dona Corral's palatial house. The sweet old lady showed the artefacts she had preserved and displayed in a glass case in her living room. The centrepiece of the exhibit was Pancho's sword with a hand-printed note in Spanish that read, 'When this snake bites you, there is no survival.' I had to suppress a smile at the melodramatic words.

On 26 January 1967, my stint in the army ended. Mex Mouse, Squeaky and Howdy were also due to get out. A recruiting agent said if we 're-upped', or re-enlisted, for three more years, we'd become sergeants immediately with an enhanced pay package of 5,000 dollars. It sounded tempting, but we all refused. I savoured the freedom to do what I wanted, when I wanted and wherever I wanted.

Once I got my discharge orders, I had my khaki army shirts screen-printed with the moustachioed French soldier, called Captain Zig-Zag, of rolling paper fame, at Wes and Jan's shop. After bidding bye to my good buddies, I packed the Ford with my meagre possessions, mainly clothes, books and records. On top of them, I set two bags with a Gila monster and a huge bullsnake for Heyward. Saying goodbye to

Claire was tough for both of us. We promised to stay in touch, and we have.

Early on a chilly morning, I left on a marathon drive across Texas, through Mississippi, Alabama and Georgia for Salley, South Carolina. I had spent six years in the States by then. This time I was truly done with the country of my birth and needed to make at least 500 dollars for my ticket to India.

25

COMMERCIAL SNAKE HUNTER

500 Dollars Worth of Rattlesnakes

A FEW KILOMETRES OUT of El Paso, the car's heater died. The winter cold chilled my bones, and I pulled on a hoodie. The only way of keeping the two reptiles warm was to set them on my lap. As if driving with them on my thighs wasn't uncomfortable enough, I had the disquieting thought of the Gila monster's jaws clamping on a vulnerable body part. I drove cautiously, avoiding any sudden movements.

Three days later, late in the evening, I arrived exhausted in Salley, South Carolina, when Mr Clamp was leaving for his job as a night watchman at the Savannah River Site, a nuclear power plant about fifty kilometres away. The family lived on twenty acres of former cotton fields, where The Snake Pit was also located. Heyward and Teddy were glad to have the Gila monster and the bullsnake. The responsibility of keeping them warm and safe had worn me out, and I was relieved to be rid of them.

While we caught up on one and a half years of news and stories, the brothers invited me to their fishing cabin on the Waccamaw River, where they planned to catch a female alligator as a mate for their big old male called Bone Crusher. Winston Brown, the Clamps' childhood friend, hooked Heyward's pickup to a trailer containing a flat-bottomed boat. The four of us loaded camping and catching gear in the back of the truck and headed east.

At a dock near Myrtle Beach, we slid the skiff into the river and transferred the stuff into it. Teddy took the controls and kept the boat at a steady pace. Although it was sunny, the wind froze my nose and made my eyes tear up. When he turned into a narrow tributary, the ride became more interesting as fat brown water snakes lay draped on the low-hanging tree branches.

'Hold on!' yelled Teddy, as he gunned it towards a huge log bobbing ahead. At the last minute, he lifted the outboard motor and we sailed over it and landed with a gut-wrenching thud.

'You scared the bejeezus out of me!' I shouted back.

He navigated through a maze of channels before slowing the engine and put-putting to a halt in front of a two-storey cabin the brothers had built themselves with salvaged wood and metal sheets from abandoned barns. The wooden pier extended from the river to the porch. After Heyward jumped out and secured the boat, we hauled the gear and supplies inside. A ground-floor room had butane cylinders, kerosene lamps and fishing rods, while the other was a kitchen with a coffee pot and battered pans covered with dust. No electricity or indoor plumbing, and the toilet was an outhouse with an out-of-date Sears Roebuck catalogue hanging by a string. Although we had a roof over our heads, we'd be roughing it. With everything stashed away, we dragged a few rickety chairs outdoors to rest our tired bodies.

Heyward threw some sausages on to a pan and soon we bit into hot dogs under the starry sky. There wasn't an electric light or traffic noise to sully the peace.

'I brought some peyote for you guys,' I said, taking a canister from my pocket.

We each ate a peanut butter and jelly sandwich laced with dry cactus powder. Winston beamed his flashlight across the river.

'There's an enormous gator over there,' he exclaimed. 'Its eyes are as big as saucers.'

We took turns holding the light close to our temples, and the pair of bright orange orbs glowed at us from the opposite bank. Winston was ready for action.

'We'll probably drown or get bit badly,' cautioned Heyward. 'Let's wait until later.'

The ripples swirled, and we savoured our visions to the sounds of the flowing water, the occasional splash of a catfish, the croaking of bullfrogs and the eerie sound of barred owls calling back and forth. Since we had consumed only a fraction of what I had in El Paso, the effect wore off in two hours.

At midnight, the gator continued to remain where it had been. We got into the skiff, and Winston paddled across. Teddy sat in front, holding a pole with a noose dangling from it. Heyward shone his flashlight without illuminating his brother. As we edged closer, Winston stopped paddling and Teddy slipped the lasso around the gator's neck. When he jerked the pole to tighten it, the animal crashed into the front of the vessel and churned the water as it disappeared below the surface.

Teddy had a good grip on the rope and Heyward moved the pole out of the way. The gator tugged hard, towing us to the centre of the channel. It was the closest I'd get to a Nantucket sleighride, when a harpooned whale tows an open whaling boat around. After the alligator spent its energy on that explosive struggle, Teddy brought it to the surface. Heyward held a sack on a short handle ready and slid it over the gator's head. I stayed on the other side of the skiff as a counterbalance, and the three of them wrestled it into the boat. Teddy sat on the eight-footer, gripping its neck. Winston removed the burlap and tied the jaws shut with a piece of parachute cord. I slipped my hand under the tail and shoved my finger into its cloaca.

'Female,' I called.

We bound her legs and carried her to the fishing cabin. This was so unlike the gator-catching experiences Heyward and I had in Florida. We had been prepared to spend two days at least, but we had accomplished the mission on the very first night. Staying another day would have meant keeping the captive animal trussed.

We headed back to Salley at daybreak and got her into an enclosure next to Bone Crusher. The plan was to give the female a few weeks to recuperate before introducing her to her new mate.

That evening, Heyward wanted help in salvaging tin sheets from a derelict barn. As we sped down the road, a highway patrolman pulled us over. The sight of someone with the authority to arrest made me nervous, but Heyward was his usual cool self.

'What would your daddy say if he knew you were driving so fast?' the cop asked.

'You oughta try to catch my daddy sometime,' Heyward replied.

I wouldn't have had the sass to reply in that manner. The amused cop let us go.

We found the farm and hauled the tin sheets to the Clamps, where we scattered them around the property. After a few months, rodents and snakes would shelter underneath them. Whenever the brothers needed any snakes for their summer shows, they only had to lift the metal sheets. We usually hunted these reptiles by turning over rocks and debris, but creating the same conditions on one's own land was ingenious.

The next day, I departed south for Miami.

'Cut your hair; you look like a damn hippie,' were Heyward's parting words of advice.

But I had no intention of looking as straight as a soldier ever again.

Dottie wasn't home, and a housemate said she was working on a Caribbean cruiser as a sailor. A snake-hunting pal, Gary Maas, let me sleep on his couch until I found a place to rent in Coral Gables. None of my old friends had any orders for reptiles. *What am I to do?* I needed money.

I got a night-shift job at a meat-packing plant. The other workers and I sprang into action when a reefer truck arrived every two hours. We loaded it with frozen shoulders of beef, pork and boxes of sausages from the warehouse freezer. Until the next truck drove in, we smoked, sipped beer and watched skin flicks on a rattling 8 mm projector the owner had set up in the waiting room. We made eighteen dollars a night, but I couldn't stand the work after a week.

The pay from a job at the serpentarium wouldn't cover my living expenses, and I'd have to slog for years to earn enough for a ticket to India.

Attila got an order from Bill Chase for a hundred cane toads at fifty cents each. These amphibians from South America had been introduced in Florida, and high school biology classes wanted big ones for dissection. With large sacks slung over our shoulders, we tramped across the lawns of the University of Miami campus after dark. The biggest ones weren't hard to find as they hopped in the open. Attila warned me not to rub my eyes while catching the beasts because the pair of parotid glands on their backs leaked milky secretions brimming with neurotoxins.

'It stings like a shot of cobra venom,' he said as if he knew from experience.

In two hours, we had filled the sacks.

Next came an order for Cuban anoles at five bucks apiece, good money since we'd make the same sum catching ten of them as grabbing a hundred cane toads. The beautiful green lizards had been brought to Florida as pets and were breeding on their own in gardens and parks. But the demand for them was high in pet shops up north. They were easy to spot at night when they were asleep on the tops of palm trees on the university campus. *But how are we to catch them?* Fishing rods were not long enough. Skip Pierce, another hunter, had a clump of bamboo growing in his garden. We traded weed for two lengths of stems, which Attila and I rigged with fishing-line nooses. It took a few hours to get used to the weight of the poles, and our success rate was low at first. By the second night, we had caught a dozen of them.

Bill was prepared to pay fifty cents for each five-lined skink and a buck for a broad-headed skink. Who wanted these skinks and for what? Neither of us knew. Perhaps for the pet trade, which was as fickle as fashion. We lifted rocks and old pieces of tin at the nearby junkyard, but the reptiles zipped away like greased lightning. We woke up early, aiming to catch them when they were sleepy and slow from the cool air. Even then, they were too fast. For the first time, we were stumped.

Skip had more experience with skinks, and we asked his advice. He handed us two yellow pills each.

'Speed,' he explained. 'It'll make you quick enough to grab the little buggers.'

I remembered my previous ordeal with the drug and wasn't interested in a repeat performance. He insisted we wouldn't be able to fulfil the order without it. Reluctantly, I swallowed a tablet and struggled to quell the anxiety when my heart raced like a hare running away from a cat. It was an unpleasant few hours, but we caught several dozen skinks. Skip was right, but I didn't care for the stimulant or these small orders.

Then we got a big order of the kind I was desperate for. Gordon Johnstone, in New Jersey, wanted fifty large timber rattlers for venom.

'Let's drive to Binghamton and meet Crazy Evens,' suggested Attila.

Paul 'Crazy' Evens, a hunting guide, lived in a shack behind an inn on Highway 17 all the way up in northern New York State. *Is Attila serious?*

'It'll take us a good two days to get there,' I replied without enthusiasm.

'If Dottie comes along, we can make it in a day,' he said. 'The weather's fine, so we won't need tents.'

By then, Dottie had returned from her Caribbean trip, but I had kept my distance. Perhaps she had a boyfriend, and she might feel awkward if I showed up. But we couldn't think of anyone else to go with us. At the Stone House, she greeted me with a warm hug, and it felt like old times. She had a week off before her next cruise to the Bahamas and was excited about taking a break in New York. We loaded Attila's 1955 Plymouth station wagon with hooks, plenty of bags and several wooden boxes drilled with air holes to cart the snakes. To save time, we stocked bread, salami, cheese, lettuce, mustard and mayonnaise for sandwiches. No matter how well we made them, Attila called them 'choke sandwiches', but he never volunteered to make them.

We hit the road when the sun barely peeked above the horizon. At Santee, South Carolina, we bought moonshine for Evens from one of Heyward's contacts. By nightfall, as the temperature dropped, we crossed from Virginia into Pennsylvania with Attila driving. Dottie sat beside me, breast pressing against my arm and hand on my thigh, keeping that side of me warm and tingling.

The inn's sign came into view well after midnight. As the car pulled into a gravel driveway leading to the back, our headlights illuminated Paul's shack.

'Welcome,' he called as he sleepily stumbled out. 'Been expecting you. How's that old sonofabitch Attila Beke?'

It felt good to stretch our limbs after being cooped up for more than eighteen hours. Paul opened the moonshine and took a large swig while we ate a dinner of beans and franks. Dottie and I left the two guys to chat and unrolled our sleeping bag on soft pine needles.

I didn't know when or if they drifted off to bed, but Attila and Paul were already up and about when I woke up feeling cold. The fragrance of brewing coffee wafted from the shack. By the time we washed up in a basic washroom indoors, which had no heating, Paul had broken eggs on a heavy iron skillet greasy with pig fat. Attila sat on a log preparing a joint.

'To search for camouflaged snakes, take two tokes of grass,' he said. 'It helps you find them.'

He had inverted Skip's advice about speed pills and skinks. He may well be on to something, but then, he didn't need an excuse to smoke. Every morning he collected the joint ends, or roaches, lying on the ground and snubbed out in ashtrays from the previous evening, and rolled a whole one to start the day as he was doing right then.

Without a moment to lose, we gobbled up breakfast. Tucking bags into our belts, we grabbed our hooks and picked our way through slabs of shale up the steep mountain slope behind the inn.

'We gotta get over that yonder hill and then climb across to the south-facing slopes,' Paul said when we stopped to catch our breaths.

Timber rattlers would be stirring after five to six months of hibernation in dens deep inside crevices protected from the winter cold. Once sunlight filtered through clouds and heated the rocks, the snakes would emerge to soak up the warmth. Since it wasn't deer hunting season, nobody else was in sight. Well-camouflaged ruffed grouse startled us when they fluttered off the ground at the last minute, and white-tailed deer scattered as we climbed the slopes.

Paul's shout shook us out of our reverie. He stood stock-still until we reached him. A gorgeous five-foot rattler shone golden with a dark zigzag pattern along its velvety back. Either it was torpid or thought we hadn't seen it. It didn't taste the air with its tongue, nor did it rattle.

When Attila scooped it up with his hook, it jerked as if startled, and I helped him bag it. Paul led the way to an opening in the forest, where the light-coloured rocks glittered in the sun.

'There's one here!' Dottie exclaimed.

A dark timber rattler lay coiled asleep in the sunlight. After that nasty prairie rattler bite in El Paso, I had given thought to single-handedly catching large rattlers without endangering myself. I unfurled the bag tied to the stringless frame of an old tennis racquet, hooked the timber and dropped it into the wide open bag, a simple and safe way of grabbing big venomous snakes. Pinning the head was risky for the catcher and bad for the snake. Holding the bag open with one hand and coaxing the snake with a hook was also hairy. Attila stood further up the slope watching me, but I could tell by his snicker that he didn't think much of my method.

'Come here fast,' Paul called.

Dottie and I stumbled to where he crouched next to a massive outcrop. Four rattlesnakes emerged from their cool dens.

'You get the two big ones on your side, and I'll snag the two at the bottom of the pile,' he said.

'Make sure you hook them away from the cave, or they'll be gone.'

After Dottie had tied another bag to the tennis racquet, I caught the biggest. The loud, distinctive buzz of the rattlesnake cut through the air. I knotted the bag while she rigged the racquet again. After we bagged the second one, I helped Paul capture the other two.

Throughout the morning, snakes emerged in twos and threes as the hillside warmed. We walked past the small ones. We were on our thirty-sixth snake, a velvety black timber, when it happened, like always, in slow motion. Attila put his hand under a slab of shale to lift it, without realizing a large rattler lay hidden behind a smaller stone next to his arm. It struck his wrist. He unleashed a volley of profanities, swearing at himself and the snake in equal measure.

'Let's sit and think about what to do,' he said, wiping the drops of blood with his sleeve.

I was worried. Both fangs of the snake had punctured his hand. Several minutes went by. Two magpies squabbled in the tree above us and a red-tailed hawk screeched. *If he shows symptoms, what will we do next?* We couldn't carry him all the way to the road. *Instead of wasting time, perhaps we ought to head back.*

'Strange as it seems, there isn't any pain,' Attila broke the silence. 'It's a dry bite.'

That was a relief. We returned to the job of catching snakes. By evening, we had our fifty. In addition, I had bagged two colourful timbers to take to India.

We bid farewell to Paul and stopped at Hoosick. In the attic, I found an old trunk in which I pounded a few holes with a hammer and screwdriver and lined the inside with newspaper. With a full water bowl to keep them hydrated, the snakes would be fine for a few weeks. They could go without food for a while longer.

We drove to New Jersey to deliver the rattlers to Gordon and collect our money. Then we sped non-stop to Miami. I needed another large order for the ticket home.

After Dottie left for the Bahamas, I met a cute, petite girl at a coffeehouse in the Grove one evening. She seemed familiar. I introduced myself.

'Didn't we meet at Skip's house two years ago?' I asked. 'You had a head of long hair then.'

'I cut my hair last year,' she replied. 'I'm Linda. Where have you been?'

I told her about being drafted into the army and visiting Japan.

'Tell me about Japan,' she said. 'I always wanted to go to a place where people aren't towering over me.'

By the end of the evening, we had promised to be in touch.

Catching kingsnakes and rat snakes for animal dealers earned an average of twenty dollars a day. At that rate, it would take me forever to get my ticket. I was in a funk when a letter from Kauffeld arrived, asking for species from the south-west—twin-spotted, green rock and Willard's rattlesnakes, besides a few blacktails and Mojaves. This was my passage to India.

At a coffee house that evening, I asked Linda on a whim if she'd visit me in India.

'India is high on my list,' she replied. 'Send me your address and I'll let you know.'

She was to make good on her promise.

My car wasn't in great shape for the long drive to Arizona, so I sold it. Instead of wasting my time hitch-hiking, I bought an air ticket to Tucson for eighty dollars. After bidding my farewells to Attila, the Haasts and other friends, I left.

At Tucson Airport, I hitched a ride to Bisbee and then to Nicksville. At Nick's Place, Ace Reynolds perched on a bar stool, like a permanent fixture. I brought him up to speed with my plans and mentioned needing a car. Besides his battered pickup truck, he had an ancient Pontiac parked outside, which he offered me.

'Make sure you return it to me with a full tank of gas,' he said with a wink, dangling the keys from a finger.

I arrived at Nell's house in a roar of noise, which brought her outdoors. The car's muffler had a hole, which made it sound like an elephant farting. She welcomed me with a big grin and a hug.

'That's got to be Ace's car,' she commented wryly.

She said nothing about ill-fated faces on windowpanes that evening, and I didn't ask. After a simple but filling dinner, I retired to the barn and fell asleep thinking of my imminent departure.

Early in the morning, I lay in bed by the open door, watching seven peccaries rooting in the apple orchard. With them were two coatimundis searching for ripe fruit. One peccary ambled up before realizing how close I was. It looked at my face in surprise, coughed once, and all of them took off like midget racehorses. I savoured the moment, but there were snakes to be caught. I busied myself making four peanut-butter-and-grape-jelly sandwiches with thick slices of wheat bread, which went into a clean snake bag.

I headed straight up the canyon, crawling through barb-wire fences and into the woods along a well-worn trail that took me through the narrow Box Canyon and through the pine forest. Deer scattered through the brush, and the occasional one streaked away with its white tail flashing. Insect sounds reverberated through the air. The sun rose high, brightening the floor of the canyon.

I walked carefully across a massive rock slide, alert for the soft buzz of a small rattler. At the first sound of one, I excavated the rocks, but the rattle grew fainter. The snake had retreated inside. I had to be faster next time.

Careful not to start a landslide, I made my way. Another snake disappeared under a flat rock. On lifting the stone, I caught sight of a slate grey coil near my hand. Too late. The small lance-shaped head of a green rock rattler shot out and bit deep into my left thumb.

'You dumb shit,' I berated myself.

My thumb burnt like a hot iron drilling into flesh. This was no dry bite. Although in pain, I wanted the snake. I grabbed it with my tongs and dumped it into a bag. Not knowing how bad the snakebite was going to be, I didn't waste my time in that remote spot and retraced my steps for the three-hour hike back to Nell's barn.

Exhausted from the agony, I slumped beside a stream and drank deeply. I made an improvised sling with a bag for my throbbing hand and rested in the shade of a tree for a few minutes. The swollen thumb had turned blue like an overripe fruit, stiffened and oozed fluid from the puncture wounds. I wiped it with a damp handkerchief and tied it loosely around the bite to keep the flies away. My small medical kit contained no painkillers. I did, however, have a stash of marijuana. I tamped a thimble-full into a corncob pipe for a smoke. The familiar high took the edge off the agony.

I felt better enough to continue on my way. About a mile later, I began sneezing non-stop, which made me even more tired. Then my armpits, crotch and head started itching. I had no time to dwell on this new, unfamiliar symptom of an allergic reaction to venom.

The distance passed in a blur. The sneezing abated, but I continued to scratch as if bedevilled by fleas. A parked car stood in Nell's yard, and the sound of people's voices came from the house. If her guests saw my puffy face with a snotty nose while I raked my privates like an uncouth simpleton, they would run a mile. I stumbled behind the barn without being spotted and sat under an apple tree with my back resting against the trunk. Sweat trickled from my brow and my shirt was damp.

I toked on the corncob pipe, which eased the pain. Two snake bags stuffed with dry leaves made good pillows, and I stretched out, gazing into the branches. I sank into a deep sleep, listening to redstarts warbling among the overhead foliage. On waking up, I had no sense of how much time had gone by since my watch had busted days earlier. A troop of coatimundis surrounded me, chewing on fallen apples. *Am I hallucinating?* They kept a wary eye on the prone human. When I propped myself to a sitting position, they scattered and watched me from a distance.

The swelling had now reached the elbow. A deep, dull ache that throbbed with my pulse replaced the burning pain. I peeked around the barn. The car had left. I knocked on the door and told Nell about the bite. My swollen arm concerned her, and she urged me to leave for the hospital. The nearest one at Bisbee was an hour's drive away, and my last excruciating experience at Beaumont lingered in my memory.

'It was a tiny snake,' I reassured her. 'It couldn't be dangerous. The swelling has stopped, and it's not even painful any more. I'll be fine.'

'It doesn't look good,' she said. 'Anyway, you better stay in the house.'

After we had a sumptuous dinner of deer steak and baked potatoes, she pointed me to her guest room. At night, I got up in the pitch dark to take a leak, but lost my balance and fell down. I was blind. A hundred worries assailed me as I lay there. *I should have taken Nell's advice and gone to the hospital. Now it's too late. Should I call for help? Am I dying?* Nell hadn't seen my face on her windowpanes, so I must be all right. I smiled at the thought. *Should I ask her to drive me to Bisbee?* I had already worried her enough. I sat upright, paralysed by fear and uncertainty.

About an hour later, my vision started returning, like an old TV set warming up. The night light and the furniture were blurred at first, and then they came into sharper focus. Unsteadily, I stood up and leaned against the wall, waiting for my balance to return. I staggered into the bathroom and returned to bed.

I woke to birdsong and the morning sun streaming in through the window. My hand was stiff and sore, but much better than the previous day. After a breakfast of French toast with maple syrup washed down with strong coffee, Nell bandaged my thumb. Against her advice, I went into the mountains to catch snakes despite the discomfort. During the following two days, I caught three more green rocks, two Willard's and two black-tailed rattlers with my right hand.

On the mend, I said a fond farewell to Nell and headed for Tucson to visit Dick and Nan. We spent my twenty-fourth birthday hiking a hillock not far outside the city and getting scratched by cacti and thorn scrub. It wasn't long before we caught a hefty Mojave rattler. I was excited by my first tiger rattlesnake, a strange-looking snake with a fat body and small head. Although Kauffeld hadn't placed an order for it, I knew he'd pay big bucks. We found two more tigers before sunset.

The walk down to their pickup was hell as clouds of mosquitoes descended on us, and the more we hurried, the more we got torn by thorns. It had been a successful week of hunting, with at least 500 dollars worth of snakes in bags. I packed them in a box and sent it to Kauffeld from Tucson Airport and returned the Pontiac to Ace.

One of Ace's friends gave me a ride to El Paso, where I dropped in at Beaumont Hospital. My sudden appearance surprised a few remaining old pals.

'Spec 4 Whitaker reporting for duty, huh?' asked one guy.

'Got bitten again!' exclaimed another.

'Come on in and we'll fix you up.'

A doctor inspected the bite and excised the dead dark tissue.

'Don't let it become any worse or you could lose that thumb,' he warned. 'See a doctor every two days to get the dressing changed.'

'I'll be on a ship sailing for India and won't have access to a hospital for a month or more.'

He prescribed a course of antibiotics and had a nurse prepare a month's supply of sterile dressing kits.

At El Paso, I boarded a plane for New York.

26

HOMEWARD BOUND

India on My Mind

Elly AND DUGALD WERE at Hoosick, but the doorman had instructions to let me into their apartment in Washington Square. The next day, I got the ships' schedule at the Port of New York harbour. The comfort of a passenger liner was out of my reach. Freighters sold tickets to a few poor travellers prepared to tolerate the minimal facilities. I scanned the list, and my finger stopped when my eyes lit on the word 'India'. A Greek freighter, the *Hellenic Leader*, was headed for the country in a fortnight. The confusion between Pakistan and India was still fresh in my mind, and I double-checked if the ship would anchor in Bombay. After booking my passage for an affordable 400 dollars, I could relax.

The symptoms of my green rock rattlesnake bite worried me. The sneezing had been an allergic reaction to the venom. *Is the intense itching, which reminded me of the crab infestation, also indicative of hypersensitivity?* The brief blindness had been the most startling and not mentioned in any of the books. I wrote to Dr Findlay Russell in the hope he'd reply before I left the country. The wound healed slowly.

Bernice, Elly's friend who made fancy wigs and hairpieces, invited me to a party. I was an odd fit among the other guests dressed in posh clothes. My hair was long and my attire was clean but scruffy. The bandaged snake-bitten hand was a good conversation starter. I spent most of the evening with Marlyn, a tall, lovely woman about my age who worked for Bernice. We drank wine and nibbled on canapés. Before calling it a night, I had a date with her for the following evening.

While ambling through Greenwich Village, I stopped at a record store to buy *Sgt. Pepper's Lonely Hearts Club Band* for brother Neel. Ma had mentioned he had quit school to become a guitarist. Although I detected a note of despair, she seemed proud when she said, 'All he does is play the guitar or think up names for the rock band he plans to start. He practises twelve hours a day.'

I took Marlyn to a burger-and-beer joint on the corner. My adventures in Texas and Arizona fascinated this Dublin girl, who had grown up in snake-less Ireland. After dinner, we walked arm in arm to Elly's apartment. She didn't comment on the incongruity of a hard-up hippie in the tastefully appointed pad.

The next morning, Marlyn was making cinnamon toast when I ripped the cellophane and placed the needle on the new vinyl. The title song, *Sgt. Pepper's Lonely Hearts Club Band*, surged from Razzack's big Vox speakers. Marlyn's eyes were enormous when she came to the kitchen door.

'That's the new Beatles album!' she exclaimed.

With our arms around each other, we sank into the plush sofa and listened, cinnamon toast forgotten.

Get by with a little help from my friends,
Get high with a little help from my friends.

That was all the encouragement I needed to roll and light a spliff of good Texas weed. We traded smoke as we French-kissed. By the last song, *A Day in the Life*, we were high on grass and each other.

I read the news today, oh boy,
About a lucky man who made the grade.

And when they sang 'I'd love to turn you on', we both agreed it was the trippiest track yet, an anthem for the times.

I walked her to the studio and stayed to chat with Bernice. When another employee, Gerlinde, mentioned she was driving to Hoosick on the weekend to deliver Elly's artwork, I volunteered to accompany her, since I had to collect my snakes. On Saturday morning, Gerlinde and I headed north in her car, smoking some of her potent weed.

The rattlers had lost some weight but were otherwise healthy.

'Something incredible happened after you left the snakes here, Breezy,' Elly said. 'The bats fled.'

'The snake smell was probably too much for them,' I replied.

The bats would not return for several decades.

After cleaning the trunk of their waste and lining it with fresh newspaper, I set rat traps in the attic and cellar. I had four rodents the next day, and the snakes had a feast before the voyage. On Sunday afternoon, I bid a fond farewell to Elly and Dugald, and we drove back to New York, stopping on the way for a sandwich and a toke.

A letter from Dr Russell, which wasn't reassuring, arrived on Monday.

'The venom of the green rock rattler has not yet been studied, and it's possible the neurotoxic fraction in the venom caused the blindness and loss of balance.'

The sneezing and itching were symptoms of an allergic reaction called anaphylaxis.

'A severe anaphylactic reaction can kill you faster than the effects of the venom,' he cautioned. 'Make sure you have adrenalin handy when you work with snakes.'

In a worst-case scenario, my lungs would have filled with fluid and drowned me in minutes. His letter was a wake-up call reminding me to be careful. Indeed, that was the last serious snakebite of my career. Years later, Professor David Warrell of the University of Oxford suggested that a rapid and sudden drop in blood pressure was the likely cause of the loss of vision and balance. Neither of the good doctors commented on the use of marijuana for relieving pain and anxiety. Today I can't even shake a dirty snake bag. Venom dust and dry shit make me sneeze, my nose drip and my eyes tear.

During my last week in the States, Marlyn and I were wrapped in each other, walking around Washington Square slurping ice-cream cones or sitting on a bench in a patch of the cool sun near the chess players. I was also dating Gerlinde without letting Marlyn know. I was having a good time, but home beckoned.

On the day of departure, Marlyn helped me load my trunks into a taxi and accompanied me to the docks. I didn't expect to see Gerlinde, since we had already said our goodbyes the previous evening. But there she was, waiting to bid me farewell. They had caught me two-timing, and I feared a scene. But the ladies laughed in surprise while I turned red.

I felt strange boarding a ship as a passenger. We wove past cargo being loaded and hatches getting battened down. After we stashed the trunks in my cabin, Marlyn appraised the tiny space.

'I can't believe you're gonna live here for a month,' she commented, hinting I was crazy.

She opened the bottle of champagne she had brought for the occasion and we sipped straight from it.

'What'll you do with the rattlesnakes?' Gerlinde asked.

'They'll be fine. The rats they ate in Hoosick will be enough.'

My python at school had gone four months without eating, so I was confident these healthy rattlers would be none the worse for wear.

'You're cuckoo,' Marlyn commented, looking at me as she sipped from the champagne bottle.

'Wouldn't it be great if you gals could come with me to India?' I joked.

Both women laughed.

'Here's a present for you,' said Gerlinde, handing me a packet of grass and a pack of rolling papers.

When the ship's horn blew, the ladies disembarked. I waved to them until they receded into the distance.

Waking up in my cabin during the first few days was disorienting.

Although it had been four years since I had last sailed as a seaman, I rose in a hurry, groping in the dark for my work pants and gloves. It took me a full minute to realize there was no work, and all I had to do was lounge and pretend to be on a cruise liner.

The Greek officers and seamen spoke little or no English. The cook made pasta and a variety of spicy Indian curries, which the messman served with a sweet red wine. I often chatted with them in the galley as they were from Goa. As luck would have it, the only other passenger was a Baptist missionary from Boston heading to Hyderabad, Pakistan. Perhaps he recognized I was a godless heathen by merely setting eyes on me, as he wasted no time and opportunity in preaching the gospel. I was transported to the religious education classes in Kodaikanal and felt no compulsion to tolerate his presence. When he appeared in the distance, I ducked below deck, and even in the engine room once. Suddenly the 400-foot ship that had seemed vast shrank in size. There was no escape at mealtimes, when we had to share a table in the officer's saloon. He didn't get the message that his sermons were unwelcome. When ignoring him failed to shut him up, I regaled him with my LSD and peyote experiences. I offered Roseman's *The Peyote Story* to him, saying, 'Here, you might be interested in reading this.' His facial expression changed from righteous affront to resignation. Thereafter, we ate our meals in silence.

In my cabin, I dressed the healing snakebite and let the rattlesnakes out to stretch themselves. They explored every corner with their sensitive tongues. *Are they disappointed by the sterile and clean room, with no scent of rodent, bird or lizard?* They drank from a plate of fresh water by working their jaws, chewing the liquid into their gullets.

With no comfortable deck chairs, I settled myself against the stern railing with life jackets as cushions, reading and rereading my books while enjoying the sunny weather and the cool breeze. When my mind drifted, I watched the sea. Two species of flying fish kept me company. The bigger kind with broad wing-like fins took lengthy flights above the waves, launching themselves through the air for several metres with the quick flapping of their tails. The smaller one couldn't stay airborne for long. I daydreamt of home while staring at the horizon. A booby coasted a bare inch above the surface, its sharp wings almost touching the water. *Where does it roost at night, thousands of kilometres away from land?* As if in answer, the next morning it perched on the rigging above the forward hatch.

We were halfway across the Atlantic when we got the news that Egypt had closed the Suez Canal with the start of the Six-Day War. The ship had to take the long detour around the Cape of Good Hope, South Africa, adding about 4,000 nautical miles and at least ten more days to the journey. I cursed my luck and kicked the railings. I'd go crazy if I spent any more time at sea. After the frustration passed, I resigned myself to the change in plans.

I begged the bosun for two pieces of canvas. One became a hammock on deck and the other I rigged as a canopy over it. I was more comfortable, but the lack of anything to do got to my nerves. I wandered at a loose end, like the eight-year-old me on that voyage aboard the SS *Independence*. I was as cooped up in the ship as my snakes were confined to their trunk. The anticipation of getting home sent a frisson of excitement through me and brightened my mood.

In the evenings, I sipped a shot of bourbon while leaning on the railing and watching the phosphorescent waves slap against the side of the vessel. *Had Gerlinde and Marlyn come along, the trip would have been fun.* With nothing to do, I was ready to chip and paint the entire deck rather than wallow in boredom.

While having a cigarette, Alphonse, the officer's messman, said there was a turntable in the cupboard above the dining table. I stacked half a dozen records on the 33 rpm record changer—Joan Baez, Bob Dylan, Jefferson Airplane, Donovan, The Who and Frank Zappa. Every cabin had a speaker, so I stretched out on my bunk and lost myself in the music, which offered some respite from the tedium.

In the bookshelf of the officers' mess, I was thrilled to discover a book in English. The first line was, 'His name was Romulus, and his friends called him Rom.' With a yelp of surprise, I read it again in disbelief. The cover was missing, so I didn't know the book's title.

The opening sentence in a nameless book on a Greek freighter cruising south along the west coast of Africa gave me chills. In the cheap adventure yarn, Rom, a British soldier, fought the Pashtuns in the Khyber Pass. If only I had brought a pile of books to read.

I'll go insane if I don't step on dry land soon. Worse, the weed that had buoyed my spirits ran out. As the *Hellenic Leader* cruised close to the coast of South Africa, the early-morning sun lit the veld stretching back from the white beach to a line of low purplish hills. Seals floating in the water watched us pass. I was tempted to jump overboard and swim to the shore. But the thought of arriving in Bombay in a few days, a moment I'd been anticipating for six years, kept my morale up. The beautiful open land disappeared as we headed north up the east coast of Africa.

The ship slipped through Bab-el-Mandeb Strait into the calm Red Sea with tall sandstone escarpments and endless dry country with hardly a sign of human life for much of the way. More than forty days after embarking in New York, we chugged into Port Sudan to offload cargo. Docking and undocking had been my favourite jobs as a seaman, and I joined the surprised deckhands. One of them chucked me a pair of leather gloves to protect my hands from getting snagged by 'fish hooks', bits of sharp wire in the metal lines. By then, my thumb had healed. It felt good doing something after weeks of sitting on my ass. I spun the monkey's fist ashore to the Black longshoremen with wild hairstyles who hauled the heavy mooring lines tethering ships. If the line had fallen short and landed in the water, there would have been derision. I was gratified to still have the touch.

At the bottom of the gangway, I flashed my seaman's ID card. No one knew I was a passenger on this freighter. My mission that hot mid-afternoon was to buy dope. A small kiosk at the dock sported the sign 'Money Changer', where I changed fifty dollars for Sudanese pounds. A taxi driver accosted me.

'Do you want beautiful girl?' he asked. 'Black or Brown, young and clean?'

He was all business, without a hint of sleaze in his demeanour. Pimping seemed to be an honourable profession here. I shook my head.

'I want to buy some *dagga*,' I replied, using the southern African name for marijuana, and hoped I wouldn't be ripped off.

'I can get for you,' he said. 'But you hire my taxi, long drive, twenty pounds.'

We haggled it to fifteen pounds and set forth in his rattling old Fiat, which seemed ready to fall apart.

The dusty streets were empty of traffic. We drove through the edge of town and into the countryside. After half an hour on a bumpy road, we arrived in a shantytown and stopped beside a small shack built with cheap dealwood. He knocked hard on the door and spoke to the young woman who answered.

'Ten pounds,' the driver translated.

I handed her the money and she gave me a newspaper-wrapped packet. On the way back, I opened it, and the potent aroma of the sticky, resinous buds assailed my nose. I hadn't been swindled.

After the dock hands finished unloading textile bales from the two forward hatches on the second day, the *Leader* headed south to Massawa, Eritrea, one of Italy's last African outposts. I strolled through the bustling harbour and sat at a rough-hewn table under a tamarind tree outside a bar, expecting that a waiter would come out with a cold beer. Within seconds, a pretty, dark young woman pulled up a chair.

'Buy me a beer?' she asked.

I was pleased to see her, but I was more interested in a chilled beer. Peeling a few pounds from the roll bunched in my pocket, I asked her to buy us each one. We sipped our beers and chatted. After finishing my drink, I headed towards what looked like the centre of town.

A girl staring at a store window surprised me by calling out.

'Are you from the Greek ship?'

I nodded.

'But you look English.'

I smiled at the pretty lady with pale skin and straight brown hair, obviously of mixed parentage.

'What will you do in Massawa?' she asked. 'There's not much to do here.'

I shrugged in response.

'Do you like movies?' Rosila asked, pointing to a billboard of a French film, *The Wages of Fear,* starring Yves Montand. 'I'd love to see it. What about you?'

'When does it start?' I asked.

It wasn't on for another hour, so we walked to a park and got a soda. In the tropical heat, I had become thirsty already. We chatted about the States and India. She wanted to come with me to Bombay, since she was bored with Massawa. I laughed in reply, and her foot rubbed against mine under the picnic table.

'Isn't it time for the movie to start?' I reminded her.

We chose the best seats in the empty movie house and became engrossed in the action. Two desperately poor truck drivers have to transport nitroglycerine to put out a massive fire on an oil rig in the middle of the desert. Any sharp jolt on the long and dangerous road would blow them to hell. Rosila began kissing me, and I forgot all about the rising tension in the movie. We drew apart when someone pushed open the door and bright daylight streamed into the hall. She looked behind us and hissed, 'My father.' A short, stout Italian stood by the exit. When his eyes got used to the darkness, he walked past us and sat down a row ahead. He didn't acknowledge Rosila. Maybe he hadn't seen her. We sat still, our attentions focused on the man sitting a mere three feet in front of us. *Is it bad for a woman to go to the movies with an unrelated man? Would her father create a scene when the film ended?* I needn't have worried. When the lights came on at the end of the movie, the man walked out without a word. Rosila shrugged and joined him.

At the bar, I bought a rum and Coke. The girl I had met in the morning took a seat beside me.

'So you met Rosila?' she asked. I nodded. 'She is a whore like all of us here. She pretends she's better than us because her dad has the cloth store, but don't be fooled. She'll do it for money.'

Massawa was like any other small town, where everyone was nosy and loved a good gossip. I chatted with her as long as my drink lasted and returned to the vessel.

Next morning, before we departed, I was paying for roasted peanuts and fried snacks at the harbour store when someone tapped on my shoulder. It was Rosila.

'I know your ship is leaving today,' she said. 'I brought you a present.'

She gave me an envelope and a hug.

'Write to me, will you? Invite me to India so I can get out of Massawa.'

I nodded as she spun on her heel and walked away.

Inside was a photograph of her and a folded perfumed paper.

It said, 'Hi Romulo, don't forget me, huh? I'm waiting for you to invite me to India. I'm serious. Love always, Rosila.'

I knew her for only a few hours, but for some mysterious reason, she captivated me.

The *Leader* berthed at Djibouti for two days. With every passing day, my impatience rose. The longshoremen appeared to work in slow motion and took long breaks. After an interminable wait, we swung around the Arabian Peninsula and made for Karachi. The preacher disembarked without returning my book. I was happy to let him keep it if there was a chance he'd convert from being a missionary to a stoner. The closer we approached India, the slower time flowed. After an eternity, we departed on the last leg of the voyage.

I couldn't contain my excitement as the coast appeared on the horizon. The hours ticked sluggishly as the lights of the Bombay skyline, my childhood home, came into view, bringing memories racing back. A boat from the port sped towards us and pulled alongside. A pilot scrambled aboard on the ladder that the deckhands lowered. He'd steer the vessel through the shallows into the harbour. He brought disappointing news. The berths were all occupied by other ships, and it might take a day or two before one would be available. I paced the deck, beside myself with frustration to be anchored within sight of home but unable to reach it. Nothing, no book or music, could hold my attention. The desperate need to walk on solid ground overwhelmed me. I might sound like a wimp for complaining about spending a couple of months aboard a ship, but I had done my innings on rusty ships, crossing the Atlantic in mid-winter squalls.

I baited a fishing line with chicken guts and threw it off the stern. The calm sea stilled my mind. When there was a tug, I pulled it up. My jaw dropped at what I'd hooked. A spiny lobster. I remembered attempting to catch one at the Worli Sea Face as a lad. The surprise was a pleasant distraction. I carried the crustacean down to the galley, where the cook prepared it for dinner. After dark, I stood on the deck watching the lights of the shoreline, brooding about the delay and consoling myself that it was only a matter of a couple of days.

We had covered over 17,000 nautical miles at 14 knots per hour. With the stops at Port Sudan, Massawa, Djibouti and Karachi, I had already spent fifty-four days onboard.

The next day, I still remember the date, 31 July 1967, another boat brought a health inspector to the ship.

'Pay him ten dollars,' urged Alphonse. 'He'll take you ashore. You don't have to wait here.'

Thanking him for the advice, I approached the official.

'Can I ride with you to the port?' I asked.

'Hmm …' he replied noncommittally as he looked me up and down.

'I'm happy to pay you for your trouble,' I said, handing him a ten-dollar bill.

'Of course, of course.'

With the help of the seamen, I loaded my trunks on to his boat, and we zipped ashore. Since I was returning after a six-year gap and 'transferring residence' as the customs officials so kindly put it, I didn't have to pay duty. When the examiner was about to poke his hands into the trunk with the rattlers, I cautioned him about my pets. There were hardly any other passengers, and the bored officers crowded around wanting to see them. I spent the next hour talking about snakes and why rattlers have rattles. The Indian Wildlife Act was still a decade away and the Convention on International Trade in Endangered Species of Wild Fauna and Flora (CITES), which governed the movement of animals across national borders, hadn't come into being yet. So there was no law prohibiting the import of live American rattlesnakes into India. The customs officers waved me onward.

A porter helped me carry the trunks out of Sassoon Dock to the line of waiting black-and-yellow taxis. I didn't haggle with the taxi driver over his price in my excitement at meeting the family soon. We loaded one trunk in the boot and tied the other on the roof carrier. I directed the driver to head to Nataraj Hotel on Marine Drive, as Ma had instructed.

'You stay in Nataraj Hotel?' he asked as the taxi sped into the city.

'No, Chateau Marine.'

'*Nargis ka ghar* [Nargis's house]*?*'

'*Pataa nahin* [I don't know].'

Ma and the kids had moved to this new address after the divorce. Later, I discovered the driver had been correct. The famous actors Nargis and Sunil Dutt were our upstairs neighbours.

Bombay's smells and sounds carried me back to my first arrival here in 1951. The cacophony of blaring car horns, cows munching through a pile of waste paper and pedestrians walking by. Either there were many more people on the road, or I had forgotten how crowded and crazy Indian roads could be. A black kite dodged electric wires, swooped down and snatched a scrap of food from the pavement.

The taxi pulled up in front of the yellow-fronted building with the name Chateau Marine above the hallway. A teenage lad leaned over the second-floor balcony, watching me alight from the car. We stared at each other for a moment.

'Neel,' I called.

'Breezy!' he yelled and disappeared. Moments later, he burst from the entrance. As a fourteen-year-old, he had wisps of facial hair and his voice had turned gruff. He was older, taller and skinnier. We hugged and slapped each other's backs. We unloaded the trunks and carried them to the lift.

Ma and sixteen-year-old Nina stood beaming at the open door.

'Welcome home, stranger,' Ma said, and I gave them both a big hug.

I had to borrow Indian rupees from Ma, and Neel raced downstairs to pay the driver. Nina had turned into a gorgeous young lady with waist-length blonde hair. Both kids were bursting with questions about my trip, about what I did in America, what was in the trunk with holes in it.

'Let the poor boy relax,' Ma said. 'Bring him a glass of nimbu pani [lemonade].'

It seemed like I had been away for at least two decades. Everything looked very different from a mere six years ago. Every muscle relaxed in a way it hadn't in the country of my birth. I was home at last.

EPILOGUE

M Y FIRST WEEK AT home passed in a blur. Sitting on the balcony of Chateau Marine, which overlooked the sweeping curve of Marine Drive one early morning, I was content. There wasn't much traffic and a slight sea breeze ruffled my hair. Haze obscured the horizon and the Arabian Sea lapped against the rocks. The family was still asleep as I watched seagulls, pigeons, crows, stray dogs and joggers on the wide esplanade across the road. *What to do next?*

The brief spell at college hadn't taught me a thing. But I didn't need any more classroom education. My many jobs, from being a salesman and waiter to a seaman and lab technician, were forgettable. The only career experience that mattered to me was working for the man I had idolized since high school, Bill Haast. *Perhaps I can set up something similar here, keeping snakes, showing people how marvellous they are and extracting venom.* The Bombay Snake Park. *Where would I establish it?* I'd need land and then build snake rooms. *Where would I go for the large stash of cash needed to start this enterprise? Who'd give a loan to a twenty-four-year-old hippy with no education?* The idea was daunting, but promised to lead me on the adventure of my wildest dreams.

ACKNOWLEDGEMENTS

Thanks are due to many people.

M.D. Madhusudan and Pavithra Sankaran are the main movers behind this effort. Madhu gifted me a voice recorder to narrate my stories, and Pavithra offered comments on the early drafts. Without their constant encouragement, this book wouldn't have been.

Sadanand Menon and *Business Standard* for giving permission to use the excerpt in Chapter 2. Vijaykumar Thondaman of the Pudukkottai royal family for reminding me of his father's incredible talent at shooting.

Mathew Anthony, Viju Parameshwar and Joseph Thomas for help in fact-checking the chapter on Lawrence School, Lovedale. But any errors that remain are mine alone.

Bob Ashley, Joe Wasilewski and Trent Adamson for photographs of beautiful snakes, and Evan Wilson for the photo of the Hoosick house.

Diane Diekman for critiquing the manuscript. Chinmayee Chandra for legal advice.

Jaya Bhattacharji Rose, our first reader, for her enthusiasm.

Ranjana Sengupta and Hemali Sodhi at A Suitable Agency for making this book possible. At HarperCollins India, Ujjaini Dasgupta for asking the right questions, and spotting missing words and grammatical errors, and Swati Chopra for shepherding the manuscript towards the final product that's in your hands.

Siblings Gail Wynne, Nina Menon, Neel Chattopadhyaya and Penny Booher for remembering details and for always being there. Former wife Zai, and sons Nikhil and Samir for their encouragement. Cousins Joan Eaves and John Babson for digging through old letters and photographs. It goes without saying that any lapses of memory are mine.

Dear reader, should you wish to see more pictures of my adventures in those early years and the songs that punctuated my life, please click this link https://t.ly/h2yfn
This is for the snakes and rock 'n' roll. As for the drugs, just say no! 😆

BIBLIOGRAPHY

——Rayond L. Ditmars, *Snakes of the World* (New York, US: The Macmillan Company, 1944).

——Percy A. Morris, *Boy's Book of Snakes: How to Recognize and Understand Them* (New York, US: The Ronald Press Company, 1948).

——Edwin H. Colbert, *The Dinosaur Book: The Ruling Reptiles and Their Relatives* (New York, US: McGraw-Hill Book Company, Inc., 1951).

——Frank Wall, *A Popular Treatise on the Common Indian Snakes* (Bombay, India: Bombay Natural History Society, 1900).

——Henri Cartier-Bresson, *The Decisive Moment* (New York, US: Simon & Schuster, 1952).

INDEX

Abdulali, Humayun, 122

Abdullah, Sheikh, 76

Abdullah Jan, driver, 75, 107, 119

adrenalin, 55, 244, 249, 314, 347

ads, 182, 186; Burma Shave, 17;
  for fish, 66; for Future Homes
  Incorporated, 195; job listings,
  207; rentals, 173

Agritoxins Venom Lab, Florida,
  277

aircraft: A-4 Skyhawks, 325;
  C-130 Hercules cargo plane,
  299; F-4 Phantoms, 325; T-39
  Sabreliner, 299

Air India DC-3 Airplane, 21

Airplane, Jefferson, 350

Akhter, mechanic, 145–147, 162

Alabama, 231, 331

Alcoa Pilgrim, cargo carrier, 223–
  226, 229, 231

Ali, trout fishing guide, 94

Alice, 127, 231

Alif Laila, 52

Ali, Salim, 83

Allen, Ross, 247

alligators, 233, 236, 248, 251, 261,
  332, 334; gators, 250–254,
  333–334; catching, 252, *see also
  crocodiles*

Alphonse, 350, 355

American Museum of Natural
  History, New York, 13

American passport, 167

American WASPs (White Anglo-
  Saxon Protestants), 48

Amy, 314

Anand, Dev, 44

anaphylaxis, 347

Anderson, Charles, 288

Anderson, Jim, 326

Anderson, Rick, 235–236, 238,
  247, 262–263, 267, 269

And I wonder, 188

Andrew Furuseth Training School,
  Philadelphia, 210

Andrews Air Force Base,
  Maryland, 299–300

animals: antelopes, 154, 185;
  barking deer 'kaattu aadu,' 88,
  128, 162; black bear, 192, 317;

blackbuck, x, 154–155, 162;
coatimundis, 317, 341, 343;
coyotes, 185, 190; dealers in,
139, 261, 340; deer, 126, 128,
135, 145–147, 151–152, 154–
155, 158, 160, 162, 185–186,
188–189; dholes wild dogs,
160; gaur, 137, 158; hares,
162, 337; hunting jackals,
102; jackals, 80, 97, 102, 136,
162; javelinas, 317; leopard, x,
33, 129, 134–137, 139, 142,
150–153, 155, 157, 161–162;
lions, 8, 134, 137; mountain
lion, 8, 186; mule deer, 174,
178, 186–188; 192; Nilgiri
langur, 102; Nilgiri tahr, 56,
121; panther, 149; peccaries,
341; sambhar stag, 155; sloth
bear, 163; spotted deer, x, 146,
151, 160; tigers, 8, 25, 129,
134–135, 137, 139, 158, 163;
ungulates, 135, 155; wild boar,
72, 158, 160–161
antivenom, 103, 240, 313–314, 321
antiwar protest in Washington,
287
Arabian Sea, 224–225, 359
Arizona, 17, 300, 341, 346; Ajo
Road, 315; Huachucas, 315
Army of the Republic of Vietnam
(ARVN), 322
Atlantic City, 5, 221–222
Augusta, Georgia, 282, 285, 287
Australia, 26, 74
Ayo, 105

Baba Sait, mechanic, 136, 163

Bab-el-Mandeb Strait, 351
Babson, Dick, 5
Babsons, 6, 8, 42, 170, 206, 276
Baez, Joan, 260, 265, 301, 350
Baltimore, Maryland, 231
B and B—House of Wheels, 247
Bandipur elephant camp, 140, 158
Bangalore (now Bengaluru), 87,
116–117, 121
Barker, Jim, 288
Bassam, Abdulla, 75
Batista, Fulgencio, 228
Battle of the Bulge, 4
bayonet practice, 281
Beatles, 217, 254, 302
beer, 100–101, 107, 143, 147,
181, 185, 218, 224–225, 228,
264–265, 271, 346, 352;
Cerveza Polar, 229; Coors,
266; Corona, 230; draught
beer, 168; Golden Eagle, 168;
Heineken, 220; Kirin or Asahi
Gold, 326
Beke, Attila, 255–257, 260, 270,
335–341
Bernice, 345–347
Betancourt, Rómulo, 229
Beth, 221–222
Bhavanisagar, 144
Bibliography of Snake Venoms and
Venomous Snakes, Russell, 238
Biggs Air Force Base, El Paso, 299
birds, 39–40, 78, 80, 82–85, 87,
102, 104, 136–138, 146, 152,
154, 304, 306; albino crow,
136; black-headed ibises, 258;
black kite, 24, 104, 136–137,
356; blue herons, 258; booby,

223, 350; coppersmith, 79;
crested serpent eagle, 80;
crows, 24, 359; doves, 9, 79,
83, 94, 178, 251; flameback
woodpeckers, 82; grey hornbill,
144; grey junglefowl, 88;
hawk, 9, 340; hill mynas,
144; hummingbirds, 317;
magpies, 339; Malay bittern
or Malayan night heron,
115, 122; nightjars, 108, 155,
161; paradise flycatcher, 79,
85; parakeets, 84, 111, 145;
peacocks, 92; quail, 244, 248;
red-wattled lapwings, 154;
rheas, 137–139; rose-ringed
parakeet chick, 83; sage grouse,
186; seagulls, 359; imperial
pigeons, 88; sparrows, 39–40,
42, 59; spotted owlets, 108;
turkey vultures, 258; vultures,
155; warblers, 257; white-
breasted kingfisher (white-
throated kingfisher), 79; white
egrets, 258; woodpecker,
82, 285; yellow-naped
woodpecker, 82
birthday: Dad and, 16; eighth, 18;
twelfth, 76; fourteenth, 94;
eighteenth, 163; twentieth,
230; twenty-fourth, hiking on,
344
Bisbee, Arizona, 341, 343
Black Hills, 203
Bliss, Fort, Texas, 288, 290
blood-collection drives, 309
Bloomingdale, 207–208
boat rides, 120, 159

Bobbie, 245–246
Bogert, Charles, 295
Bolivia, 262
Bombay (now Mumbai), 24,
26–27, 35–37, 48, 51, 73–74,
76, 88, 91–92, 122–123,
133, 136, 225, 351, 353–354;
Breach Candy, 60, 106, 124,
202; Chateau Marine, 356,
359; Colaba, 24, 57; Crawford
Market (live animal market),
104–105; Haji Ali Dargah, 75;
Juhu, 21, 25, 27, 37–38, 44,
57, 60, 92; Matunga, 26, 42,
48, 60; Nataraj Hotel, 356;
Parel, 28; Powai Lake, 107,
123; Santa Cruz airport, 23;
Victoria Terminus, 29, 47, 95;
Worli Sea Face, 43, 52, 57, 60,
98, 104, 355;
Bombay International School, 300
Bombay Natural History Society,
83, 116, 122
Bombay Snake Park, 359
Bombelli ice cream parlour, 60,
75, 124
The Bomber's Handbook, 106,
111–112, 114, 127
The Book of Indian Birds, Ali, 83
boot camp, 289
Boston, 4, 273, 275; Wollaston
(Ma's family) in, 4–5, 17, 24,
26, 42, 206, 222, 273, 276
Bowie, Jim, 71
Box Canyon, 341
Boy's Book of Snakes, Morris, 15
Bradford, Brad, 255
Breezy Brand Firecrackers, 114

Bret Harte Elementary School, 17
Bronx Zoo, 102, 122
Brooklyn, New York, 210, 221
Brown, Nell, 297, 317, 319, 341, 343
Brown, Winston, 332
Bruce, 233, 238, 242
Bücherl, Wolfgang, 238
Buckley, Eleanor E., 238
Burbank, California, 16–18
butterflies, 5, 89, 248, 317

cacti collection, 18, 304, 317, 344
Camp Croft, 4
camping, 4, 8, 76, 99–100, 127, 129, 140, 158, 193–194, 282, 297
Camp Zama, 323
Carbon County Memorial Hospital, 179
Carmelita, 230
Carol (stepsister), 168–170, 197
Carr Canyon, 298, 317
cars: '53 Chevy pickup, 196, 282; 1955 Plymouth station wagon, 337; Cadillac Fleetwood, 211, 235; Chevy, 184–186, 200; Ford, 243, 252–253, 330; Ford, 1956, 221; Ford, maroon left-hand-drive, 23; Ford, two-door '50, 258; Ford red '63, 243; MG sports, 311; Oldsmobile Holiday, 274; Pontiac, 341; Studebaker, 175; Volkswagen Beetle, 203
Cartier-Bresson, Henri, 104

'A Case of Snakebite of Crotalus viridis viridis' by Romulus E. Whitaker III, 316
Castro, Fidel, 78, 90, 228
cat: jungle cats, 136, 162; Trichy, Persian cat, 73, 105–106, 119
Catskill Mountains, 8
Chad, 183
Chamarajanagar, 144–145
Charles, Ray, 150, 153–156, 161, 163, 187, 220, 288
Chase, Bill, 246–247, 255, 261, 335
Chattopadhyaya, Doris Norden. See Norden, Doris (Ma/ Mummy)
Chattopadhyaya, Harindranath (Baba/Granddaddy), 14, 25–28, 36, 43, 300; at Lovedale, 36; Menon on, 27–28; notoriety, 27
Chattopadhyaya, Kamaladevi (Amma/mother of Rama), 14, 18, 25; All India Handicrafts Board, 134; birthday gifts of, 76; to Delhi, 124, 160; gifting big-format book, 104; Handicrafts Board, 134; and Indian art, 52; Jammu Kashmir Prime Minister and, 93; to Kashmir, 92; in Kodai, 158; Maharaja of Mysore inviting, 159; visit to Bombay, 27, 58, 123
Chattopadhyaya, Rama (stepfather), 3, 13–14, 16–19, 22–30, 40, 43–44, 46, 74–75, 92, 94, 133, 137, 299–300;

'56 Plymouth of, 75; buying fishnet, 38; Fiat car of, 75; job in Technicolor in Hollywood, 16

Chell, Mrs, 50

chemistry lab, 112

Cherry, 216

Chinese coins, 34

Chinniah, 139, 142

Christian, classmate, 68-69, 81, 95, 98–99, 102, 111–112, 114, 116–119, 125, 127, 129, 132, 143–144; grades, 91; house, 101–102, 117; and motorized bike, 95

Christine/Nina (sister), 18–19, 21, 25–26, 30, 35, 37, 43, 51, 157–160, 299–300, 356; bicycle for, 74;

Christmas, 15, 18, 25, 50, 61, 187

Chuck, 86, 98–99, 111, 121

church services, 87, 98, see also Religious Education

Chugwater 197

cigar, Java Whiffs, 137, 147, 149, 161, 260

cigarettes, 69, 108, 114, 192, 197, 259–260, 264, 289, 350; and beedis, 120, 210; Marlboro, 210; quit smoking, 280

Claire, 310–313, 315–316, 320, 329, 331

Clamp, Heyward, 235, 237–247, 250–257, 260–263, 265, 269, 273, 277, 282–287, 319, 329–335

Clamp, Teddy, 250, 273, 277, 282–283, 285, 332–334

classmates, 36, 48–49, 53, 62, 66, 68, 77, 97–98, 103, 126–128, 173, see also friends

Clauser, John, 205

Coasters' Poison Ivy, 313

coffee, 31, 69, 107, 119, 182, 208, 216, 266

Colbert, Edwin, 18

Cold War, 255

colour blindness, 64, 91, 239, 289

commercial snake hunter, x, 255, 332–343

Connie, 221–222

consignments, 83, 224, 230, 240–241; from Bolivia, 262; 'VENOMOUS SNAKES— KEEP OUT OF SUN,' 312

Convention on International Trade in Endangered Species of Wild Fauna and Flora (CITES), 355

Coral Gables, 238, 335

Coronet magazine, 103

Corral, Dona, 330

cottontails rabbits, 178–179, 185; and tularaemia "rabbit fever", 184

cousins, 24–25, 207, see also under separate names

crabs, 57, 318

Craig, 44–46, 48–49, 52–54, 56–57, 63, 69–70, 73, 77; death of, 74; family, 44, 47, 51, 73; leaving India, 53 crocodiles, 13, 109, 143, 154, 233, 238; man-eating, 143; Nile and American, 236–37

Crombie, Mrs, 39–40, 42, 57

cryotherapy, 321

CS gas, tear gas as, 284

Cuban Missile Crisis, 255

Cumballa Hill, 92

Curtis, Ralph, 247

Custer's motorbike mechanic shop, 201–202

Daniel, Bro., as Father Tanner, 82–86, 88, 102, 115–116, 122, 132

Dave, 62-63, 66, 70, 72-73, 77, 84-85, 97, 100, 109-110, 121

Dave, visitor to the serp, 252

Dean, 175–178, 181–182, 186–189, 193–195, 208, 329

The Decisive Moment, Cartier-Bresson, 104

Delaware River, 212

Dilip Kumar, 44

The Dinosaur Book, Colbert, 18

Ditmars, Raymond L., 10, 41, 85, 102, 122, 236

Djibouti, 224, 354–355

DMM (deck maintenance man), 212–213, 223

dog food, 200, 207

dolphins, 20, 229, 241

Donovan, 350

Don Juans, 115

Dorothy (Dottie), 260–262, 265–268, 277, 335, 337–340; and La cucaracha la cucaracha, 264

Drafted into Army, 178, 271–273, 275–287, 289, 301, 326, 340; sergeants, 277–278, 280; dodgers, 273, 277; marching, 278, 281, 289

Dragonflies, 9, 171

drinking, 99, 185, 217, 255

drugs: amphetamine, 308; cocaine, 264; diet drug Dexedrine (speed), 264, 308, 336, 338; ganja, 264; heroin, 264; joint, 264–266, 292–293, 302, 321, 338; LSD, 264, 276, 301, 349; marijuana, 264–265, 342, 347, 352; morphine, 264; opium, 26, 264

dump truck, 201–202

Dutt, Sunil, 356

Dylan, Bob, 301, 322, 350

earthworms, 10, 64, 89, *see also* fishing

Edisto Island Serpentarium, South Carolina, 277

Edna (Aunt), 5

Egypt, 223, 350

Ekberg, Anita, 219

Elaine, 312

Elena, 220

elephants, x, 121, 134–135, 139–140, 144, 147–151, 153, 155–156, 158, 163; khedda operation, 159; kumkis, 159

Elly (aunt), 3, 5–6, 11–13, 42, 171–172, 187, 207, 209, 275–276, 345, 347; apartment, 208, 221, 293, 300, 346; commercial artist, 170; cutting down elms, 205–206; with her new husband, 205

El Paso, 288–289, 293, 296, 299–300, 312–313, 316, 318, 329, 332, 334, 339, 344

El Paso zoo, 292, 316

epinephrine. *See* adrenaline

Ericsson, Augusta (grandmother/ Mumma), 4–5, 42, 50, 206–207

Ericsson, John, Capt., 4

Estrella, 293–294

eucalyptus, 30, 55, 70, 101, 131

Eucalyptus, 131; tobacco as dirty weed, in, 101, *see also* cigarette

Evens, Paul, 337, 337–340

experiments, 81–82, 239, 304

explosives, xi, 70, 82, 112–113, 115, 117, 119, 281, *see also* firearms; guns

Facente, Jack, 277, Agritoxins Venom Lab, 277

Fauna & Flora International (FFI), ix

Fighting Caravans, Grey, 50

film laboratory, 24; film-processing operations, 52; motion-picture colour-processing, 16

fire, 25, 32–33, 39, 82, 113–114, 149–151, 178–179, 190, 192–195, 224, 280–283, 316–317, 319, 321, 328

firearms, 87, 150, 174, 190, 281, *see also* guns; rifle

fishermen, 26, 45, 57, 65, 224, 270

fishes, 37, 44–45, 67, 104, 108, 175, 195, 230; barramundi, 9; bonito, 228; brookie, 177; brook trout, 175; carp, 65–66, 68, 93, 107–108, 327; catfish, 59, 334; catfish wallago, 143; catla, 107–109; channel catfish, 9; crayfish, 8; cutthroat trout, 199; eel, 57–58; at Juhu beach, 38; kingfish, 228; king mackerel, 229; large mirror carp, 68; largemouth bass, 9; long-nose sucker, 194; mahseer, 9; rainbow trout, 178, 194; rohu, 107, 109; sardines, 38, 200; sunfish, 8; tarpons (silver king), 270; tiburon (shark), 228; trout, 93–94, 99, 177, 193–194; yellow perch, 8–9

fishing, x–xi, 5, 9–10, 59, 63, 65–68, 73, 75, 123, 175–176, 193, 203, 206; in Cauvery River, 143; foul hooking, 194; ground baiting, 108; learning from Mogla, 93; ledgering, 108; at Powai Lake, 107, 123; spear guns, 98; treble hooks, 194; worms for, 8, 32, 92, 171, 285, 306

fishing rods/fish hooks, 9–10, 55, 57, 59, 65, 67–68, 93, 99, 107–109, 143, 177, 193, 270, 333, 336

fishwives, 37–38, 58

Fitter, Richard, ix

Florida, x, 227, 231, 243–248, 255, 257, 265–266, 276–277, 334, 336; City, 243, 245, 248,

266; Everglades, x, 243, 250, 261–262, 268

Florida Armed Forces Induction Station, Miami, 271–274

flyfishing equipment, 199

flying squirrels, 101–102

Fort Gordon, Fort Garbage, 277, 282, 287, 289

Foster, Richard, 19

Freak Out, 80, 329

friends, 6, 26–27, 43–44, 50–51, 53–55, 59–60, 63–65, 70–73, 113, 126–127, 131–132, 139–141, 184–185, 197–198, 254–255, 260, 277, 301–302, 305, 346

frogs, 8, 11, 94, 171, 253, 269, 316

Gail (elder sister), 3–6, 8, 10, 12–15, 17, 19, 21–23, 26–28, 30, 36, 46–47, 49–51, 72–73, 91–92, 170–171, 205; graduation ceremony, 91–92; at Syracuse University, 92

Gandhi, Mahatma, 14

gas, 118–119, 182–183, 185, 199, 206, 260, 275, 341; chlorine, 284

Georgia, 233, 277, 331

Gerlinde, 347–348, 350

German, 68

Germany, 95, 139, 144, 152, 219

gharials, 154

Gibbs, Mrs, 78, 84, 91, 100, 111, 121, 145

Gibraltar, 20, 223

girls, 72, 75, 85, 96–98, 103, 114–116, 127–130, 149, 152,

172, 195, 197–199, 218–222, 260, 352–353

GIs, 289, 300, 314, 323–325

Give a cheer, give a cheer, 100–101

God of Idiots, 70–71, 112, 180

gold dust, 203

Goris, Richard, 328

Green River Ordinance, 198–199

grenade, 127, 279, 281, *see also* firearms

Greyhound, 12, 170, 172, 222, 275

Grinder, Joe de, 218

Guevara, Che, 78, 90, 119, 228

Gumtapuram, 145, 148, 151–153, 155, 159–160, 170

Gundar Valley, 99

guns, (*see also* rifle): 7.62 mm cartridges, 278; 12-gauge shotgun, 68, 174, 185, 211; .22 revolver, 174, 178; .38 Special, 211; .44 Magnum revolver, 180; .222, 188; .500 Express double-barrel, 150, 153, 157; airgun, 77, 92, 122; BB gun, 25–26, 39, 59; double-barrelled shotgun, 147, 151; Eley Kynoch cartridges, 161; LG cartridge, 146, 161; muzzle-loaders, 151; Remington, 174; semi-automatic weapon, 278; single-shot Winchester .22 rifle, 147

Gutierrez, Florence, The Lizard Lady, 257, 265, 267–268

Gwen, 103–104

Haast, Bill, 89–91, 103, 232–242,
    244, 247, 250, 252–254,
    256–257, 260, 263, 267,
    270–271, 274, 277; divorce
    and marrying Nancy, 261;
    venomous snakebites, 239; as
    Wild Bill, 239
Haast, Bill Jr, 247
Haast, Clarita, 234–235, 237, 239,
    261
Haast, Naia, 277
Haast, Shantih, 277
The Hague, Netherlands, 220
Haines, John, 288
Haley, Bill, *Rock around the
    Clock...*, 72
Happy Wanderer song, 130–131

Hautz, Lawrence/Larry, 271, 274
Hemingway, Ernest, 61
Hendrix, Jimi, 301
HERP, Bulletin of the New York
    Herpetological Society, 316
Herz, Alice, 287
Highclerc School. *See* Kodaikanal
    International School
highway, 183, 191–193, 203–204,
    232, 235, 243, 250, 252, 287,
    323, 337, *see also* hitchhiking/
    thumbing
hiking, 55–56, 68, 70–72, 99–100,
    128–129, 207, 210, 230, 232,
    317, 320, 341–342, 344
Hillary, Edmund, 70
hippies, 254, 276
hitchhiking/thumbing, 34, 41,
    66–67, 72, 200–204, 207,
    209–210, 232, 259–260, 274,

    274–275, 296–297, 341–342,
    344, 351
Hoffa, Jimmy, 211
Holland, 219–220
homesickness, 50, 185, 187, 208,
    329
Hoosac River, 206, 222
Hoosick, New York, 6, 14, 16–18,
    30, 42, 54, 56, 73, 155, 170,
    183, 185, 204, 206, 209, 217,
    220-222, 225, 323, 340, 345,
    347-348
hope chest, 196–197
Huachuca Mountains, southern
    Arizona, 315
hunting, ix–xi, 84–85, 121,
    133–134, 145, 147, 150–151,
    155, 157, 160, 184–188, 193,
    243–244, 270–271; army men
    on, 162; deer, 146, 162; gators,
    252–253; imperial pigeons, 87;
    snakes, 245; stories, 169
Hunting for Tyrannosaurus Rex, 61
Hurricane Cleo, 269
Huxley, Aldous, 301

I Ching, 301
I don't wanna get drafted, Zappa,
    271–272
iguanas, 233, 257, 270; as 'bamboo
    chicken,' 236; green, 236, 277;
    rhinoceros, 236, *see also* lizards
Indian Wildlife Act, 355
Ingrid, (stepmother), 168
insects, 149, 156, 171, 248;
    ladybugs, 297
Ionides, C.J.P., 240
Iran, 223–224

Irene *Goodnight, Irene*, 141–142
Ivory poachers, 151

Jack, as 'Howdy' 292–293; 295, 297, 303, 314, 330
Jack, Gunboat, 87
jacklighting, 146, 162, 184
jackrabbits, 184, 190
Jaime, fisherman, 228
Janaki, 261
Japan, 197, 322–331, 340
Japanese china, 197
Japan Snake Centre, Yabuzuka, 326
Jill, 124, 127
Jim, mechanic, 190–193, 201, 275, 326–328
Jimmy, 151–152, 157; black Labrador, 151; rat snake enmeshing, 156
Joanie, cousin, 5–6, 206
Joe, Italian foreman, 210–211
Joe, salesman buddy, 195–208, 223
Johnny (cousin), 6, 17, 34
John Paul (JP), 62–63, 66, 69–70, 72-73, 77, 81, 84–85, 97, 100, 109–110, 117, 121, 144
Johnson, Ben, 261–263
Johnson, Lyndon B., 271
Johnstone, Gordon, 247, 337
Jones, Davy, 216
Josefina, 227–229
Jose 'Mex Mouse', 292–295, 302–303, 306, 308, 314, 330
Journal of the Bombay Natural History Society, 102
Juárez, 303, 308, 318
Junior High School Dance, 72

Kannada, 134, 140, 152
Kapoor, Raj, 43–44
Kapoor, Shammi, 109
Karachi, 224–225, 354–355
Kashmir, 76, 92–94; Dal Lake, 93; Pahalgam, 94; Shangri-La, houseboat, 92–93, 104, 106
Kasi, Robert, 87, 102, 130
Kauffeld, Carl, x, 247, 282, 295, 298, 315, 317, 319, 340, 344
Ken, classmate, 173–174, 178, 181–182, 184–187, 189, 195; studious, 178
Kennedy, J.F., assassination of, 250
Kesey, Ken, 264
King Cobra Conservancy, 277
kitchen police (KP) duty, 281
kite-flying, 42, 52, 59–60, 74, 109
Kodaikanal (Kodai)/Kodaikanal hills, ix, 46–47, 49, 51, 53, 60, 62, 64, 71, 74, 93–94, 109, 119–120, 137, 143, 156–157, 349; bullying, 54; left, 132; Banday Brothers, 77, 83; Bear Shola, 87, 100; Berijam lake, 88; Brahmin hotel, 69, 101, 144; Budge/bazaar, 56, 69, 81, 83, 87, 95, 98–99, 101, 131, 144, 233; Carlton Hotel, 48, 68; Coaker's Walk, 70, 73, 115; Doveton's Photo Studio, 98; German Settlement, 68, 117; Highclerc School, 46, 48, 50, 100–101, 131; Jacob's Bakery, 99; Kodai Road, 47, 73, 110; Kookal Caves/ Leech Shola, 127–128; Kistnamma

Naik Tope, 70, 79, 85–86, 89, 131, 158; Maharaja's Boat House/Boat Club, 66, 68, 127; Observatory Hill, 55, 99, 129; Pudukkottai royal mansion, 86; Seven Roads, 78; Shembaganur, 82, 87–88, 102, 136; Shembaganur museum, 86, 129

Kodaikanal International School, commencement address for, 132; annual dance, 103; bell ringer, 49, 125; graduation ceremony, 130; hayride, 120; high school as Highclerc School, 46, 48–50, 64, 73, 76–77, 90, 96, 100–101, 131–132, 198, 359

Kodai Missionary Union, 87

Krause, principal, 122, 129

Kumar, Malayali cook, 26, 38, 40, 186

lab technicians/techs, 294, 309, 322, 324, 326

LaGuardia Airport, New York 167

Lakshman, 43

Lama, Dalai, 140

Lambretta scooter, 110, *see also* motorbikes/motorcycles

LaPorte, Roger Allen, 323

Laramie, 172, 174, 177, 181, 183–184, 186, 193, 195, 198, 200, 202

Laszlo, Joe, 255

Leary, Timothy, 301

Le Havre, 219

Leon, 211

leopard, x, 129, 134–135, 137, 139, 142, 150–153, 155, 157, 161; cub, 136; in Lovedale, 33; shot at, 162, *see also under* animals

letters, 35, 93, 103, 121, 126, 168, 183, 203, 208, 235

Liberty ship, 210, 215

lifeboat winches, 214

Lilly, John, 241

Linda, 340

Line of Duty "LoD no", 314

liquor/alcohol, 67, 98, 100, 181, 187, 265, 282; Bacardi Añejo rum, 308; Colt 45 malt, 187, 282, *see also* beer

Little Hoosac river, 8

lizards, 18, 63, 86, 257, 265, 298, 316–317, 319, 336; Cuban anoles, green lizards, 336; Draco, flying lizard, 86; garden lizard, 39; gila monster, 330; skinks, 336, 338; tegus, 257; Texas horned, 266

lobsters, 58, 355

Longfellow, Henry Wadsworth, *Paul Revere's Ride* by, 84

Long Island Sound, in Long Island Sound, 5

longshoremen, 224, 227, 229, 354

Lovedale, Lawrence School, 28–31, 33, 35–36, 42, 44, 90, 135, 174, 278; quitting, 53

Lundberg, Col., 296, 310

Luther (Squeaky), 292–293, 302–303, 306, 310, 315, 318, 330

M★A★S★H, about Korean War, 308

Maas, Gary, 255, 335

machan, 107–109, 149, 155

MacLachlan, Dugald (uncle), 205, 221–222, 276, 323, 347

Mad magazine, 79

Madras, 29–30, 36, 47, 74, 110

mahouts, 139–140, 159

Malaitis, 290–291

mammals, 102, 137; bats, 108, 171, 347; civet cats, 155

Mara River, 237

Mariappan, blacksmith, 71

Marie, 304, 306

The Marijuana Papers, Solomon, 301

Marlyn, 346, 348, 350

Masako, 327–328

Massawa, 352–355

math deficiency syndrome, 62

Mathis, Johnny, 207

McGrew, Paul, 173, 190

McGuire Air Force Base, New Jersey, 323

McGuire, Barry, 322

McKelligon Canyon, 315

McNamara, Robert, 323

McQuatters, Jim, mobike repair shop, 184

McVay, Scott, 241

meat locker, 195, *see also* hunting

Medicine Bow National Forest, 190–191

Meems, Albert, 139, 152

memories, 5, 11, 13, 85, 90, 107, 144, 171, 176, 223, 315

Menon, Sadanand, 27

Meredith, 207

Merrick, sophomore, 80, 95, 121

Mettupalayam, 30

MI (Military Intelligence Corps), 288

Miami, 232–233, 235, 251, 255–256, 271, 276, 295, 312, 335, 340; Hurricane Cleo over, 269

Miami Seaquarium, 265

Miami Serpentarium, 103, 232–233, 235–253

Mike, bird mimic, 80, 84, 97, 121, 303

Miller Peak, 316–317

minerals (rocks) collection, 18–19, 26

missionaries, 46–47, 50, 53, 71

Mohammed, Bakshi Ghulam, 93

mongoose, 40, 107

mongrel/mutt, Jellybean, 35, 43

Montand, Yves, 353

Morrison, Norman, immolation of, 323

Morris, Percy, 15

motel, 17, 199, 204, 223, 235, 238, 242

Motel, Mariner, 235

motion picture processing lab, 16, 24; building design by Mummy, 28

motorbike/motorcycle, 95, 116, 119–120, 122, 136, 143–145, 148–149, 183, 189–191, 193, 196, 202, 247, 250–252, 261, 266–267; 350 cc Triumph, 43, 96, 137, 143, 148, 163, 182, 247; 1939 500 cc Norton, 116–117, 119–120, 137, 144;

1955 BSA 350 cc single, 247; AJS, 500 cc single, 182–183, 188, 190, 196, 201, 203, 247; British, 95; BSA twin-cylinder, 190, 247, 274; cheater sprocket, 190–191, 193; clanking, 201; knobby tyres, 191; riding, 110; in Wyoming, 182

motorcycle bug, 63

Mount Rushmore, 201, 203

movies, 52, 54, 67, 90, 97, 114–115, 117, 124, 141, 261, 353

Mudumalai, 158

Mukund, carpenter, 52, 105

Munnar, 98–99, 152

Muthu, barber, 96

Mysore, 133–147, 152, 157, 159–160, 163, 170, 184, 247; Dasara celebrations, 137–139; Ganesh Talkies, 141; Golden Age Café, 134, 137, 141; KR Sagar dam, 143; Srirangapatna, 143

Nadudorai (Maharajkumar Radhakrishna Thondaiman), 68, 86–87, 150

Nan, 319–321, 344

Nancy, 114–116, 120, 122, 125–127, 132–133, 143–144, 261

Naren (cousin), 26, 42, 52, 60

Nargis, 356

National Cadet Corps (NCC), 32

National Maritime Union (NMU), 211

Natural Selections, Florida, 277

Neelakantan (brother)/Neel, 43, 50–51, 106–107, 123, 157, 159–160, 202, 206, 299–300, 356; 'Madiga' language of, 75; *Sgt. Pepper's Lonely Hearts Club Band* for, 346; and temple in the sea, 75

Neelakantiah, 134–135, 137–138

Nehru, Jawaharlal, 14, 27, 58

nettles, 56, *see also* poison ivy

neurotoxins, 240, 328, 336, 347, *see also* venom

New Guinea, 9

New Jersey, 5, 200, 207, 247, 288, 312, 323, 337, 340; Three Bridges, 5

Newman, Arnie, 255

newt, 328, *see also* reptiles

New York, 18, 20, 22, 167, 170–171, 208, 217–218, 222, 225, 274–275, 323, 344, 347; Hoosick, 6, 14, 17–18, 52, 170, 183, 185, 187, 217, 220–222, 225, 345, 347–348

Nick's Place, Huachucas, 316, 341

nicotine withdrawal, 280, *see also* cigarette

Nilgiri hills, 30

Nimmi, 43–44

Nita, 292–293, 301–303, 330

Norden, Doris (Ma/Mom/Mummy, 3, 7–15, 18–19, 21–24, 26, 28, 30, 35–36, 40, 42–44, 46–47, 50, 57–59, 61, 64, 67, 71–75, 91–92, 96, 104–106, 116, 118, 121–124, 158; become Doris Norden Chattopadhyaya, 16; blueberry pie, 9; coming with Nina and Neel, 157; and Dad divorced

again, 16; divorced from Rama,
300; interior decoration, 59;
Johnnie Walker Black Label,
lies and, 21; marrying Rama,
16; road trip with Rama,
16–17; Rolleicord camera,
159; separation of, 4; wooden
toys manufacturing, 52; writing
from New York, 299
Nordens, 4, 124
Norden, Samuel (grandfather/
Pappa), 4–5, 42, 206
Norgay, Tenzing, 70
Nova Scotia, 215

Okeetee, South Carolina, 283,
285, 315
Old Mam Wine Company, 326
Old Yeller, 186
Oliver, James, 102
on-the-job training (OJT), 289
Oothu, 47, 84, see also Kodaikanal
optirectomy, 293
ornithologists, 85

pachyderm, 151, 155–156, see also
elephants; tusker
Padma, the cook, 58, 92
paediatric lab, 291
palaeontologist, 61, 173; as assistant
to, 13
Palani Hills, 47, 122, see also
Kodaikanal
parasitologist, 318
Parker, Fess, Ballad of Davy Crockett
by, 72
paw prints, 129, 161
Paxton, Tom, 322

pear wine, 95, 100
Peckham, Sonny, 171
Peckham, Billy, 171
The Penitent Butchers, by Richard
Fitter and Sir Peter Scott, ix
Penn, Jan, 300–301
Penn, Wes, 301, 330
Penny (half-sister), 168, 248
Periyakulam road, 158
Periyar Wildlife Sanctuary in
Kerala, 98
pet, 95, 105, 123, 255; black kite,
136; dog, 203; kitten Trichy,
74; Mandapam parrot, 131;
mouse, 56; Parakeet, 84;
Pomeranian, 129; python,
105, 116, 123–124, 130, 262;
Sammy (basset hound), 186–
187; Texas horned lizard, 266;
Tempest (dog), 4, 6; trinket
snake as, 41; Zephyr, 4
pet-market, 105
pet shops, 336
pet trade, x, 255, 317, 336
peyote, 301, 303–304, 306–307,
333, 349
Phil, classmate, 77–78, 221
photographs, 10, 52, 92, 98, 104,
116, 120, 122, 139, 159, 168
photography, 52, 98
Pierce, Skip, 336–338, 340
pigeons, 39, 83, 359
Pillai, V.T., general merchandise
store, 69, 81
PL-480, or Food for Peace, 231
Pleshette, Suzanne, 242
poison ivy, 8

A Popular Treatise on the Common Indian Snakes, Wall, 102
Port Everglades in Florida, 231
Port Sudan, 351–352, 355
Pradhania, V., 134–139, 141, 155, 157
pranks/misgivings, 55, 58, 72, 81, 93, 97, 113, 131, 133, 261–262, 265
predator, 128, 151–152, 160–161
Presentation Convent, Mother Superior of, 129–130
preservation, 86, 143, 330; of birds, 82, 137; snakes 122;
prostitutes, 219, 229, 231; Mama Sis, 210–211
Puerto Rico, San Juan, 230
Putz, Annie, Miss, 67, 72
PX, 293, 308, 329; tax-free supermarket, 289

racism, 107, 202, 213, 231
radio stations, 187
Raghava, 145–146
Raja, jeweller, 115
Raju, mechanic, 96, 116–118, 120
Ramdas, driver, 43
Ramnord Research Laboratories, 28, 43–44, 52, 57, 59–60, 75, 81,104, 107; Maharaja of Baroda investing in, 51; relocation of, 57
Ramsey Canyon, southern Arizona, 297, 317, 319
Rat Tail Falls (Thalaiyar Falls), 89, 144
rat/ mouse traps, 56, 105, 111, 347
Rat Wars, 19

Rawlins, 178–179, 197
Razzack, H.H. Abdul (uncle), 3, 6, 12–13, 19, 23, 42, 170–171, 187, 209, 346; death of, 187; on holy cow, 19, 23; mansion of, 6
Religious Education, 50, 62, 349
Renoir, Jean, 19
reptiles, x, 240–241, 245, 251, 263, 270, 292, 295, 328, 332, 335–336
Reptile World Serpentarium, Florida, 277
Reserve Officers' Training Corps, or ROTC (pronounced rot-cee), 178, 273, 299
revolver, 174, 178; *see also* guns
Reynolds, Ace, 316, 341
Rhodesia, 271, 275, 277
rifle, 74, 87, 147, 150, 154, 186–188, 192–193, 196, 209, 278–279, 281–282; .22 rifle, 87, 147, 162, 174, 186, 193, 209; 30.06, 178; air rifle, 24–25, 39, 79, 87; Diana air rifle, 87, 133, 136; German Diana air rifle, 74; M-14, 278, 281–282; Remington single-shot rifle, 88, 174, 188 (*see also* guns)
Rinkel, Dieter, 139–140, 152
The River, Renoir, 19, 143, 159, 193, 285–286, 333
road cruising, 243, 295, 311
Robbins, Marty, 103, 293
Robertson, Robbie, 13
Robeson, Paul 12; *John Henry* by, 69
Robinson, Dave/Little Dave, 273

Robot camera, 35 mm still camera, German-made, 92, 98
rock beehive, 113
rock 'n' roll, 205, 220
rodents: bandicoot rats, 92; mole rats, 111
The Rolling Stones, 308
Rome, 21, 167
Romulus, Brother, 147, 149–154, 156–157, 160–161, 163
Root, Principal, 125, 128–129, 195
Roseman, Bernard, 301
Rosila, 352–354
Ruhe, Herman, 139
Russell, Findlay Ewing, 238, 321, 345, 347

Saleh, M., 74, 92
Salim, 59–60
Salisbury Snake Park: as curator, 274; Southern Rhodesia, 271
Salley, South Carolina, 250, 282, 331, 334
Salt Lake City, Utah, 199
Sara (stepmother), 168
Sarge, I'm only eighteen, draft dodger song, 273
Sasebo Naval Base, Nagasaki, 324
Sawai, Yoshio, 326, 328
Schoder, Erik, 107–109, 123
Schrafft, catering company, 208
Schubel, Richard, 298, 319-321, 328, 344
Schubert, 256–260, 265–270; and cobra bite, 266; death of, 268, 270
Scott, Peter Sir, ix

Seafarers International Union (SIU), North America, 209, 216
seals, 351
seaman, 208–210, 214, 221, 226, 235, 349, 351, 359; AB - able-bodied, 213–214, 216, 225; B card, 212; C card, 211–212, 218, 351
serpentarium, 235–236, 238, 240–241, 245, 247, 249, 254–255, 263–264, 269, 275, 277, 282
Shadrach, 64–68, 129; bike rental, 63
Shanti, 152–156, 160, 163
shield-tail snakes, 89
Shinjuku, 326–327
ship, 4, 19–20, 22, 210–212, 214–220, 223–226, 229, 231, 235, 345, 348, 350–351, 354–355; bosun, 212–213, 215, 219, 225, 227, 350; deck maintenance man (DMM), 212; fo'c'sles, 212–213, 225; sea legs, 214–215; torpedoed, 210
shipmates, 218–219, 225, 229
shotgun, 8, 68, 87–88, 95, 101, 130, 145–146, 150, 153–155, 157, 162; barrels, 161; shells, 88, 92; shooting my leg, 179–181
signboards, 78; Burma Shave ad boards, 17; *see also* ads
Silverheels, Jay, 5
Sitamma, 25, 28, 299; tales of, 43
skating, 54–55, 63
skinning, 82, 86, 88, 102, 137–138, 152; lesson in, 82

skins, 11, 82, 85, 87, 99, 102, 108, 120, 124, 130, 134–138, 224, 228

skunks, 7–8, 10

Smiley, Col., 310

snakebite, 58, 89, 255–257, 266, 268, 313–316, 320–321, 339, 342–344, 347; American Boy Scout first aid protocol for, 90; from anaconda, 263; Bill's life-saving blood, 240; dry bite, 240, 259–260, 340; green rock rattlesnake, 345; necrosis (dry gangrene), 90, 315; pattern by python, 262; two-fang, 258–259; venomous, 260

snake boy, 89, 129, 136, 221

snake-catching trip, 243

snake charmers, 24, 40–41, 122, 133, 263; Asmeth, 41, 133

snake hooks, 236–239, 241, 244, 249, 252, 258–259, 262, 266, 270, 313, 321

snake hunting, x–xi, 240, 244–245, 247, 253, 255–257, 260–262, 268, 286–287, 297–298, 312–313, 315, 332–343

snake park, 264

The Snake Pit, 250, 282, 332

snakes: anaconda, 263; black cobras, 266, 268; indigos, 236, 243, 245-248; black mambas, 15, 240–241; black racers, 245; blacktail rattler, 312, 317, 344; brown water snakes, 333; bullsnake, 311, 331; Burmese pythons, 262, 277; canebrake rattlers, 283, 285–287; coachwhips, 245; cobras, 15, 19, 27, 40–41, 233–235, 237, 241, 244, 256, 263, 265–267; coral, 240, 244, 277, 326; eastern diamondback rattlesnakes, 243–244, 248–249, 259, 270, 282–283, 286, 311; feeding, 103; gaboon vipers, 271; garter snakes, 10–11, 18, 245; Cape cobra, 234; green rock rattler, 297, 317, 342, 347; of hills, 64; keelback water snake, 41, 107; king cobras, 85–86, 138, 237; kingsnakes, 244–245, 247, 320; krait venoms, 237, 244; mambas, 103, 241, 271; massacre after Hurricane Cleo, 269; mamushis, Japanese pit viper, 326, 328–329; Mexican cantils, 256, 266; milksnakes, 10; Mojave rattler, 317, 340, 344; non-venomous, 246; Okinawan habu, 326; pit viper, 64, 90, 119, 326; prairie, 312; python, 15, 105–106, 109, 111, 116, 122–124, 130–131, 133, 154, 262, 348; rat snakes, 27, 42, 86, 89, 92, 156, 243–245, 270; rattlesnakes, 176, 178, 237, 244–245, 311, 316–317, 321, 326, 332, 338-339, 348–349; red-bellied mud snake, 269; red rat snakes, 243, 245, 247, 256, 258, 270; red-tailed boa, 229, 256; reticulated pythons, 236, 262; Russell's viper, 89–90, 105; sand boa,

41, 105; scarlet kingsnakes, 247; shieldtail, 56; sidewinder rattler, 325; species, 236; taipan, 234; tiger rattlesnake, 344; timber rattlers, 337–339; trinket snake, 41; twin-spotted rattlers, 298, 316–317, 321; venomous, 41–42, 64, 89–90, 103, 234, 237–241, 243–245, 247–249, 251, 256–261, 263, 265–267, 282; vine snakes, 64; vipers venomous, 89–90, 103, 237, 244; water moccasins, 243, 245, 248–249, 251, 256–259, 261, 263, 265–267, 282; water snakes, 105, 243, 245, 247, 251, 269; western diamondback rattlesnake, 312, 317, 330; Willard's rattlesnakes, 298, 320–321, 340, 344; yellow rat snakes, 243, 245, 247, 255–256, 270

Snakes and Snake Hunting, Kauffeld, x, 247, 278, 282, 295, 298, 315

snake shows, 282

Snakes of the World, Ditmars, 10, 102

snake missionary, 10

Social Evenings, 54–55, 90

solo camping, 99, 127, 162

Solomon, David, 301

Someswara, 136

Song of Myself, Whitman, 132

Southampton, 217–219

South India Taxidermy Studio in Mysore, 134

Spanish, 218, 228, 230–231, 330

Spanish pine, 55

Sparks, 213, 215

Spec 4, 329, 344

spiders, 8, 286, 295

SS *Independence,* 21, 223, 350; to India, 19

SS *John C,* 212, 221

Stafford, Jim, 286

staging plays, 85

Stahnke, Herbert, 314

Staten Island Zoo, 247

St. Luke's School, kindergarten at, 15

stray dogs, 104, 359

stuffed birds, 82, 84, 91, 122, 133

Suez Canal, 223; closure of, 350

Sundar (cousin), 26, 42, 52, 60

Sunday services, 62, 67, 110

Susan, 197

swamp rabbits, 248–249

Swiss Army knife, 189

Sylvia, 72–73, 85

Talavadi, 144

Tamiami Trail, 257, 269

Tamil, 64, 68, 135, 152

Tanner, Father. *See* Daniel, Bro.

Tara Aunty (Rama's cousin), 26, 42

tarantulas, 295–296

taxidermy studios, 87, 133–134, 136, 152, 157

TDY (temporary duty), 328

Teamsters Union, 211

Tennyson, Alfred Lord, *The Charge of the Light Brigade and Ozymandias* by, 85

termite mound, 138, 163

terrariums, 11, 254, 256, 259–260
Thakur, 157
Thomas, K.I., principal of Sishya,
    35–36
Thondaiman, Maharajkumar
    Radhakrishna, 68
Thondaman, Vijaykumar, 87
toads, 8, 269, 335–336
Tokyo, 324, 326, 328
tortoises, 233; Aldabra and
    Galapagos, 236
trailer, 293, 295
train, 9, 21, 29–30, 84, 92–93,
    124, 133, 139, 157, 170, 326;
    cat from Trichy to Bombay,
    73–74; to Kodai Road, 47, 73,
    110; to Madras, 110; *Pandian
    Express*, 47; travelling in the
    engine, 73
training movies, 279
Tredis, 68, 87
trek, 64
truck, 140, 174, 178–179, 185,
    199, 201–202, 282, 332, 335
Tucson, 298, 319, 321, 341, 344
turtle, 12, 252, 261, 316;
    Cherokee Indian, 16; white
    soapstone, 20
tusker, in musth, 150, 156
*Two children on their natal day
    awaken*, Harin, 14–15
*225,000 Indians Can't Be Wrong:
    The Peyote Story*, Roseman,
    301, 349
Tyson, Wayne, 255, 260

university admission, 130
University of Wyoming, 126

Unruh, Miss, 73
US Army, 4, 36
USS *Enterprise*, nuclear aircraft
    carrier, 325

vadai, 65, 69, 119
Val, 168
Van Horn, George, 277
Van Ingen & Van Ingen, 134
Vanivilas Mohalla, 134
VC (Viet Cong), 280
Veerappa, toymaker, 136, 139
Velu, 65–66
Venezuela, 227, 229; Puerto
    Cabello, 229–230
venom, 90, 234, 238–240, 244,
    259, 314–315, 326, 337, 342,
    345, 347; dust, 348; extracting/
    milking, 103, 233, 237,
    263, 359; extraction Miami
    Serpentarium, 233; neurotoxic
    snake, 240
*Venomous Animals and Their
    Venoms*, Bücherl, 238
Vera, 138, 140
Veracruz, Mexico, 227, 229–230
Vermont, 6, 170,
Vietnam, 80, 255, 272–273,
    276–277, 281, 284, 287–288,
    310, 321–322, 324–325, 329;
    Da Nang Air Base, 325; War,
    80, 255, 281, 287
vinyl record, 265; 33 rpm, 79; 78
    rpm, 12
Violet [Ma's sister], 11
Vyjayanthimala, 43

The Wages of Fear, 353

Wall, Frank, Maj., 102
Warrell, David, 347
Wasilewski, Joe, 277
'Way down south, not so very far off', 129
Wes and Jan's shop, 330
whale, 334
Whitaker and Higgins, 4
Whitaker III, Romulus Earl/ Breezy/ Breecy/Rom/Whitey, 3, 5, 14, 44, 46, 61, 131, 133, 140-141, 147, 167–168, 176, 190, 192, 206–207, 213–214, 216, 218–219, 221, 226-227, 237, 29, 241, 255, 257, 261, 263, 273, 283–284, 320 ; birth of, 3; escapades, 57, 113; jeans, 51, 96, 179, 181, 183, 257, 268; leather jacket, 116, 18, 122; messman, 226, 230, 349; Medical pathology, 288; part-time employment, 190; sailors, 126–127, 217, 224, 324, 335, see also seamen); salesman, 196–198, 207, 233, 247, 359; as waiter, 93, 141, 169, 226, 352, 359
Whitaker Jr, Romulus Earl (Dad), 3–6, 16, 92, 133, 167–169; as chiropractor, 168; he'd pay my tuition fees, 126; marrying for third time, 168; remarried, 16; ten-dollar cheque, 16, 18, 303
Whitman, Walt, 132
wildlife, 169, 175, 193; international wildlife conservation, ix
William Beaumont Hospital, El Paso, 288–289, 301, 313, 329, 343–344
Winston, 333–334
Woodchucks, 8
World War, First, 187, 284; Second, 6, 93, 106, 137, 139, 178, 210, 284
Wyeth Laboratories, antivenom manufacturers, 256
Wynne, John, 171, 205
Wyoming, x, 13, 172, 176, 181–182, 198, 217, 220; boys, 175, 194; ID and liquor, 181; university admissions office, 134

Yer left, yer left, yer left, right left, 279
Yokohama, 324
You gotta get up, 278

Zappa, Frank, 80, 271, 329, 350
Zephyr, 4
zoo, 135–139, 141–142, 145, 152, 157, 160, 247, 299, 310

ABOUT THE AUTHORS

Romulus Whitaker (b. 1943) is unquestionably one of the best-known figures of the wildlife conservation scene in India. He is famous for establishing the Madras Snake Park, the Madras Crocodile Bank Trust and the Andaman and Nicobar Environmental Team, as well as for his work conserving India's rainforests—the habitat of so many endangered species. Internationally, he has received the Rolex Award for Enterprise and the Whitley Award for his contribution to nature conservation. In 2018 he was awarded the Padma Shri. Whitaker has co-authored the definitive *Snakes of India: The Field Guide* and produced several wildlife documentaries, including the Emmy Award-winning *King Cobra*.

Janaki Lenin writes about wildlife and conservation, and the intermingling destinies of humans and animals. She was a columnist for *The Hindu* and is the author of the two-volume memoir *My Husband and Other Animals*, and *Every Creature Has a Story*.

Whitaker and Lenin live in Karnataka.

HarperCollins *Publishers* India

At HarperCollins India, we believe in telling the best stories and finding the widest readership for our books in every format possible. We started publishing in 1992; a great deal has changed since then, but what has remained constant is the passion with which our authors write their books, the love with which readers receive them, and the sheer joy and excitement that we as publishers feel in being a part of the publishing process.

Over the years, we've had the pleasure of publishing some of the finest writing from the subcontinent and around the world, including several award-winning titles and some of the biggest bestsellers in India's publishing history. But nothing has meant more to us than the fact that millions of people have read the books we published, and that somewhere, a book of ours might have made a difference.

As we look to the future, we go back to that one word— a word which has been a driving force for us all these years.

Read.

 Harper
Collins

 HARPER
PERENNIAL

 HARPER
BUSINESS

 HARPER
BLACK

 हार्पर
हिन्दी

 HarperCollins
Children'sBooks

 HARPER
DESIGN

 HARPER
VANTAGE

 Harper
Sport